Roberto Rossellini

D'une simple bouffée de cigarette l'héroïne déclenche, sur les pentes du Vésuve, une nuée de fumerolles: ainsi Rossellini, maître sorcier, fait-il mieux que rendre sa matière absolument docile, il compte sur sa complicité comme un musicien qui donnant un concert dans une grotte jouerait avec l'écho.

(With a simple puff of a cigarette the heroine releases, on the slopes of Vesuvius, a cloud of hot vapours: so Rossellini, master magician, does more than make his material absolutely docile; he counts upon its complicity as a musician giving a concert in a cavern might play with the echo.)

Eric Rohmer, 'La Terre du Miracle' [review of *Journey to Italy*],
Cahiers du Cinéma, vol. 7 no. 47, May 1955, p. 40.

Il suo abbandono nei confronti della realtà, sempre attento, limpido, fervido, quel suo situarsi naturalmente in un punto impalpabile e inconfondibile tra l'indifferenza del distacco e la goffaggine dell'adesione, gli permetteva di catturare, di fissare la realtà in tutti i suoi spazi, di guardare le cose dentro e fuori contemporaneamente, di fotografare l'aria intorno alle cose, di svelare ciò che di inafferrabile, di arcano, di magico, ha la vita. Il neorealismo non è forse tutto questo?

(His abandonment in the face of reality, while remaining attentive, clear-headed, engaged, his natural ability to place himself at an imaginary but exact point in between indifferent detachment and clumsy identification, enabled him to pinpoint and to capture reality in all its dimensions, to look at things from inside and outside at the same time, to photograph the air around things, to uncover the intangible, arcane, magical aspects of life. Is this not what neo-realism is all about?)

Federico Fellini, *Fare un film* (Turin: Einaudi 1980), pp. 45–6.

Roberto Rossellini

Magician of the Real

Edited by
David Forgacs, Sarah Lutton
and Geoffrey Nowell-Smith

 Publishing

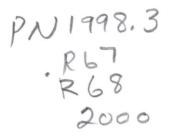

First published in 2000 by the
British Film Institute
21 Stephen Street, London W1P 2LN

The British Film Institute promotes greater understanding of, and access to, film and
moving image culture in the UK.

Cover design: ketchup

Cover image: Rossellini directing Ingrid Bergman in a location sequence in Rome for
Europe '51 (Joel Finler collection)

Set in Minion by Fakenham Photosetting, Norfolk, United Kingdom

Printed in Great Britain by St Edmundsbury Press, Suffolk, United Kingdom

British Library Cataloguing-in-Publication Data
A catalogue record for this book is available from the British Library

ISBN 0–85170–795–5 pbk
ISBN 0–85170–794–7 hbk

Contents

Foreword by Martin Scorsese   vi

Notes on Contributors   viii

Chronology   x

Introduction: Rossellini and the Critics

David Forgacs   1

1 North and South, East and West: Rossellini and Politics

   Geoffrey Nowell-Smith   7

2 The Fascist War Trilogy

   Ruth Ben-Ghiat   20

3 Rossellini and Neo-realism

   Christopher Wagstaff   36

4 Rossellini's Landscapes: Nature, Myth, History

   Sandro Bernardi   50

5 Saint Ingrid at the Stake: Stardom and Scandal in the Bergman–Rossellini Collaboration

   Stephen Gundle   64

6 *Francis God's Jester*

   Alan Millen   80

7 Vesuvian Topographies: The Eruption of the Past in *Journey to Italy*

   Laura Mulvey   95

8 *India*

   Sam Rohdie   112

9 Rossellini's Historical Encyclopedia

   Adriano Aprà   126

Documents   149

Filmography   172

Select Bibliography   196

Index   205

Foreword

Martin Scorsese

When you're discussing a filmmaker's career, its important to stay focused on the work itself, and not to get sidetracked on personal details. Its doubly important with Roberto Rossellini, because there have been very few filmmakers of his stature whose lives were so overrun with drama and incident: the emergence of Neo-realism, which Rossellini supposedly 'betrayed,' after the war; the scandal of his relationship with Ingrid Bergman; his intimate association with the filmmakers of the French New Wave; his rejection of 'normal' movies in favor of so-called 'didactic,' or historical projects; his unorthodox approach to the filmmaking process, which was sometimes difficult for his actors to adjust to. If you know the stories and the legends about Rossellini – and many people know them better than they know the films themselves – it can take some effort to put them aside and just concentrate on the work. But the fact remains that Rossellini's films speak for themselves. Many of those films have been very important to me over the years, as a filmmaker and as a person – they've moved me, inspired me, and influenced me.

I'm in the middle of making a documentary about Italian cinema, and I'm beginning with the first Italian movies I ever saw: *Open City* and *Paisan*. I saw them as a child in the late 40s, on television, with my family around me. Everyone agrees that Rossellini accomplished something extraordinary with *Open City* and *Paisan*, and I know he did from first-hand experience: I will never forget my grandparents crying as they watched these movies. Rossellini brought the plight of his country alive in these movies; he gave us both the tragedy of the war and the spiritual fortitude of the Italian people. It was an indelible achievement.

There's been a great deal said and written about the films he made in the late 40s and throughout the 50s, particularly the ones with Ingrid Bergman. At the time they came out, most of these films were box-office disasters (only *Europa '51* was a success in Italy). Italian critics took offense to their melodramatic plots, to the presence of Bergman, and they claimed that Rossellini had sold out Neo-realism. To the French filmmakers and critics for whom these movies were so influential, Rossellini was an eminently moral filmmaker who could do no wrong. These are both extreme, blanket judgments: the fact is that every movie is an individual case, and that most of the films from this period – I'm thinking particularly of *Flowers of St Francis, Stromboli, Europa '51* and *Voyage to Italy* – are genuinely great. Here you have three intensely moving explorations of sainthood and spirituality, and one of the most honest portraits of a marriage ever put on film.

The 'didactic' period that more or less began in the 60s with *Viva l'Italia!* has also been the subject of some extreme judgments. Few filmmakers at this stage of their lives or their careers were as adventurous or ambitious – when you really think about it,

Rossellini's goal was nothing less than to educate the entire world. Some of these titles are more than just great educational films; some, the *The Messiah*, are great films, period. They have their own unusual forms of suspense – you could call it 'philosophical suspense'. My own favorite is *La Prise de pouvoir par Louis XIV*, which is as close as Rossellini ever got to the gangster genre – it was definitely on my mind when I was making *Goodfellas*.

For me, Rossellini is a source of never-ending inspiration – for his adventurousness, his sense of experimentation, and his unique, powerful grasp of the film image. Images are alive in Rossellini's films, because he understood how to let people and places speak for themselves. Sometimes his simplicity can take your breath away. When Ingrid Bergman's character wakes up on the volcano in *Stromboli*, she's framed against the black of the volcanic earth and the white of the sky, an unforgettable image of elemental power. But there are many images like this throughout Rossellini's work: St Francis preaching to the birds or following the leper in *Flowers of St Francis*, George Sanders and Ingrid Bergman watching the excavation of the couple in *Voyage to Italy*, or the rejection of the pork in *La Prise de pouvoir par Louis XIV*. These are images and films of majestic simplicity. Very few artists, in film or any other medium, had the confidence, the nerve or the genius to keep things as simple as Roberto Rossellini.

October 2000

Notes on Contributors

Adriano Aprà is Director of the Cineteca Nazionale, Rome. He founded and edited the quarterly *Cinema & Film* (1966–70) and directed the film festivals at Salsomaggiore (1978–89) and Pesaro (1990–8). He is editor of the collection of Rossellini's writings and interviews *Il mio metodo* (Venice, 1987), a selection of which has appeared in English as *My Method* (New York, 1992), and director of the film *Rossellini by Rossellini* (1992).

Ruth Ben-Ghiat is Associate Professor of Italian Studies at New York University. She is the author of *Fascist Modernities: Italy, 1922–45* (Berkeley, 2000; also published in Italian as *La cultura fascista*, Bologna, 2000) and co-editor (with Mia Fuller) of *Italian Colonialism* (New York, 2001). She has contributed articles on Italian fascist and post-fascist culture and film to *Critical Inquiry*, the *Journal of Modern History* and other publications.

Sandro Bernardi is Associate Professor of Film History and Criticism at the University of Florence. He writes for the journals *Bianco e Nero*, *Positif*, *Cinémaction* and *Drammaturgia*. His books include *Le Regard esthétique, ou la visibilité selon Kubrick* (Paris, 1994), *Introduzione alla retorica del cinema* (Florence, 1998) and *Marco Bellocchio* (Florence, 1999).

David Forgacs is Professor of Italian at University College London. His recent publications include 'Spettacolo: teatro e cinema' in the Garzanti *Guida all'Italia contemporanea, 1861–1997* (Milan, 1998), an updated edition of *L'industrializzazione della cultura italiana, 1880–2000* (Bologna, 2000) and the book on *Rome Open City* in the BFI Film Classics series (2000).

Stephen Gundle is Senior Lecturer and Head of the Department of Italian at Royal Holloway, University of London. He is the author of *Between Hollywood and Moscow: The Italian Communists and the Challenge of Mass Culture, 1943–91* (Duke University Press, 2000) and has written widely about Italian history, politics, culture and the mass media. He is currently working on a study of glamour and an analysis of feminine beauty and national identity in nineteenth- and twentieth-century Italy.

Sarah Lutton works for the British Film Institute, where she is currently part of the team responsible for organising the London Film Festival. She completed her Master of Philosophy in Film Studies at the University of Kent at Canterbury in 1996 with a thesis on Rossellini.

Alan Millen is Emeritus Fellow of the School of Drama, Film and Visual Arts in the University of Kent at Canterbury.

Laura Mulvey is Professor of Film and Media Studies at Birkbeck College, University of London. Her essays have been published in *Visual and Other Pleasures* (London, 1989) and *Fetishism and Curiosity* (London, 1996). She is also the author of the book on *Citizen Kane* in the BFI Film Classics series (1992). She co-directed six films with Peter Wollen, including *Riddles of the Sphinx* (1978) and *AMY* (1980) as well as *Disgraced Monuments* with Mark Lewis (Channel Four, 1994).

Geoffrey Nowell-Smith is Professor of Cinema Cultures at the University of Luton. He is Director of the Joint European Filmography (JEF) and editor of *The Oxford History of World Cinema* (1996) and the Cassell/BFI *Companion to Italian Cinema* (1996). He is currently writing a book on the aesthetics of art cinema.

Sam Rohdie is Professor of Film Studies at The Queen's University Belfast. He has written books on Pasolini and Antonioni for the BFI. He has just completed a book on French modernism entitled *The Promised Land*. He is currently writing a Fellini lexicon.

Christopher Wagstaff is Senior Lecturer in Italian Studies at the University of Reading. He is co-editor (with Christopher Duggan) of *Italy in the Cold War* (Oxford, 1995). Recent articles include 'Il cinema italiano nel mercato internazionale' in Gian Piero Brunetta (ed.) *Identità italiana e identità europea nel cinema italiano dal 1945 al miracolo economico* (Turin, 1996) and 'Il nuovo mercato del cinema', in Gian Piero Brunetta (ed.), *Storia del cinema mondiale* (Turin, 1999).

Chronology

Date	Biographical events	Other events
1906	Roberto Rossellini born in Rome (8 May) to Elettra Bellan and Angiolo Giuseppe Rossellini	
1908	Brother Renzo born (2 Feb.)	
1909	Sister Marcella born (9 Sept.)	First Manifesto of Futurism published in *Le Figaro*, Paris (20 Feb.)
1915		Italy enters First World War (May)
1918	Father builds Corso Cinema, Rome.	First World War ends (Nov.); subsequent peace treaty (1919) rejects Italian nationalist claims to territory in Istria and Dalmatia
1922		Benito Mussolini becomes Prime Minister (28 Oct.)
1923	Drops out of school at 16	
1924	Great uncle dies leaving a considerable fortune to Roberto and Renzo	First regular radio broadcasts in Italy
1925		Mussolini begins building single-party regime
1929		Conciliation (Lateran Pacts) between Italian state and Catholic Church (Feb.)
1930		First Italian sound film: *La canzone dell'amore,* directed by Gennaro Righelli, produced by Cines
1932	Begins casual running-work on *Tre uomini in frack* (directed by Mario Bonnard). Takes dubbing assistant work at Caesar films, Rome. Staged wedding to actor Assia Noris with fellow actors as priests (the marriage is never formally validated)	

Date	Biographical events	Other events
1933	Assists in dubbing and editing of imported films. Takes position at ICI (Industrie Cinematografiche Italiane). Ghost-writes some scripts for Cesare Vico Lodovici	Protectionist law passed in Italy making it obligatory for all imported films to be taxed and dubbed into Italian. The revenues are used to subsidise domestic film production
1935	Begins work on first short film *Dafne*	Italy invades Ethiopia (Oct.); action is condemned by League of Nations
1936	Meets (May) and marries (26 Sept.) Marina Marcella (known as Marcellina) De Marchis. Works uncredited as scriptwriter and assistant director on *La fossa degli angeli* (directed by Carlo Ludovico Bragaglia)	Abyssinian war ends (May) with declaration of Italian empire in East Africa, comprising Ethiopia, Eritrea and Italian Somaliland. First issue of the journal, *Cinema*, edited by Mussolini's son Vittorio. Spanish Civil War begins (July): Italy intervenes on Franco's side; Italian anti-Fascists join International Brigade
1937	Begins co-writing script for *Luciano Serra pilota* (directed by Goffredo Alessandrini), the action of which culminates in Abyssinian war. First son, Romano, born (July)	Ministry of Popular Culture founded. Cinecittà inaugurated in Rome by Mussolini (21 Apr.). Death of anti-Fascists Antonio Gramsci (27 Apr.) and Carlo and Nello Rosselli (murdered in France, 9 June)
1938	Shoots short film *Fantasia sottomarina*. Begins work at story and script department of ACI (Anonima Cinematografica Italiana)	'Monopoly Law' leads to drastic reduction of US films imported into Italy. 'Alfieri Law' gives commercial boost to Italian film production. Laws for the Defence of the Race: first anti-Semitic legislation under Italian Fascism, followed by further restrictive laws up to 1945
1939		Italy occupies Albania (7 Apr.)
1940	Begins work on three short films *Il tacchino prepotente*, *La vispa Teresa* and *Il ruscello di Ripasottile*. Begins shooting first feature *La nave bianca* for Navy Film Unit	Italy enters Second World War on the side of Germany (10 June)

Date	Biographical events	Other events
1941	Second son, Renzo Paolo (Renzino), born to De Marchis and Rossellini (Aug.). *La nave bianca* screened at Venice Film Festival (Sept.) then released in Rome (Oct.). *Un pilota ritorna*, about bombing raids over Greece, goes into production (Oct.)	By April, German and Italian troops control Balkan peninsula from Yugoslavia to Greece. Soviet Union enters war (June). USA enters war after Japanese bombing of Pearl Harbor (Dec.)
1942	*Un pilota ritorna* released (Mar.). Works uncredited on developing subject for *I 3 aquilotti* (directed by Mario Mattòli). *L'uomo dalla croce* in production (July to Sept.), about a military chaplain and Italian soldiers taken prisoner in Russia (the location sequences are filmed north of Rome). Separates from Marcella De Marchis, continues affair with German actor/dancer Roswitha Schmidt, who plays Irina in *L'uomo dalla croce*	Massive Soviet offensive repulses invasion of German and Italian troops (winter 1942–3). 75,000 Italian soldiers die in this and the subsequent retreat on foot through snow
1943	*L'uomo dalla croce* released (June). Production starts in Rome of *Scalo merci/Rinuncia* but is interrupted by 19 July bombing and subsequent fall of Mussolini government. Cast and crew relocate in a village east of Rome	Italian troops surrender in North Africa (May). Allied landings in Sicily (9 July) (later depicted in first episode of *Paisà*). Rome bombed (19 July). Mussolini forced out of office (25 July); Pietro Badoglio (formed chief of armed forces) becomes prime minister. Armistice between Italy and Allies announced (8 Sept.). Italian army disbands; King and Badoglio retreat from Rome to Brindisi. German troops occupy north and central Italy. Armed resistance begins. Mussolini, rescued from imprisonment by Germans, announces formation of new Fascist government ('Republic of Salò') in the north (23 Sept.). German troops take direct military command of Rome (23–30 Sept.). Insurrection in Naples forces Germans to abandon the city before Allies arrive (1 Oct.)

Date	Biographical events	Other events
1944	Work starts on script of *Rome Open City*, initially called *Storie di ieri* (Stories of Yesterday) (Aug.–Oct.)	Execution of Don Giuseppe Morosini, one of the models for Don Pietro in *Rome Open City* (3 Apr.). Allies occupy Rome (4 June), Germans retreat northwards
1945	Starts shooting *Rome Open City* (18 Jan.). Works starts on script of *Paisà* (initially called *Seven from the US*) (June). *Rome Open City* premiered in Rome (24 Sept.), released there on 8 Oct.	Partisans liberate northern Italian cities (25 Apr.). Mussolini executed by partisans (28 Apr.). Christian Democrat (DC) Alcide De Gasperi becomes Prime Minister and heads coalition government including Communists (PCI) and Socialists (PSI) (Dec.)
1946	*Paisà* in production (Jan.–June). *Rome Open City* released in New York (as *Open City*) (25 Feb.). *Rinuncia* completed with Marcello Pagliero directing; released in Rome with title *Desiderio* (Aug.). Death of son Romano after short illness (14 Aug.). *Rome Open City* wins Grand Prix at Cannes jointly with ten other films. Screenplay nominated for Academy Award (won by *The Best Years of Our Lives*). Released in Paris (1 Dec.)	Referendum (June) abolishes monarchy in Italy. Paolo Cappa (DC), Undersecretary of State with responsibility for cinema, invites producers to turn 'to more noble themes and ideas'. Repeal of 1938 Monopoly Law; around 600 US films imported into Italy
1947	*Open City* released in London (4 July). Begins relationship with actor Anna Magnani; travels with her to Paris and meets Jean Cocteau. Encouraged by Magnani, he films her in a version of Cocteau's stage monologue *La Voix humaine*. Visits Berlin to obtain ideas for a script (becomes *Germany Year Zero*). Returns to Berlin to film location sequences of *Germany Year Zero* (Aug.–Sept.). Interiors shot in Rome (Nov.–Feb. 1948)	Truman Doctrine (Mar.) makes containment of Communism the cornerstone of US foreign policy. De Gasperi expels left parties (PCI, PSI) from government (May). Cinecittà reopens. Giulio Andreotti (DC) becomes Undersecretary of State for cinema. European Recovery Program (Marshall Plan) launched, giving financial aid to reconstruction and promoting ethos of economic freedom and growth

Date	Biographical events	Other events
1948	Release of *Germany Year Zero*. *Paisà* opens (as *Paisan*) in New York. Receives letter from Ingrid Bergman stating her desire to work with him after seeing *Rome Open City* and *Paisà* (May). Negotiates with David Selznick over possible future projects with Bergman and Jennifer Jones. Films 'Il miracolo' at Maiori, south of Naples; it is released in Italy together with 'Una voce umana' as *L'Amore*, shown at Venice Film Festival, then released in Rome (2 Nov.). Begins filming *The Machine to Kill Bad People* in Amalfi area. *Germany Year Zero* released in Italy (Dec.)	Critical theorisations of neo-realism. Bazin's 'Le réalisme cinématographique et l'école italienne de la Libération' published in *Esprit* (Jan.); *La Revue du Cinéma* publishes special issue on Italian cinema (May) including Antonio Pietrangeli's article 'Panoramique sur le cinéma italien'; articles in *Bianco e Nero* (Apr.–June). Fierce election campaign in Italy results in landslide for DC, who win 48 per cent of the vote (Apr.). Assassination attempt on PCI leader Palmiro Togliatti (14 July). Umberto Barbaro, a Communist, is fired from directorship of Centro Sperimentale di Cinematografia. Censorship of Pietro Germi's film *Gioventù perduta (Lost Youth)*. Thirty-five directors sign letter of protest against censorship and 'uncontrolled invasion of foreign films'
1949	Visits USA to meet Bergman (Jan.). Begins negotiations with various Hollywood studio bosses to get funding for their project. Money eventually obtained from Howard Hughes, RKO. Rossellini–Bergman production company Berit formed. Bergman arrives in Rome to work on *Stromboli*. Her relationship with Rossellini and the announcement of her pregnancy causes media scandal. Annulment of marriage to Marcella De Marchis (Dec.)	Rally in Piazza del Popolo, Rome, in defence of Italian cinema, addressed by Anna Magnani and others (20 Feb.). Italy joins NATO (Mar.). 'Andreotti Law' (July) introduces new fiscal measures which increase governmental support for (but also control of) Italian film production

Date	Biographical events	Other events
1950	*Francis God's Jester* starts shooting (17 Jan.). Son, Robertino, born to Bergman and Rossellini (2 Feb.). RKO version of *Stromboli* (edited with voice-over inserted) released in USA (15 Feb.). Bergman gets divorce from Petter Lindström (9 Feb.) and marries Rossellini (24 May). *Stromboli, terra di Dio* (original version) and *Francis God's Jester* screened at Venice Film Festival (26 Aug.). 'The Miracle' released in New York as third film in compilation *Ways of Love*, with shorts by Renoir and Pagnol. Film denounced by the Legion of Decency and picketed by Catholic activists. Resulting court case eventually leads to US Supreme Court ruling that films should be covered by the free-speech clause of the First Amendment. Italian release of *Francis God's Jester* (15 Dec.)	Andreotti's open letter to De Sica about *Umberto D* (1950), critical of the negative image of Italy projected abroad by neo-realism, appears in DC weekly *Libertas* (24 Feb.) and is republished in the magazine *Tempo*
1951	First release of Italian version of *Stromboli, terra di Dio* (18 Mar.). Begins work on *Europe '51* (Sept.). Films 'Envy' episode for *Seven Deadly Sins* (Oct.)	Appearance in Italy of *Cinema Nuovo*, journal edited by Guido Aristarco, and in France of *Cahiers du Cinéma*

Date	Biographical events	Other events
1952	Begins filming *Dov'è la libertà?*; production later completed by Carlo Ponti and Dino De Laurentiis. *The Machine to Kill Bad People* released in Italy (May). Works on development of subject for *Rivalità (Medico condotto)* (director Giuliano Biagetti). Twins Isabella Fiorella Giovanna Frida and Isotta Ingrid Giuliana Elettra born to Bergman and Rossellini (18 June). *Europe '51* is closing film at Venice Film Festival. Shares international prize with John Ford's *The Quiet Man* and Kenzo Mizoguchi's *Life of Oharu* (12 Sept.). Films the episode 'Ingrid Bergman' ('The Chicken') for *Siamo donne* (*We, the Women*) (autumn). Stages production of Verdi's *Otello* at San Carlo Opera House, Naples (Dec.)	
1953	Films episode 'Napoli '43' for *Amori di mezzo secolo*. In France, *Cahiers du Cinéma* critics urge a reassessment of *Europe '51*, claiming it as a masterpiece of European cinema. Begins filming *Journey to Italy* with Bergman and George Sanders (Feb.–Apr.). Release of *Dov'è la libertà...?*, Rome (Mar.). Directs production of opera *La gioconda* at Arena Flegrea, Naples (July). Directs Bergman in stage production of oratorio *Giovanna d'Arco al rogo*, which later travels to London, Paris and Stockholm, 1954–5	End of De Gasperi premiership (July). Aristarco publishes in *Cinema Nuovo* Renzo Renzi's script of *L'armata s'agapò*, giving a critical portrayal of Italian army's conduct in Greek campaign during Second World War. Aristarco and Renzi are arrested and given prison sentences for libelling the armed forces. The opposition parties and press denounce the arrests as a further attack by the state on freedom of expression in the cinema. Conference on neo-realism in Parma

Date	Biographical events	Other events
1954	Films *Giovanna d'Arco al rogo*, first colour feature-length work. Travels to Munich to film *Fear* starring Bergman (Sept.), first released in Germany (*Angst*) on 5 Nov. Italian release of *Journey to Italy* (7 Sept.); film widely attacked by Italian press. Publication of François Truffaut's articles in *Cahiers du Cinéma* in praise of Rossellini's work	RAI (Radio Audizioni Italia) begins a regular television service (Jan.). Death of De Gasperi (Aug.)
1955	First release of *Giovanna d'Arco al rogo* in Rome (29 Mar.). *Journey to Italy* opens in France to great critical response (Apr.). André Bazin publishes open letter to Guido Aristarco, 'Defence of Rossellini', in *Cinema Nuovo*, generating a series of debates in film journals. Bergman travels to France to work with Jean Renoir on *Eléna et les hommes* and announces her creative split with Rossellini	Manifesto of the Circolo Romano del Cinema on freedom of expression (23 Apr.). All-time peak of cinema ticket sales in Italy (819 m.)
1956	Bergman signs contract to begin work on *Anastasia* in Hollywood (Jan.). Rossellini works on French project *Le Psychodrame* (unfinished). Arrives in India (Dec.)	Events in Soviet Union and Eastern Europe (Khruschchev's criticisms of Stalin, Soviet repression of uprisings in Poland and Hungary) split PCI and break PCI–PSI alliance
1957	Meets Indian Prime Minister Nehru to discuss government-funded film projects. Films documentary material and *India Matri Bhumi*. Sonali Senroy, married to film-maker Hari Das Gupta, works as screen-writer on the latter, and enters relationship with Rossellini. Their daughter, Raffaella, is born 29 Dec.	Treaty of Rome establishes EEC (Mar.): Italy is one of the six original member states. Advertising introduced in Italian television (Feb.)

Date	Biographical events	Other events
1958	Bazin organises colloquium on cinema to which Rossellini contributes (Oct.). Bazin dies in November	TV licences in Italy exceed 1 m. RAI buys Perry Como Show from NBC (first shown May)
1959	*L'India vista da Rossellini* broadcast in parts on Italian television (7 Jan.–11 Mar.). *India Matri Bhumi* screens at Cannes Film Festival out of competition, with Rossellini and Sonali Senroy in attendance (May). Begins filming *General Della Rovere* at Cinecittà (3 July). At Venice Film Festival (Aug.–Sept.) it wins Golden Lion jointly with Mario Monicelli's *La grande guerra*. Rossellini tells a journalist, 'It wasn't a good choice. I don't think it's that important a film'. Presides over 'New Cinema' conference at Venice. Writes open letter to Umberto Tupini, the minister responsible for cinema (7 Sept.): 'cinema and television ... have stimulated the mental development of children but restricted the mental horizon of adults'. *General Della Rovere* released (7 Oct.)	Fidel Castro becomes President of Cuba (1 Jan.). East-West *détente* furthered by Khrushchev–Eisenhower summit at Camp David
1960	Begins filming *Era notte a Roma* (*Blackout in Rome*) at Cinecittà, making extensive use for the first time of Pancinor remote-control zoom (Feb.). Film screens at Cannes (13 May); released in Italy (7 Oct.). First release of *India Matri Bhumi*, Milan (12 Mar.). Completes *Viva l'Italia* for the centenary of unification	Tupini's letter to the president of Associazione Industriale Cinematografica made public (June): he warns he will prevent the release of films on 'scandalous and morbid subjects'. The letter provokes protests in parliament and the film world

Date	Biographical events	Other events
1961	First release of *Viva l'Italia*, Rome (2 Feb.). Filming *Vanina Vanini*. Screens at Venice Film Festival (27 Aug.); released in Italy (12 Oct.) to poor reception. Films *Torino nei cent'anni* for television. Broadcast on RAI (10 Sept.). Supervises direction on *Benito Mussolini*	Patrice Lumumba, leader of new state of Congo, deposed by *coup d'état* and murdered by Belgian neo-colonialist forces. John F. Kennedy attempts to undermine Castro régime by Bay of Pigs invasion (Apr.). Second RAI television channel (RAI 2) begins transmissions (Nov.). TV licences in Italy now 2.9 m. Ettore Bernabei becomes Director General of RAI (Jan.–Sept. 1974): maintains DC control of television but decentralises and hires non-party people
1962	Begins filming *Anima nera*. Leaves project before completion (finally edited by Gillo Pontecorvo). First release in Milan 5 Sept. Films 'Illibatezza' episode of *RoGoPaG* at Cinecittà (Nov.)	DC prime minister Amintore Fanfani forms first centre-left government with Social Democrats and Republicans (Mar.). Cuban missile crisis (Oct.)
1963	*RoGoPaG* released in Milan (21 Feb.). Films material for *The Iron Age* (summer–autumn)	Socialists join government (Dec.) headed by Aldo Moro (DC)
1965	Develops film project on the history of world food for UNESCO. Contributes to UNESCO conference in Brazil and implores artists to use their art to contribute to society. *The Iron Age* broadcast on Italian television (Feb.–Mar.); later broadcast in France (1966–7) and Spain (1971)	Police in Rome suspend performances of Rolf Hochhuth's play *The Representative (Der Stellvertreter)*, critical of Pope Pius XII's inactivity over Nazi extermination of the Jews in the Second World War (Feb.)
1966	Founds own production company Orizzonte 2000 Inc. (22 Apr.). Visits Paris to begin work on television film *La Prise de pouvoir par Louis XIV*. Film screens at Venice Film Festival out of competition (10 Sept.), the first television film to be screened at the festival. Broadcast on French television and then released on film on 9 Nov.	Floods in Florence destroy a portion of the city's artistic heritage (Nov.)

Date	Biographical events	Other events
1967	Begins work with son Renzo on multi-part television film *Man's Struggle for Survival*. *Louis XIV* broadcast on RAI (23 Apr.). Films *Idea di un'isola* with assistance of Renzo	Student protests in Trento and Milan (Oct.–Nov.). Che Guevara killed in Bolivia. Six Day War in Israel
1968	Films *Acts of the Apostles*. Meets John and Dominique de Menil at Rice University, USA. *Idea di un'isola* broadcast in USA on NBC (29 Dec.)	Tet offensive in Vietnam initiates Vietcong retaliation against US (Jan.). Student protests in various Italian cities, as well as many other parts of Europe (Apr.–May). Demonstration at the Venice Film Festival (Sept.); no prizes are awarded between 1969 and 1979
1969	Italian release of *La presa di potere di Luigi XIV* (Jan.). Nominated President of Centro Sperimentale di Cinematografia (Jan.). Resigns 1 Nov., but continues teaching at CSC. *Acts of the Apostles* shown on RAI 1 (May); broadcast in Spain (Mar.) and France (Oct.–Nov. 1970)	Workers' occupation of Istituto Luce (18 Feb.). Film critics' club (Club della Critica) formed in Milan, nucleus of the subsequent Sindacato Nazionale dei Critici Cinematografici Italiani (SNCCI). 'Hot autumn': wave of strikes and workers' protests over contracts. Bomb in Piazza Fontana, Milan, kills sixteen people and inaugurates 'strategy of tension': violence assisted or protected by elements in the state and armed forces to generate public anxiety and discredit the left
1970	*Idea di un'isola* broadcast by RAI (Feb.). Goes to Spain to film *Socrates* (Apr.–May); shown at Venice Film Festival (19 Sept.). Begins collaboration with Rice University Science Faculty (to 1974), and starts researching television series on science. Holds seminars and assists the Menils at their Media Center, Rice University. First parts of *Man's Struggle for Survival* shown by RAI (Aug.–Sept.); later broadcast in Spain (1972)	Statuto dei lavoratori (Workers' statute) guarantees workers' rights. Divorce law passed in Italy (Oct.)

Date	Biographical events	Other events
1971	Interviews President Salvador Allende in Chile (May) (the film is first broadcast in Sept. 1973 after military *coup* in which Allende dies). Begins filming *The Age of the Medici* (June). Films *Blaise Pascal* in 17 days (Aug.–Sept.). *Socrates* broadcast in two parts on RAI 2 (17 and 20 June) (shown on French television Oct. 1974). Final parts of *Man's Struggle for Survival* broadcast by RAI (Sept.–Oct.)	PCI adopts pro-European policies
1972	Begins shooting *Augustine* (Jan.–Aug.); completed and broadcast in two parts on RAI 1 (25 Oct. and 1 Nov.). Plans ten-hour film on science (never completed). *Blaise Pascal* shown by RAI 1 in two parts (16–17 May). Broadcast in totality on French television (29 May). First part of *The Age of the Medici* shown on RAI 1 (26 Dec.). Publishes defence of state television ('Plaidoyer pour la télévision d'Etat') in *Le Monde*	Nixon's visits to China (Feb.) and USSR (May) aid *détente*
1973	Final parts of *The Age of the Medici* shown on RAI 1 (Jan.). Begins work on *Cartesius*. Delivers series of lectures on science and communication at Rice University (some are filmed). 'Dialogues with Rossellini' seminars at Yale University (spring). Begins relationship with producer Silvia d'Amico, daughter of screenwriter Suso Cecchi d'Amico	Death of Salvador Allende during army *coup d'état* led by Augusto Pinochet (11 Sept.). PCI leader Enrico Berlinguer publishes 'Reflections on Events in Chile' (23 Sept.), launching strategy of 'historical compromise' between Communists and Catholics. Death of Anna Magnani (26 Sept.)

Date	Biographical events	Other events
1974	Separates from Sonali Senroy. Silvia d'Amico claims she marries Rossellini in Mexico in Feb. Films *Anno uno*, released in Italy (Nov.) to poor reception. *Cartesius* shown in two parts on RAI 1 (20 and 27 Feb.). Films *A Question of People* for the United Nations Conference on World Population. Publication of first book *Utopia Autopsia 10^{10}*	Referendum in Italy (May) votes to retain divorce law, which DC had sought to abrogate. Bombs planted by neo-Fascist terrorists kill eight people in Brescia (May) and twelve on a train near Bologna (Aug.)
1975	Begins filming *Il Messia* mainly in Tunisia (June–July)	Law reforming the RAI transfers effective control from government to parliament, initiating division of public broadcasting into spheres of party influence. Pier Paolo Pasolini killed in Ostia (2 Nov.)
1976	First release of *Il Messia* in Paris (18 Feb.) and Rome (30 Sept.). 70th birthday party organised by Ingrid Bergman in Rome.	Ruling of Constitutional Court opens door to private broadcasting in Italy (June)
1977	Films *Concerto per Michelangelo* in Sistine Chapel (shown on RAI 2, 9 Apr.) and *Le Centre Georges Pompidou* for French Ministry of Foreign Affairs (filmed in April; broadcast in France by ORTF on 4 June and in Italy by RAI 3 on 1 Oct. 1983). Presides over main jury at Cannes Film Festival (May). Creates furore by inspiring judges to award Palme d'Or to Paolo and Vittorio Taviani's *Padre padrone*, a television film produced for RAI, and for choosing not to award the two other main prizes, the Special Jury Prize and Best Director Award. Dies in Rome (3 June) aged 71. Buried in the family mausoleum (6 June)	Law depenalising abortion passed by Chamber (lower house of parliament) (Jan.) but blocked by Senate (June). Youth and student protests in Bologna against repression (Aug.)

Introduction: Rossellini and the Critics

David Forgacs

Rossellini's critical fortunes have been rocky. Almost universally considered a great director for some of his films, including *Rome Open City* and *Paisà*, made at the end of the Second World War, and *La Prise de pouvoir par Louis XIV*, produced for French television some twenty years later, he was panned in almost equal measure for others, such as his film with the fine comic actor Totò, *Dov'è la libertà . . . ?* (1952/4), several of his collaborations with Ingrid Bergman, most notably *Fear (Angst/La paura)* (1954) and his film about the Christian Democrat statesman Alcide De Gasperi, *Anno uno* (1974). Most directors experience swings of critical opinion at some time in their careers. What makes Rossellini's case unusual, and interesting, is that it was often the same films that were praised and trashed by different critics. This was true, for instance, of *Germany Year Zero* (1948), most of the Bergman films and *General Della Rovere* (1959). Rossellini, moreover, has always been a director's director, admired and emulated by other film-makers around the world, more than a critic's director. Even sympathetic critics found him erratic, capable of making bad or indifferent films as well as good ones, and many of them lost patience and interest when he climbed onto the hobby-horse that would occupy him for the last fifteen years of his life: the series of educational films he made for Italian television about the history of western civilisation. Film-makers, on the other hand, tended to worry less about this erratic quality. Rossellini's films, at their best, had a freshness, a power, an ability to make one rethink cinema and television as if from scratch; at worst, they pursued false trails. He seemed to be at once an inspired genius and an *ingénu*, a holy fool, somewhat like Saint Francis in the extraordinary film he made about him in 1950 (examined in Chapter 6 of this volume by Alan Millen). Since his death in 1977, the conflict of opinion has remained. It is probably true to say that no wholesale critical reappraisal of Rossellini's work has taken place during the last quarter century, despite the publication of two major biographies and some important studies.

Why has Rossellini remained a controversial figure? Why has so much of his work consistently been ignored? Why reopen his case now? One might try to answer all these questions by saying that he was a highly individual and idiosyncratic film-maker, one who doggedly developed and pursued his own agenda during a series of key transitions in the history of the moving image, and that his career was for this reason at once uneven and exemplary. The transitions in question were not so much technological, even though there were some notable innovations in Rossellini's working lifetime, from lightweight cameras and portable sound-recording equipment to faster colour stocks, widescreen processes and videotape, and even though film-making technique certainly interested him. They were primarily changes in the way film-making was approached, and changes in attitudes to the role of the cinema: first the trend towards location film-

La Prise de pouvoir par Louis XIV, produced for French television in 1966, was filmed in non-studio locations using direct sound. The dying Mazarin (Giulio Cesare Silvani) is bled by doctors; Colbert (Raymond Jourdan) stands on the left.

ing and documentary realism, which started before the war in Italy; then the renewed hegemony in the 1950s of a 'rationalised' production model and the rise of European co-productions, often with US capital invested in them; finally, the impact on film-making and the cinema of the development of television.

Rossellini's career was uneven in that moments of brilliance alternated with moments of failure, when an experiment went wrong or his enthusiasm for a project flagged in midstream. It was exemplary in that it drew attention by its example to a series of important questions: about the truth value or otherwise of the photographic image, about whether films really needed large budgets, detailed shooting scripts and long production schedules, or whether all these things might be a hindrance; about the differences between trained and untrained actors, commercial and independent cinema, between television as a means of distraction and as an educational tool. From the vantage point of a later phase of moving-image technology, centred on computers and digital images, we may now look back at these questions in a new light and per-haps understand, more easily than some of Rossellini's contemporaries did, why they mattered.

Roberto Rossellini was born into a comfortable middle-class family in Rome in 1906. His father owned a construction firm which built, among other things, a number of first-run film theatres. According to his own account, his love and knowledge of the cinema began in his adolescence when he got free entry into these and devoured films by Grif-fith, Chaplin, Stroheim and Vidor. In 1932 he worked as a dubbing assistant. A few years later (1936–7) he made his first films – fantasy shorts about marine and animal life – and also worked as assistant screenwriter on Goffredo Alessandrini's film *Luciano Serra pilota* (1938), the climax of which was set in the Italian war of colonial conquest in Ethiopia (1935–6). The first films he directed were also war films (overall, a considerable number of Rossellini's films are set in one war or another): *La nave bianca* (*The White Ship*: the title refers to a hospital ship) in 1941, on which he shared the direction with Francesco De Robertis, then *Un pilota ritorna* (1942) and *L'uomo dalla croce* (1943), both of which he directed himself.

This phase of Rossellini's career has always been controversial. New generations of film students are always surprised and not a little disconcerted to discover that the director of *Rome Open City* had been making propaganda films for the Fascists a couple of years earlier. From a historical point of view, however, his early features are interesting for just this reason. In her chapter in this book, Ruth Ben-Ghiat (Chapter 2) carefully reassesses the 'Fascist war trilogy', situating the three films among a wider trend towards a realist and documentarist cinema in Italy and Europe, whose 'hybrid aesthetic' of documentary crossed with fiction fed straight into postwar neo-realism, but at the same time showing how they were at once consistent with certain Fascist ideological themes and thematically pointed forward to Rossellini's later work.

It was of course the next films he directed, those which came to be described as neorealist, notably *Rome Open City* and *Paisà*, which made Rossellini's reputation, both in Italy and internationally. But it was also these films, or to be exact a particular way of seeing them as radical social films, which made it hard for some critics and audiences to accept and appreciate what Rossellini went on to do afterwards. The ostensibly relentless negativity and concentration on inner character of *Germany Year Zero*, released in 1948, was already a shock. Then, starting with *L'Amore* (1948), *Francis God's Jester* (1950) and the satirical fantasy *La macchina ammazzacattivi* (*The Machine to Kill Bad People*) (filmed 1948, released 1952), and continuing with the Bergman cycle (1949–54), critical responses were deeply mixed, and the critics who had lauded Rossellini in 1945–6 as the standard-bearer of a new realist aesthetic and a new kind of committed cinema now saw him as guilty of 'involution', a turning inward, away from a social aesthetic into a rather dubious sort of spiritualism. Or, at any rate, this was the case in Italy, where criticism was strongly politically overdetermined, where critics on the left had taken up neo-realism as a more authentic and serious kind of cinema than the commercial 'escapism' served up by Hollywood and were deeply suspicious of anything that smacked of spiritualism, Catholicism, individualism or 'formalism'.

The timing here was fundamentally important. This was 1948 when the cold war really started to bite, when the Italian left was trounced in the general election by the Christian Democrats, whose campaign the Truman administration in the US had helped fund, and when the Soviet Union again took a hard line towards 'deviationist' Communist parties in the west. Rossellini was never a committed leftist, and his film-making agenda was shaped not by these events but by his own artistic outlook and his own judgment of what the deeper problems of the contemporary world were. He came to see these problems as loss of values, loss of faith, failures of communication; symptomatic of all of these were the problems of marriage and sexual relations. Marital crisis, infidelity or frustration provides the theme, or one of the themes, of nearly all the films he made with Ingrid Bergman as well as his short films 'Envy' (1952) and 'Illibatezza' ('Chastity') (1962). There was at the same time an insistent attention in these films to problems of modernity: to the disorientation and desolation of reconstruction Europe, to the collective repression of the trauma produced by Fascism and the war, which remained internalised within adults or was transmitted by them to their children. Indeed, the profound novelty of Rossellini's films of the 1950s might be said to consist in their tight interweaving of personal anxiety and collective trauma. But, at the time, critics on the left either could not understand or did not accept this, and therefore could not endorse the direction in which the films were tending.

It was at just this moment, however, when Rossellini's critical fortunes were start-ing to flag badly in Italy, not to mention in the USA, after the scandal produced there by Rossellini's liaison with Bergman (analysed in this book by Stephen Gundle in Chapter 5 as a media event) and the critical and commericial failure of the RKO-pro-duced *Stromboli* (1949), that his new films began to be enthusiastically received in France. It was the critics of *Cahiers du Cinéma* – Bazin, Hoveyda, Rohmer, Rivette, Truffaut, Godard – who not only salvaged Rossellini's reputation as a major film-maker in the 1950s but propelled it to even greater heights than in the first, neo-realist, period. A second Rossellini came to prominence, one who was to have a fundamental, and widely acknowledged, influence on the new wave in France. Again, the timing is very important. What left critics in Italy interpreted as political involution the *Cahiers* critics in France saw as a fresh and liberating approach to film-making, a complete break with the conventionalism and artistic poverty of much of their own national cinema. The enthusiasm can be seen bubbling over in their articles and interviews with Rossellini in this period. 'Since we like your films and feel we understand them,' Rohmer and Truffaut told him in 1954, 'it is almost as difficult for us as it is for you to make sense of why some people don't like them'.[1] Rivette compared the modernity of Rossellini's visual style to that of Matisse.[2] Bazin, in 1955, praised his extraordinary sharpness of 'line', calling his art 'linear and melodic' rather than painterly and har-monic.[3] Rossellini's influence was even more apparent in the subsequent film-making practices of the new-wave directors: Truffaut's *Les Quatre cents coups* (1959) is pro-foundly indebted to *Germany Year Zero*; Godard's *Le Mépris* (1963) is at one level a conscious remake of *Journey to Italy*, and so forth. Yet the fact that some of these crit-ics positively identified what they saw as Rossellini's Catholic spiritualism as a source of his artistic power (Rohmer said in 1955 *à propos* of *Journey to Italy* 'what makes Catholicism so great is its extreme openness')[4] only served to confirm, for Marxist crit-ics in Italy such as Guido Aristarco, that attitudes to the director were essentially divided up along ideological lines and had little to do with any intrinsic properties of his 'art'. The detailed analyses in the present volume of *Journey to Italy* and *India*, respectively by Laura Mulvey in Chapter 7 and Sam Rohdie in Chapter 8, look at these major films outside the context of those conjunctural critical debates, while Christo-pher Wagstaff's chapter on neo-realism (Chapter 3) suggests a line of continuity between the new dramaturgy first developed in *Paisà* and the films of the 1950s.

In the mid-1950s, Rossellini began to develop an interest in television that would remain for the rest of his life and would mark the beginning of what is still the least well-known, and least well-understood, phase of his career. Interviewed by Bazin together with Jean Renoir in 1958, when both were preparing films for television (Rossellini was editing the material he had shot in India the year before), he said 'Modern society and modern art have been destructive of man; but television is an aid to his rediscovery'.[5]

Rossellini had several reasons for being attracted towards television. One was his critique, in evidence since the early 1950s, of various aspects of modernity and 'mass society', and with them of a certain kind of cinema, driven by profit, over-expensive and technically over-complex, where 'the producers have ended up by creating ersatz substitutes for human emotions'.[6] Another was his excitement over television's potential for intimacy, its capacity to observe human character closely – something he had been exploring in his films at least since *Germany Year Zero* and 'Una voce umana', both filmed in 1947, and in the interior sequences of the Bergman films, all of which are already 'televisual' in this respect. A third reason, and the one that was to become of overriding importance for him, was television's ability to serve as an educative tool, its capacity to bring a critical understanding of the world and of history, through images, to a mass public. He would later compare this function of the medium with that of the *universités populaires* of the late nineteenth century. European television provided the opportunity for this mass-teaching project because of its public service remit, which was still taken seriously by most broadcasting organisations until commercialisation and new technologies of delivery began to transform television throughout western Europe from the late 1970s, a transition which Rossellini did not live to see take effect.

Like his films of the 1950s, Rossellini's television work in the 1960s and 1970s was viewed with incomprehension, dismay or disapproval by a number of critics: not just those on the left, for whom Rossellini was now choosing to work with what they saw as a state-controlled and politically compromised medium in order to promulgate naïve or questionable 'humanistic' ideas about 'man' and human history, but now also some of those who had been most passionate about the radicalism of his cinema in the 1950s. Many of these critics judged the films he made in 1959–61 – *General Della Rovere*, *Era notte a Roma*, *Viva l'Italia*, *Anima nera*, *Vanina Vanini* – as a slide back into a more conventional dramaturgy and could not understand why he wanted to spend his time thereafter making what looked like a version of popularised television history programmes for schools. Even Federico Fellini, his friend and former collaborator, suggested that Rossellini had let the ascetic, purist side of himself get the upper hand over his pleasure-loving side in making the television films.[7] Yet this phase of Rossellini's activity, as Adriano Aprà points out in Chapter 9 of this volume, occupied him for over twelve years, accounted for approximately half his total output as a film-maker and involved him in an elaborate project to film large parts of human history, accompanied by extensive theorisations and repeated reaffirmations of his commitment to film as a teaching instrument. In reappraising this work, Aprà makes a strong case for seeing it also as highly modern and experimental, consistent with Rossellini's long-standing rejection of a cinema of fiction and distraction and his exploration of new forms and techniques.

Against the view of his career as made up of a series of sudden new departures or swerves of direction, Rossellini himself argued in his numerous interviews that he had remained consistent over time, that his work as a whole was linked by the theme of spirituality, or his interest in human character, or his pursuit of documentary inquiry. Some admirers of his work have supported this view, and have argued that his alleged inconsistencies were largely projections of the incomprehension of critics and of the over-narrow categories into which they tried to box his work. The trouble with this view is that it produces too smooth an account of his career, ironing out its awkward contradictions and overestimating the director's ability to shape the world in which he works. It is true that Rossellini, at least from *Paisà* onwards, had an unusual degree of control over most of his film projects, because he did without detailed shooting scripts, because he was often his own producer or co-producer and, from the early 1960s onwards, because of his direct control of many of the set-ups and camera movements with the aid of the Pancinor zoom. It is also the case that there is a consistent interest, running through most of Rossellini's career, in place and landscape, which Sandro Bernardi in Chapter 4 of this volume identifies with the sacred. One may also argue, as Geoffrey Nowell-Smith does persuasively in Chapter 1, that there was a deep consistency in Rossellini's political outlook, which has generally not been recognised. But he made films, to adapt Marx's expression, in conditions not of his own making, and these conditions – the political climate of the time, the prevalence of certain modes of production in the cinema, the development of television and the critical discourses which grew up around these media – shaped his choices, sharpened his passions and his aversions, as much as he shaped his own film-making practice. Inevitably, not all the choices he made were good ones and we would render him a dubious service if we pretended they were or defended everything that he did. But the persistence, and passion, with which he pursued his goals as a film-maker were quite unparalleled and at best – as many of the chapters in this book argue – they produced some of the most extraordinary, intriguing and moving works ever made for the screen.

Notes

1   Maurice Schérer [Eric Rohmer] and François Truffaut, 'Entretien avec Roberto Rossellini', *Cahiers du Cinéma*, no. 37, July 1954, p. 2; translated in Jim Hillier (ed.), *Cahiers du Cinéma*, vol. 1: *The 1950s: Neo-Realism, Hollywood, New Wave* (London: Routledge & Kegan Paul, 1985), p. 210.

2   Jacques Rivette, 'Lettre sur Rossellini', *Cahiers du Cinéma*, no. 46, April 1955, pp. 14–24; translated in Hillier, *Cahiers du Cinéma*, vol. 1, pp. 193–8.

3   André Bazin, 'Défense de Rossellini', in *Qu'est-ce que le cinéma?*, vol. 4, *Une esthéthique de la réalité: le néo-realisme* (Paris: Cerf, 1971), p. 356; the whole text is translated in the Documents section below, pp. 157–61.

4   Maurice Schérer [Eric Rohmer], 'La Terre du miracle', *Cahiers du Cinéma*, no. 47, May 1955, p. 41; translated in Hillier, *Cahiers du Cinéma*, vol. 1, pp. 205–8 (p. 207).

5   'Cinéma et télévision. Un entretien d'André Bazin avec Jean Renoir et Roberto Rossellini', *France Observateur*, 4 July 1958, pp. 16–18; translated as 'Cinema and Television: Jean Renoir and Roberto Rossellini Interviewed by André Bazin', in Roberto Rossellini, *My Method: Writings and Interviews*, edited by Adriano Aprà, translated by Annapaola Cancogni (New York: Marsilio, 1992), p. 94.

6   Rossellini, 'Cinema and Television', p. 96.

7   See the passage from *Fare un film* (1980) translated in the Documents section below, pp. 169–70.

1

North and South, East and West: Rossellini and Politics

Geoffrey Nowell-Smith

Roberto Rossellini was 'discovered' as a figure in world cinema in 1946 with the international release of *Rome Open City*, first shown in Italy late in the previous year. With *Paisà* (made in 1946 and released worldwide in 1947) and *Germany Year Zero* (released in 1948) he capitalised on this initial success, though with diminishing returns. After that, his career suffered a number of shocks. His next film, *L'Amore* (1948), veered sharply away from neo-realism into an area of spiritual exploration which the majority of left-leaning Italian critics regarded as a betrayal. He then entered into a deal with RKO for a film with Ingrid Bergman which proved a disaster in all possible ways. The film's full title, *Stromboli, terra di Dio* ('Stromboli, Land of God') hinted at high spirituality, but the ambiguous morality of the film's ending – a wife leaving her husband – and the scandal of the director's off-screen romance with his star during the making of the film triggered off a disastrous sequence of events. RKO re-edited the film, cutting out twenty minutes in the process, in the hope of making it more palatable to American audiences, and Rossellini's reputation in Italy suffered a serious blow not so much because of his affair with the popular Bergman as because of his desertion of the even more popular Anna Magnani, his companion since the days of *Rome Open City*. His political and moral reputation equally sullied in his home country, he persevered with making films with Bergman, now his wife, to be rewarded with acclaim from a small band of critics centred on the French magazine *Cahiers du Cinéma* – first André Bazin and then Jacques Rivette, Eric Rohmer and Jean-Luc Godard. To the 'first' Rossellini of *Rome Open City* and *Paisà* there came to be added a 'second' Rossellini of the Bergman cycle – *Stromboli* (1949), *Europe '51* (1952), *Journey to Italy* (1954) and *Fear* (1954). Even so, his role continued to be marginal. The support of a few French critics could not make up for commercial failure both at home and in major export markets. For a long time he had difficulty making the films he wanted and was only successful with films (such as *General Della Rovere* in 1959) which he himself didn't like. Then a dramatic change of tack in the late 1960s created a 'third' Rossellini, that of the historical tele-films beginning with *La Prise de pouvoir par Louis XIV* ('The Taking of Power by Louis XIV') made for French television in 1966.

About the moralism, whether in Italy or in America, which contributed to Rossellini's loss of prestige after the astonishing success of *Rome Open City* and *Paisà*, I do not want to add anything to what has already been written. It damaged his reputation but it cannot be used as an explanation of the changes in his career – up and

down, side to side – that took place after the *Stromboli* débâcle. The question of
Rossellini's politics – or possible lack of them – is more interesting. Ideologically boy-
cotted by the left after (and indeed before) *L'Amore* in 1948, Rossellini was rescued on
aesthetic grounds by his French admirers and it is the aesthetic and non-political
interpretation of his work that has held sway ever since. On this account, Rossellini
was an essentially apolitical figure: his films from the Fascist period (he made three,
one about each of the armed services) are not Fascist; his neo-realist trilogy stands
aloof from the politics of the Resistance and postwar reconstruction; the Bergman cycle
is about the camera's search for the spiritual moment in human relations; his tele-films
are non-partisan monuments to the history of mankind; and so on. The continuity of
his spiritual gaze – the account continues – has been obscured by misguided attempts
to reduce him to the level of the transient world that formed his political environment.
Rossellini's great misfortune, indeed, was to be born into a world that was too political. Politics did him no good and the ideological pettifogging of the post-war leftist
critics in Italy not only harmed his career materially but prevented his true greatness
from being made manifest.

The rescue operation which led to the creation of an apolitical Rossellini began with
a debate between André Bazin and the Italian critic Guido Aristarco in 1954 (reproduced
in this volume on pp. 156–61). After Aristarco had criticised *Europe '51* for a lack of
social analysis, Bazin wrote an open letter to Aristarco's magazine, *Cinema Nuovo*,
defending Rossellini in general and his most recent film, *Journey to Italy*, in particular.
The letter culminates in the now famous metaphor of the stepping stones and the bricks,
in which Bazin compared ordinary film-making to crossing a river on a bridge constructed from man-made bricks and saw Rossellini's unique realism as more akin to
hopping across it on stepping stones provided by reality itself. With this now famous
flight of rhetoric, Bazin expresses a phenomenological attitude to reality as the cinema
can present it, finding in Rossellini a model not only for the neo-realist film but for the
cinema in general. For his colleagues on *Cahiers*, and especially for those who were about
to embark on their own careers as film-makers, *Journey to Italy* was also a model of how
to make a film which created its own truth of a kind which the film-maker could feel
happy with as his own. The proof of the power of example exercised by Rossellini and
Journey to Italy in particular is there for all to see in the work of the new wave, most
clearly perhaps in Godard's *Le Mépris* (*Contempt*, 1963), with its dual homage to the
'phenomenological' Rossellini and to the 'classical' Fritz Lang, but also in *Les Carabiniers*
and other films.

Bazin's approach shied away from attributing to an essential Rossellini qualities he
discerned specifically as linking *Paisà* and *Germany Year Zero* with the 1950s Bergman
cycle of *Stromboli, Europe '51, Journey to Italy* and *Fear*. For Bazin, Rossellini existed (to
adapt his own terminology) *a posteriori*. Rossellini was what was to be found in
Rossellini's films. Subsequent critics have been less cautious and have created an *a priori* Rossellini – one who was always phenomenological, always spiritual, always above
the fray – using this *a priori* authorial unity to gloss over the accidental changes in the
work of an artist whose career nevertheless remains a puzzle to sceptical observers.

It seems to me, however, that while the rescue of the spiritual and phenomenological Rossellini from his politically motivated detractors was an important event, not only
for criticism but for subsequent film-making, his elevation to the status of an author

whose work constitutes a unity *a priori* represents a step backwards. The case I want to argue here is that there are both consistencies and inconsistencies in Rossellini's work and that politics, so far from being a distraction, throwing off course his essential, spiritual, human quest, was actually a major source of consistency in his career. Throughout his career, Rossellini was a profoundly political artist – a fact which has been obscured in equal measure by people who were aware of (but opposed to) his political project and those who denied its existence in the name of higher values.

To understand this, it is worth going back to the debate between Aristarco and Bazin. For Aristarco, the validity of neo-realism lay in its attempts to grasp contemporary and historical reality. But by his standards the majority of neo-realist films were aesthetically deficient, too observational and external, too closely tied to chronicling the everyday to offer a coherent form of historical narration. Rossellini's films of the 1950s represented for him an abject falling away from the ideal of what neo-realism might have become. For Bazin, by contrast, they represented precisely what was most original about neo-realism, a move beyond 'classic realism' which only the cinema could take (but rarely did). Behind this aesthetic difference was a political–ideological one. Aristarco was a Marxist, drawing his aesthetic ideas from Georg Lukács even more than from Marx and Engels themselves, and politically aligned with a political left in which the Italian Communist Party was the senior partner. Bazin, by contrast, was a Catholic whose politics (in the cold war context) were those of the left wing of Christian Democracy. The debate between them had strong political overtones. Bazin was trying to wrest away from Marxism what seemed to him best and most original about the neo-realist experience. Aristarco was trying, along with the left, to situate neo-realism more strongly in the 'progressive', Marxist camp. For Aristarco, as for others on the left, Rossellini was a defector. Politically, he had broken with the unity of all anti-Fascist forces stemming from the Resistance. But he had also lost his way aesthetically in that his films had come to content themselves with mere surface description, at the cost of their power to explain, through coherent narration, the wellsprings of human action in given circumstances.

The debate between Aristarco and Bazin was only possible, however, because neo-realism was not, and had never been, a unitary phenomenon. What held it together was not a shared aesthetic but the political will to create an 'other' cinema for Italy in the immediate postwar context. There was room in this other cinema for many variations on the idea of realism and for many variants of otherness. There was also, at the beginning, room for different political approaches, but the spectrum of difference was contained within the alliance – of Communists, Socialists and Christian Democrats – issuing from the Resistance. So long as this alliance held, neo-realism was able to pretend to a unity as the original voice of a nation emerging out of the ashes of Fascism and German occupation to rebuild itself on new lines. When the Christian Democrats came to power in 1948, and the Socialists and Communists found themselves in ineffective opposition, neo-realism became the object of political contention. The left claimed it as its own, while the right and the centre saw it as a distraction: its petty, artisanal production methods ran counter to the project of rebuilding a proper national film industry, while its constant harping on themes of poverty and backwardness were an embarrassment to a government busy pleading with the Americans for Marshall Aid to help to modernise the economy. Yet the notion of a realist cinema did not have to be a left-wing one. If the Italian cinema were to compete with Hollywood, it might indeed be well advised not to do so by imitating Hollywood genres and production methods, but by following a path of its own less constrained by studio artifice.

Faced with the choice between mending his bridges with the neo-realist left or try-ing to place himself in the mainstream of resurgent commercial production, Rossellini opted to do neither. He knew what he wanted to do, and set out to do it very much on his own and in his own way. The production of each of his films was a *coup*. It was a *coup* to make *Rome Open City* at all, in the improvised conditions of Rome immedi-ately following its liberation. It was a *coup* to secure, as he did, American para-governmental funding for *Paisà*. It was even more remarkable to set up *Germany Year Zero* as a tripartite production, basically Italian but with French and German inputs, and it was certainly innovative (and, in the neo-realist context, a bit shocking) to combine location shots in Berlin with studio work carried out in Rome. Improvis-ation again prevailed in the making of *L'Amore*, which consists of two quite separate parts, 'Una voce umana' ('A Human Voice', adapted from Cocteau's *La Voix humaine*) and 'Il miracolo' ('The Miracle'), shot at some months distance from each other, and yoked together to make a releasable package. The biggest *coup* of all would have been *Stromboli*, which he and Bergman produced themselves, bankrolled by RKO. Had *Stromboli* been a success, he would have outsmarted the professional producers, men like Carlo Ponti and Dino De Laurentiis, not to mention Goffredo Lombardo at Titanus and Riccardo Gualino at Lux, any of whom would have loved to lay their hands on American capital and get guaranteed release in the American market.

In the event, it was Ponti and De Laurentiis who helped to put Rossellini back on his feet after the *Stromboli* débâcle by rescuing (though also mangling) *Dov'è la libertà...?* and offering to produce *Europe '51*, the second of the Ingrid Bergman cycle. But he con-tinued to be a maverick throughout the 1950s, and indeed beyond, never subordinating himself to the demands of the industry and always seeming to keep financially afloat – if only just.

If one asks what animated this extraordinary project, the simple answer would be sheer cussed individualism: he wanted to make films the way he wanted them, and was prepared to risk economic insecurity and even disaster in order to do so. But what sort of films did he want to make? Was there a coherence to the project that saw him through from film to film, a line he wanted to pursue through thick and thin? A possible answer would be that he wanted to continue to pursue the vein of realism he had discovered for himself in the neo-realist trilogy of 1945–8.

Whether this is a satisfactory answer depends on one's definition of realism. Some critics – for example Peter Brunette in his book on Rossellini[1] – have argued that Rossellini's project cannot be subsumed under a realist heading because of the central role played by imagination and fantasy both in his films and in his explanation of them, particularly in the period around the making of *L'Amore* and *La macchina ammazza-cattivi* ('The Machine to Kill Bad People' – shot in 1948 but not released until 1952). But realism versus fantasy is a rather abstract criterion which does not really fit the bill as far as Italian film history is concerned. For many film-makers, including De Sica and Zavattini as well as Rossellini, fantasy did not stand in an antithetical relationship to realism and the introduction of fantasy elements into a film remained perfectly con-sistent with a broadly realist project.[2] The central issue, for these film-makers, was whether they would remain free to explore reality in their own way, looping off in the direction of fantasy as they saw fit, or whether they would be obliged to subordinate their approach to the rules of genre convention. And here there can be no doubt that Rossellini, who was an intuitive artist rather than a theorist, not only chafed against the restrictions of genre but used his freedom to follow an inspiration which was real-ist in a sense which, while admittedly loose, was of a kind which artists themselves recognise. Equally, there can be no doubt that Bazin – an intuitionist himself – was right to see in Rossellini's films of the 1950s a continuation and a bringing to fruition of a kind of non-conventional realism more radical than that of his more overtly pol-itical contemporaries.

The originality of Rossellini's realism, in Bazin's account, lay not only in its ability to make bridges where other people only saw stones, but in a sensing of the moment when something happened and turned into narrative before the camera. In these moments, something was privileged which critics had difficulty in describing in other than spiri-tual or religious terms. For Bazin this was grace. Even for less religiously minded critics the moments had a quality of revelation; in them something was there to be seen, an intuition that otherwise might have been missed. Thematically, the moment of revel-ation, of intuition, revolved around communication. In a world marked by non-communication, suddenly something would be communicated, a flash of insight enabling the audience to see what the characters themselves saw or maybe were too blind to see, or enabling the characters themselves to go forward from an impasse. The theme of communication (or the lack of it) is constant in Rossellini's work, though it is only here and there that he sets up mechanisms which enable something to be revealed about it and banality to explode into the sublime.

A procedure whereby a general thematic of communication is brought to life in privi-leged moments can be located throughout Rossellini's work, though I am sceptical if it really appears in any of the films before *Rome Open City*, where the suffering of Don Pietro, condemned to watch, and understand, the torture of the Communist militant Manfredi before facing his own execution, is the centrepiece of the film. It is certainly central to *Paisà*, to *Germany Year Zero* and to the Bergman cycle, and reappears in the tele-films, most notably in *Blaise Pascal* (1972).

The case of *Paisà* is particularly interesting, because failed communication, and a very rare transcendence of this failure, is at the heart of each of the six episodes into which the film is divided. In the first, Joe 'from Jersey' tries to overcome the linguistic differ-ence that separates him from Carmela; while attempting to do so he neglects the most elementary safety precautions, and is shot while lighting a match. In the second, the black American sergeant does not understand the behaviour of the Neapolitan street-urchin, is robbed of his boots, but at the end understands something about the conditions under which the Italian victims of the war were living. In the third, Fred and Francesca create for themselves imaginary worlds of love which do not survive the encounter with the reality of the relations between man and woman, occupier and occu-pied. In the fourth, Harriet, separated from her partisan lover, tries to cross the German lines to join him, but only succeeds in receiving news of his death. In the fifth, the monks live in a universe for which the Jews are beings deprived of the light of the Saviour and they cannot understand the non-sectarian fraternity of the military chaplains billeted in their monastery. In the final episode, the sense of non-communication is even more devastating; few words are spoken, most of them at cross-purposes, serving only to hide the fundamental silence, which is that of God.

Communication/non-communication is again the theme of the Bergman cycle, though here it is more narrowly focused around the Bergman character herself, who is shown as isolated from the world around her and alienated in particular from her husband. Unusually for Rossellini, the films of the Bergman cycle – certainly *Stromboli, Europe '51* and *Journey to Italy* and to some degree also *Fear*[3] – adopt a form of narration which not only makes of her the central character but in various ways privileges her point of view. Not only does *Journey to Italy* in particular contain a number of shots taken from, or close to, her (optical) point of view, but even the shots which have her as the object perform the function of interrogating her thoughts and feelings. The films therefore have a dual narrative standpoint: that of Bergman, who is seen from the inside and whose inner world is revealed; and that of Rossellini, who shows her from the outside. Both narrations, however, function equally to stress her social and psychological isolation and non-communication with her surroundings.

There is, however, something very significant about the characters she is called upon to play and the circumstances in which she finds herself, which makes the films more than just instances of the theme of communication/non-communication in general. This has to do with her role as a foreigner, a northern European, in Italy. By looking more closely at this peculiarity I hope to throw light on the vexed question of Rossellini's politics in the 1950s.

In *Stromboli*, Bergman plays Karin, a Lithuanian in a displaced persons camp in postwar Italy. When her request to emigrate to Argentina is rejected, she gets out by marrying a southern Italian fisherman and goes to live on his island, a move she soon comes to regret. In *Europe '51* she is Irene, a rich society lady of not very clearly specified nationality, living in Rome with her English husband (played by Alexander Knox).[4] And in *Journey to Italy* she is Katherine, a cultured Englishwoman,[5] whose marriage with her equally English but rather less cultivated husband Alex (George Sanders) undergoes a crisis in the course of a visit the couple make to Naples. Each of the films marks out various lines of differentiation between Karin/Irene/Katherine and the other characters and their environments. In *Stromboli*, apart from the obvious (and accentuated) differences of sensibility between a man and a woman, there is a difference of nationality between Karin and her husband, and a class difference between her and the island population (male or female). In *Europe '51*, there is again a difference of nationality with her husband, there are ideological differences with a Communist cousin, there is a sexual contrast between her and the world of masculine power, and class differences between her world and that of the Roman workers and prostitutes; at the end of the film, communication breaks down entirely. Irene's family cannot understand her at all and can only think she is mad, while the ordinary people think she is a saint.[6] In *Journey to Italy*, there is a linguistic and cultural difference between the couple Katherine/Alex and the Neapolitans, but there are also differences among the Neapolitans between the aristocracy and the ordinary people, and a sharp contrast of sensibility emerges within the couple. In almost every case, the function of the differences and contrasts is to isolate the Bergman character, who neither understands the world around her nor is understood by it. At a personal level, the Karin/Irene/Katherine character cannot communicate with anyone else; at a cultural level she is blocked by her sexual, national or class belonging from any possibility of communion with other individuals and other modes of being in the world.

So pervasive is the problem of non-communication, even if in these films it is centred around a single character, that it might still seem as if the problem was presented as a universal, ahistorical and even metaphysical one. But looking more carefully at who it is who does not communicate, both in the Bergman cycle and in *Paisà*, it becomes clear that, alongside the age-old non-communication between woman and man and rich and poor, there is an insistent theme of non-communication between the Italian and the Nordic and Anglo-Saxon worlds.

In *Paisà*, there are two levels of non-communication: one which is contingent and due to the war conditions opposing Italians and the Allies on the one side and the Germans on the other; and one which is more serious in that it persists even between people on the same side, opposing the Italians to the Americans and (to a degree) the British.

The Bergman figure in the 1950s films offers a more complex figuration. In *Journey to Italy* she, together with Alex, clearly represents England and the North in opposition to Naples which is a representation (by synecdoche) of the Mediterranean world – the South. In *Stromboli* too she represents the North, but in a very generic way. (It is possible that making Karin a Lithuanian hints at the displacements caused by the Soviet Union's takeover of eastern Europe, but no commentators have ever picked up on this: indeed, the tendency is to describe the character – incorrectly – as Swedish.) In *Europe '51*, her position is ambiguous since Irene, whatever her precise origin, seems to be settled in Italy, and it is more by her marriage to the Englishman George that her difference is marked out.

However, in addition to the national origin of the characters she plays, Bergman herself as an actress also had, and carried with her into her roles, a distinct aura of her own. She was Swedish, but for ten years she had been making films in Hollywood (where she was married, until Rossellini came along, to a fellow Swede, Petter Lindström). In her Hollywood films, she tended to play characters of vaguely European provenance. With her distinctive accent (which she never lost), she represented to American audiences a type of European sophisticate in contrast to the all-American girl typified by, for example, Betty Grable. For Italian audiences, however, she was not so much European as Nordic. In her films for Rossellini – which were all shot with English dialogues and directed as much to Anglo-Saxon audiences as Italian – she fits both stereotypes.

What is constant in these cultural–national configurations is a differentiation/ opposition between an 'Italy' and a 'non-Italy': a demarcation whose frontier is situated to the North and the West, across the Alps or across the Atlantic. This non-Italy is the setting of two further films which reflect a further aspect of the cultural thematic. *Germany Year Zero* was planned (as already mentioned) as an Italo-Franco-German co-production with locations in Berlin and studio work completed in Rome, and attempted to look at the experience of Italy's former Axis partner after the 1945 defeat. A cruel and unsentimental film, *Germany Year Zero* was received at the time with some hostility because it did not reflect the prevailing mood of optimism. Retrospectively, its determination to look so unsparingly at the fate of Germany after Nazism seems exceptionally courageous and the film can be read, without forcing the sense, as a statement of the necessity – and at the same time, extreme difficulty – of creating a new Europe from the ground and extricating the positive side of the European idea, its shared culture, from the negative of political nationalism.

Rossellini returned to Germany in 1954 to make his fourth film with Bergman, *Fear*, adapted from Stefan Zweig's short story *Angst* and also known under that title since it was a co-production shot originally in German with subsequent English and Italian soundtracks.[7] Although the cross-cultural content of this film is minimal, the facts of its production are interesting. For a start, it is evidence of Rossellini's interest in European literature in the period. Following 'Una voce umana' (1947), from Cocteau, in the 1950s he used Colette as his source for *L'Envie/L'invidia* ('Envy'), an episode of the compilation film *Les Sept Péchés capitaux* (*The Seven Deadly Sins*, 1952), and Paul Claudel for *Giovanna d'Arco*, while his only adaptation from any Italian text is *Francis God's Jester* in 1950, loosely derived from two fourteenth-century works, *The Little Flowers of St Francis* and *The Life of Brother Juniper* (see Chapter 6). Second, it is yet another example, and an extreme one, of Rossellini's dedication to international co-production initiated with *Germany Year Zero* and *Stromboli*. After *Stromboli*, in fact, all Rossellini's cinema films with the exception of *Europe '51* were technically co-productions until *Anno uno* in 1974. And, third, there is the fact that *Fear* was shot with an English-language soundtrack, as were the other films of the Bergman cycle.

It would be a mistake to read too much into these facts. An interest in European literature was far from unique in Italy at the time (though adaptations from 'literary' literature were infrequent in the cinema). Co-production was also widespread, and was indeed regarded as a necessity by producers wanting to share costs and extend the 'home' market to more countries. And making films in English in the hope of attracting English-speaking audiences intolerant of either subtitling or bad dubbing was also

Anno uno (1974): Alcide De Gasperi (Luigi Vannucchi, centre) visits Matera to promote the government's plans to develop poor agricultural regions.

a fairly common practice. But Rossellini's position was nevertheless extreme. What is cumulatively striking about his practice is the extent to which his gaze seems to have been directed only relatively speaking to Italy and far more to somewhere else. There is a sense of this already in *Paisà*, which was made with the USA in mind, but it is most emphatic in the 1950s with the Bergman cycle which was targeted clearly at inter-national audiences.

What interested Rossellini, I would suggest, both in the 1950s and later with the tele-films, was the relationship between cultures, between civilisations. On one side of the equation was Italy, an Italy already divided in itself between popular Italy and bour-geois Italy; and on the other side was the rest of the western world, European and North American. (Later, as we shall see, the equation was to be expanded to take in the South: India in the 1958 film of that name, North Africa in the 1972 tele-film *Augustine*.) Between the Italian world, notionally the cradle of European civilisation and the place where the remains of Graeco-Roman antiquity were still omnipresent (see in particu-lar *Journey to Italy*), and the world to the north and west of it, which was the new centre of western civilisation, an abyss had grown up. On both sides, customs and sensibili-ties had changed, and dialogue had become difficult. Channels of communication had to be opened, and people on each side had to learn to understand each other again. Italy had to be made to understand America and northern Europe, and, conversely, Americans and northern Europeans had to be made to understand Italy and what it represented.

Why was this important? Because politically the western world had once again become a unity. It was called the Free World and was the world of the Pax Americana, of the Marshall Plan and NATO and the first steps towards European integration and the preparations for a Common Market. This western world, within which there remained a gap between North and South, was the environment in which people now had to learn to live. Politics, economics, ideology (that of human rights and the free market) had, in the postwar years, acquired a new set of boundaries, which stretched not (as De Gaulle would have wished) 'from the Atlantic to the Urals' but from San Fran-cisco to Berlin and from Trondheim to Trapani.

From *Paisà* in 1946 to *Fear* in 1954, the field of action to which Rossellini's vision was directed was the new post-Yalta, postwar, Marshall Plan world. This, as much as his 'spiri-tuality', instantly marked out his difference from the mainstream of the neo-realist movement, whose political horizons were those of the Communist-dominated neutral-ist Left and whose cultural politics took the form of an aspiration to be 'national–popular' (in Gramsci's phrase)[8] coupled with a certain diffidence towards foreign, particularly American, political and artistic models. But although differentiated from the Left, Rossellini was not aligned with the traditional right. He was never a right-wing nationalist, not even in *Viva l'Italia*, his 1960 epic made for the centenary of the unification of Italy, nor even in his war films of the Fascist period.[9] Rather, his vision was that of a group of far-sighted, mainly Christian Democratic, European politicians and thinkers who understood the need for a new *modus vivendi* between the United States and 'Europe' and were determined to construct a collective Europe strong enough to deal with the United States on equal terms. In Italy, one man more than any other represented this new vision of Europe, and that was the Christian Democrat leader Alcide De Gasperi, Prime Minister of Italy from December 1945 until July 1953.

Rossellini's vision was De Gasperi's, and what he added to De Gasperi's vision was a cultural and personal dimension, a sense of the communication and understanding that had to be developed if the components of the new western world were to be able to live together with mutual respect. Proof – if proof were needed – of Rossellini's devotion to this political vision was to be supplied in 1974 with *Anno uno*, his last cinema film, devoted to celebrating the achievement of De Gasperi.

In the years leading up to *Anno uno*, however, Rossellini had more or less abandoned the making of films for cinema and had also embraced a wider geographical and historical perspective which, in appearance at least, put his Atlanticism in a new framework. Beginning with *India*, released in 1959, his interest began to stretch outwards to include the Third World, while from *The Iron Age* (1964) onwards he delves back into the earliest past of civilisation. His style changes too, following his discovery of the potential of the Pancinor zoom lens as a way of following dramatic action from a spatially fixed position. *Viva l'Italia*, although made for the cinema, marks the shift to the new, essentially televisual style as well as to a new didacticism. The point of *Viva l'Italia*, as of the subsequent tele-films, is to bring history to life and to bring this living history to the viewer. Understanding the culture of other times becomes as important as understanding the culture of other places. The relations between the Anglo-Saxon and Mediterranean worlds became a subset of a broader division between the 'stitched' (*cucite*) civilisations of the North and the 'draped' (*drappeggiate*) or toga-wearing civilisations of the South.

Wide-ranging though Rossellini's researches were, however, he never really abandons a world-view which, like a medieval *mappa mundi*, has a fixed point at its centre. This centre for Rossellini is provided by what in the earlier films was 'the South' – that is to

Viva l'Italia (1960): Garibaldi's troops engage the Bourbon army at the Battle of Calatafimi, 1860.

say, the world of the Mediterranean. Other civilisations are measured by their closeness or distance from the presumed centre. The films he made or planned to make tell a story which begins in Greece with Socrates, takes in Christ and St Paul, was originally planned next to include the Roman Empire (the abortive Caligula project),[10] then crosses to North Africa to look at Augustine and early Christianity, and resumes after a millennial gap with the Renaissance in Italy and its consequences across the Alps in the persons of René Descartes and Blaise Pascal. This historio-geography of civilisation looks at first sight like the conventional Graeco-Judaean one as found in school primers across the western world, but it contains certain intriguing differences. One difference on the historical side is the stress that Rossellini puts on material factors and the uneven development of the material and the spiritual. History is not a pure progression of the spirit, it is, indeed, as in the title of the tele-series he and his son Renzo made in the 1960s, 'man's struggle for survival', and this struggle is aided by technological progress and impeded by strange dysfunctional practices such as the medical interventions applied to the unfortunate Blaise Pascal in the film about him. Second, Rossellini's, understandably Italo-centric geography privileges the zones of the world which were part of the Roman Empire, which is a Mediterranean rather than European entity. The Italo-centric map of the Empire was a staple of Italian Fascist propaganda and therefore full of resonance for an Italian audience, or at least that part of it old enough to have gone to school in the Fascist period. At times, Rossellini seems cheerfully unaware of the extent to which he had uncritically absorbed and was regurgitating a bunch of clichés, including some inherited from Fascism. But at other times his southernness encourages him to confront stereotype head on. For example, his Mediterranean world is emphatically not Aryan. It is proudly multi-racial and Rossellini's Augustine is not some whey-faced saint from a missal but a dark-skinned Berber, played by Dary Berkany, of clearly marked African origin (as the historical Augustine probably was).

   In the last analysis, Rossellini's grand historical project stands or falls not so much on its particular Mediterranean-centredness as on the form by which centredness is assumed in the first place. Adoption of the zoom can be used as a metaphor for Rossellini's activity in general throughout the latter part of his career. Although his vision encompasses more things, he himself remains the fixed reference point. The film-maker's vantage point is one from which the film can home in on details or pull out to elucidate the context. The world is out there and film-maker and viewer are exploring it (or pretending to explore it) together. As a didactic strategy, this has great merits. The films are wonderful sources of information, particularly rich in material detail. They present the development of civilisation with a concreteness unparalleled on television. They do however remain open to a 'post-colonial' criticism to the effect that they do not really challenge the basic notion that in the hierarchy of knowledge there's a 'we' and there's a 'they' and we are the West and We Know Best.

   There are many things to be said about Rossellini besides what is said here and I would not like anything I have said to be used to diminish his reputation as one of the most imaginative film-makers of the second half of the twentieth century. But I think that his career emerges in a more coherent light if it is recognised that behind his constant thematic of communication/non-communication between persons and between cultures one sees not a vague apoliticism but some precise political choices. I also think, furthermore, that these choices did Rossellini great credit – although it was not always acknowledged at the time – and that seeing them for what they were enhances rather than decreases one's appreciation of his work.

Notes

1 Peter Brunette, *Roberto Rossellini* (New York: Oxford University Press, 1987), notably p. 95 ff.

2 De Sica and Zavattini also used fantasy in their *Miracle in Milan* in 1950 and Zavattini often combined 'realistic' and fantasy elements in his early short stories. No one could really claim that Zavattini, of all people, was not a neo-realist. And more recently the term 'magic realism' reminds us that there is more to realism than just taking snapshots of what happens in real life.

3 Apart from these four films, in 1954, Rossellini also directed Bergman in an adaptation of Paul Claudel's dramatic oratorio *Jeanne au bûcher*, under the title *Giovanna d'Arco al rogo* ('Joan of Arc at the Stake'). Although stylistically different from Rossellini's other films, its theme is the usual one: the mutual non-comprehension between Joan and her persecutors.

4 In the Italian (dubbed) version of the film, she is represented as belonging to some vague Anglo-American high society. In the English-language version, as in *Journey to Italy*, her distinctive accent clearly connotes a non-Anglo-American origin. Even without the give-away accent, Italian audiences would clearly have perceived her as 'Ingrid' (and therefore part-Swedish, part-Hollywood) first and as 'Irene' or 'Katherine' second.

5 English by adoption if not necessarily origin.

6 The character of Irene is, as Bazin pointed out, in part based on the French philosopher/activist Simone Weil; see 'Europe '51', *Qu'est-ce que le cinéma?*, vol. 4, *Une esthéthique de la réalité: le néo-realisme* (Paris: Editions du Cerf, 1958); English translation in *Bazin at Work: Major Essays and Reviews from the Forties and Fifties*, edited by Bert Cardullo (New York: Routledge, 1997). Rosalind Delmar has pointed out to me that, in addition to the Weil parallel, when Irene goes religious towards the end of the film, Rossellini represents her conversion by having her seem to perform the 'seven acts of mercy' as described in the Gospel (*Matthew* XXV, 25-35).

7 English and Italian versions also seem to have had different endings. The English version ends happily (and unconvincingly), but at least one unhappy end was also shot, and may survive on German or Italian prints of the film.

8 The extent to which the ideas of Antonio Gramsci, the Italian Communist leader who died in 1937 shortly after his release from prison, were a direct influence on cultural policy in the immediate postwar period is much debated. The contents of his posthumous *Prison Notebooks* became known quite slowly and those on culture, where the notion of national–popular is elaborated, were not published in book form until 1952. The general drift of his thinking, as interpreted by Palmiro Togliatti and other Communists, undoubtedly did filter through from quite early on, but sometimes the ideas were Togliatti's rather than Gramsci's own and were given weight because his name was attached to them rather than as a result of any critical evaluation of them.

9 I would not go so far as to claim that his Fascist-period war films were in any way incompatible with, let alone oppositional to, the ideological dictates of the time. But it can be argued that *La nave bianca* (*The White Ship*, 1941), which is about a hospital

ship, is remarkably free of nationalistic or militaristic rhetoric, while *L'uomo dalla croce* (*The Man with the Cross*), set on the Eastern front, subordinates national values to religious ones very much in the same way that *Rome Open City* subordinates the political values of the Resistance (expressed through the Communist Manfredi) to its religious–humanitarian ones (expressed through the priest, Don Pietro).

10 Besides the ones he actually completed, Rossellini also planned tele-films on the Roman emperor Caligula and on Karl Marx. The Caligula film project is discussed in an interview published in the Spanish magazine *Nuestro Cine* in 1970 (English translation in *Screen*, vol. 14, no. 4, Winter 1973/4). A sketch for the Marx film, originally published in English in *Framework* 11, 1979 and reprinted in BFI Dossier No. 8, Don Ranvaud (ed.), *Roberto Rossellini* (London: BFI, 1981), is reproduced in this volume, pp. 166–9. According to Rossellini in the *Nuestro Cine* interview, the Caligula film would have been for the cinema since Caligula's incest with his sister was too hot a theme for TV. Rossellini also retrospectively regarded his film on Garibaldi, *Viva l'Italia*, as part of the historical series, although it was made much earlier (1960) and for the cinema.

2
The Fascist War Trilogy

Ruth Ben-Ghiat

This chapter examines the three military films made by Rossellini between 1941 and 1943, often referred to as the Fascist war trilogy. Each of these films showcases a branch of the Italian Fascist armed forces: *La nave bianca* (The White Ship, 1941) and *Un pilota ritorna* (A Pilot Returns, 1942) advertise the capabilities of the navy and air force; *L'uomo dalla croce* (*The Man with the Cross*, 1943) concentrates on the army's contributions to the Eastern Front campaign. Rossellini's importance in the history of neo-realism has inspired several investigations of the aesthetic and ideological continuities that bind these pre-1945 films with the post-1945 war-themed works from *Rome Open City* onwards.[1] Here, I shall view these earlier war films as products or endpoints as well as precursors. I shall situate Rossellini's military movies within the context of Italian Fascism, considering them in relation to a decade of experimentation with and debate about realist aesthetics during the dictatorship. In order to address questions of authorship and politicisation that are often raised about these movies, I shall also explore Rossellini's position within a highly collaborative film culture regulated by official patronage and disciplinary structures, and I shall consider his activities from the late 1930s to the fall of the Fascist government in July 1943.

Although Rossellini belonged to the generation of Italians whom the Fascist government had targeted as its future political and cultural élite, he did not participate in official programmes designed to train the next leaders of the Fascist film industry. His choice to forgo a university education kept him out of the film sections of the Gruppi Universitari Fascisti (University Fascist Groups) and he did not attend the Centro Sperimentale di Cinematografia (Experimental Centre of Cinematography), the film school that the regime established in 1935. Like his contemporary, Mario Soldati, Rossellini received his film training the traditional way: through a series of apprenticeships as a dubbing assistant, film editor, and screenwriter.[2]

In 1936, Rossellini worked on the first of two projects that would prove important for his development as a realist film-maker with a penchant for political subjects. First, he served as an assistant director and screenwriter for his friend Carlo Ludovico Bragaglia's *La fossa degli angeli* (The Quarry of the Angels, 1937). Shot on location in the marble quarries of Carrara, with working miners as its protagonists, this film placed elements of documentary film-making at the service of a fictional drama. On the occasion of the film's release, Bragaglia identified such formal experimentation as a fruitful path for the Italian cinema, even as he pointed out the challenges it presented for film-makers. 'How to amalgamate the strictly 'documentary' part with the narrative part?' Bragaglia wondered. 'How to achieve a unity of style?' In the years to come, such questions would occupy Rossellini and other directors who combined non-fiction and feature-film aesthetics in their work.[3]

Rossellini's second project offered a hands-on introduction to the ideology and craft of the war cinema, preparing him for his future armed forces' assignments. In 1938, he worked as assistant director and co-screenwriter on Goffredo Alessandrini's *Luciano Serra pilota*, a big-budget colonial aviation epic supervised by the Duce's son Vittorio Mussolini. In October 1935, the Fascists had invaded Ethiopia and they had declared victory in May 1936, when Mussolini proclaimed the Empire of Italian East Africa. Alessandrini's and Rossellini's script focused on the air force's crucial contributions to the conflict, and it presented combat and the colonial experience as redemptive experiences. The pilot Luciano (Amedeo Nazzari) is transformed from a daredevil expatriate of the Liberal (pre-Fascist) era into a disciplined patriot who dies in Ethiopia for the Fascist cause.[4] *Luciano Serra pilota* also offered Rossellini his first opportunity to direct battle scenes. In charge of the second unit, he travelled to Ethiopia to film on location. Although Rossellini's own footage cannot be isolated from the rest of the film, a similarly dynamic *mise-en-scène* would mark parts of *Un pilota ritorna* and *L'uomo dalla croce*, as would the use of blinding dust clouds which convey the chaos of combat. In the short term, the critical and commercial success of *Luciano Serra pilota* greatly strengthened Rossellini's position in Fascist political and film circles. He consolidated his friendship with Vittorio Mussolini, who henceforth served as his informal patron, and he became a regular at the salon run by Vittorio's sister Edda and her husband, the Foreign Minister Galeazzo Ciano. Employed as a screenwriter by Franco Riganti, the producer of *Luciano Serra pilota*, Rossellini spent his off-hours directing his own brief nature-themed films. By 1940, he had a contract with Scalera Films to make ten other such shorts.[5]

Italy's entry into the Second World War in June that year interrupted these pursuits. Now, both fiction and non-fiction film were conscripted for battle. The demands of permanent mobilisation (Ethiopia, Spain) had blurred the boundaries between military and civilian film-makers, as had the diffusion of devices such as the 'cinema-machine gun' (*cinemamitragliatrice*), designed to 'shoot' images at the same pace as bullets. Even before the war began, a new class of operatives had been created, many belonging to Rossellini's generation, who were 'soldiers among soldiers ... well acquainted with the practice of war'. Over the next few years, as the air force outfitted Italian bomber planes with movie cameras, the regime intensified its efforts to make film *and* film-makers perform in the service of the war, exploiting the conflict's 'cinematic possibilities'.[6] In this climate, Rossellini's love of flying and his familiarity with documentary techniques and the military genre were a valuable combination. He would ultimately direct several military-associated projects that had been approved by the regime's Committee for War and Political Cinema, working with non-fiction and fiction film in ways that expanded the boundaries of each.[7]

In these wartime projects, Rossellini could draw on years of formal experimentation by others with both fiction and non-fiction that had elucidated the propaganda potential of realist aesthetics. Although no unified school of realist theory and practice emerged during the dictatorship, many in the film world had championed realism since the late 1920s as the basis for a national film style. With its emphasis on outdoor shooting and non-professional actors, they reasoned, realism would constitute an Italian

alternative both to artificial diva-driven American movies and to European art films
with avant-garde pretensions. Realism also appealed to those who wished to communicate political messages through the medium of feature film. As the young director
Raffaele Matarazzo argued in 1931, the integration of documentary footage and location
shots of recognisable places into dramatic narratives would endow them with a collective, national resonance. Over the next decade, directors such as Matarazzo, Mario
Camerini, Giovacchino Forzano, Guido Brignone, and Augusto Genina utilised newsreel footage and documentary conventions in fiction films on military and non-military
themes. Rossellini and others further developed this hybrid aesthetic during the Second
World War, satisfying those who called in the press for a 'warlike cinematography ...
that unites documentary footage with a story that can be filmed in the studio'.[8]

The interest in realism also produced innovations within the documentary genre by
1940. Mussolini had at first considered non-fiction films to be 'the best and most sug-
gestive means of education and persuasion', and the Istituto LUCE, which he founded
in 1923, had celebrated every Fascist initiative in newsreels and propaganda shorts. The
Ethiopian war mandated a new level of image management, though, and occasioned
experiments with the documentary mode designed to maximise its political impact with
domestic and foreign audiences. The 1936 compilation film on the conquest of Ethiopia,
Il cammino degli eroi, is an interesting product of this climate. Made by Corrado D'Errico, who came to military film-making from the ranks of the cinematic and theatrical
avant-garde, the movie alternates footage shot by LUCE's Africa Unit with graphics that
set the mood and context for the images to follow.[9] By the Second World War, state documentary centres in other countries were also utilising the talents of film-makers who
came out of the crucible of interwar modernism. Walter Ruttmann, whose *Neue Sach-
lichkeit* ethos informed both his documentary *Berlin, die Symphonie der Großstadt*
(*Berlin: Symphony of a City*, 1927) and his non-fiction films for the Nazi Bureau of
Labour, contributed documentaries such as *Sieg im Osten* (*Victory in the East*, 1941).[10]
In Britain, Alberto Cavalcanti, whose own city film *Rien que les heures* (*Nothing but
Time*, 1926) reflected his association with the French avant-garde, worked for the Ministry of Information's Film Division during the Second World War. The Ministry's
Crown Film Unit produced feature-length 'narrative-documentaries' which integrated
studio shooting and other elements of the commercial cinema.[11] A few years into the
war, a chain of mutual stylistic influences and citations linked the non-fiction military
films of allies and enemies: German war documentaries, for example, were studied
closely not only by Italians, but also by the British and the Americans.[12]

In Fascist Italy, much of this wartime experimentation with documentary and fictional genres took place in association with the armed forces' cinema production centres.
The army, navy, and air force each had long employed cinematographers who shot newsreels and documentaries, often sharing their material with the Istituto LUCE and with
commercial studios. The Navy Ministry was particularly open to innovation, thanks to
the presence of navy officer and film-maker Francesco De Robertis, a director of the Ministry's Centro Cinematografico. Since the early 1930s, the Navy Ministry had envisioned
a documentary, made with the Istituto LUCE, that would 'appeal to Italian and international markets through the integration of a love story and dignified and humane
comedy'.[13] The project was picked up years later by De Robertis, who in January 1939
penned a series of treatments for a naval film to be made 'with the most scrupulous sense

of truth'. Approved for production by the Navy Ministry in February 1939, these treatments formed the basis of two films that the press would call 'fictionalised documentaries' (*documentari romanzati*) for their use of non-actors and real locations.[14] De Robertis's *Uomini sul fondo* (*Men on the Seabed*, 1940), with a cast of full-time navy men, recounts the drama of sailors whose damaged submarine has sunk to the sea floor. *La nave bianca*, which Rossellini directed under De Robertis's supervision, employs a cast of navy operatives to demonstrate the operations of a warship and those of a hospital vessel, but also introduces a romantic involvement between an injured sailor and his nurse.[15]

It is worth exploring De Robertis's guidelines for these military 'fictional documentaries' as expounded in his treatments, since they influenced the ideology and the aesthetic of both *La nave bianca* and *Uomini sul fondo*. The treatments also clarify an issue that critics have long debated: the respective contributions of De Robertis and Rossellini to *La nave bianca*, and, in particular, responsibility for the romantic scenes that dominate the film's awkward second half. For different reasons, both directors have intimated that Rossellini had little to do with its filming, although the latter offered conflicting testimonies on this subject. Yet both treatments reveal that De Robertis had always intended the love story to be an integral part of the film. It is doubtful that Rossellini was unaware of this when he took the job, since De Robertis had a detailed storyboard, and even more unlikely that he chose to shoot only the film's 'documentary' first half. Both De Robertis and Rossellini were perhaps less than truthful in their retrospective assertions that the love story had been added as an afterthought.[16]

At the same time, the treatments help to discern Rossellini's contribution to *La nave bianca* and De Robertis's influence on the director's stylistic development. First, both treatments underscore the importance of *coralità* (chorality), a principle that would underlie Rossellini's own realist aesthetic. 'A film about the Navy must be *a film about atmosphere*,' De Robertis asserted, one that would set its protagonists 'within a very broad background that extends to and highlights the life of other men'.[17] Second, De Robertis proposed minimising battle scenes to highlight the corps' everyday discipline and dedication. Writing before the outbreak of the Second World War, he argued that to focus on the efficiency of auxiliary vessels (such as the hospital fleet), and on standard military manoeuvres, would suffice to convey the navy's 'spirit of adaptation, inventiveness, and aggression'. De Robertis wished less to document combat heroism than to narrate 'the most normal and common story possible . . . devoid of all rhetoric.'[18] These ideas are preserved in *La nave bianca*, which was made after Italy's entry into the war. Eschewing lengthy battle footage, the film focuses on the navy professionals (doctors, nurses, officers, sailors) who keep the war machine running.

Finally, although De Robertis believed in the superior educative value of the documentary short, he also recognised that 'propaganda, commercial and artistic reasons' mandated attention to 'narrative unity and psychological development' in full-length films made for theatrical release. Thus 'emotional conflicts', particularly the clash between collective obligations and personal relations, figure strongly in both his treatments. The first one features a young protagonist who is torn between his obligations to the mother of his child and his desire for a navy career. The second and more important one maps out a two-part film that corresponds closely to *La nave bianca*. This movie's first half was to depict the daily routines of shipboard life 'with looseness and spirit' to show that 'Italians are not as sad and serious as they are perceived abroad'. This directive accounts for the comic and light tone of the early scenes of *La nave bianca*, which communicate camaraderie among the corps and foreground the love story between the sailor Basso and his wartime pen pal or *matrigna* (literally, 'stepmother') Elena, a nurse and teacher.

The second part, De Robertis wrote, was to take on more drama and urgency, incorporating 'so-called theatrical elements ... to satisfy the public's curiosity and passion'. Here the crew is to take on a risky peacetime mission, which is transformed in *La nave bianca* into an aerial attack on the warship; here, too, we are to witness the development of 'emotional ties' between the protagonist and a woman, as happens in *La nave bianca* when the injured Basso is transferred to Elena's hospital ship. The finale, De Robertis specified, was to have a 'spiritual' content, which in *Uomini sul fondo* is provided by a sailor who sacrifices his life to save his companions. In *La nave bianca*, the sacrifice is made by Elena, who recognises Basso as her amorous correspondent but disguises her feelings out of a professional duty not to favour any of those in her care. Their romantic involvement remains unresolved, since De Robertis had vetoed an on-screen marriage as contrary to the film's theme, which he defined as 'the overcoming of individualism through a sense of honour for the military and a sense of duty and love for the Fatherland'.[19] *La nave bianca* thus draws its plot, tone, and pace from De Robertis's second 1939 treatment. De Robertis's stylistic influences are also evident in the initial spareness of dialogue, the attention to detail and to quotidian actions, the clipped montage that emphasises the navy's efficiency, the emphasis on the interaction of men and machines, and the blending of documentary footage and studio shooting, non-actors and actors. All these elements link *La nave bianca* to *Uomini sul fondo*.

Yet, *La nave bianca* is also recognisable as Rossellini's work. An attention to formal composition, which is present from the first Eisenstein-influenced frames; a more expansive *mise-en-scène* in the film's second half, which works with the slower pace of the melodramatic and intimist segments; the use of music (by Rossellini's brother Renzo) to signal these changes of tempo and mood; a certain wittiness, best shown in a scene that cuts from a shot of a cat and dog warring for food to Italians and Germans together on deck – these qualities are instead specific to Rossellini and figure in his subsequent films.[20] The space given to the iconography and doctrine of Christian humanism also separates *La nave bianca* from De Robertis's texts. Elena, a carrier of rectitude and charity as well as a love interest, is a prototype for characters in later Rossellini films. The movie's last frames reinforce her symbolic status. The camera zooms in and holds on the red cross that adorns Elena's uniform, voiding the screen of all reference to surrounding reality, until the film's dedication (to 'the wounded of all the ranks' and to those who 'attenuate their sufferings and nourish their faith') is superimposed. The on-screen message is reminiscent of *Uomini sul fondo*, but the shot is pure Rossellini, and it sets off his own dedication to the cause of Christian humanitarianism. It also underscores the consolatory ideology that pervades *La nave bianca*, which was made during a war that produced a devastating number of Italian casualties and the temporary loss of half of the Italian battleship fleet before Rossellini even finished his picture. Ultimately, the controversy over the film's authorship cautions against an overreliance on auteur-based critical models to understand films that came out of highly collaborative environments such as the Centro Cinematografico.

La nave bianca met with great success when it was first shown in September 1941 in special screenings for civil and military officials and two thousand naval officers.[21] Its public première came at the Venice Biennale, where it won the Fascist Party Cup. Critics praised its homage to 'military duty,' but were especially struck by its stylistic innovations. They fêted *La nave bianca* as the perfect blend of art and propaganda and a film that 'made use of elements that are entirely new for its genre'. For Guido Aristarco, the film, along with *Uomini sul fondo*, appeared as the harbinger of a new kind of non-fiction cinema in which the documentary element became 'not merely background, but a fundamental and active factor in the narration'.[22] The glowing reception of *Uomini sul fondo* one year earlier had created an audience for *La nave bianca*; now the praise heaped on Rossellini cemented his reputation as a director. It also improved his political standing in a regime that, especially during the war, encouraged artists to make topical films, regardless of their private beliefs. The performative value of *La nave bianca* can be understood in this context, as can the film's striking initial shots. A dark screen is revealed to be the barrel of a huge navy warship gun, which is pointed squarely at the viewer, and then raised to show off an equally intimidating warship. Rossellini's citation here of Eisenstein, a master of the art of cinematic propaganda, is significant. The big guns target Italy's enemies, but also the audience, reinforcing Mussolini's slogan (borrowed from the Bolsheviks) that cinema was to be the Fascists' 'strongest weapon' of indoctrination and influence.

Rossellini's considerable imaginative and persuasive talents would be called on for his next project, *Un pilota ritorna*. The film takes place during a military campaign – the 1940–1 Italian invasion of Greece – the outcome of which had been at best unsatisfying and at worst humiliating. By the time Rossellini started shooting in October 1941, repeated unsuccessful advances had caused heavy Italian casualties and had prompted an intervention by the Fascists' Nazi allies. The Germans eventually allowed the Italians to occupy western Greece, but left no doubt about their control of what was to have been the 'Italian Mediterranean'.[23] *Un pilota ritorna* partially reflects this reality. Based on a story by Vittorio Mussolini, who had participated as a pilot in the Greek and Albanian invasion, it follows the experiences of an Italian aviator who becomes a POW in Greece. Mussolini also supervised the film and was in charge of the air force cinema centre that provided some of the aerial footage used in the movie.[24]

In *Un pilota ritorna*, as in *La nave bianca*, the realist and documentary tone gradually yields to melodrama. The film's first part advertises the appeal of aviation service, integrating spectacular footage of bombing operations taken by LUCE, the air force, and Rossellini's film crew. When Lieutenant Rossati (Massimo Girotti) carries out his first airborne missions, the director shows off the sophisticated technology and manoeuvres of Italian fighter planes through a combination of gliding pan shots, real-time action, and dynamic cross-cutting. We observe the privileges putatively enjoyed by air force officers, who are served by a phalanx of white-coated waiters and valets and also the camaraderie of the men when tragedy strikes. The second half, which takes place mostly in Greece, is structured around the twin narratives of Rossati's growing love for the Greek-Italian Anna (an expatriate Italian doctor's daughter, played by Michela Belmonte), who comforts the prisoners, and his public saga as a POW who joins the ranks of the war's displaced. The latter narrative has a happy ending that owes something to Fascist and Hollywood film cultures; Rossati steals a

British warplane and navigates back through Italian air space, receiving a hero's welcome when he lands at his home base. The resolution of the love story is foiled by
the war, which brings the two together and just as quickly pulls them apart. Rossati
returns to Italy dogged by his feelings for Anna, who could not leave her besieged
land, and the extreme close-up of his face in the film's final shot conveys his inner
conflict.[25] The sense of drama is maximised in this half of the picture by a Sturm-
und-Drang-infused score (again by Renzo Rossellini), high-contrast lighting
(especially in Rossati's escape scene, which includes some striking chiaroscuro
effects), and a drawn-out tempo that builds tension around such maudlin events as
the unanaesthetised leg amputation of another POW.

Rossellini's depictions of war's universally devastating effects, in particular the
material toll of its bombings and invasions, are more successful. Shunted from British
to Greek captivity, Rossati is forced to wander through villages and fields with Greek
peasants whose own homes have been destroyed. The film-makers give the British some
soft touches – they keep kittens and share drinks with their prisoners – but also present
them as by-the-book warriors who don't hesitate to 'make a desert of the enemy', as one
of their officers succinctly states. The Greek soldiers are also relatively tolerant captors,
and the Greek people a defeated nation of ragtag nomads who search futilely for shelter. Interestingly, the Germans do not receive this humanising treatment; they are
present only as unseen pilots of screaming Stuka bombers that threaten Rossati's life as
well. As a POW, Rossati moves out of the partisan position he occupied in the film's first
half and becomes a witness to war's horrors, which we experience through his eyes.
Trudging through British-razed villages with his amputee comrade on his back, diving
for cover from German bombs, Rossati bears the burdens of the war along with the

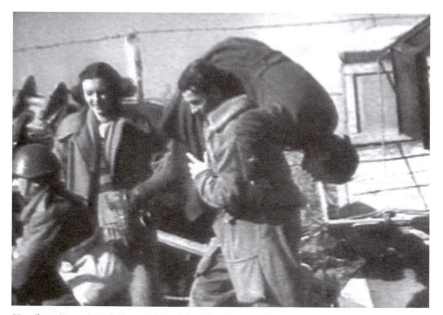

Un pilota ritorna (1942): Rossati (Massimo Girotti) carries his wounded comrade through a
Greek village destroyed by the British army.

Greek peasants. He appears as a victim among victims, rather than a bomber who contributed to the destruction that now surrounds him.

This transformation of Rossati from aggressor to aggrieved, which builds on established rhetorics of victimhood within Italian Fascist ideology, complicates interpretations of *Un pilota ritorna* as simply an anti-war film.[26] Certainly, Rossellini's Christian humanitarianism is present here throughout the movie, chiefly through the mediating figure of Anna, who dispenses first aid and moral support to both Greeks and Italians. Nor does Rossellini gloss over the war's disruption of habit and history. His images of decimated villages and smoking ruins initiate a visual meditation on war's effects on everyday reality that will be more fully realised in *Rome Open City* and *Paisà*. Still, the film-makers' positioning of Rossati as a man caught in the middle of the war is disingenuous at best. It begs the question of the Italians' own culpability as the architects of the tragedies which are so movingly depicted. The movie's presentation of the Germans as a menace rather than as co-belligerents of the Greek invasion is consonant with this ideological operation, although it also reflects Italian anxieties about their subalternity within the Axis alliance that found an echo in other areas of cultural production.[27] The disavowal of Italian responsibility in *Un pilota ritorna* may indeed express Rossellini's own ambivalence about what was undoubtedly an unpopular war, but it also supported claims about Fascism's 'humanitarian' and 'spiritual' qualities that intellectuals and policymakers had advanced since the start of the regime.[28]

Premièring in April 1942 before high state and military officials, *Un pilota ritorna* won the 36-year-old Rossellini more accolades and bigger audiences. Critics termed his style 'free from all rhetorical concessions' and lauded the 'humanity' of his depictions of war. Rossellini's growing personal status was signalled by a rather sycophantic article in Vittorio Mussolini's *Cinema* by Rosario Leone, Mussolini's assistant and a fellow screenwriter on the project. Leone portrayed a Rossellini who had so far logged 'two hundred flight hours in the skies of Africa, Italy, and the Mediterranean', often risking his life for the perfect shot.[29] Yet, *Cinema* also published a less positive piece by the anti-Fascist Giuseppe De Santis, who admired *Un pilota ritorna*'s anti-rhetorical ethos but felt that its 'documentarism' was not 'transfigured into essential poetry'. De Santis accompanied these stylistic criticisms with a veiled political message that urged Rossellini to reflect on the path he was taking. Instead of becoming further involved 'in a tumultuous struggle that risks overcoming our souls', Rossellini might consider making films that would function as a 'recall to the senses', oriented to 'a future for which we should all consider ourselves responsible'.[30]

Although Rossellini would soon turn his talents to the cause of anti-Fascist film-making, for the time being he continued to link his name to the Fascist military film. The success of *Un pilota ritorna* had opened up many opportunities; a film on the composer Franz Liszt was among the projects announced in the press that never came to fruition. Instead, Rossellini chose to work on the scripts of two more military-themed movies before starting to shoot *L'uomo dalla croce*, a drama about the experiences and eventual martyrdom of an Italian military chaplain on the Russian front.[31] For this project, Rossellini once again collaborated with some of the regime's most influential figures. The driving force here was the journalist Asvero Gravelli, who wrote the story and collaborated on the script. On the radio and in the press, Gravelli advertised Fascism as the agent of a 'spiritual' regeneration that would cleanse Italy and the world of the forces of political and cultural decadence. This translated into a ferocious crusade against democracy, but especially against Communism and its potential carriers – who included not only Russians, but also Jews in and outside of Italy.

Some critics have tended to apportion responsibility for *L'uomo dalla croce* in ways that minimise Rossellini's contribution. In this scheme, Rossellini, who also co-wrote the script, provided the film's Catholic–patriotic ethos and artistic direction, and Gravelli its blatant anti-Bolshevism.[32] Yet, Christianity had long been lauded by Gravelli as the ideological component that would distinguish Fascism's 'universal' civilisation from that of Communism.[33] And the warrior brand of Catholicism espoused in *L'uomo dalla croce* is not inconsistent with Rossellini's personal convictions, but merely reflects a sharpening or hardening of an existing mentality. The desperate situation Italy faced by mid-1942 may have contributed to this shift and to the film's slightly apocalyptic feel. By this time, Italian East Africa had been lost to the British for a year, spelling the end of the Italian empire. The débâcles in Greece and elsewhere had raised the distinct possibility of Italian postwar subordination to the Nazis, who seemed to scorn Christianity almost as much as the Russians. In this context, Italian participation in the Russian campaign, which involved almost a quarter of a million men by 1942, took on the significance of a last bid for Italian influence, understood in spiritual as well as military terms. It was also a last-ditch defence of values and beliefs that were broader and older than those of Fascism. Recognised as a transition film in the director's *œuvre*, *L'uomo dalla croce* marks the emergence of a Manichaean mode of thought (most visible in the portrayal of Italy's enemies) that will figure heavily in *Rome Open City* as well.

Shot at Rome's Cinecittà studios and in the Roman countryside, the film opens with tranquil and light scenes: birds sing, brooks babble, Italian soldiers relax in the rustling grass. The reassuring tone carries through to the introduction of the chaplain, played by Rossellini's architect friend Alberto Tavazzi. In the film's early scenes, he calms young recruits and gazes at the stars with a wounded soldier in his arms. This opening section targets viewers' emotions to facilitate an immediate identification with the main character, a strategy that De Robertis summed up as 'giving full development to *human factors* through a well-defined theatrical narrative about an individual story: making the audience feel the war, not just see it'.[34] It also clarifies the narrative function of the chaplain, who serves as a healer, mediator, and captive, unifying the characters of Anna, Elena, and Rossati from Rossellini's preceding films. Yet, the increased space given to melodrama in *L'uomo dalla croce* does not prevent Rossellini from completing his tripartite celebration of Italy's armed forces. The chaplain's missionary work is paralleled by the army's attempt to conquer a Russian village, and the director shows off tanks, flame-throwers, and more tanks, which are filmed in action from every possible angle. With respect to *La nave bianca* and *Un pilota ritorna*, though, the director shows a surer hand in the composition and movement of his battle scenes. The striking geometries and conflicting planes that he creates with troop formations will be echoed in *Rome Open City*, where rigid rows of marching Germans offset the irregular volumes and spaces of the Italian capital.

The film changes its focus and mood when the chaplain becomes a Russian prisoner. As in *Un pilota ritorna*, an expatriate Italian sets the tone for the experience of captivity. Instead of a humanitarian doctor, we are confronted with a hard-bitten interrogator

L'uomo dalla croce (1943): frame enlargement (Joel Finler Collection).

who ends Italian lives rather than saving them. This Italian Marxist who, it is intimated, fled Fascism for Russia years ago, scoffs at the chaplain's cross and orders the execution of an Italian soldier who holds a Fascist Party card. Significantly, the film-makers depict this turncoat as afflicted with a repulsive skin disease; he has stained bandages covering his head and his hands, and he scratches himself compulsively as he confers with his scruffy Russian comrades. This strategy of defamiliarisation will be utilised in *Rome Open City* to portray Nazis and their Italian collaborators as carriers of sickness and sexual deviance. The interrogation scene is the first of two enclosed spaces in which the spiritual war between atheistic Communism and Catholic Italian Fascism is waged. The second is a hut (*izba*), occupied by a mix of peasant families, Italian soldiers, and their Russian prisoners, where the chaplain takes refuge after the schoolhouse is bombed. Inside the *izba*, the Italians drop their martial bearing, and the chaplain exchanges the role of the Russians' captive for that of their 'impartial' spiritual liberator. 'No, I am not the enemy', the chaplain tells Irina, a Russian fighter who at first resists his pastoral attentions. 'I am a minister of God who is father to all men and who considers all men brothers even if they are antagonistic.'

In *L'uomo dalla croce* the ideals of Christian fraternity and anti-Communism work together, making the former an arm in the battle against the latter.[35] The chaplain seeks communication with the Russians less as a humanitarian end in itself than as a prelude to the recuperation of the Catholic faith. The *izba* proves to be a propitious environment in this regard. The peasant women drop to their knees and utter Christ's name when they see the chaplain, and ask him to baptise a newborn Russian child. Even the fiercest men and women seem ready to rethink or abandon the atheistic and materialistic attitudes inculcated by Communism, as the scenes dedicated to Irina (Roswitha Schmidt) and Fyodor (Attilio Dottesio) demonstrate. Wearing a dashing headband instead of a babushka, fighting alongside the men, Irina is the Communist New Woman who dismisses romantic love as an obsolete bourgeois notion. The death of her companion Sergei (Aldo Capacci) in the *izba*, though, brings forth a speech about her life that reveals her to be a casualty of Communism's anti-familial politics. Here Rossellini uses extreme close-ups and high-contrast lighting to underscore emotional intensity in ways that presage the expressionistic torture sequences of *Rome Open City*. The birth of a baby during this scene seals the sense of catharsis and repentance: Irina's scowl is replaced by a soft smile as she caresses the infant.

The death of Fyodor, another disfigured hardline Communist, provides a final missionary opportunity as well as the film's climactic moment. The hut goes up in flames from a bombing attack, and the chaplain is shot while he rescues Irina. Dragging himself through crossfire to reach the wounded Fyodor, he lives just long enough to teach the dying Communist the Lord's Prayer and to witness Italian troops' triumphant advance. As in *La nave bianca*, the ending clarifies the referents of the film's Catholic ideology: a close-up of the cross on the chaplain's uniform is overlaid by a dedication to Italian clergy 'who fell in the crusade against the godless, in defence of the country, and in order to bring the light of truth and justice even to the land of the barbarian enemy'. Indeed, the film's final focus is not on the unnamed chaplain, but on the faceless hordes of Italian soldiers who practically trample his body as they rush by on foot and on horseback.

Although Rossellini had always known how to make the most of the opportunities offered him, his timing was not the best in the case of *L'uomo dalla croce*. The film's release was delayed until June 1943, by which time the bitter winter campaign in Russia had reversed Axis fortunes and made a mockery of this and other propaganda films set on the Eastern Front. Mussolini's regime then fell from power at the end of July. Six days earlier, Rossellini had started on his first non-military picture, *Scalo merci*. Filming was interrupted by the bombing of Rome, and it was ultimately completed by Marcello Pagliero and released in 1946 as *Desiderio* (*Desire*). By the end of 1944, with Rome under siege by the Germans, Rossellini had turned his attentions to the anti-Fascist resistance, which formed the subject of *Rome Open City* and *Paisà*. During this period, he also served as the Christian Democrat representative to the Committee of National Liberation's new Film Workers' Union. This political affiliation reflected the continuing importance Catholic tropes and themes held for Rossellini after 1945 as a means of understanding human beings and the histories they create through their actions.

One of the first movies to portray the partisan struggle, *Rome Open City* became a model for other movies that approached the Resistance at the level of everyday life and rendered a sense of its historical importance. Viewed from the perspective of Rossellini's Fascist war trilogy, though, *Rome Open City* appears less as an *ex nihilo* neo-realist creation than as a transition film, one that builds on the aesthetics and themes of Rossellini's previous movies and works out his relationship to past ideologies and identities. The film's most striking similarity to *L'uomo dalla croce* – both feature a priest who becomes a martyr for a political cause – highlights how Rossellini's understanding of Catholicism was evolving in the transition from Fascism to democracy. Whereas the military chaplain on the Russian front aimed to convert those who did not espouse his own belief system, Don Pietro, the partisan-allied priest of *Rome Open City*, holds a more pluralist outlook. This change of context is emphasised by a curious continuity: the priest who prepares Don Pietro for his execution by Italian Fascist soldiers is the same man (the non-actor Alberto Tavazzi) who played the military chaplain in *L'uomo dalla croce*. Rossellini's resurrection of this figure as a negative presence in this crucial scene suggests a renunciation of Fascist-linked paradigms of Christian practice and thought.

Critics have only recently begun to locate the Fascist war trilogy within the continuum of Rossellini's *œuvre*, and a full evaluation of the director's activities during the dictatorship is only now taking shape. This is, in part, a function of Rossellini's important status as an anti-Fascist film-maker, which caused many critics to gloss over his relationship with the regime. Most now conclude that opportunism, rather than political fervour, motivated the director's professional decisions during the dictatorship. Many years later, Rossellini would describe his situation then as follows: 'I employed all my talents to make films without falling prisoner of [the Fascist] system. True, I had to engage in extraordinary contortions. At the end, I had become as strong, supple, and ungraspable as an eel'.[36] This explanation undoubtedly reflects a partial truth, but it also glosses over the complexity of Rossellini's position within Fascist film culture, given his close ties with Mussolini's family and his choice to specialise in propaganda films on the armed forces. Only 25 out of 400 Italian movies made between 1940 and 1943 dealt directly with the war, and Rossellini made three of them and scripted a fourth.[37] What is clear is that Rossellini's flexibility, together with his enormous talent, allowed him to emerge quickly as one of anti-Fascism's most effective propagandists. Internationally acclaimed upon its release, *Rome Open City* helped to rehabilitate Italy and Italians from association with the dictatorship. Ultimately, the films of the Fascist war trilogy merit attention as important moments in Rossellini's artistic formation. They laid the foundations of a neo-realist film-making style that would influence directors from India to Spain to America, bringing the Italian cinema the audiences and prestige that had eluded it throughout the long years of Mussolini's rule.

Notes

I thank Elliot Jurist for his insightful comments on drafts of this article. I am also grateful to MacGregor Knox, who patiently answered my questions about Fascist military technology, to Christopher Wagstaff, who facilitated video viewings, and to Paola Castagna of the Cineteca Nazionale, Rome. John Gooch, Robert Mallett, and Giorgio Rochat kindly aided my access to the Ufficio Storico della Marina Militare in Rome, where Dr Ester Pennella proved helpful and efficient.

1 See Peter Bondanella, *The Films of Roberto Rossellini* (Cambridge: Cambridge University Press, 1993), Gianni Rondolino, *Roberto Rossellini* (Turin: UTET, 1989), Peter Brunette, *Roberto Rossellini* (New York: Oxford University Press, 1996), Gian Piero Brunetta, *Storia del cinema italiano, 1896–1945* (Rome: Riuniti, 1993), pp. 152–6. Adriano Aprà's bibliography in *Rosselliniana* (Rome: Di Giacomo, 1987) offers the most comprehensive coverage of the vast body of Rossellini criticism.

2 Tag Gallagher, *The Adventures of Roberto Rossellini* (New York: Da Capo, 1998), pp. 28–30, 39; Bondanella, *Films*, pp. 1–2.

3 Carlo Ludovico Bragaglia, 'Narrazione e documentario', *Cinema*, 10 October 1937.

4 Rossellini would seek to minimise his involvement with this film after the war, pointing out that Fascism's authoritarian cinema culture accorded absolute power to the director. Yet the dictatorship's preventive censorship policies assigned screenwriters

such as Rossellini considerable responsibility, since production advances depended on officials' judgement of a script's 'moral and professional qualities'. Roberto Rossellini, interview in Francesco Savio, *Cinecittà anni trenta. Parlano 116 protagonisti del secondo cinema italiano*, 3 vols (Rome: Bulzoni, 1979), vol. 3, p. 962. On Fascism's film censorship policies, see Jean Gili, *Stato fascista e cinematografia. Repressione e promozione* (Rome: Bulzoni, 1981).

5 Rondolino, *Rossellini*, p. 46; Gallagher, *Adventures*, pp. 55–6. *Luciano Serra pilota* won the Mussolini Cup at the 1938 Venice Biennale, along with Leni Riefenstahl's *Olympia*. On Rossellini's early shorts, see Marta Teodoro, 'Perduti e ritrovati. Due cortometraggi di Rossellini, *La vispa Teresa* e *Il tacchino prepotente*', in Teodoro (ed.), *Il nuovo spettatore*, 1 (Milan: Franco Angeli, 1997), pp. 116–44.

6 Fernando Cerchio, 'Servizio di guerra', *Cinema*, 10 July 1940; Ugo Casiraghi, 'Cinema e vita militare', *Cinema*, 25 July 1941. On the *cinemamitragliatrice*, see Fernando Volla, 'Cinema: arma di guerra aerea', *Cinema*, 28 July 1936; also Guido Bagnani, 'Cinema, occhio della guerra', *Cinema*, 25 August 1936. Paul Virilio offers a theorisation of the nexus between the perceptive apparatus of cinema and modern war in *Guerre et cinéma* (Paris: Editions de l'Etoile, 1984). The majority of the documentarists who worked for the cinema centres of the air force, navy, and army were born between 1905 and 1915, as revealed in the *Almanacco del cinema 1942–3* (Rome: Società Anonima Editrice Cinema, 1943), pp. 45–6. On Fascist wartime cinema policies, consult Mino Argentieri, *Il cinema in guerra. Arte, comunicazione, e propaganda in Italia, 1940–4* (Rome: Riuniti, 1998), and Gianni Rondolino, 'Italian Propaganda Films, 1940–3', in K.R.M. Short (ed.), *Film and Radio Propaganda in The Second World War* (Knoxville: University of Tennessee Press, 1983), pp. 220–9.

7 Rossellini's *Un pilota ritorna* and *La nave bianca* formed part of a nine-film plan by the Committee for War and Political Cinema, an entity created in 1941 by the regime. See Guglielmo Cerani, 'Nove film di guerra', *Lo Schermo*, August 1941. *L'uomo dalla croce* formed part of a new round of military films approved in 1942.

8 Sandro Reanda, 'Cinematografia di guerra', *Cinemagazzino*, 20 March 1941; also Lando Ferretti, 'Il film documentario e gli altri', *Lo Schermo*, February 1939; Raffaele Matarazzo, 'Roma avrà un suo centro di cultura e di studi cinematografici', *Tevere*, 20 March 1930. Matarazzo's 1933 film *Treno popolare*, Giovacchino Forzano's 1932 film *Camicia nera*, Giulio Brignone's 1938 *Sotto la croce del sud*, and Camerini's 1932 *Gli uomini, che mascalzoni!* and 1936 *Il grande appello* all utilised newsreel footage. The Spanish Civil War-themed *L'assedio dell'Alcazar* (Augusto Genina, 1940), which was described as a 'fictional documentary' by officials, is an important precedent. See Bondanella, *Films*, pp. 9–11, on this film. Debates from the 1930s about, and practices of, cinematic realism are discussed in Ruth Ben-Ghiat, *Fascist Modernities; Italy, 1922–45* (Berkeley and Los Angeles: University of California Press, forthcoming), Chapters 3 and 6; Massimo Mida and Lorenzo Quaglietti (eds), *Dai telefoni bianchi al neo-realismo* (Bari: Laterza, 1980), gives a selection of primary texts.

9 Mussolini, quoted in Giuseppe Rossi, 'La propaganda agraria cinematografica svolta dall'Opera Nazionale Combattenti', *La Conquista della Terra*, February 1930. On the Istituto LUCE and the function of documentaries in Fascist Italy, see James Hay, *Popular Film Culture in Fascist Italy* (Bloomington: Indiana University Press, 1986), pp. 201–32; for Corrado D'Errico and *Il cammino degli eroi*, see Ruth Ben-Ghiat,

'Envisioning Modernity: Desire and Discipline in the Italian Fascist Film', *Critical Inquiry* (Autumn 1996), pp. 130–5.

10 For Ruttmann's path from Weimar to the Nazis, see Barry Fulks, 'Walter Ruttmann, the Avant-Garde Film, and Nazi Modernism', *Film and History*, May 1984, pp. 26–35. On the influence of Russian Communist montage theories and compilation films on German military documentaries, see Hilmar Hoffmann, *The Triumph of Propaganda: Film and National Socialism, 1933–45* (Providence and Oxford: Berghahn, 1996), pp. 135–69.

11 Wartime British documentary and the Crown Film Unit are analysed in James Chapman, *The British at War: Cinema, State and Propaganda 1939–45* (London: I.B. Tauris, 1998).

12 On the international circulation of war footage and documentaries, see Elizabeth Sussex, *The Rise and Fall of British Documentary* (Berkeley: University of California Press, 1975), p. 114, Argentieri, *Il cinema in guerra*, pp. 104–5, and David Culbert, 'Social Engineering for a Democratic Society at War', in Short, *Film and Radio Propaganda*, pp. 180–1. Vittorio Mussolini, 'Cinema di guerra', and Giuseppe Isani, 'Forza del documento bellico', both in *Cinema* (25 June 1940), proposed German documentaries as models for the Italians.

13 Letter from the Istituto LUCE to the Ministero della Marina, 30 November 1933, in the archive of the Ufficio Storico della Marina Militare, Rome (USMM), t. [titolario] 8, f. [fascicolo] 2820. On the armed forces' cinema production centres, see Argentieri, *Il cinema in guerra*, pp. 10–14.

14 Domenico Meccoli, 'I nuovi registi', *Cinema*, 25 December 1941, is among those who use the term to refer to the works of Rossellini and De Robertis.

15 Francesco De Robertis, 'Pro-memoria circa un film sulla R. Marina Militare', sent to the Naval Ministry on 18 January 1939, De Robertis, 'Criteri di indirizzo per la realizzazione di un film sulla regia marina', and the 1 February 1939 approval memorandum from the office of the Navy Undersecretary, all in USMM, t. 8, f. 2820.

16 The Centro Cinematografico's collectivist ethos mandated the elision of individual on-screen credits for *Uomini sul fondo* and *La nave bianca*. On the conflict over authorship of the latter film, see Gallagher, *Adventures*, pp. 67–70, and Brunette, *Roberto Rossellini*, pp. 12–13. De Robertis's claim that the love story in *La nave bianca* had been added after the fact dates from 1943. See his article 'Appunti per un film d'aviazione', *Cinema*, 25 February 1943.

17 De Robertis, 'Criteri di indirizzo', and the treatment summary that accompanied the Navy Ministry's 1 February 1939 memorandum, both in USMM, t. 8, f. 2820.

18 Ibid.

19 Ibid. See also 'Pro-memoria'.

20 Brunette, *Roberto Rossellini*, pp. 11–18, Argentieri, *Cinema di guerra*, 120–3, analyse *La nave bianca*'s relationship to *Uomini sul fondo*.

21 USMM, t. 8, f. 2820, sf. [sottofascicolo] 2.

22 Pietro Bianchi, 'La nave bianca', *Bertoldo*, 31 October 1941, in Bianchi, *L'occhio di vetro. Il cinema degli anni 1930–43* (Milan: Il Formichiere, 1978), pp. 94–5; Giuseppe Isani, review in *Cinema*, 10 October 1941; Guido Aristarco, 'La scuola dei registi', *Corriere padano*, 19 November 1942.

23 See MacGregor Knox, *Mussolini Unleashed. Politics and Strategy in Italy's Last War*,

1939–41 (Cambridge: Cambridge University Press, 1982), for an overview of these débâcles.

24 Rossellini, Ugo Betti, Gherardo Gherardi, Michelangelo Antonioni, Margherita Maglione, and Massimo Mida worked on the script, which initially called for a non-actor in the male lead. They turned to Massimo Girotti when an amateur talent search proved inconclusive.

25 On this point, see Brunette, *Roberto Rossellini*, p. 21; Rondolino, *Rossellini*, pp. 55–8.

26 Ibid., p. 57; Gallagher, *Adventures*, pp. 79–81.

27 See on this subject Ben-Ghiat, 'Fascist Italy and Nazi Germany: The Dynamics of an Uneasy Relationship', in Richard Etlin (ed.), *Culture and the Nazis* (Chicago: University of Chicago Press, forthcoming).

28 In this regard, one might note that the Greek and British men who play Rossati's captors in the picture were themselves Italian POWs. The Italians' disavowal of their own violence during the war has been addressed by Enzo Collotti and Lutz Klinkhammer, *Il fascismo e l'Italia in guerra. Una conversazione fra storia e storiografia* (Rome: Ediesse, 1996).

29 L. (Rosario Leone), 'A R.R.', *Cinema*, 10 February 1942; Francesco Callari, 'Tre autentici registi', *Lo Schermo*, April 1942; Guido Piovene, review in *Corriere della Sera*, quoted in Stefano Masi, *Roberto Rossellini* (Rome: Gremese, 1987), p. 15.

30 Giuseppe De Santis, 'Un pilota ritorna', *Cinema*, 25 April 1942. De Santis's ideas about realism and cultural practice would be incorporated into Luchino Visconti's *Ossessione* (*Obsession*, 1942), to which he contributed as a screenwriter and assistant director. On the different factions of *Cinema* and their competing visions of realism, see Argentieri, *Il cinema in guerra*, pp. 124–5, 269–96, and Millicent Marcus, *Italian Film in the Light of Neo-Realism* (Princeton: Princeton University Press, 1986), pp. 14–29.

31 These are: *I 3 aquilotti* (*Three Pilots in Training*, Mario Mattoli, 1942), a Vittorio Mussolini creation about three cadets at Caserta's Air Force Academy, and the historical movie *L'invasore* (*The Invader*, Nino Giannini), which dramatises the invasion of the Kingdom of Sardegna by Habsburg troops and which Rossellini also supervised. *L'invasore* ran into financial problems and was not released until 1949. Rondolino, *Rossellini*, pp. 59–60; Gallagher, *Adventures*, pp. 84, 97.

32 This view is espoused most strenuously by Rondolino, *Rossellini*, p. 61, who lists Gravelli as the 'true author' of the film; Gallagher, *Adventures*, pp. 84–5, oscillates between removing Rossellini from responsibility and justifying his presence on the film. Bondanella, *Films*, pp. 32–44, Brunette, *Roberto Rossellini*, pp. 25–32, and Argentieri, *Il cinema in guerra*, pp. 128–32, offer more complex readings.

33 Gravelli based the story that gave rise to *L'uomo dalla croce* on the experiences of Don Reginaldo Giuliani, a priest who served in the Second World War, the Fiume expedition, and the Ethiopian invasion before dying in battle.

34 De Robertis, 'Appunti per un film d'avazione'.

35 For a range of views on the function of Rossellini's Catholicism in the film, see Brunetta, *Storia del cinema italiano*, pp. 152–6; Argentieri, 'Storia e spiritualismo nel Rossellini degli anni quaranta', *Cinemasessanta*, January–February 1974, pp. 28–37; Bondanella, *Films*, pp. 38–9; Michele Serceau, *Roberto Rossellini* (Paris: Cerf, 1986), p. 17.

36 Gallagher, *Adventures*, and Brunette, *Roberto Rossellini*, both make this point;

Argentieri, *Il cinema in guerra*, and Bondanella, *Films*, point out how Rossellini's films converged at many points with Fascist ideologies. Rondolino, in 'Italian Propaganda Films', p. 52, and *Rossellini*, p. 38, argues that Rossellini was 'indifferent' and claims that his beliefs and aesthetic lie 'beyond any ideological scheme.' The Rossellini quotation is from *Fragments d'une autobiographie* (Paris: Ramsay, 1987), pp. 116–17.

37 Figures on wartime film production are from Rondolino, 'Italian Propaganda Films', p. 238.

3
Rossellini and Neo-realism

Christopher Wagstaff

At some point in the making of *Paisà* (1946) Rossellini abandoned one form of dramaturgy for another, and that adoption of a new dramaturgy is a more essential
characteristic of neo-realism than has generally been acknowledged. A number of different approaches could be taken to the definition of neo-realism in the cinema. One
approach might be to collect contemporary reviews of the films and distil a 'reception'
from them; another might be to collect the statements of the film-makers themselves
and of film-makers who have been influenced by neo-realism, in order to distil from
those statements a cinematic practice. An approach widely adhered to is that of sur-
veying the way film critics and historians have defined the term. Unfortunately, few of
these critics have *analysed* the films very closely. The earliest and still the best critic,
André Bazin, is so attached to the notion of the indexicality of cinematography (discussed below) that he often fails to *read* the films, content with the power of what he
calls the 'facts' on-screen.[1] Perhaps the best approach is to look closely at the films
themselves. In this case we shall take *Paisà* and, for reasons of space, one episode in
particular.

It might be helpful, before going any further, to discuss briefly the relationship a feature film has with the reality it purports to represent. The American philosopher C.S.
Peirce distinguished between signs on the basis of their connection to their referent (the
thing in reality to which they refer – not the same as what Saussure called the *signifié*;
the *signifié* of 'tree' is a concept in my mind, whereas the referent of the sign 'tree' would
not fit inside my head). He identified three types of sign: the symbol, the icon and the
index.[2] The symbol is connected to its referent by a rule or an agreement: the words 'two
cats' could be replaced by other agreed signs such as 'due gatti'. The icon is connected to
its referent by some characteristic of the sign itself: a street plan of London has a characteristic that links it to its architectural and urban referent; an onomatopoeia like 'moo'
for the lowing of cattle also has an iconic character. The index is connected to its referent by a causal or logical link: the fingerprint on the dagger in Colonel Prendergast's
chest was caused by the murderer's fingertip. Photographs are caused by light rays from
the referent striking a silver nitrate emulsion, and so are indexical (the viewer who did
not know that the image they were viewing was photographically produced might still
identify the referent because of the iconic character of photographs). Peter O'Toole,
dressed up as, and behaving as though he were, Lawrence of Arabia, is an icon, of which
the cinema projects an indexical sign for the ticket-paying public. *Within* the narrative
of a film, *meanings* can be signified indexically: if a little boy bursts into tears in a given
narrative context, the *meaning* might be that he is frightened, disappointed or angry –

the emotion *caused* the behaviour; but in 'reality' the actor (whether 'professional' or not) cried because the director told him to.

Hence, the cinematic sign is at two removes from its referent: it is an index of an icon of a referent. The referent, in turn, exists in a conventionally coded iconic narrative, which *may* have its own referent in historical fact – though by now the links are tenuous. There is nothing 'real' in a neo-realist film, except (sometimes) the locations in which it is shot (when these are indexically recorded). Yet *Paisà*, a film in which the locations are sometimes iconic (the monastery in the Appenines was actually on the Amalfi coast), and in which the narrative often has no precise referents in historical fact, is generally considered more profoundly neo-realist than *Rome Open City* (1945), in which locations are sometimes precisely those belonging to the historical facts that are the referents of the narrative. *Rome Open City* is a 'true' story, in many ways; though it would be better to call it a collage of more or less true stories manipulated in such a way as to transform them into a legend. Because the legend is intimately connected to very real aspects of the social and political experience of Italians at a certain point in time, it has been recognised as a 'real' portrayal of life in German-occupied Rome. The film is a startling innovation in relation to his previous films, but it does not break away from conventional genre cinema nearly as radically as *Paisà*.

For too long, neo-realism has been defined by means of a description of unintended superficial characteristics, for example non-professional actors, poor film stock, low costs and location shooting. Yet non-professional actors were not a matter of principle in the case of *Paisà*: the film's co-producer Rod Geiger considered Burgess Meredith for a while, and asked his father to line up Miron McCormick of the Group Theatre, Canada Lee from two Hitchcock films, Frances Farmer and William Gargan. He added: 'We need two more actors. Good actors, but not necessarily stars.'[3] The 'look' of *Rome Open City* has been attributed to poor film stock, yet the film was beautifully photographed by Ubaldo Arata on entirely appropriate film stock, one kind for the interiors and another for the exteriors. Production costs were determined by the potential domestic theatrical market: the Italian domestic market was relatively small, most of it was taken up with American films, so production costs had to be low. Yet *Bicycle Thieves* (*Ladri di biciclette*) (Vittorio De Sica, 1948) was a high-cost production and only recouped its costs after an intense and carefully planned promotional campaign. As for location shooting, studios had been bombed or requisitioned for military storage or refugee housing; equipment had been removed either to Venice or to Germany; the unreliability of electricity power supply meant that only sunlight could be counted on for the maintenance of a shooting schedule.

It cannot be denied that neo-realist cinema had material determinants: low production costs meant the avoidance of stars and spectacle; shooting on location or in poorly equipped studios meant using the Italy that the war had left as the setting for the stories; temporary political and social destabilisation and decentralisation meant that there was no 'establishment' and no recognised status quo around which to construct stories. However, it is easy to be misled – by the heroic picture of struggle against adversity that neo-realist film-makers themselves have promulgated – into thinking that the contingent material characteristics of their films are what define their essence.

Neo-realism grew out of a historical moment, and embraced literature (both poetry and prose), non-fiction publishing, painting, photography and cinema. What neo-realists have always insisted is that their art was a response to a moment in time. For them the problem was not so much the *a priori* one of changing their aesthetic, but that of *finding a way* to convey what they had to *express*. The content demanded the form. The function of their art was to give expression. But to what? The answer has nearly always been the same: to their experience – of suffering – and to the need to understand it, hence to a search for values which would prevent a repetition or perpetuation of the suffering. Visconti even made a film to express the suffering brought about by the cinema: *Bellissima* (1951). Rossellini, Antonioni and Fellini were deemed by some Communist intellectuals to have 'betrayed' neo-realism for pursuing that mission (to give expression to suffering) through the 1950s and into the 1960s.

For those Communists, as Rossellini himself shows in *Europe '51* (1952),[4] values were not up for grabs: the problems were clear, and even clearer was their solution. The function of the cinema was to give expression to conflicts that had already been decided upon (for example, the class struggle, or the search for full employment). It is easy to see how, once they had so defined neo-realism, they would accept as neo-realist *Bicycle Thieves*, *La terra trema* (Visconti, 1948), *Il sole sorge ancora* (Vergano, 1946), *Bitter Rice* (De Santis, 1949), *Il grido* (Antonioni, 1957) or even *I vitelloni* (Fellini, 1953), and how they would feel profoundly uncomfortable in the presence of *Stromboli* (Rossellini, 1949), *L'avventura* (Antonioni, 1960) or *La strada* (Fellini, 1954).

To continue this procedure – of accounting for what the function of cinema *was* for the neo-realists, by opposing it to what it was *not* – it is helpful to look briefly at how the state saw the function of cinema. In 1952, Giulio Andreotti, Director General of the Cinema in the Cabinet Office, published an open letter to De Sica in response to *Umberto D*, in which he said:

> We are not really asking De Sica to base his film making on the writings of Don Sturzo or the affairs of the Partito Popolare ... We are just asking this man of culture to accept his social responsibilities. ... De Sica shows clearly – and who could challenge him? – that he does not consider the present order to be the best order possible on earth ... but nothing in his film offers that modicum of teaching which might help in reality to make tomorrow's world less cold for the multitudes who waste away, suffer and die in silence ... It has been said in this post-war period that the cinema must realistically portray the truth by not representing society in an unreal, false and sugar-coated way. A principle that is acceptable in itself for a certain kind of production, but always within the limits of balance, objectivity and proportion.[5]

In 1955, Luigi Scalfaro addressed a meeting of the General Directorate of the Cinema thus:

> The cinema is first and above all a sector of industry, and the prime goal of an industry is to keep that industry strong ... [T]he cinema's first duty is to entertain on the human level. A film must offer the public relaxation after the toils of the daytime, it must interest it and entertain it in a simple way, without creating the torment of complicated states of mind, but rather relieving the weariness of the day with a greater optimism, with a more joyful vision of the world.[6]

What these two politicians – men with considerable power over the purse-strings for production finance – are saying to neo-realism is: 'Enough!' But they are also clearly declaring that the function of cinema, as a popular, mass medium, is consolation and propaganda (just as it was for the industrially and commercially successful US cinema, which they wanted the Italian cinema industry to emulate). That is *not* what the function of cinema was for the neo-realists. The person who tried most seriously to articulate what neo-realism *was* is a writer. In 1964, Italo Calvino tried to explain what had motivated the writing of his 1947 novel *Il sentiero dei nidi di ragno* (*The Path to the Spiders' Nests*):

> The literary explosion of those years in Italy was not so much an artistic phenomenon, more a physiological, existential, collective fact ... a sense of life being something which could begin again from scratch ... The fact of having emerged from an experience – a war, a civil war – which had spared no one, established an immediacy of communication between the writer and his public: we were face to face, on equal terms, bursting with stories to tell ... the explosive charge of freedom which inspired young writers in those days resided not so much in their urge to provide documentary information, as in the urge to *express*. Express what? Ourselves ... For the fact is that those who now think of 'neo-realism' primarily as a contamination or coercion of literature by non-literary forces are really shifting the terms of the question: in reality the non-literary elements were simply there, so solid and indisputable that they seemed to us to be completely natural; for us the problem appeared to be entirely one of poetics, of how to transform that world which for us was *the* world into a work of literature ...
>
> For many of my contemporaries it had been solely a question of luck which determined what side they should fight on; for many of them the sides suddenly changed over, so that soldiers of Mussolini's Fascist Republic became partisans and vice versa; they shot or were shot at on either side; only death signalled an end to their choices. It was Pavese, caught between remorse for not having fought and the urge to be sincere about the reasons for his refusal, who managed to write, in the closing pages of *La casa in collina*: 'every casualty resembles the survivor and demands to know the reason for his death from those who survive'.[7]
>
> If I say that in those days we made literature out of our condition of poverty, I am not really talking about some ideological programme, but rather about something far more profound that was inside all of us ... the spirit which animated our attempts to establish a new tradition of fiction which had to be built entirely from scratch.[8]

Calvino's last sentence is illustrated by Fellini's account of the making of *Paisà*:

> Following Rossellini around when he was shooting *Paisà* provided me with the sudden joyous revelation that you could make a film with the same freedom, the same lightness of spirit, with which you might draw or write, enjoying it and suffering with it day by day, hour by hour, without agonising too much about the final result; and having the same, secret, anxious and exciting relationship with it that one has with one's own neuroses; I realised too that the blockages, the doubts, the second thoughts, the dramas, the travails were not that different from those suffered by the painter trying to fix a tint

on the canvas or a writer crossing out, rewriting, correcting and starting again, looking
for a mode of expression hidden, impalpable and elusive, as one possibility among a
thousand.[9]

Perhaps we need to explain why a film industry which had hitherto been essentially concerned with bourgeois genre entertainment issuing from a centralised (in Rome)
studio-bound production system should, for a limited period, concern itself with the
suffering of every social stratum of a widely dispersed community. Perhaps Andreotti
and Scalfaro were right to call a halt to it. In 1945, Carlo Levi published *Cristo si è fermato a Eboli* (*Christ Stopped at Eboli*). The Fascist regime had had a practice of
convicting political opponents to *confino*, or exile in the far provinces. Levi's memoir
recounts his experiences of *confino* in the deep South, and specifically asks what it can
mean about a community for it to be able to *exile* a member of that community to a
part of what is putatively *the same community*. The urban petty bourgeoisie, in the midst
of which writers and film-makers and most of their audience lived their lives, wanted
its comforts, and did not care too much about the suffering of others. But the German
occupation brought political subjection and material deprivation (*exactly* the experience of the South, for example) to those hitherto protected groups. In a word, suffering.
Literature and the cinema became the urban petty bourgeoisie's means of expressing
and understanding its own suffering and that of others. The liberation temporarily
decentralised administration, and deprived Rome of its logistical supremacy in film-
making. The stage was set for a cinema of suffering located all over the peninsula (the
Genoese Germi and the Milanese Visconti went south, the Romans Zampa and De Santis went north; in *Paisà*, the Roman Rossellini went north and south, and in 1947, for
Germany Year Zero, to Berlin). *Stromboli* becomes clearer to an Anglo-Saxon viewer in
the light of this explanation: Rossellini subjected Karin to a sort of *confino*, and watched
what she made of it.

Neo-realism, however, is not so much a matter of choice of subject and setting, as a
new dramaturgy in the cinema; it replaces the dramaturgy of 'givens' contained in genre
cinema with a dramaturgy of search and discovery. Cinematic narratives had inherited
from a generic and formulaic tradition a dramaturgy of *conflict* between two 'given' positions: one right and one wrong, one good and one bad, one leading to progress and one
leading to doom. Rossellini's *Rome Open City* is one of the few neo-realist films that
clings to an old dramaturgy which he will definitively abandon in *Paisà*. Otherwise,
nothing is 'given' at the outset in a neo-realist film: values have to be explored.

The *function* of cinema became enquiry. Directors and scriptwriters knew instinc-
tively that this prohibited closure in their narratives, though they did not necessarily
articulate the logic behind their feelings. Neo-realist films ask, rather than confirm; they
wonder, rather than reassure. That is why Rossellini, Fellini and Antonioni could say
that there was no real rupture between their work of the 1940s and that of the 1950s
and 1960s. Their films had never depended on choice of setting, on matters of class, on
the purely material (for instance, economic and political) determinants of society, even
though those had played a large role in *causing* the change in dramaturgy. Many have
observed how neo-realist films eschew the conventional cinema's obsession with narrative. In fact, the neo-realists developed a *new* narrative. In many ways, the road movie
is the neo-realist narrative, with its special dramaturgy not of conflict but of discovery.

Often the very titles themselves suggest the road movie, and one can point to the lack of closure in the following very different films by very different directors: *Bicycle Thieves*; *Umberto D.* (De Sica, 1952); *Paisà* (the first three episodes); *Stromboli* (Rossellini's edition); *Europe '51*; *Journey to Italy*; *Le amiche* (Antonioni, 1955); *L'avventura*; *I vitelloni*; *La strada*; *Il bidone* (Fellini, 1955); *Le notti di Cabiria* (Fellini, 1957); *La dolce vita* (Fellini, 1960). They are all rather like road movies; they have plots that involve repetition and circularity; they end with no concrete resolution, but rather with the suggestion that something has been found or rediscovered (or lost). The concern with the superficial characteristics of neo-realist films that derive from the material conditions of their production has obscured what has a far stronger claim to being the essence of neo-realism.

At what stage in the preparation of *Paisà* Rossellini changed his dramaturgy we may never find out. That it took place can be demonstrated by comparing early treatments with the finished product. An undated version of the synopsis for the whole film, treatments for six proposed episodes, and the scenario for the first episode (Sicily) were found in the archives of the Cinémathèque Française.[10] In the synopsis, each episode is built around one representative type of American, each of whom dies at the end of their episode: 'The six heroes of the six episodes die, and each episode ends with a white cross in a military cemetery'. The treatment of the second episode (that of the military policeman in Naples) is as follows:

A black MP is on duty at a petrol dump on the outskirts of Naples. He has made friends with a Neapolitan shoeshine boy, Pascà [Pasquale].

Pascà often asks him about America, and the black man describes it. Pascà also asks him to take him to America with him, and the black man promises to. On this basis, they are very good friends.

One night, the black man is on guard duty. Pascà is keeping him company. In the dark, the boy sings Neapolitan songs which the black man tries to repeat with his deep, vibrant voice.

Two unsavoury characters turn up out of the dark, and draw near. They start out obliquely, then they offer the black man money: they want petrol, and they are prepared to reward him. The black man chases them away and resumes singing with the boy.

The other two rejoin their mates, and together decide to do without the black man's help. They have all they need: the truck, the cans, a length of rubber tubing, and something to pierce one of the petrol tanks.

Suspicious, the black man gets up and calls 'Who goes there?' Two or three shots ring out, the black man falls to the ground. While other soldiers arrive, opening fire, Pascà throws himself on the body of his friend, desperate with grief: he must not die; if he dies he won't take him to America. Dying, the black man smiles, and tells him not to make too much of a thing of it. He is a poor negro, in America he counts for nothing, he's like a shoeshiner. He's better off not going with him to America. It wouldn't amount to much going there with a poor negro. He's better off staying in Naples . . .

First, it is necessary to point out that between the invention of the stories and the filming of the first three episodes a new theme has entered the first half of the film – the flight of the Americans from the suffering of the Italians – just as in the second half the theme becomes the solidarity of the Americans with the suffering of the Italians. In the material from the Cinémathèque Française, this change has already taken place between the treatment and the scenario of the first episode (in the treatment, the Americans restrain Carmela from attacking the Germans – now prisoners – who shot Joe; in the scenario, the American soldiers think she betrayed Joe, while we see that the Germans have killed her for avenging him). In other words, the film has swung round to being an expression of the suffering of the Italians as experienced by the Americans, but with that experience observed by us, the viewers, who do not necessarily share it – Rossellini's famous 'detachment' transforms the film into a learning experience for the viewer. A closer look at *Paisà*, starting with the Naples episode, may show us how this has been achieved.

Whereas *Rome Open City* represented and affirmed the 'national' vision of the Resistance, *Paisà* evolved, during the shooting, into an unmasking of the ambiguities involved in the liberation. Both films retain, as a central theme, the expression of the suffering of the Italian people, and both attribute it to the war between the Germans and the Allies. While the first can lay the blame squarely and (almost) unambiguously at the feet of an unexplained evil visited upon the Italians in the form of the German occupation, the second has a far more difficult and subtle task to perform, because the Allies were both liberators and conquerors, and the Italians were both passive victims and active participants. Carmela evolves in the first episode from victim to participant to victim – in the last instance, victim of the Americans' ignorance; Francesca in the Rome episode is the distillation of the victim – both of the occupation and of the Americans' ignorance. Making his characters victims of another character's ignorance (dramatic irony, in other words) is the procedure Rossellini uses to impart knowledge to the viewer, and it requires of the viewer *both* identification with the suffering of the victim *and* the detachment of the observer. This procedure is taken to its highest refinement in *Stromboli*, where the viewer's dual perspective makes ultimate judgement – of the modern sophisticated individualism of the North and of the traditional conservative stoicism of the South – impossible.

We first see Joe, the military policeman, from Pasquale's point of view (in a reverse-angle sequence), having his upper lip drawn back to examine his teeth (as though he were livestock) by the boys bidding for the right to exploit him (his shoes, his jacket and the wallet somewhere in an inside pocket). An adult intervenes, and declares himself the winner in the auction ('Teccot'e tremila lire' ['Here, take three thousand lire']), even though Pasquale has bid more ('Aggio ritto tremila lire e ddui pacchett'e sigarette' ['I bid three thousand lire and two packets of cigarettes']). The man says 'Vattene, vattene. Tremila lire abbasteno' ('Go away, three thousand's enough'); Pasquale feels cheated ('Ma te n'abusi che so' piccirillo ['But you're taking advantage because I'm little']), which motivates his ruse of pretending that the police are coming in order to scatter his rivals. Thus the ambiguity of this tall, strong, wealthy representative of a conquering army coming from a background of slavery and oppression is introduced from the very first moment we, the viewers, see him, while at the same time Pasquale's youth is presented as an obstacle to his survival in the Neapolitan economic jungle. Joe's power is diminished by drink; Pasquale's lack of power is compensated for by intelligence. As they go through Naples, the pair are very similar to Antonio and Bruno in *Bicycle Thieves*, both as a visual motif (their contrasting height and gait) and psychologically: Antonio's wits are dulled by obsessive anxiety while Bruno is alert, resourceful and protective of his father. Costume is important in *Paisà*: Rossellini has dressed Pasquale differently from the other little boys, in a coat that is far too big for him, emphasising his smallness and his vulnerability, and with a military cap – the two together function as an index of his admiration and *need* for the paternal, which he projects onto the American military. Joe will interpret Pasquale's clothes as an index of his predatoriness. In both films the adult is too self-absorbed to notice the needs of the child, and both films use that dramatic irony to generate meaning.

After the episode in the puppet theatre has alerted Pasquale to the human identity of his 'prey', they sit on a pile of rubble and talk. At a certain point, it looks as though the original intention may have been to film their entire dialogue in one sequence-shot with direct sound: the boy's harmonica-playing changes from being dubbed to being directly recorded, and the rest of the sequence consists first of one sequence-shot and then of another in a slightly different light (or with better film stock), with the camera slightly closer to the couple, and with a few inserted close-ups still in direct sound (there are a couple of lines of dialogue obviously post-dubbed). Acting errors with the dialogue or intrusive sounds from the city may account for some of the inserts (one of which is of Joe singing 'Nobody Knows the Troubles I Have Seen'), and the use of two sequence-shots instead of one. The close-ups of Pasquale are cutaway reaction shots. The scene ends with a return to the (second) sequence-shot, Pasquale leaning over the supine Joe, urgently telling him: 'Joe! Joe! Si tu ruorme io arrubb'e scarpe' ('If you fall asleep, I'll steal your boots').

The first half of the film, therefore, establishes Pasquale's point of view on Joe,

Joe (Dotts M. Johnson) drives Pasquale (Alfonsino Bovino) across Naples to get his boots in the second episode of *Paisà* (1946).

through which the viewer gains knowledge about Joe. The dialogue on the pile of rub-ble (almost a monologue by Joe) may have evolved, during the shooting and the editing, from a single, quite distant, sequence-shot to a more intimate montage incorporating close-up cutaways of Pasquale's reaction.

There is a fade to black followed by a fade into an establishing shot of Joe's jeep enter-ing the frame and proceeding down a wide street, followed by a through-the-windscreen shot of Joe intent on battling with the traffic, then a dissolve into a high-angle shot of traffic in a street, and then a return to the through-the-windscreen shot of Joe looking up (shading his eyes), this time at something that has caught his attention just ahead. This last is the first in a reverse-angle sequence of six shots alternating between the viewer (and it is important that it is *not* Pasquale) looking through the windscreen at Joe, and Joe's point of view (the camera jerks) on Pasquale, the pilferer. After the reverse-angle sequence there is a master shot of Joe's jeep drawing alongside the truck, which then dissolves into a through-the-windscreen shot of Joe driving in his jeep with Pasquale in the passenger seat.

The fade into and out of black and the dissolve denote elision, a jump in time and space, and the consequent omission of 'action'. What has been elided is Pasquale's theft of Joe's boots, and Joe's arrest of Pasquale – the key actions in a dramaturgy of 'given' rights and wrongs. André Bazin famously remarks on the elision, in the final episode, of the German attack on the Casal Maddalena, but for the purpose of characterising Rossellini's narrative style.[11] He does not *interpret* that elision. If Rossellini is interested in expressing the American *experience* of the suffering of the Italians, rather than the German *infliction* of that suffering, there is no real elision (indeed, to show directly to the viewer the Germans at work would both raise distracting issues – 'bad' Germans, for example – and would destroy the point of view he was carefully establishing as thematic).

The ensuing dialogue between Joe and Pasquale is, this time, shot in a single sequence-shot lasting 52 seconds, through the windscreen of the jeep, from the 'observer's' point of view that Rossellini has created for the viewer. What Joe says rein-forces our understanding of his viewpoint on Pasquale which has been established in the immediately preceding reverse-angle sequence: he is a systematic, opportunist thief, ungrateful for what the Americans have brought with them. Our 'detached' observation of Joe's viewpoint continues while Joe goes through Pasquale's pockets (saying 'Why do you steal? Why do you steal?'), until we are offered another shot from Joe's point of view, of Pasquale running away crying. Joe himself then enters this shot to catch the boy, and brings him back to the jeep for a 34-second sequence shot from a detached viewpoint, in which he now starts to treat Pasquale as a little boy ('Put this coat on before you catch cold'). When he finds the harmonica, his anger returns, and Pasquale once again defends his integrity (as he had done over the 'auction') saying 'Te l'aggio ditto che nun aviv'a durmì ('I told you not to fall asleep'). By now, however, the disproportionate power between the adult and the child has come home to Joe, who demands to be taken to the boy's parents at home. Pasquale protests: 'Io nun a' tengo' ('I haven't got one').

We can move to the entry of Joe and Pasquale into the cave at Mergellina. Outside, Joe has been surrounded by children, has distributed sweets, has been offered one of, evidently, many pairs of boots – all filmed from the observer's point of view. When he enters the cave, the camera alternates between Joe looking and what he sees (one of the shots of Joe being 20 seconds long), establishing his point of view. At a certain point, the procedure changes. There is a shot from behind Joe taken at the level of Pasquale's head – it is a head and shoulders close-up of Pasquale, with Joe's left hip out of focus in the right-hand edge of the frame; Pasquale's head is tilted back to point up at Joe's face, but his eyes are lowered to look at the boots held at thigh level in Joe's hand; Joe is swivelling away from the view of the interior of the cave. There is a cut to a close-up of Joe's head from the adult height. He has turned past Pasquale below him, and lowers his eyes to the ground, asking: 'Where's your mother an' father?' There is a cut to Pasquale's level, where he moves round Joe's body to face him, looks up and says 'Nun te capisco' ('I don't understand'). There is a cut up to Joe's head and shoulders in which he raises his eyes away from the boy who has come round in front of him, and starts turning away from him towards the interior of the cave. A cut down to Pasquale who, looking up, sees that Joe is turning away, and lowers his gaze to the boots. A cut back up to Joe continuing his turn away, and saying, now with his back to the boy, 'Dov'è mamma e pàppa?', is followed by a cut back down to Pasquale, who walks round Joe to his front, to face him from below, looks up at his face and says 'Mamma e papà non ce stanno chiù. So' morti. 'E bombe … ('Mum and dad aren't here anymore. They're dead. The bombs …'). The camera cuts up to Joe again, while the voice of Pasquale continues off camera to say: '… Bum, bum! Capisci? 'E bombe. Bum, bum!' – Joe's head is turning back away from Pasquale, his eyes looking up and down. The camera cuts back down to a close-up of Pasquale looking up once more at Joe's back. Then it cuts to a three-quarters shot of the two of them in that position, Joe leaning away from Pasquale, dropping the boots and starting to move out of the frame to the left, meanwhile Pasquale's eyes going from Joe's head to the boots in his hand, then on the ground, and bending forward to pick them up, the camera tilting down to follow him. As he begins to rise from his bending position, the camera cuts to a close-up of him rising back erect, looking towards the camera in the direction Joe left, motionless with huge wide eyes. There is a cut to Joe in his jeep driving fast away from the camera down the hill through a tunnel of arches, gradually being obscured by the dust thrown up by the wheels, and this shot fades to black.

The sequence in the cave is carefully choreographed, with the lighting very accurately set to illuminate Pasquale's face in particular, and his little figure outlined against the gloom by back-lighting. Though the camera rises to Joe's level to shoot him, and descends to Pasquale's level to shoot him, we neither see Pasquale from Joe's point of view nor Joe from Pasquale's. Pasquale's attention is equally divided between trying to get Joe to look at him (in which he is unsuccessful) and keeping the boots, which Joe evidently no longer wants.

The elisions in the narrative, the choice of camera angles, decisions about *mise-en-scène* and editing have all been directed towards delving behind superficial appearances and exploring the complexity of the two protagonists' experience. The viewer watches the characters learn: Pasquale, that the power and wealth of the American is only temporary and apparent, that Joe is no 'father' and that he must rely on himself; Joe, that his belief that he, as liberator, was bringing bounty and security to inveterate thieves hid the reality of the Allied bombing and its consequences for the civilian population, and that Pasquale and others like him were young, orphaned and destitute. What 'happens' in Rossellini's new narrative is that the viewer progressively sees more clearly; in his dramaturgy a complex understanding gradually displaces simple appearances. It would be difficult to overestimate how influential the opening up of such possibilities for the cinema has been. Understandably, however, it was never going to make much money for producers. The divide between art cinema and commercial cinema starts to become significant as directors learn Rossellini's lesson.

Critics have censured the use of the flashback in the Rome episode as being a conventional Hollywood device. In early versions, the story was to have been told chronologically. Instead, the flashback serves to *reveal* the world of suffering and struggle that lies behind Francesca's present state, using once again dramatic irony: the viewer's perspective on Fred's point of view, and Fred's – like that of Joe and of the soldiers in Sicily – flight from a suffering that they cannot fully comprehend and cope with. Similarly, the episode set in the monastery in the Appenines comes into focus when it is understood how the episode gradually evolved around the centrality of *food* (Sergio Amidei's original story involved a contest between American and Italian cooking). It is the *hunger* of the monks, who renounce their first proper meal in months for the souls of the unbaptised, that motivates the Catholic chaplain's admiration for their valuing the spiritual above the material (a binary opposition typical of Fellini who rewrote the episode). In the Florentine episode, the dramatic irony is of the British officers on the southern banks of the Arno, blithely indifferent to the domestic slaughter going on across the river (particularly shocking – and delicate for Rossellini to portray in 1946 – is the summary execution of some terrified Fascists, viewed in the margins, as it were, of Harriet's quest). The final episode in the Po delta was from the start planned to observe an American secret service agent as he helped the partisans to implement General Alexander's order for them to lay down their arms for the winter while the Allies (once again) delayed – an order that took no account of the Germans' determination (and capacity) to wipe them out unless they were adequately supplied. The Americans' outrage at the end is a rebellion against this 'irony', and is the only moment in the film in which the conventional dramaturgy of 'givens' emerges (though by sharing the Italians' experience, these Americans have learned its meaning), to be covered, in its turn, by the irony of the final voice-over. The episode starts and ends, in a circular fashion, with the bodies of partisans in the river.

Rome Open City, in contrast, offers the familiar pleasures of a tight, suspenseful narrative told in parallel montage (intercutting between events taking place simultaneously), spiced with humour. The viewer is offered a point of view from within the narrative, first by Pina, and then, when she is killed, by Don Pietro (his viewpoint is exploited to great effect in the torture scene at the Gestapo Headquarters in Via Tasso). The drama is one of conflict between 'givens': positive and negative are unambiguously coded. Negativity is coded in terms of sexual deviancy, or opportunism, and sadism; the 'positive' is attributed to the spontaneous goodness of the common people, rising in revulsion against the outrages of the German occupation, and is coded in terms of the maintenance of family values in extreme circumstances (the spanking that the youthful saboteurs receive on their return home comically reinforces that coding, as do other little details, such as that of the Austrian deserter tucking the blanket around the sleeping Marcello in the sacristy). Rhetorical and generic contamination reaches a climax when Pina's passionate and foolhardy pursuit of the truck carrying away her bridegroom is punished with a burst of machine-gun fire, whereupon Don Pietro cradles her body in an overt allusion to the iconography of the deposition from the Cross – all this following on immediately from the Hitchcockian parallel montage of Don Pietro carrying

Overtly coded negativity in *Rome Open City* (1945). Bergmann (Harry Feist) shows the torture of Manfredi (Marcello Pagliero) to Don Pietro (Aldo Fabrizi, off camera). Frame enlargement (Cineteca Nazionale, Rome).

arms down from the top of the stairs while the Fascist soldiers climb up from the bottom, and as they meet in the middle the comic 'business' of the fake extreme unction.

The coding of good and evil and the exploitation of iconography are devices proper to propaganda and to genre cinema. The politics advanced by the film are overtly populist: the alliance between a Communist leader, a Catholic parish priest and a woman of the people – the film's explicit articulation of the ideology is comically put in the mouth of Marcello in an exchange full of dramatic (and comic) irony:

> *Don Pietro*: Come mai non ti si vede più all'oratorio?
> *Marcello*: Come se fa, de 'sti momenti, a venì a perde tempo all'oratorio?
> *Don Pietro*: Ma cosa stai dicendo?
> *Marcello*: Lei fa il prete, e nun po' capì. Ma bisogna strigne un blocco compatto contro 'l comune nemico.
> *Don Pietro*: Ma dì un po', chi te le dice queste cose?
> *Marcello*: Me l'ha detto Romoletto.
> *Don Pietro*: Ah, Romoletto dice queste cose.
> *Marcello*: Don Piè, mi raccomando, non lo dica a nessuno!

('How come we never see you at the oratory [parish school]?' 'At a time like this, how can one go and waste time at the oratory?' 'What on earth are you saying?' 'You're a priest, and you can't understand. But we must form a tight bloc against the common enemy.' 'Wait a minute, who's been telling you these things?' 'Romoletto told me.' 'Ah, Romoletto's been saying these things.' 'Don Piè, please, don't tell anybody!')

However, the portrayal is not without subtleties, just three of which, for reasons of space here, we shall list with a minimum of comment. First, Bergmann upbraids his officer for 'tactlessly' searching Don Pietro's sacristy (which has all sorts of implications concerning the position of the Church towards Nazism, mediated, as it was, by the Concordat with Fascism). Second, when Bergmann asks Don Pietro why he is protecting this 'Communist', this 'subversive', this 'senza Dio', Don Pietro replies: 'Io sono un sacerdote cattolico, e credo che chi combatte per la giustizia e la libertà cammina nelle vie del Signore, e le vie del Signore sono infinite.' ('I am a Catholic priest, and I believe that whoever fights for justice and freedom [the English subtitles mistranslate this as 'truth and justice'] walks in the ways of the Lord, and the ways of the Lord are infinite.') Bergmann is homing in on the enmity and incompatibility between Catholicism and Communism, but Don Pietro's words contain a reference to an anti-Fascist organisation – Giustizia e Libertà – which was incorporated into the Partito d'Azione, a coalition of Liberals, Republicans and Socialists that fought alongside, but were separate from, the Communists in the Resistance. A little later, Bergmann points out to Manfredi the incongruous and inevitably temporary nature of his party's support from the monarchists.

Third, the most interesting scene in the film, from a political and historical point of view, is a brief exchange between Sturmbannführer Bergmann (representing the historical Gestapo officer Herbert Kappler) and the Questore (chief of police) of Rome (historically Pietro Caruso). Bergmann is irritated by the screams of pain coming from the torture chamber next door, and gets up to say contemptuously: 'How much they scream . . . ' (there is a cut to the seated Questore who would like to change the subject) '. . . these Italians'. The Questore looks up, pauses, and says 'Right'. In the immediate post-war period and during the reconstruction, the treatment of Fascists was a delicate matter (their execution in the Florentine episode of *Paisà* is a rare exception, disguised as being almost *en passant*, which would probably not have passed the censors a year later) and *Rome Open City* treats them tenderly, more with burlesque than with anger. When the Fascist soldiers search the apartment block near the Via Prenestina, they are easily over-awed by Don Pietro's liturgical performance, and the firing squad at his execution deliberately aims away from him. For the group film *Giorni di gloria* (edited by Mario Serandrei and Giuseppe De Santis in 1945), Visconti shot documentary footage of Caruso's trial, and of his head being blown apart by a firing squad, as well as the lynching, by the public in the courtroom, of the governor of the Regina Coeli gaol, Carretta.

In an Italy that had been defeated and occupied by both sides in the war, and had suffered its own civil war, the spontaneous goodness of the people seemed the only thing that could regenerate civilised community life. In 1945, with a coalition of anti-Fascist parties which spanned the political spectrum co-operating in reconstructing the nation, it seemed as though that spontaneous humanity *was* Italy. *Rome Open City*, for all its artifice, *expressed* something very real in the Italy of that precise moment. But *Paisà* changed film-making.

Notes

1 See André Bazin, *What is Cinema?*, trans. Hugh Gray, vol. 2 (Berkeley and Los Angeles: University of California Press, 1971), p. 37. It would not be at all a bad idea to read the present chapter in conjunction with two essays in that volume: 'An Aesthetic of Reality: Neo-Realism' (pp. 16–40) and 'In Defense of Rossellini' (pp. 93–101) (the latter is also included in the present volume in a new translation: see pp. 157–61). For an orthodox Communist critique of Bazin, see Guido Aristarco, *Neorealismo e nuova critica cinematografica* (Florence: Nuova Guaraldi, 1980), pp. 56-68 (see the article reproduced in this volume, pp. 156–7) . For an analysis of sequences from *Bicycle Thieves* which takes issue with Bazin, see Christopher Wagstaff, 'Comic Positions: Detailed Shot analysis of *Ladri di biciclette*', in *Sight and Sound*, vol. 2, no. 7, November 1992, pp. 25–7.

2 C.S. Peirce, *Collected Papers* (Cambridge, MA: Harvard University Press, 1932), vol. 2, pp. 134–73.

3 Adriano Aprà (ed.), *Rosselliniana. Bibliografia internazionale. Dossier 'Paisà'* (Rome: Di Giacomo, 1987), p. 132.

4 Andrea says that employment will put an end to the suffering of the poor; Irene replies that working on an assembly line is another form of suffering.

5 In the Christian Democrat weekly *Libertas*, 24 February 1952.

6 Quoted in Marco Salotti, '1957–1964. L'industria cinematografica gonfia i muscoli', in Enrico Magrelli (ed.), *Cinecittà 2: Sull'industria cinematografica italiana* (Venice: Marsilio, 1986), p. 147.

7 Cesare Pavese, *La casa in collina* (1949) (Turin: Einaudi, 1967), p. 185. It is striking how succinctly Pavese's reflection encapsulates the function of Primo Levi's *Se questo è un uomo* (*If This is a Man*, 1947) and the first and last episodes of *Paisà*.

8 Preface to the second edition (1964) of *Il sentiero dei nidi di ragno* (Milan: Garzanti, 1987), pp. 7–9, 20, 23.

9 Federico Fellini, *Fare un film* (Turin: Einaudi, 1980), p. 44; this passage is also included in the longer extract from this text on pp. 169–70 of this volume.

10 Aprà, *Rosselliniana*, pp. 92–137.

11 Bazin, *What is Cinema?*, vol. 2, pp. 34–5.

4
Rossellini's Landscapes: Nature, Myth, History

Sandro Bernardi

If we look again at the cinema of Rossellini, with our own eyes rather than through the critical debates over realism of the 1950s, we will have to admit it has very little to do with realism. Certainly not the realism that Aristarco, Rivette or even Bazin were talking about. If Rossellini's cinema is realistic, then it is in the sense that it reflects on the state of western culture and evokes, in order to comprehend it, the experience of the sacred: not in its religious meaning but in the way that Pasolini (who was deeply indebted to Rossellini) or Bataille spoke of the sacred.[1] There is nothing transcendental, supernatural or divine about the sacred in this sense. It is completely immanent. It appears at its clearest in everyday life, or in nature, but also in ruins, or in interactions between people or cultures. The sacred, for Rossellini, is not just what happens in exceptional circumstances, or to superior beings, but what lies before everyone every day and what they live within, the world in its totality, which manifests itself to each person differently yet is always the same and only a small part of which can be comprehended by the conscious mind.

This experience of the sacred certainly has much to do with religion, but not with Catholicism or Christianity. It has to do with the search for the fundamental and archaic principles of religion (*religio* in the sense of 'bond'), such as the relationship of individuals with the universe of which they are a part, a part which can only be fulfilled through an overcoming of the self. In this discovery of the sacred, for Rossellini, the theme of landscape is central. It is in landscape that characters, in their experience of vision, come out of themselves and discover the world they are part of. The relationship of the individual with the whole, the cult of the dead, love, the discovery and observation of the world – these are the aspects that link landscape to myth as an epiphany of the sacred.

Rossellini made a 'descent to the Mothers', in Goethe's sense, a descent into the heart of darkness of contemporary man: a very solar, luminous heart of darkness, which has remained archaic beneath the veneer of modernity. He was looking for the residues of that ancient world which European anthropologists and philosophers then virtually unknown in Italy, such as Mircea Eliade, Lucien Lévy-Bruhl or Walter Benjamin, were examining. We might even say, anticipating our conclusions, that Rossellini is the principal Italian anthropologist since he carries out through cinema the research which the European anthropologists and philosophers of the twentieth century pursued by other means. It is not anthropology understood as the observation of primitive peoples from a Eurocentric and logocentric standpoint, but an anthropology which digs in the past, which is also archaeology, understood as a journey of discovery of the primitive soul hidden in the heart of modern man. It is a type of research that puts into question the very foundations of Eurocentric and logocentric culture.

Rossellini's work, in this sense, consisted above all of a 'cleansing of the eyes', an attempt to free cinema, vision, and therefore knowledge from the stereotypes accumulated over time, over centuries. This was a complex and endless task because each time one got rid of an old stereotype one necessarily created new ones, without which it would not be possible to see anything. In this respect, Rossellini's work is primarily negative and it possesses all the 'positivity of the negative' described by Hegel: the opening up of meaning produced by criticism, the destruction of old, dead models which are no longer adequate to make sense of what is happening.[2] The cinema becomes the instrument of a type of thought which passes directly through observation and vision, the latter understood as engagement with an object, as curiosity and awareness of difference.

What emerges from the war trilogy onwards is the sense of loss experienced by the individual living in the contemporary world, the lost sense of the unity of the world, of the unity of humans with the world and, consequently, the individual's loss of identity too. Rossellini's reflection begins from the war, but only as epiphenomenon, macrophenomenon of the identity crisis and the general regression. In the description of this loss of a relation with the whole, the landscape becomes epiphanic, albeit often in a negative sense. Think of the anxiety that grips Katherine (Ingrid Bergman) in *Journey to Italy* when she climbs up to the Temple of Apollo and remains alone, almost frightened by the simple sight of the trees being blown by the wind. What is this about? Who is it that appears and then disappears in that small clearing where the old guide refuses to accompany her, saying: 'there is too much wind'? And why is the discovery of the landscape for Rossellini's characters so profoundly linked to the experience of the sacred?

The reading of Rossellini I am going to propose here is different from any of the usual interpretations: the old critical demolitions or the old eulogies. The idea of Rossellini as philosopher and anthropologist may seem tendentious. However, this argument will appear less 'new' if one considers the strong ties Rossellini had with European culture, more so than with Italian culture. His reading of Simone Weil or of Edgar Morin, for example,[3] and later of Comenius, from whom he took and developed the concept of 'autopsy' (seeing with one's own eyes),[4] and others, lends some weight to the claim that Rossellini was a philosopher, or a director who used the cinema to think, on the same intellectual level as Walter Benjamin, Hannah Arendt, Simone Weil or Elias Canetti. However, if we want to emphasise the continuity of his work and his research it is best to start at the beginning.

Paisà: landscapes of death

In *Paisà* there are two episodes – the first (Sicily) and the last (the Po delta) – in which landscape assumes a determining role. Rossellini begins to look at landscape linking it to the theme of death. There is, however, another landscape, which is only such in a manner of speaking because it lies beneath the ground, but which is the fundamental discovery of *Paisà*. We get a brief but, for this reason, dazzling glimpse of it in the Naples episode: the vision at the end of the displaced people in the Mergellina caves. The black

Shooting the final episode of *Paisà* in the Po delta.

soldier Joe, deeply disturbed, rushes away. The scene has all the characteristics of a *nékya* – a descent to the underworld – and it may be taken as a symbol of all Rossellini's landscapes. *Paisà*, that much-praised film, choral and grandiose, as Cocteau said, is, in reality, a dark and uncertain film, which slips away from us at least as much as its characters do. Its meaning changes in each episode, it oscillates like a pendulum between liberation and catastrophe, epic and tragedy. From a barely sketched depiction of a world, the film continually moves to a vision of people without a world.

Let us start with the Sicilian episode, from the scene at the window where the soldier Joe is shot dead. It is a famous example of a sequence-shot, interrupted only by an edit on movement at the beginning, in which Joe (Robert van Loon) and Carmela (Carmela Sazio), left alone to guard the tower, cross the room and sit by the ruined window. This scene is not only a reflection on life, on the external world, on waiting, which is waiting for death; it is also a reflection on the relationship between people and the world, where the landscape which appears and disappears behind the two characters, through the window, is indicative of an unknown presence, of which they are unaware, but which is so important that it is from the landscape that death finally comes. Rossellini himself said that waiting was one of the things that interested him most. Here, we could add, waiting constitutes the very form of cinema; the sequence-shot makes it possible to see time passing.

The sequence is divided into two parts which correspond to two shots, one moving, the other strictly without movement. Two strangers confront each other. The landscape, at the beginning, is effectively the director in what starts out as a traditional idyll. Joe turns to look at the sea: 'What beautiful scenery'. Carmela tries to escape but Joe restrains her: 'You can't leave now. There's fighting out there! Understand? Boom boom!' This is the stereotype I mentioned, the idyll where the landscape, still invisible because of the dark, influences them like a romantic backdrop, dissolving their tensions and anxieties as they make an attempt at communication. But this stereotype will be destroyed immediately in the course of the sequence. Rossellini's realism always follows this procedure: it builds up a stereotype then suddenly demolishes it. The result will be, as we shall see, an epiphanic instant when the film stops because it is impossible for it to go on any further.

If, in the first part of the sequence, the two young people move restlessly, in the second they stop at the ruined window. The camera squats close by, fixed on them, making only small movements in order to follow theirs. The sea is illuminated in the dawn light and Joe remembers his home: 'You know ... I can almost imagine I'm home'. Here, the landscape that begins to open up behind their backs, in the morning light, is already an unreliable, treacherous presence. Rossellini really is able to photograph the air that surrounds things.[5] Carmela and Joe are sitting on the broken windowsill, on the boundary of two different worlds: inside and outside. He is nervous because he cannot make himself understood and she is ever more attentive. The camera lens examines in close-up the faces of the two young people talking. It then looks at the distant murmuring sea in the half-light, far but also near. The tension reaches breaking point: everything is still; something has to happen. The rupture of the stereotype (the idyll) leaves an open wound in the eyes. The bullet that comes from the sea does not only kill Joe but also reaches us, killing our expectations of a love scene. A cut follows immediately: we only just manage to see Joe falling. It is one of Rossellini's most famous ellipses. It gives the story a slow breathing and yet makes it breathless, able to execute a feline leap after a long rest.

We encounter another of these ellipses at the end of the next episode with the escape in the jeep of the black soldier, also called Joe. This Joe is destined to make a terrifying discovery. He follows the boy who has stolen his boots with the intention of punishing him (here too there is a stereotype: theft and punishment, norm and transgression). However, what Joe discovers is a scene that takes one's breath away. The huge and chaotic crowds of people camped in the Mergellina caves defy common sense. Theft, punishment, the law, no longer make any sense; nor does the 'beautiful scenery' of the first episode. We are now in a hell similar only to that evoked in *Faust*, but a real one, a result of that huge regression which is war. In this flash vision, Rossellini's eye is an organ of thought because it manages to extract from just one image the entire sense of a period of history. This subterranean landscape is far stronger than the one preceding it, thanks to the sudden ellipsis which ends the story, as if words were pointless after one has seen this.

Let us jump to the end of the film. A corpse floats downstream buoyed up by a lifebelt, with a sign over his shoulders saying 'Partisan'. This first shot is enough to restore all meaning and space to the story: the distant corpse within the long shot, an insignificant object; the grey of the sky, of the water and of death merging into one. Rossellini *shows us* the cold. The sight of Porto Tolle, the small dark village in the distance, merely confirms the harshness of the landscape, the coldness of death, enclosed between the grey and the black, in the desolation of the water whose coldness we can see through its colour. The people watching from the bank, dressed in black, who are afraid to step further forward, reinforce the sensation of solitude. Between the reeds, others watch, hidden. They are Cigolani and Dale, the partisan and the American, the two friends whose deaths will mark the only kind of encounter possible in this story, like Joe and

Germany Year Zero (1947/8).

Carmela. Even in this final episode, the landscape plays a fundamental role in producing meaning, or rather the lack of meaning which constitutes the film's meaning.

The episode is all about observing and carefully scrutinising the surrounding space,
for signs of the enemy and possible escape routes. From an observation tower, the Germans look around ('Schau!') and shoot on sight anything that moves in the marshes or
on the river. The camera is constantly moving, like the partisans and the American soldiers, always low, in a hurry, brushing the surface of the water between the reeds that
block the horizon, in a prolonged semi-subjective shot, to use Mitry's terms. It seems to
be not just looking but also fighting, escaping, searching, following. It is a film, as Paul
Eluard said, in which we too are actors; we see and are seen.[6] The sudden ellipsis on the
slaughtered family, with the baby crying, is so strong and harsh that we do not have time
to notice a striking error in the lighting: the sun is rising in front of us, in the distance,
but the shadows fall at right angles to it, from left to right. What matters here, though,
is the opening up of vast spaces, desolate, flat scenes without direction and meaning,
like the events portrayed in the film. The low, Eisensteinian sky (Eisenstein's influence
on Rossellini can be seen already in *La nave bianca*, with its shots of gyrating cannons
which recall, indeed quote, *The Battleship Potemkin*) threatens the characters, crushing
them as if with an unending oppression. The grey sky is confused with the grey of the
water and the slightly darker grey of the reeds.

Landscapes of ruins

With death, Walter Benjamin wrote in his essay on Bachofen, what had been part of history falls back into the domain of nature; what had been natural falls back into the
domain of history.[7] *Germany Year Zero* constitutes a journey into the world of death and

of ruins. Realism is even further away here. The picture we are given of Germany, though taken from reality, is entirely symbolic. Rossellini shows a dead, ghostly city, with buildings in ruins, their windows smashed, uninhabited, jagged with spires like a glacier. He concentrates on the rubble, the disconnected streets, the piles of detritus. A handful of people scutter about, but the long shadows of the buildings cast across the streets, broken by the holes of the windows through which the rays of the morning sun pass, reveal that many of the exteriors, both at the beginning and at the end of the film, were filmed at dawn, perhaps to increase the impression of an uninhabited city. The picture that Rossellini tries to gives us is that of a world destroyed, whose shattered monuments are no more than the ruins of a culture swept away by an infernal ambition. The opening titles comment on the catastrophe of ideology but widen the horizon: the ruins we see are not only of Berlin but allude to that immense ruin which is, for Rossellini, the western world, overturned by the same ambition of reorganising the world according to human law. Basil Wright said the film contained metaphysical images like those of De Chirico.[8] The landscape of ruins which Rossellini shows us is abstract and symbolic, a first journey into the realm of the dead.

In this film it would seem inappropriate to speak of landscape, at least in the traditional sense, since everything takes place in Berlin. However, 'landscape' seems paradoxically the most apt term here: the war and the catastrophe of ideologies have brought the world back to its starting point and have plunged the space that was once a city back into the state of nature. Among the ruins, grass grows. Again, as Benjamin noted, when a culture no longer has any use in understanding the world, and indeed produces only power and destruction, then its monuments fall into ruin;[9] nature and culture alternate in history through that moment of exchange which is death. *Germany Year Zero* is perhaps Rossellini's most symbolic film, the one in which reality is raised to the infinite power. The ruins englobe all of the western world, desolation rules uncontested and absolute. The war and history turn the world to stone, transform the inhabited buildings into a vast necropolis, such as we will find again only in Katherine and Alex Joyce's visit to Pompeii.

Clashes of cultures

If we set out from this view of the ruins of Naples and Berlin as great metaphors, we can perhaps better understand Rossellini's itinerary after the war as a search for other inner ruins. *Stromboli* is the film where this historical reflection becomes an anthropology of contemporary society, which Rossellini looks at through an inverted telescope in order to get further away rather than nearer. He sees two cultures. The first is that of Karin (Ingrid Bergman), a modern woman, free, accustomed to equal, uninhibited, open relationships but essentially alone, deprived of the world, an 'uprooted' person, a *déracinée* in Simone Weil's sense. The second is an archaic culture, surviving in small enclaves, islands outside the world, still full of values of truth, characterised by a strong bond between its components and an intense relationship with the forces of nature, but for this reason primitive, violent, cruel, repressive. In this intense relationship, which the archaic world maintains with nature as totality, with the absolute, the landscape plays a fundamental part. The volcano is the authentic representative of the absolute, of nature as indifferent (very much in the way it was seen by Leopardi) and cruel because of its indifference. It is the incarnation of the negative sublime, as Eric Rohmer called it in his review.[10] *Stromboli* is also another descent to the underworld because Rossellini, in his search for values of truth, naturally pushes himself to the edge of the dizzying abyss which separates the modern world from the primordial, which we glimpsed in the caves of Mergellina.

Let us consider the couple's arrival on the island after their wedding in the displaced persons camp at Farfa and their departure. It consists of twenty-one shots recounting a genuine 'rite of passage'. From the departure of the train to the landing on the beach at Stromboli, we watch a symbolic journey, condensed into a few images, representing a much more significant crossing than the real journey. Here, Karin, annoyed, tired, cold in the boat that is taking her to another world, starts to look at the volcano, with Antonio's guidance: 'Look. The stones are falling in the sea!' From here on, the entire film will be a journey of visual education to discover the volcano, the epiphany of nature and the absolute, an education of Karin's eyes and those of the spectator. Later, she arrives at her husband's house. It is an empty broken-down hut. Karin runs away and starts towards the rock with Antonio behind, while the camera follows them with a travelling shot. He emphasises the theme of seeing: 'See ... lava che viene giù da 'u monte' ('lava coming down the mountain'). 'I understand!' is Karin's response, still more irritated; her eyes, squinting with rage, are two impenetrable fissures. The next day Karin complains about their lack of money and the poverty of the place. Antonio leaves for work, and she, crying, draws up to the window. One of the most beautiful landscapes in the world stretches out beyond the window, but she does not yet see it. The cruel scenes continue: the tuna fishing, where Karin is again a spectator; then the eruption. This encounter with the natural sublime terrorises Karin completely and she tries to escape. But on the summit of the volcano, overwhelmed, seduced, subdued by nature, Karin for the first time gives in to tears, exclaiming 'God, God! What mystery, what beauty!' *Stromboli* is a visual journey in which the maturing of the protagonist coincides with that of the cinema, which is also learning how to see. But the conflict remains, there are no easy answers, because the problem is that of the relationship between human beings and nature, between modern and archaic culture.

Bodies under the sun

If the idea of sanctity, as Rossellini said, was already implicit in the character of Karin, an ambiguous saint, struggling against God and herself, then Francis, in the film of the following year, *Francis God's Jester* (1950), is also particularly ambiguous. This film, based on *The Little Flowers of Saint Francis* and the *Life of Brother Juniper*, is remarkable in the way it looks both forward and backward, towards a cosmic and natural religiosity that is at once modern and ancient. The sanctity of Francis is wholly physical, it lies in his ability to see what we cannot, what also escapes the camera. Francis finds himself in a world which is in fact the one we live in, not that of legend. Rossellini seeks to remove from Francis and his world any marks of the supernatural or superhuman. Francis is a saint not because he is superior to other humans but because he is like everyone, totally similar to them, indeed because he is more human than everyone else (only Pasolini will understand this lesson perfectly: that the whole world is sacred, including pimps, prostitutes, thieves and murderers). And Francis is a saint because he sees God in the world. The sacredness of the world is obtained by a use of photography to level and equalise everything: earth, sky, grass, animals, people. Good and bad, young and old, educated and ignorant, clever and stupid, peasants, villagers, soldiers: all are equal, people and things under the sun, everything is great and everything at the same time is banal, common, modest.

This sacredness of the common world, however, cannot simply be taken for granted as an established fact. It can be seen clearly only by Francis and it entails an immense suffering. We see this in the episode with the leper. Francis is lying on the ground weeping for the passion of Christ. A bell alerts him that a sick man is coming. Francis spies him through branches, then looks up in his search for God. A point-of-view shot shows the tops of the trees and the sky, nothing else. No sign from God; the sky remains the same. When the sick man has passed, Francis follows him, looks at him and finally embraces him, only to fall back onto the ground murmuring: 'God, God of all, great God, God of all'. This is followed by a slow tilt upwards, which abandons Francis on the earth, then it abandons the earth too until it shows only sky. It is just the ordinary sky, but its beauty lies exactly in that: in its being the ordinary sky that is always there.

In this deconsecration, Rossellini discovers the sacred even deeper down, in its very roots. Francis invokes God but he turns to the sun, the earth, the water. The sacred is the body, the human face, the animal, the plant, the pig, the leper. Every single thing, living and not living, is a symbol of the world.

This sacredness is the rediscovery of the world, its epiphany without epiphany, since it depends on seeing what is before our eyes. Francis is the subject-gaze for whom chaos becomes cosmos. He is the subject of the gaze, both because the point-of-view shots are attributed to him and because we see him looking around, as in the final scene. Francis is within the world and outside it, as an observer is virtually inside a painting, is presupposed by it, even if he or she is not depicted in it. We stand with him, next to him, we see and we do not see. We are not able to see what he sees. Perhaps there is nothing, but for Francis this nothing is full of things. We the spectators are humans, like the other characters, and, in the words of Béla Balázs, 'we see that we do not see'.[11]

Loss of landscape

The problem of secular sanctity and otherness, or sanctity as consciousness of alterity, returns in the protagonist of *Europe '51*, which is a secular version of *Francis*. This time the landscape in which the Ingrid Bergman character moves is urban. The fictitious cosmos of her bourgeois world returns to the state of chaos. *Europe '51* is a true adventure of the gaze, in which the new conception of Rossellini's cinema matures. The strength of the film lies not in its story, which, although certainly dramatic, is not really all that different from many others, but in the extraordinary series of shots from Irene's point of view scattered throughout her journey, which make the film as a whole a genuine voyage through visible and invisible reality. There is for instance that magnificent, short but terrible pan with which Irene looks around her on her first arrival at 'block seven' of Rome's Garbatella district. Her gaze discovers long, drab modern tenements, new yet already crumbling, devoured by poverty and humidity. The shot marks a real moment of feeling lost, for Irene and also for the cinema. A few children are playing in the mud, between the newly laid streets and the 'rubbish mountains' as Pasolini would later call them.[12] Or there are the point-of-view shots with which Irene discovers the factory, the enormous buildings bearing down with their crushing mass, the enormous rolling tubes, correspond to a type of transfiguration of the negative sublime into what we might call the industrial sublime, evoked later by Antonioni in *The Red Desert* (1964). These are images where it is the machine of production that is the crushing power. *Europe '51* is also an odyssey of the look.

A descent to the underworld: *Journey to Italy*

At this point in Rossellini's work, we encounter what many have considered his master-piece: *Journey to Italy*. This film, which numerous directors, critics and historians have lauded as an authentic discovery of the real world, is a cine-poem, an account of a sym-bolic journey, the least realistic of all, or, at most, realistic in as much as it is symbolic. It traces the most symbolic of itineraries: a journey into myth at least as much as into reality. Its literary references are to Goethe for the title (the *Italienische Reise*, the account of Goethe's journey to Italy in 1786–7, first published in 1816) and Joyce for the name of the principal couple and for an episode which suggests that the film is a sequel to Joyce's short story 'The Dead'. If Ulysses' journey to the underworld in the *Odyssey* is the *nékya* of Greek literature, Aeneas' journey in the *Aeneid* is the *nékya* of Latin literature, and the *Divine Comedy* that of Italian literature, then *Journey to Italy* may be considered the *nékya* of Italian cinema.

Yet this journey into the realm of the dead is at the same time also the opposite: a journey into light, the sun, the realm of the living and love. In this world, still so impreg-nated with archaic heat and sunlight, life and death embrace in a continuous exchange. They are not opposites but are tied by a simple quantitative relationship: death is only a subtraction from life, and life too perhaps is only a subtraction from death.

Why has *Journey to Italy* been considered for many years a realistic film? And why do I suggest seeing in it a profoundly symbolic journey, to the roots of Mediterranean cul-ture? Certainly, everything that has been said about it is fundamentally true: Bergman crying, the destruction of the image of a star of classic American cinema, the discovery of the surrounding world, the suffering and the everyday pleasure of living – these are all elements of a new realism. But Katherine's visits to the museums, the sulphur pits, the Fontanelle cemetery, and the Temple of Apollo are about something else, difficult both to grasp and to see. It is death that Katherine continually encounters on her path, or rather the cohabitation of death and life, by which one germinates the other and vice versa. It is the same with the relation between reality and myth: one feeds off the other and vice versa. Through Katherine's eyes, Rossellini ventures to discover that deep level of Mediterranean culture buried under millennia and under a veneer of fragile and apparent modernity.

According to Alain Bergala, in his excellent recent analysis of *Journey to Italy*, the film really is 'a miracle', a secular miracle, and also the first film in the history of cinema to construct a new type of spectator, responsible, active, deeply involved in the process of production of meaning.[13] Take one of the initial scenes. After having admired the panorama on the terrace, the Joyces recline in the sun. Katherine starts talking about the allure of the country: 'Temple of the Spirit. No longer bodies, but pure ascetic images.' The words, she tells her husband, are those of the young poet Charles Lewing-ton, a former lover of hers who, the night before he left for London, had waited for her outside in the garden to say goodbye, shivering, in the rain, and had died soon after-wards from tuberculosis. This is the episode taken from 'The Dead', and it explains the meaning of the whole film, which is a variant, or rather a continuation, of Joyce's story.

Alex, who is jealous, although he hides it, snubs this memory and becomes even more bad-tempered. The next day, Katherine begins her journey around Naples, starting at the Museo Nazionale, where she is deeply disturbed by the sight of some of the statues. In a series of false point-of-view shots, the camera follows the series of dancers, pauses on the satyr, moves around the drunken faun and tracks towards the discus-thrower, who seems to look without seeing, from an infinite distance. Katherine is struck by this proximity and this huge distance. We are within reality and at the same time within myth. The whole sequence is an introduction to the next epiphany.

This procedure creates an even more disturbing effect in the visit to the cave of the Cumaean Sibyl, where nature intervenes to heighten the uncertainties. Here, as the guide says, after the death of the Sybil and after the Greek and Roman eras, the cave was transformed into a great fortress against pirates. Aeneas landed there after the Trojan War and the Americans also landed there during the war. History and myth are one.

Katherine then climbs up alone to the ruins of the Temple of Apollo, where the revelation occurs. The trees, moved by the wind, create a sort of curtain, a waving *skené* that hides the landscape (in the classical theatre, the *skené* was the curtain behind which the actor stood before coming on stage). The only thing that we see is the wind, a manifestation of the invisible, like that which impressed the audiences of early cinema (for instance Georges Méliès, when he first saw the Cinématographe Lumière). What is important here is what does not happen, what cannot be seen. Katherine approaches the terrace and looks at the sea. Cut. The interruption of the sequence comes at the exact point. Rossellini creates an epiphanic machine that leaves us with a sense of having seen and not seen. Once again 'we see that we do not see'.

The instrument of this epiphany without epiphany is, precisely, the landscape, in which Rossellini manages to suggest a presence without showing anything. Bergman's sunglasses make her appear curiously like the statues she saw earlier, eyes without a look. Our eyes are like this too. The landscape offers itself to them as a scene, in its etymological sense of *skené*. We too are confronted with a landscape which is like a curtain (*skené*) that does not open, whose truth lies precisely in its being a curtain.

The situation is repeated at the sulphur pits at Pozzuoli with the phenomenon of ionisation, an effect of natural sympathy, and then on the visit to the Fontanelle cemetery, with its huge pile of anonymous skulls, where death seems richer than life. Finally, the visit to Pompeii brings the culmination of this vertigo, with the last 'miracle'. *Journey to Italy* is a completely private and public, singular and universal, story. It is a story of the living and the dead in which, as in Joyce's story, the dead are more alive than the living. And nature is the site of this mysterious cohabitation of two worlds that culture has violently separated. The rustle of the branches, the sun and the sea, the silence and the confused noise equivalent to silence, lead to a sort of general equivalence. Everything turns into everything else; life and death are very close together. Nowhere more than here is nature an invisible totality, present–absent. To use Hölderlin's oxymoron, we could say that *Journey to Italy* is a film full of 'dark light'.[14]

There is, however, another film which confronts us with the reversal, the parody of the mystery and religion. This parody is not cynical or derogatory but, on the contrary, deeply moving: its aim is to display the cruelty of the world and the impossibility of distinguishing between sainthood and folly. The film is 'Il miracolo', the first of the two episodes of *L'Amore* (1948). The sudden appearance of Federico Fellini, dressed as a tramp on the clifftops of the Amalfi coast, in front of the poor shepherdess Nannina (Anna Magnani), has the force of a genuine epiphany, for her, whose senses and mind are dazzled by the sun. Not the least of the causes of this equivocation, this dream which destroys the last remaining shred of Nannina's reason, is nature, wild nature, which is the protagonist of the first part of the film: the rocky coast, the violent sun that blinds even the spectator, the sea and the sky, the earth and the grass which fuse into a single fire. Even here we cannot fail to notice a trace of Greek myth. Nannina is like the ancient shepherd who, if he got lost in the open during the noonday hours, sometimes had the privilege of seeing naked nymphs with the god Pan in their midst, but he returned with his mind altered, gone mad.

And in the midst of this wild nature, in these very long tracking shots which follow Nannina in the hot sun, ascending and descending, with her bundle of madness and life, among the stones, steps, trees, paths, rocks, terraces, gardens, in this *via crucis* before and after the act of love, accompanied only by the insistent voice of the goats intoning their monotonous tune, the real protagonist, Nannina's true companion, is the landscape, and we too could lose our reason. We might say that Nannina has been impregnated by the landscape. Here too everything has a double meaning: on the plane of perceptible reality Nannina makes an error: she has a dream and she mistakes a tramp for Saint Joseph; but on the other plane, that of metaphor, where what is important is what cannot be seen, it is the people, the village, who are wrong, and Nannina who is right, because she really has seen the world, the god Pan. To adapt what Kafka wrote about parables, on the plane of reality Nannina has lost, but on that of metaphor she has won, because the plane of reality and the symbolic plane run in opposite directions.[15]

Only what is realistic is mythical: *India*

If Godard wrote that *India* is 'beautiful like the creation of the world', we can assume he had his reasons, not least because Godard's statements are never intended to be taken literally.[16] We could say that the film is a discovery of the world by the movie camera, very similar to that of the Lumière brothers. Everything is real and at the same time everything is fiction, everything is old and at the same time everything is new, everything is found and everything is invented. Rossellini's camera, faced with an unknown and immense world like India, rediscovers what Rohmer, talking of the Cinématographe Lumière, calls 'the first astonishment'. It is probably in this sense that we can understand Godard's statement. Rossellini's eye experiences the same amazement as someone looking at the world for the first time: the eye of a child or of cinema which has become a child again. From the great long shot of the crowds in Delhi from above, which opens and closes the film, to the long tracking shots and travelling shots among palm trees and boundless plains, immense rivers, paddy fields, sunsets, lakes, forests, plains dried up by the sun, snow-capped mountains, statues and infinite decorations of bodies interwoven into the temples of love which are 'the delirious explosion of a people's love of life', according to the voice-over, the camera moves inward towards the 580,000 villages where the 'real India' lives, the astonishment is renewed, both in what is seen and in the movements of the gaze. As with Giuseppe Promio's early tracking shots or the dispatching of camera operators round the world by the Lumières and Kahn to film scenes of real life, the camera here returns us to the simple pleasure and surprise of those first movements. There is, moreover, not just the gaze of the cinema; the whole film is made up of gazes. The mahout who tends his elephant and lives in symbiosis with it catches sight from the top of the tree of the girl he wants to marry, whom he had seen for the first time at a puppet show the evening before. The elephant that works lifting tree trunks and then allows itself to be looked after, scrubbed and groomed immersed in the water, almost as an exchange of favours, looks around pleased after its efforts. The love stories of humans and elephants, recounted in parallel, become correlative, each a metaphor for the other. Nokul, the worker, goes to look for the last time at the dam that he has spent seven years building and then leaves to find work elsewhere. Then there is the look, as much surprised as attentive, of the old man who meets the tiger in the jungle, another epiphany of the sacred. Finally, the tame monkey, Ramu, left alone because of the death of his owner, who has collapsed with heat stroke, looks around not understanding, alone. They are all human and animal gazes directed at a world, a nature of which they are part, gazes which are aware and unaware at the same time.

However, *India* is not a simple and banal return to myth, to the infantile and idealised gaze of primitive man. Rossellini is not a romantic to the point of pursuing an imaginary state of nature and exclaiming, like Hölderlin's Hyperion, 'the ideal is what was once nature'. On the contrary, he is well aware that this gaze does not exist, or exists only as the trace of a great suffering. The contemporary Indian, the worker who bids farewell to the dam, is in no way a noble savage, nor is he modern man. He is, once again, a mind in conflict between two world-views and two cultures. The conflict between staying within the landscape or staying outside it, in culture, is a conflict between looking from the inside and looking from the outside, between myth and technology, which contend for the human heart. The modern Indian, Nokul, observes the hydroelectric power station next to the dam; his thoughts are relayed in the voice-over: 'Electricity. Electricity. Magic. Magic. But everything can be explained. It can be explained. One only has to reflect. Reflect. There is no more magic. There is no more magic. There are no more miracles. There are no more miracles. Knowledge. Knowledge.' The inner conflict between the old, magical, superstitious world, tied to the rhythms of nature, and the new rational world is also expressed in the editing, which alternates between close-ups of the amazed Nokul and shots of the dam from his point of view. But it is expressed even more by his inner voice which repeats everything. Every statement is said twice as if it were an echo, producing an effect of redundancy, as if two people were speaking within Nokul, the old and the new, as if the old were not sufficiently convinced and the new were not sure. Nokul's gaze is a double gaze, the amazed look of the child and that of the knowing adult, that of the ancient man and that of the modern man, a fusion of two gazes which see in nature the sacred, the eternal mystery, but also simply a system which, according to determinate laws, one can dominate and control. One only has to reflect. The power of man is too much and too little, as is shown immediately after in the story of Ramu the monkey, who is the other side of the coin of technological man, and who could be the man-monkey of Kubrick's *2001 – A Space Odyssey*. Nature, so powerful in the epiphany of the tiger, once it has been subjugated by man is revealed to be small and weak like a little monkey who does not know what to do. The sacred disappears from the face of the earth. All that remains are poor defenceless animals, mountains, woods, energy to be harnessed. But is it really like that? Has the mystery really disappeared? Certainly not, because suddenly the sacred, chased away by reason, reappears in the very heart of man. Everything is overturned and we come back to the starting point, with the mysterious crowd, that one great body without a face or with a thousand faces: 'And again the crowds, the immense crowds'. The mystery remains.

But it is not enough, because all these linked gazes, so true, so profound and intense, upon which the film's meaning is constructed are also excessively false: the old man who is watching the tiger is only an effect of editing, a fable, a story – we can see this easily from the crudeness of the editing and the fire, which are almost ridiculous. The old man's voice is false: it is the voice of a young man imitating the shaky voice of an old man. Everything is cinema, construction, editing. The monkey is not watching the other wild monkeys at all, who in any case pose no threat to her, nor is the mahout of the first episode looking at the house of his beloved. There is no shot in which these characters or animals are seen together. We are in the same position as the worker Nokul who cannot believe in magic any more, but neither can he stop believing in it. We see and we do not see. For Rossellini, culture cannot replace nature; it stands alongside it. Nature and culture continue to exist in parallel in the human mind. Mystery remains once again.

Notes

1 Pier Paolo Pasolini, 'Il codice dei codici', in *Empirismo eretico* (Milan: Garzanti, 1972), pp. 277–84; Georges Bataille, 'Le Sacré', in *Œuvres complètes* (Paris: Gallimard, 1971), vol. 1, pp. 559–63.

2 G.W.F. Hegel, *Die Phänomenologie des Geistes*, VI, B: 'Der sich entfremdete Geist. Die Bildung'; *The Phenomenology of Mind*, translated by J.B. Baillie (London: Allen & Unwin, 1931), VI, B: 'Spirit in Self-Estrangement: The Discipline of Culture and Civilization'.

3 The title *Germany Year Zero* was inspired by Morin's book *Berlin année zero*, according to Roger Boussinot, 'A Berlin, après avoir trouvé un ange grâce au désespoir d'amour d'un éléphant, Rossellini tourne dans les rues, le métro ... et sous les ponts', *L'Ecran Français*, no. 119, 7 October 1947. On Simone Weil as one of the inspirations for *Europe '51*, see Maurice Schérer [Eric Rohmer] and François Truffaut, 'Entretien avec Roberto Rossellini', *Cahiers du Cinéma*, no. 37, July 1954, p. 8, translated by Annapaola Cancogni in Roberto Rossellini, *My Method*, edited by Adriano Aprà (New York: Marsilio, 1992), p. 54.

4 Roberto Rossellini, *Utopia Autopsia 10^{10}* (Rome: Armando, 1974).

5 At the opening of Godard's *Pierrot le fou* (1965), Ferdinand (Jean-Paul Belmondo) reads from Elie Faure's book on Velázquez: 'Velázquez, après cinquante ans, ne peignait plus jamais une chose définie. Il errait autour des objects avec l'air et le crépuscule, il surprenait dans l'ombre et la transparence des fonds, les palpitations colorées dont il faisait le centre invisible de sa symphonie silencieuse.' ('Past the age of 50, Velázquez stopped painting definite things. He hovered around objects with the air, with the twilight, catching in his shadows and airy backgrounds the palpitations of colour which formed the invisible core of his silent symphony.')

6 Paul Eluard, 'Paisà', in *L'Ecran Français*, no. 73, 9 November 1946, p. 13.

7 Walter Benjamin, 'Johann Jakob Bachofen', *Les Lettres Nouvelles*, no. 1, 1954, pp. 28–42.

8 Basil Wright, 'Germany Year Nought', *Documentary Film News*, no. 65, May 1948, p. 53.

9 Benjamin, 'Johann Jakob Bachofen', p. 32.

10 Maurice Schérer [Eric Rohmer], '*Stromboli*', *La Gazette du Cinéma*, no. 5, November

1950, republished in E. Rohmer, *Le Goût de la beauté* (Paris: Cahiers du Cinéma/Editions de l'Etoile, 1984).

11 Béla Balázs, *Theory of the Film (Character and Growth of a New Art)*, translated from the Hungarian by Edith Bone (London: Dobson, 1952), Chapter 8, pp. 25–6.

12 Pier Paolo Pasolini, *Ragazzi di vita* (Milan: Garzanti, 1955), Chapter 1, 'Il Ferrobedò'.

13 Alain Bergala, *Voyage en Italie de Roberto Rossellini* (Crisnée, Belgium: Editions Yellow Now, 1990).

14 See 'Andenken' ('Remembrance'), lines 26–7: 'Es reiche aber,/Des dunkeln Lichtes voll,/Mir einer den duftenden Becher' ('But someone pass me/The fragrant cup/Full of the dark light', Friedrich Hölderlin, *Poems and Fragments*, translated by Michael Hamburger, 3rd bilingual edition (London: Anvil Press, 1994), pp. 508–9. Compare 'Brod und Wein' ('Bread and Wine'), Part 9, lines 1–2: 'Ja! Sie sagen mit Recht, er söhne den Tag mit der Nacht aus/Führe des Himmels Gestirn ewig hinunter, hinauf' ('Yes, and rightly they say he reconciles day with our night-time,/Leads the stars of the sky upward and down without end' (ibid., pp. 270–1). In 'Brod und Wein' Hölderlin says the gods have abandoned the world but have left a trace of themselves in two things – bread and wine – which give joy to humans. Henri Langlois also said that Rossellini made cinema as one makes bread, in other words like a poor but essential food, the only one that is really indispensable for humans.

15 Franz Kafka, 'On Parables' ('Von den Gleichnissen'), in *Parables and Paradoxes* (bilingual edition, New York: Schocken, 1961), pp. 10–11. A quotation from this text is used as an epigraph in Gérard Genette's *Figures III. Discours du récit* (Paris: Seuil, 1972).

16 Jean-Luc Godard, '*India*', in *Cahiers du Cinéma*, no. 96, June 1959, p. 41.

5

Saint Ingrid at the Stake: Stardom and Scandal in the Bergman–Rossellini Collaboration

Stephen Gundle

Between March 1949, when Ingrid Bergman arrived in Rome to begin her personal and professional collaboration with Rossellini, and February 1950, when the couple's first child was born, the pair were at the centre of an unprecedented whirlwind of negative publicity. Bergman shocked Americans by abandoning her Hollywood career to work with a little-known Italian director. She horrified them by beginning a romance with this director despite the fact that she was a married woman with a young daughter. When it emerged that she was expecting Rossellini's baby, she was branded 'a free love cultist, an apostle of degradation' and 'a powerful influence for evil'. Scarcely less a victim of vituperation was Rossellini himself. Accused of sneaking 'like a viper ... into the bed of others' and of being 'vile and unspeakable ... a love pirate', 'a money-mad home-wrecker ... a degenerate',[1] he was eventually blamed for ruining one of Hollywood's brightest stars in a series of film roles that were not well received and which flopped at the box office. The scandal finally petered out when the couple married some months after the birth of their son.

As long as it lasted, the scandal was intense and persistent. It was fuelled by a cast of characters which stretched well beyond the couple themselves (and Bergman's husband) to include photographers and gossip columnists, American senators, churchmen, movie industry producers and spokesmen, public relations experts, the news media of two continents, and ordinary filmgoers. Even today, many years after the critical re-evaluation of the films made by the Bergman–Rossellini couple, it is probably true that far more people are aware of the partnership as a personal liaison born of scandal than have ever seen the resultant films, all of which had either a brief or a limited release. Over the past forty years, the scandal has been revisited many times and continues to resurface in memoirs, biographies and analyses of the motion picture business as well as popular magazine articles.

The purpose of this chapter is to examine the dynamics of the scandal that was unleashed by Bergman's failure to conform to accepted American norms of behaviour. As the first major media scandal of the postwar years, the affair presents various facets that are worthy of analysis. Particular attention will be paid to the role of Bergman's star persona and status and to the chain reaction which resulted when – to borrow publicist Bill Davidson's expression – the 'Unreal' that was the usual product of Hollywood's publicity departments suddenly and unexpectedly succumbed to the 'Real'.[2] To understand the events of 1949–50, it is necessary to consider the particular relations between press, public relations and society in America, but also the equivalent set of relations in Italy. The Italian view of the scandal has not hitherto received much attention, yet it is important both in contextualising it and in exploring its impact on the Bergman–Rossellini partnership.

The Flight From Hollywood

As a Hollywood star who had established her appeal in such box office successes as *Casablanca, For Whom the Bell Tolls and Notorious*, Ingrid Bergman did not face any immediate threat to her career in the post-1945 years as a consequence of the decline in movie-going and the break-up of the studio monopolies. However, after her period under contract to David O. Selznick, she made three films as an independent actress in 1948–9 which did not do well. In her autobiography Bergman describes her dissatisfaction with the glossy unreality of Joan of Arc and her yearning for something more authentic: 'All the battle scenes were done in the studio: the towers of Chinon and the French villages were painted backdrops. I didn't think I looked like a peasant girl at all. I just looked like a movie star playing the part of Joan. Clean face, nice hairdo.'[3]

It was in this general frame of mind that she saw *Rome Open City* on a Spring evening in 1948. Not surprisingly, the raw realism of the film was a revelation; it opened her eyes to a different way of making films.[4] The deep emotional impact that the film made on her was confirmed a few months later when, alone in New York, she saw *Paisà* on Broadway. Bergman was amazed that 'this man had made two great films and he was playing to empty houses'. Movies like this, she felt, 'simply *must* be seen by millions, not only by the Italians but by millions all over the world'.[5] 'If this man had someone who was a *name* playing for him', she reasoned, 'then maybe people would come and see his pictures'. Later the same day, after consulting her friend Irene Selznick, wife of David, Bergman decided to write to Rossellini to offer her services and to express her desire to make a film like *Paisà*. This oft-reproduced letter was intended to be brief and light-hearted, although it was also mildly flirtatious:

> Dear Mr Rossellini
> I saw your films *Open City* and *Paisan*, and enjoyed them very much. If you need a Swedish actress who speaks English very well, who has not forgotten her German, and who is very understandable in French, and who, in Italian knows only 'ti amo', I am ready to come and work with you.
>
> Best regards,
> Ingrid Bergman[6]

This was not the first such letter Bergman had written. Davidson reveals that she later confessed to having offered her services for an 'artistic' film to Elia Kazan, Fredric March and Frank Capra.[7] But her feeling for Rossellini was nonetheless strong. Unaware that *Paisà* was 'the most-discussed movie in town',[8] she regarded the Italian as an unknown, romantic figure whom she could help discover.

Sent to the offices of Minerva Film in Rome, the unopened letter was found in the aftermath of a fire by staff who conveyed it to Rossellini. The director reportedly had never heard of Bergman, or at least could not recall her name, and had to be told that she was one of the leading stars in Hollywood.[9] The haste with which he responded, assuring her that a film in which he had in fact planned to cast his then lover and leading lady, Anna Magnani, was conceived with her in mind, was motivated not only by the obvious allure of Bergman's beauty but by the opportunity that her collaboration would offer to progress beyond the war-related cinema with which he had made his name. By 1948 Rossellini was seeking to develop his cinema in new ways, exploring for the first time what he would call the 'neo-realism of the person' in the two episodes of *L'Amore*.

After having sent Bergman a long letter outlining his ideas for what would become *Stromboli*, Rossellini flew to America to meet the actress and discuss the project. During this stay, part of which he spent as a house guest of Bergman and her husband Petter Lindström, he sought financial backing for his film from Samuel Goldwyn and others. Resistance was strong, however, and Goldwyn pulled out after a private viewing of *Germany Year Zero*. With Bergman's assistance and her personal intervention with Howard Hughes, RKO agreed to produce the film. In March 1949, the actress arrived in Rome to fulfill her dream. She was collected from Ciampino airport by Rossellini, who drove her in his red Cisitalia sports car to the Excelsior Hotel, where he maintained an apartment and where a press conference was held. Accounts of this event tell of a crush of photographers eager to capture the first images of the actress who had once been groomed to be 'the new Garbo' and who was abandoning Hollywood for Italy. The attention did not diminish in the following days. In a journey that took nearly a week, Rossellini drove Bergman to the southern tip of Italy. 'The whole thing was messy from the first', Peter Brunette writes; 'paparazzi had followed them everywhere along their automobile trip down the Italian coast; a *Life* photographer caught them, in an unguarded moment in Amalfi, holding hands.'[10]

Rumours of a romance had begun even while Rossellini was in America, but now there was confirmation. If news of Bergman's 'defection' caused consternation in America, publication of this photograph fuelled the flames of scandal. The filming of *Stromboli* was thus surrounded by intense controversy. Although conditions on the island were extremely primitive and filming dragged on well beyond the projected six weeks to nearly four months, the level of interest scarcely diminished. Photographers and journalists visited the island at repeated intervals, together with press agents and public relations experts sent by the production company. 'For the first time in my life I discovered with surprise that there exist in the world incredible jobs, such as those highly specialised "specialists"', Rossellini later said. 'The wave of sensational stories undoubtedly had a sole purpose: to scare us. Faced with the flow of "sensational" news, the "experts" suggested that we adopt one attitude only: denial'.[11] The most powerful such call came from the head of the Production Code Administration, Joseph Breen, who wrote to Bergman warning that tales of adultery, if not denied, would be disastrous for her career and imperil her status as first lady of the screen. Her apparent actions had caused profound shock, he asserted, and flew in the face of values held dear by ordinary people.[12]

The first to be told that Bergman and Rossellini had fallen in love was the former's husband, who bombarded her with cables and eventually came to Italy for an unpleasant showdown in Messina. Apart from this episode, the couple endeavoured to maintain a modicum of discretion. However, this attitude became untenable when it transpired, after the conclusion of filming, that Bergman was expecting Rossellini's child. As the scandal began in earnest, the couple were virtually kept under siege in the Rome apartment where they lived openly together by photographers prepared to stage round-the-clock stakeouts in the hope of getting pictures of Bergman. The publicity explosion surrounding the impending 'out-of-wedlock' birth roused moralists to the heights of indignation. One of the American film industry's foremost congressional critics, Senator Edwin Johnson of Colorado (who was also a leading figure in the Swedish-American community), launched the most vituperative attack. He denounced Rossellini as 'a narcotics addict, Nazi collaborator and black market operator'.[13] He took the couple's brazen affair as a symbol of the disrespect with which Hollywood regarded proper moral standards. Fired by this and the controversy surrounding Rita Hayworth's hasty marriage to Prince Aly Khan in 1949, he

Ingrid Bergman and Robertino (born 1950) on cover of *La Settimana Incom*, December 1952.

developed his draconian proposal for a federal licensing system for actors, directors and producers. As for Bergman, he argued for the adoption of a resolution that would bar her on the grounds of 'moral turpitude' from returning to the United States.[14]

Rossellini threatened violence if any photographs were taken of Bergman or baby Robertino, born on 2 February 1950. In fact, despite strenuous efforts, no photographers succeeded in gaining access to the hospital and the Italian weekly *La Settimana Incom* was forced to create a photomontage featuring the imagined bedside scene.[15] Taken by many to be an official picture, the photomontage appeared to confirm the shamelessness of the couple. After this hiatus, the obsessive interest in Bergman and Rossellini declined, although publicity surrounded the couple through their respective divorces, marriage by proxy in Mexico in May 1950, the birth of the twins Isabella and Isotta in June 1952, and their eventual separation and divorce in 1957.

Although it benefited from unprecedented pre-release publicity, *Stromboli* was not a success. Re-edited in America by RKO, it was issued in a form that departed from Rossellini's intentions. Virtually all the reviews were negative. In *The New York Times* Bosley Crowther described it as 'a startling anticlimax'. 'This widely heralded film', he wrote, 'is incredibly feeble, inarticulate, uninspiring and painfully banal'. For the *New York Herald Tribune* 'the much-discussed *Stromboli* is neither good Bergman, good Rossellini, nor good anything'.[16] Audiences reportedly whistled and booed at showings. None of the subsequent films they made together received anything better than a mixed reception. French critics praised *Journey to Italy* but the general response was not positive. *Films in Review* described it as 'poorly written, incompetently directed, atrociously edited'.[17] Sheer lack of resources eventually forced Bergman to accept the offer of the leading role in the Hollywood film *Anastasia*. This led to a renaissance in her career but to the end of her personal as well as professional relationship with Rossellini.

Sources of Scandal

The scandal was not a 'natural' or 'spontaneous' phenomenon but one which owed much to the image of Bergman, the situation in the film industry and in American society at the end of the 1940s, racial stereotypes and the internal circumstances of the press. All of these facilitated the construction of a media narrative which framed the scandal and gave it characters, a structure and longevity. As James Lull and Stephen Hinerman argue, 'A media scandal occurs when private acts that disgrace or offend the idealised, dominant morality of a social community are made public and narrativised by the media, producing a range of effects from ideological and cultural retrenchment to disruption and change'.[18]

What astonished film industry insiders as well as guardians of official morality most was the lack of shame and secrecy with which Bergman and Rossellini conducted their affair. 'Americans everywhere went purple at the thought that the good girl, the saint, the nun of pictures, should flaunt her adultery in their faces,' wrote veteran actress Gloria Swanson in her memoirs.[19] Hollywood studios had press departments whose job it was to protect stars from scandal, in some cases by suppressing evidence or persuading journalists that the interests of the community would be better served by drawing a veil over transgressions. Offenders were only too ready to comply with these efforts because it preserved them from the public pillory and enabled them to continue untroubled with their careers.[20] In this case, the parties escaped such control, with the result that the type of scandal designated by Lull and Hinerman as a 'star scandal' came about.[21] There was an attempt, through the strategy of denial, to save the situation and reestablish some conformity to the dominant morality, but this failed.

Donald Spoto points out that 'an appallingly narrow, conservative smog darkened the entire landscape of the entertainment industry just when Ingrid Bergman fell in love and became pregnant. For many Americans, movie actors were strange, immoral, no-account scoundrels. Newspapers had recounted the antics of Lana Turner, Charles Chaplin, Mickey Rooney and Errol Flynn ... Ingrid Bergman was held above all that.'[22] Bergman's virginal image was crucial to the development of the scandal. Although violations of the prevailing morality by any star provoke criticism, 'they are simultaneously relativised in terms of the moral character and boundaries of the star's complex image system'. According to Lull and Hinerman, 'The star scandal forges an intersection composed of three semiotic trajectories: society's dominant morality, the particular image system of the star in question, and the actual events as reported in the news. The dynamic interplay of these factors gives each star scandal its particular platforms for interpretation.'[23] In relation to Bergman, the issue of image has been explored most thoroughly by James Damico.[24] From the beginning, Bergman was perceived as 'radiant', 'spiritual', 'natural' and 'pure'. Moulded and promoted by David O. Selznick as an unaffected, authentic alternative to the artificial 'glamour girls' usually produced by Hollywood, she confirmed her wholesome image by her stable family life and avoidance of pin-up publicity shots. Damico shows that this image, while not entirely false, hid Bergman's bad temper and extramarital involvements (for example with the photographer Robert Capa) and even bypassed 'the specifically sexual character of the largest portion of her roles and, even more essentially, the almost totally sexual nature of her screen persona'.[25]

Before she became identified in the public mind with Joan of Arc, a role she played on Broadway before taking the lead role in Victor Fleming's 1948 film, she had made twelve American films. Damico notes that she was a prostitute or promiscuous in four of these (*Dr Jeykll and Mr Hyde, Saratoga Trunk, Notorious, Arch of Triumph*), has or has had an affair in another four (*Intermezzo, Casablanca, For Whom the Bell Tolls, Spellbound*), and is virtually a slave of sexual dependency in another (*Gaslight*). Questions of infidelity are involved in a further two (*Rage in Heaven* and *Adam Had Four Sons*), while her portrayal of a Mother Superior, Sister Benedict, in *The Bells of St Mary's* relies on sex appeal.[26] What characterised Bergman's film roles was not aloof contemplation and radiant morality but total emotional involvement. 'The close relationship that an all-encompassing and finally transcendental romantic sexual love bears to spiritual love of an equal intensity is critical to the misapprehension of Bergman's film persona,' Damico continues; 'for those physical and emotional attributes that constitute her screen personality could just as easily be read as expressive of the spiritual torment of a soul reaching for communion with and salvation from God.'[27]

Bergman's publicity image stressed almost entirely this latter aspect, with the result that many filmgoers took her virtually to be a modern day incarnation of Joan of Arc. Precisely because Bergman took on a totemic function at a time when the drive to restore morality after the turbulence of the war years was in full swing, the sense of betrayal when she abandoned her family was pronounced. The level of shock can be gauged by the fact that such well-placed figures as Joseph Breen and Bergman's sometime publicity agent Joseph Steele simply did not believe the stories when they first broke. In this context, at least part of the anger was directed against *Stromboli*'s producers, who were seen as having engineered the controversy to generate publicity.

The announcement that Bergman was pregnant was first made by Hearst journalist Louella Parsons in January 1950, at the start of the Vatican's Holy Year. There has been much speculation about the source of the scoop, which Parsons used to stage a comeback after years of losing ground to her arch-rival, Hopper. Hughes, Steele, the Hearst correspondent in Rome, Mike Chinigo, and Hearst himself have all been indicated as possibile sources.[28] What is certain is that, within days of the announcement, RKO launched a campaign to stimulate interest in a film whose content was extremely tame.[29]

This does not mean that the press was a neutral factor in the development of the scandal. Lull and Hinerman note that the media are always interested players who directly contribute to turning news events into scandals. This they do by ensuring that revelations are widely circulated and are effectively narrativised into a story.[30] 'Managers of modern news media actively try to turn stories into scandals', they argue. 'To call a story a scandal is to give it a bizarre kind of journalistic appeal and integrity ("This must *really* be something!")'.[31] Undoubtedly, the ethnic element in the scandal was also significant. There was a charge of national pride in the anger and surprise that Hollywood could lose one of its biggest stars to Italy. It was sometimes forgotten that Bergman was a Swede with European sensibilities. In their study of ethnic and racial images in the American media, Allen Woll and Randall Miller argue that American popular culture stole from English traditions to give rise to an image of 'Italian men and women … [as] overly sexual, passionate and mysterious'. Gothic fiction and modern melodramas 'teemed with dark, Mediterranean men and women exuding passion and plotting intrigues, threatening English virginity and liberty'.[32] In addition, Italian-Americans acquired a reputation for crime or clownishness. Rossellini fitted the stereotype of the dark, latin man who wrested a pure, white woman from the bosom of her family. Senator Johnson's description of him as a 'love pirate' conjured up precisely this imagery, as did *Time* magazine's reference to 'Italy's swarthy, balding director'.[33].

A further dimension to the scandal was added by the rivalry between the productions of *Stromboli* and another film, *Vulcano*. Indignant and profoundly wounded by the way she had been cast aside by the man with whom she had established an intense artistic and personal relationship, Anna Magnani pursued revenge by accepting the offer of an American producer to make a film on Vulcano, another Aeolian island. Directed by William Dieterle, this film was not a work of any artistic merit; its sole purpose was to exploit for financial ends the wave of publicity generated by *Stromboli*. *Vulcano* was ready for release before Rossellini's film, but unfortunately Magnani's attempt to upstage Bergman turned into a boomerang. The evening of the Rome preview of *Vulcano* was disrupted by news of the birth of the latter's son, a news event that completely eclipsed the film (Magnani, forewarned, actually stayed away from this show).[34]

Finally, the role of church groups in the USA should not be overlooked. Many ministers denounced Bergman as a disgrace and a symptom of moral decline. The Federal Council of Churches condemned the Bergman–Rossellini affair as 'sex exhibitionism which is a symbol of the moral decline of the West', while the Salvation Army withdrew the recordings the actress had made in 1949 in support of its annual charity appeal. The Roman Catholic Church in America conducted an orchestrated campaign against the actress and was 'her most vicious attacker'.[35] This campaign brought extraordinary pressure on Bergman, who, Spoto claims, received no fewer than 40,000 letters from the USA, the vast majority unfavourable, between her departure and the birth of her child.[36]

Bergman's Italian reception

The Bergman–Rossellini affair was by any definition a global scandal. It involved three countries – the United States, Italy and Bergman's home country, Sweden – and it excited the interest of the world's media. However, as John Tomlinson has argued, 'though moral standards are nominally universal (the moral content of a scandal *should* travel), in fact censure, disgrace, and moral indignation wane with time and distance'.[37] It may be argued that the centre of this particular scandal was the United States. In Italy the indignation was less pronounced. Although the country was the site of the unfolding of the scandal, it differed from the United States in the structure of its press and public opinion, its conception of public and private, and the position occupied by film stars in society. In addition, as the country was a longstanding haven for those forced to flee the judgement of the community in their own countries, a tolerant atmosphere towards foreigners prevailed. Finally, the Catholic Church was not a pressure group as in the USA but an institution of consolidated power and influence.

From the evidence available, it appears that Ingrid Bergman was given a warm reception in Italy. She was not a Catholic and her marriage to Lindström therefore had no special value in the eyes of the Church. Moreover, Joan of Arc was not a figure of any historical or particular religious significance in the country and in any case the film had not yet been released there. At a time when indebtedness to the USA was strong, there was almost national pride in the fact that an Italian director had managed to capture one of Hollywood's brightest stars.[38] 'Arriving in Rome was just like something out of a dream,' Bergman later wrote. 'I've never experienced a welcome like it anywhere else in the world. It was a fiesta – everyone laughing and shouting and going mad. There were so many people at the airport you'd think it was a queen arriving, instead of just me.'[39] The enthusiasm continued during the car journey South. In Catanzaro, the mayor had been warned of the couple's arrival and the inhabitants were packed six deep down both sides of the main street ready to welcome them.[40]

This of course was prior to the explosion of the scandal and Bergman's testimony reveals that she and Rossellini were not yet conducting themselves as a couple. Yet the attitude of indulgence does not seem to have changed later. Although photographers regarded Rossellini and Bergman as highly newsworthy from the moment the actress arrived in Rome, in general the Italian press was quite circumspect. It was not until the couple reached Stromboli that rumours of their love turned into eager speculation. Bergman's co-author, Alan Burgess, points out that the 'speculation had begun as soon as Ingrid had reached Rome and looked at Roberto with eyes of love. It had increased as they journeyed to Capri, and was given impetus by *Life* magazine's full-page photo of them holding hands in Amalfi.' Yet Lamberti Sorrentino of *Tempo* was the only journalist to accompany the couple on their car journey through the South and he merely alluded to the developing relationship. He reported that Ingrid 'looks at Rossellini with admiration and affection', while the latter 'is tender with her. He is for her a mother, a father, a brother, everything.' Buried in the final paragraphs of his article were some opaque considerations on what Ingrid's behaviour might be in the case of divorce from her husband and a second marriage.[41]

Unlike the Americans and other foreigners, whose interest in the case was determined by the burgeoning scandal, the Italians found news potential in the romance. With memories of the Rome wedding of Hollywood stars Tyrone Power and Linda Christian still fresh, they saw an opportunity to recount a great love story.[42] Sorrentino in *Tempo* of 23 April described Rossellini and Bergman as 'two characters in a romantic fable'.[43] Only on 30 April did *Tempo* publish a richly-illustrated article which, in both its title ('Tormented Love on Stromboli') and content, made the relationship obvious.[44] However freelancers were aware of the foreign market for photographs and news. 'The Italian press scenting *amore* as sharks scent blood,' Burgess observes, 'were already dispatching reporters disguised as fishermen, tourists, and on one occasion even as a monk, to the island.'[45]

In Italy, where there was a lower level of mediatisation of society than in America, such events were a novelty. When he went to the USA, Rossellini was astonished to find that 'the publication of a newspaper or certain radio programmes could keep everyone on tenterhooks. Every day people eagerly awaited the papers and life came to a stop when the programme came on.' This gave reporters a very prominent role; many of them, the director found, 'are simply defenders of a pre-established order, militia-men ready to castigate those who upset that order'.[46] This situation did not apply in Italy. The press did not generally play any agenda-setting function; thus Rossellini was surprised by a development he had not bargained for.

It may be argued that in Italy the press operated in a 'traditional' way: it pursued an approach to personal relationships that obscured or glossed over possible elements of transgression. The American press, by contrast, functioned according to modern criteria in so far as it participated in the creation and perpetuation of a moral panic in order to increase interest and sales. The rhythm it imposed on the Bergman – Rossellini scandal was an industrial one. However, through its involvement in and observation of this scandal, the Italian press underwent a change. It learned the dynamic and the profitability of scandal and began to operate in a more American way. This culture shift reached its apotheosis in 1957–9, when magazines like *Lo Specchio* and *Le Ore* regularly published paparazzi shots of film stars and aristocrats in compromising situations accompanied by moralising prose. With *La dolce vita* (1960), Fellini turned such press practices into spectacle and gave the impression, wrongly, that scandal-mongering (and perhaps the sex scandal itself) was an Italian speciality.

By the mid 1950s the Italian Church, fearing the consequences of social change, was intervening regularly to condemn transgression, but in 1949–50 it failed to play its allotted role in the manufacture of scandal. Indeed, to some extent it protected Rossellini. Tag Gallagher argues that Rossellini's interest in religious faith as a counterbalance to the cynicism of the postwar years was especially strong in the late 1940s and early 1950s.

Priests feature prominently in several films, from *Rome Open City* to *Stromboli*, and religious sentiments are central to 'Il miracolo', *Francis God's Jester* and *Europe '51*. Rossellini
mixed extensively with clerics and was regarded in Italy as a leading exponent of the
Catholic camp in cinema. Far from being convinced, like Cardinal Spellman of New
York, that the director of such a 'blasphemous' work as 'Il miracolo' could only be a
Communist,[47] Italian Catholics saw Rossellini as a welcome ally at a time when the
majority of cinema was aligned with the left. While there were some denunciations of
the couple's conduct, on the whole the Church did not turn it into a public issue. Indeed
Spoto finds many examples of indulgence. He cites the DC paper *Il Popolo*'s repudia-
tions of American condemnations of *Stromboli* and Bergman, and refers to 'a number
of non-judgmental clergymen in Rossellini's social circle [who] had offered Ingrid
friendship and sympathy'.[48] According to Sorrentino, one of these, Father Morlion, gave
Rossellini a copy of a volume entitled *Consigli agli sposi* (Advice for Newly-Weds) even
before the couple left for Stromboli.[49] Press reports from Stromboli suggested that a
priest on the island was prepared to marry the couple without delay once Bergman's
divorce in America was confirmed and that Italian clerics viewed her with benevolence.
Later the Vatican offered its encouragement to the Saint Francis project and real friars
acted in the film, some the same as those in *Paisà*. The fact that Rossellini was occupied
with the production of *Francis* at precisely the time of Senator Johnson's outburst meant
that the controversy never found a significant echo in Italy. In late February 1950, the
weekly magazine *La Settimana Incom* commented that 'the scandal of their liaison is an
American scandal. Here in Italy, because of our common sense, the matter has had the
importance it deserved and no more.'[50]

As a sex scandal, the Bergman–Rossellini affair may have meant little in Italy, but the
same cannot be said of the politico-cultural scandal. This particular genre become a
regular feature in postwar Italy, fuelled by its marked political divisions and entrenched
subcultures. From 1949 the left became increasingly sceptical about Rossellini. The real
scandal as far as the Communists and their allies were concerned was not the liaison
with Bergman but the risks for neo-realism that were implied by the director's links
with Hollywood and his shift away from social themes. Rossellini had never been part
of the inner circle of left-wing directors but he was respected and appreciated as the
founder of neo-realism, a movement which the left supported and defended against the
attacks of conservatives. Bergman's defection from Hollywood was not hailed as a triumph for the new school of film-making but rather fuelled controversy about
Rossellini's alleged defection from neo-realism. On Stromboli, there was ample evidence to confirm the left's worries. Asked by a journalist to express his agreement with
the statement that the United States was in a profound crisis, Rossellini replied: 'Americans are optimistic … Just imagine, there are no pedestrians, only glittering cars full of
flowers.' 'This valorous director … seems to me to be already very distant from his newborn neo-realism,' commented the author.[51] By his use of a Hollywood actress he
appeared to have sold out.

There was also much sympathy for Magnani. For many Italians, she was a symbol
of the spirit of the people at a time of adversity. Through her role as Pina in *Rome
Open City* and Sor Angelina, a combative heroine of the Roman working class in
L'onorevole Angelina (Luigi Zampa, 1947), she endeared herself to ordinary Italians
and became a focus of collective identification.[52] Although her abandonment by

Rosselliini was a purely private matter, it was also a sign that times were changing, that the reconstruction was over and that Italy was embarking on a new course of development which involved psychological changes, new values and more emphasis on individualism. Sympathy for Magnani was bound up with feelings of regret that the left-wing vision of the future, which had been defeated in the election of 1948, was receding rapidly.

The attitude of critics to *Stromboli* was generally negative. It was shown, together with *Francis God's Jester*, at the 1950 Venice Film Festival, but it did not get a release in Italy until March 1951. Rossellini was accused by critics, including Guido Aristarco, Ugo Casiraghi, Massimo Mida and Tommaso Chiaretti, of 'turning inward' to psychological portraits of individuals, abandoning the choral approach and concern with social issues that had distinguished neo-realism. The emphasis on the mystical in the finale of *Stromboli* was felt to be incomprehensible and in any event unlinked to any project of social improvement.[53] *Francis* was viewed more positively in Italy but negative judgements on the collaboration were not overturned. On its release, *Europe '51* was taken as further evidence of Rossellini's lack of interest in the sources of problems and conflicts. Once again an isolated, complex, foreign figure was seen as being used to explore the great problems of the European conscience in mid-century. The film was deemed contrived and anti-communist.[54] *Journey to Italy* and the other films were greeted with similar displeasure.

Rossellini and Bergman's Stardom

Rossellini, it is generally assumed, was hostile to stars and stardom. His dismissal of Hollywood as a 'sausage factory' and his vocal objections when Bergman referred to herself on Stromboli as a star would appear to confirm a vision of film-making that had little to do with entertainment and merchandising. He wanted to save Bergman from the artificiality of Hollywood and subordinate her talents as an actress to his own highly personal style of cinema. The director's anger at the media circus which sprang up around his personal and professional relationship with Bergman is well-documented. Faced with the crowd that blocked the couple's access to the Excelsior in March 1949, Bergman later wrote, 'Roberto immediately started fighting the photographers; that was his normal behaviour with photographers. There he was hitting out with his fist and trying to smash a way through to the door. He tore one photographer's jacket right off at the arm, and the next day he felt sorry about it and sent him a new jacket.'[55] Later when the photographers informed him that they would use any means possible to get a picture of Robertino, Rossellini again exploded.[56] Yet the director's behaviour merely fuelled the media attention. His expansive gestures and flamboyant lifestyle seemed almost designed to attract attention. Moreover, there were aspects of Rossellini's method which repeatedly blurred the distinction between his work and his personal life. Magnani served as an extraordinary vehicle for his vision from 1945 to 1948 as Bergman did in the following years. Magnani's poignant telephone monologue with a lover who is leaving her in 'Una voce umana' directly reflected the state of the fraught relations between her and Rossellini. In the Bergman films, it can be suggested that *Stromboli* sees her play a displaced person and *Europe '51* raises the issue of her guilt over leaving her child, while *Journey to Italy* depicts the deterioration of her second marriage. This reading, advanced by Robin Wood, is rejected as conjectural and reductive by Peter Brunette.[57] But it is not necessary to claim this as the only possible interpretative key of these films to see that an element of autobiographical transfer was at work. The fusion of fiction and documentary that characterises Rossellini's cinema in fact does not differ substantially in some of its effects from the slippage between screen character and star persona that marked many Hollywood films. Although not conceived in Rossellini's case as a marketing device, a way of establishing a knowing complicity with the audience, it introduced a dynamic that bore a resemblance to the detested celebrity culture.

Rossellini made use of Bergman's star status to obtain American backing for *Stromboli* and it may be argued that he incorporated elements of her celebrity into his films. Pierre Leprohon has argued that 'There is every reason to think that Ingrid Bergman made, as Rossellini's interpreter, a great contribution to his work, not only by her acting, but by her presence, by her *aura*.'[58] There is little doubt that Bergman's 'aura' was a significant factor in *Stromboli* and *Europe '51*, but it is interesting in this respect to consider the episode 'Ingrid Bergman' of the compilation film *Siamo donne*. As a film in episodes featuring three of Italy's best-known actresses (Alida Valli, Anna Magnani and Isa Miranda), as well as Bergman and two young hopefuls, it aimed to explore the contradictions and difficulties of the actress as a public figure. The episodes directed by Visconti, Zampa and others are scripted and conventionally executed, while purportedly being based on some 'true-life' incident in the subject's life. Rossellini's profile of Bergman is the most light-hearted and features a clash which arises between the actress and a neighbour whose hen persistently eats the roses in the former's garden. As a portrait of an actress it is inconsequential but, interestingly, it makes more use of the conflict between fact and fiction than other episodes. Bergman not only plays herself, but speaks directly to camera and also provides a voice-over. Although she is supported by a range of professional actors playing the neighbour and friends, the action takes place in the real summer home she shared with Rossellini and features their son Robertino and a pet dog. By foregrounding so prominently the 'real' Bergman, Rossellini acknowledged that he had failed to subordinate her persona to his cinema and admitted that she had a fame and recognition that were integral parts of her reality. Despite the inherent silliness of the story, Bergman is radiant and beautiful. On the lawn of her house she seems once more the Hollywood star 'bursting with health and vigor',[59] enjoying privileged leisure, upset only by elements of screwball comedy. Appropriately, the short episode coincided with the reestablishment of a more normal relationship with the press in Italy. Although Rossellini always fought shy of publicity, pictures of Bergman and young Robertino adorned several magazine covers in Italy in late 1952.

The director's failure was confirmed by the couple's next project, which involved a return to Joan of Arc, the Hollywood role with which Bergman was most closely identified. In the early 1950s, Rossellini directed several operas, mainly from financial necessity. His version of Verdi's *Otello* was well-received and led to a proposal that he should direct Bergman in the Paul Claudel–Arthur Honegger oratorio *Jeanne au bûcher* (Joan at the Stake), which had first been performed at Orleans in 1939. The production debuted successfully in Italy and a European tour was arranged which led to performances in Spain, Britain and Bergman's native Sweden. Subsequently a film version of the oratorio was made but this was a fiasco. Rossellini appears to have relished the chance to reinterpret the figure of Joan, but ultimately the whole project depended on the director assuming a subordinate role with respect to his wife's star persona. It was not Rossellini's direction that aroused public interest but rather the pre-existing identification of Bergman with the figure of Joan. For the film, Rossellini abandoned his usual working methods to accommodate the structure and dialogue of the oratorio.

The couple's final collaboration, *Fear/Angst*, was made in Germany in German and English versions. Even those who hold the other Rossellini-Bergman films in high regard have few good words for this film. Brunette describes it as 'a clear falling off from their earlier films' and witnesses have spoken of the director's lack of interest and enthusiasm for the project.[60] The conventional dramatic structure of the work left few opportunities for Rossellini to express his artistry.

Thus by 1954 Rossellini had exhausted all options for securing funding for his films and it would be three years before he would make another. The intense frustation and anger he felt when Bergman finally decided to break her exclusive professional relationship with him was an expression of this failure. Rossellini had not only failed to reinvent Bergman in his own style; he had ended up in thrall to her star quality. It did not take long for Bergman to return to her place in the Hollywood Olympus. She won much praise and an Oscar for her role in *Anastasia*, her first post-Rossellini film and a huge hit at the box office. Moreover, the sympathies she had alienated by abandoning her family in 1949 returned after Rossellini left her in 1957 for Sonali Senroy Das Gupta, whom he met when he was working on *India*. While the director was confirmed in the role of devil, and was subjected to harsher criticism than before in Italy, Bergman gradually returned to her former sainthood.[61]

Conclusion

The Bergman–Rossellini collaboration can be read in a number of ways. Rossellini had hoped through Bergman to reach a world audience. The actress, for her part, hoped to assist in making art. The collaboration was fortuitous and from the beginning highly personal. As a star of US cinema who unilaterally decided to go to Italy to work with the leading exponent of neo-realism, Bergman was unique. But from 1950 many other American actors arrived in Italy as the season of Hollywood on the Tiber began. The appearance of Hollywood-trained actors in Italian films ceased to be a rarity and became commonplace. Bergman was also a precursor in other ways. The extraordinary scandal that surrounded her first year in Italy was primarily a phenomenon of American society and the American press. But the scale of the echo events had and the deployment within Italy of so many foreign reporters, gossip columnists and photographers provoked a series of developments in the relations between the Italian press and society. Publishers and photographers could see the highly remunerative nature of scandal, the advantages of rousing established opinion to indignation and also the potential offered by stars for controversy and transgression. Italy was not a prurient or a puritanical country, but dramatic social and cultural changes in the 1950s put conservatives and religious spokesmen onto the defensive and made them readier to issue the condemnations so necessary to public outrage. Political disputes and controversies continued to remain more important in Italian public opinion than moral misdemeanors, but the latter began to assume an importance and a role. As Bergman and

Rossellini settled into family life, the photographers and hunters of scandal shifted their attention to others, creating the premises for the notorious clashes between photographers and foreign celebrities in Rome's Via Veneto that would be rendered world-famous by *La dolce vita*.

Notes

1   See Donald Spoto, *Notorious: The Life of Ingrid Bergman* (London: HarperCollins, 1998), pp. 295–6.

2   Bill Davidson, *The Real and the Unreal* (New York: Harper and Brothers, 1961).

3   Ingrid Bergman and Alan Burgess, *Ingrid Bergman: My Story* (New York: Dell, 1980), p. 226.

4   Ibid., pp. 13–14.

5   Ibid., p. 16.

6   The inclusion of the Italian phrase meaning 'I love you' was not wholly flirtatious. It was literally the only Italian phrase she knew and this was, she later wrote, 'because I played an Italian girl in Erich Maria Remarque's *Arch of Triumph*, who spoke only English until, on her deathbed, she whispered to Charles Boyer, "Ti amo"'. Ibid., p. 17.

7   Davidson, *The Real and the Unreal*, p. 161.

8   Joseph Henry Steele, *Ingrid Bergman: An Intimate Portrait* (New York: David McKay, 1959), p. 161.

9   Giancarlo Governi, *Nannarella* (Milan: Bompiani, 1984), p. 134.

10 Peter Brunette, *Roberto Rossellini* (New York: Oxford University Press, 1987), p. 112. See also Bergman and Burgess, *Ingrid Bergman*, p. 269.

11 Quoted in Franca Faldini and Goffredo Fofi (eds.), *L'avventurosa storia del cinema italiano raccontato dai suoi protagonisti, 1935–59* (Milan: Feltrinelli, 1979), p. 201.

12 Leonard J. Leff and Jerold L. Simmons, *The Dame in the Kimono: Hollywood, Censorship and the Production Code from the 1920s to the 1960s* (New York: Doubleday, 1990).

13 Ibid., pp. 157–8.

14 Steele, *Ingrid Bergman*, p. 142.

15 *La Settimana Incom*, 11 February 1950, cover picture and Alfredo Pieroni, 'Roberto Jr bimbo invisibile', pp. 6–7.

16 Quoted in Lawrence J. Quirk, *The Films of Ingrid Bergman* (New York: Citadel, 1970), p. 133.

17 Ibid., p. 140.

18 James Lull and Stephen Hinerman, 'The Search for Scandal' in Lull and Hinerman (eds.), *Media Scandals: Morality and Desire in the Popular Culture Marketplace* (Cambridge: Polity, 1997), p. 3.

19 Gloria Swanson, *Swanson on Swanson* (London: Hamlyn, 1982; first published 1981), p. 485.

20 Davidson, *The Real and the Unreal*, pp. 162–4.

21 Ibid., p. 21.

22 Spoto, *Notorious*, p. 299.

23 Ibid., p. 22.

24 James Damico, 'Ingrid from Lorraine to Stromboli: Analyzing the Public's Perception of a Film Star', *Journal of Popular Film*, vol. 4, no. 1, 1975, pp. 3–19 (p. 7).

25 Ibid., p. 13.

26 Ibid., pp. 13–14.

27 Ibid., pp. 16–17.

28 George Eells, *Hedda and Louella* (London: W.H.Allen, 1972), pp. 248–50. Spoto credits Hughes with the leak, referring to Parsons's 'lifelong symbiotic relationship' with the millionaire, *Notorious*, p. 285.

29 Leff and Simmons, *The Dame in the Kimono*, p. 157.

30 Lull and Hinerman, 'The Search for Scandal', p. 13.

31 Ibid., p. 9.

32 Allen L. Woll and Randall M. Miller, *Ethnic and Racial Images in American Film and Television* (New York: Garland, 1987), p. 276.

33 *Time*, 7 February 1949, quoted in Tag Gallagher, *The Adventures of Roberto Rossellini: His Life and Films* (New York: Da Capo, 1998), p. 312. Rossellini is also portrayed in an unflattering way in Laurence Leamer, *As Time Goes By: The Life of Ingrid Bergman* (New York: Harper and Row, 1986).

34 Governi, *Nannarella*, p. 148; Patrizia Carrano, *La Magnani* (Milan: Rizzoli, 1986), pp. 174–5. At the time Magnani was filming *Bellissima*, directed by Visconti.

35 Spoto, *Notorious*, pp. 292–3.

36 Ibid., p. 289.

37 John Tomlinson, ' "And Besides, the Wench is Dead": Media Scandals and the Globalisation of Communication', in Lull and Hinerman, *Media Scandals*, p. 65.

38 Sergio Amidei, quoted in Brunette, *Roberto Rossellini*, p. 110.

39 Bergman and Burgess, *Ingrid Bergman*, p. 253.

40 Ibid., pp. 262–3.

41 Lamberti Sorrentino, 'Nascono a Stromboli un film e un idillio', *Tempo*, 16 April 1949, pp. 4–7.

42 The Power-Christian wedding took place in February 1949. The public impact of this event is analysed in Stephen Gundle, 'Popular Culture' in Patrick McCarthy (ed.), *Italy Since 1945* (Oxford: Oxford University Press, 2000).

43 Lamberti Sorrentino, 'La prova del vulcano per Ingrid e Rossellini', *Tempo*, 23 April 1949, pp. 9–12 (p. 12).

44 'Tormentato amore allo Stromboli', *Tempo*, 30 April 1949, pp. 16–19.

45 Ibid., p. 269.

46 Faldini and Fofi, *L'avventurosa storia*, p. 202.

47 Gallagher, *Adventures*, p. 368.

48 Spoto, *Notorious*, pp. 284, 293–4.

49 Sorrentino, 'Nascono a Stromboli', p. 7.

50 *La Settimana Incom*, 25 February 1950, p. 24.

51 Mario Schettini, 'L'inventore del vulcano', *Vie Nuove*, 15 May 1949, p. 19.

52 See Stephen Gundle, 'Fame, Fashion and Style: The Italian Star System' in David Forgacs and Robert Lumley (eds.), *Italian Cultural Studies: An Introduction* (Oxford: Oxford University Press, 1996), pp. 316–7.

53 For a summary of the various positions, see Gallagher, *Adventures*, pp. 358–9.

54 Ibid., pp. 386–8.

55 Bergman and Burgess, *Ingrid Bergman*, p. 253.

56 Quoted in Pieroni, 'Roberto Jr. bimbo invisibile', *La Settimana Incom*, 11 February 1950, pp. 6–7.

57 See Brunette, *Roberto Rossellini*, pp. 155–6.

58 Pierre Leprohon, *The Italian Cinema* (New York: Praeger, 1972), pp. 132–3 (my emphasis),quoted and discussed in Brunette, *Roberto Rossellini*, p. 155.

59 Davidson, *The Real and the Unreal*, p. 153.

60 Brunette, *Roberto Rossellini*, pp. 183–4.

61 See Davidson, *The Real and the Unreal*, pp. 143–4.

6
Francis God's Jester

Alan Millen

Francesco giullare di Dio (*Francis God's Jester*) was first shown at the Venice Film Festival on the evening of 26 August 1950.[1] That afternoon, an audience had seen the full Italian version of *Stromboli* for the first time. The film on St Francis had been shot during the brief period from January to May the same year, but Rossellini had thought about the project at least since 1948; *Stromboli*, on the other hand, which had been filmed from April to August 1949, had been planned and executed during a comparatively short period. When the two films were shown for the first time in the Italian versions in Venice they became part of the publicity that had grown up around the anecdotes about Rossellini's life and the scandalous disclosures about his relationship with Ingrid Bergman. Unlike *Stromboli*, the film about St Francis had been produced by a European company and, unusually for Rossellini, the scenario was based upon Italian texts. It had had a relatively long period of preparation before its producer, Giuseppe Amato, found financial backing from the Italian publishing company Rizzoli, which distributed it through its film subsidiary, Cineriz.

During interviews throughout his life, Rossellini declared that the film remained one of his three favourites – the other two were *Paisà* and *Europe '51*. Given this, and its long gestation, it seems improbable that the film was merely part of an opportunistic design to placate the ecclesiastical authorities during 1950 (declared a Holy Year by Pius XII) after the Bergman scandal. Later, in June 1954, during an interview recorded in the journal of Catholic Action, *La Rivista del Cinematografo*, Rossellini referred back to that 'particular period of his life' as 'full of bitterness and disappointment', and he said that the making of a film about St Francis had offered a 'clear and precise model to sustain him'. He confessed that in the making of the film 'he experienced a joy that was so great that he felt the urgent need for others to share it'. With this intuitive and urgent need to communicate with his public, he was surprised and disappointed with the response and could 'scarcely believe that the public had not understood and had not participated intensely in the deep joy that he thought he had expressed in *Francis God's Jester*'.[2]

Rossellini's memory of the reception of his films was not always reliable, but in this case he was right. In Venice, the response seems to have been one of bewilderment, even among those critics who liked the film. It was a box-office failure. Since then, the critical debate about the film has not been especially rewarding. Even in Italy, where the cult of St Francis has accumulated a series of long-standing controversies about religion, politics and national identity, the critical writings about the film, although more numerous than elsewhere, seem threadbare and increasingly entrenched.[3] Throughout Europe, in the years following its release, the film failed to conform to the expectations built up on the basis of Rossellini's past work, especially as part of the debate about neo-realism. Moreover, the other films of Rossellini's second period – *Stromboli, Europe '51,* and *Journey to Italy* – seem to have broken more clearly into the area where contemporary cultural battles were being fought, even if the director was judged to be wilfully determined to remain outside the mainstream of American and European cinema and, as such, gained the reputation of a visionary artist with a radical film style. André Bazin admired *Francis*, but it was *Journey to Italy* that he harnessed to his argument against Aristarco's appropriation of film realism to a partisan view of social realism.[4] Rivette and Rohmer likewise appealed to *Journey to Italy*, and to *Stromboli*, as a focus in their defence of Rossellini's single-minded commitment to an unconventional film practice.[5] The French Catholic critics admired the film but their writings showed a greater interest in other films by Rossellini.

Perhaps the difficulties that have beset any critical approach to *Francis God's Jester* are a direct result of Rossellini's own statements about the film as integral to his own autobiographical experiences and his acknowledgement that the project was an expression of his own vulnerable idealism. In a brief interview of 1950, published as 'The Message of Francis', he traces an itinerary in which *Germany Year Zero* 'is the world that has reached the limits of despair because of its loss of faith whereas *Stromboli* is the rediscovery of faith. After which, it was natural to look for the most accomplished form of the Christian ideal: I found it in Saint Francis.'[6]

If we take these statements seriously, we may assume that they express Rossellini's own sentiments during the period of 'bitterness and disappointment' in his own life. But if we accept that the purpose of the film is to communicate the joy that Rossellini experienced in making it, then the figure of St Francis must have global or universal value or, to use the language of Catholic phenomenological critics, the film must convey the 'essence' of St Francis. Rossellini speaks about the other protagonists of the film: 'Brother Juniper and Brother John display in an almost paradoxical way the sense of simplicity, innocence and joy that emanates from Francis's own spirit'. The emotional and ethical themes of the film are clear: simplicity, innocence and joy. But it is necessary to distinguish between the emotional values, which are somehow represented in a film, and the emotional response felt by the spectator. And, as we have seen, Rossellini was surprised and disappointed in the lack of communication, the lack of a common response between himself and his audience of the film. The distinction between the representation of certain themes or values and audience response incurs the debate about the relative values of realism in a film. And Rossellini remained consistent, even obstinate, in his absolute faith that realism was a primary tool of communication for the understanding of certain truths through the response of the spectators to his films. A particular tension between Rossellini's implied idealism and the formal strategies resulting from his aesthetic of realism is one of the dominant characteristics of this film.

A more obvious empirical objection can be raised against taking too seriously Rossellini's account of his films. *Francis God's Jester* cannot be judged exclusively as the product of Rossellini's own standard of values, even less of his own sense of crisis in his personal and professional life. In Italy, the debate about this issue was concentrated less upon the production team or the distributors, and more upon the interventions made in the working out of the scenario of the film and its *mise-en-scène*. The Marxist Pio Baldelli, who disliked the film, objected that it betrayed the person and message of the

historic Francis, insofar as it had a relevance to contemporary Italy, and also was unfaith-
ful to the medieval texts which formed a basis for the scenario. In a long controversy
with the Catholic Brunello Rondi, who worked on the film, Baldelli suggests that
Rossellini was 'in thrall to the suggestions of his scenarists'.[7] I suppose that Baldelli
implies a malevolent intervention on the part of the Catholic advisors who are credited
as having participated in the elaboration of the film, Father Antonio Lisandrini O.F.M.
(i.e. a Franciscan), and Father Félix Morlion O.P. (a Dominican). Bruno Rondi insisted
that the treatment was elaborated by Fellini, Rossellini and himself, and later worked
upon by himself, Rossellini and Father Antonio Maisano O.F.M. at the time of the shooting. The early treatment of the subject by Rossellini and Fellini was published
subsequently in 1958 and differs in many details from the existing versions of the film.[8]
The controversy about who was responsible for the scenario is rather stultifying, but the
relationship between the medieval texts and the film, and the historical role of St Francis and his companions within the film, is more complex and more interesting.

The scenario of the film is based upon certain episodes in the life of St Francis and of
his earliest followers, among them Brother Juniper. Many but not all the episodes are
based upon two anonymous fourteenth-century Italian texts, *The Little Flowers of St
Francis* (*I fioretti di San Francesco*) and *Life of Brother Juniper* (*La vita di frate Ginepro*).[9]
Rossellini chose *The Little Flowers* as a model because he 'still found, intact, the perfume
of the most primitive Franciscanism'.[10] Other, possibly earlier, texts might have been
chosen; for example the thirteenth-century lives written by Tomaso da Celano and Saint
Bonaventure. *The Little Flowers* is a highly controversial text whereby the anonymous
author gives clear support to the cause of the strict Franciscan Observants (or Spirituals)
for whom the life of their founder is not only exemplary for the virtues of poverty and
simplicity but also promotes the practice of preaching through example, a practice
ignored by most of the author's opponents among contemporary friars. *The Little
Flowers* is a polemical attack upon the supremacy within the Church of the Conventual
Friars (those who settled in convents). The place of *The Little Flowers* within a long and
bitter conflict between the medieval Franciscans may have a limited interest for modern audiences of the film. Rossellini either chose to ignore or, more likely, was ignorant
of this contest (but Father Lisandrini must have known about it). For an exploration of
the effects that religious schism has upon the unity of religious belief and institutions,
we must wait for Rossellini's treatment of St Augustine's conflict with the Donatists in
the television film *Augustine* (*Agostino d'Ippona*) (1972). In the field of politics,
Rossellini's conviction for the need for a common ground, for unity, is celebrated
through his heroic portrayal of Alcide De Gasperi in *Anno uno* (1974). But it is evident
that the contest between Franciscan Spirituals and Conventuals does not play a part in
the film. However, I would argue that the controversies around the status of the text of
The Little Flowers do have consequences for the formal strategy of the scenario and the
mise-en-scène of the film.

The Little Flowers of St Francis is not a biography of the saint but a series of episodes
that serve as 'exempla'. Not only is St Francis an example of human excellence, an exemplary figure (whose actions are in turn based upon the example of Christ), but the text
has at its disposal examples of this excellence for the orator, polemicist, or, given the
specific nature of the Franciscan vocation, for preaching. To state the medieval formula,
the word 'exemplum' applies both to the act and to the account of it. An instance of this

use of the exemplum is the celebrated episode when St Francis preaches to the birds. In the text, the sermon resolves the dilemma of whether St Francis should be 'wholly intent on prayer, or should sometimes preach'. Francis's preaching not only resolves this dilemma, but also offers to us a model sermon, through an elaborate analogy between the praise of the birds for their Creator and the need for humanity to praise God. In the third episode of the film, Francis preaches to his companions ('He who knows not the Bible will learn from your deeds') facing them, while they have their backs to the camera and to the viewer. Francis then praises God by a complete recitation of two prayers: one known as the Prayer of St Francis and the Lord's Prayer. This sequence is based on a pattern of alternating shots between St Francis in prayer and praise and the birds moving and singing among the branches. The juxtaposition of these two sets of shots, the use of editing, within the sequence is continuous because the integrity of space and the duration of time (the time that Francis needs for the recitation of his prayers) is maintained. This is not like Eisenstein's 'intellectual' or discontinuous montage.[11] I do not think that the frame insertions of the birds are to be interpreted as a series of shots from Francis's point of view, which in classical American editing would offer a greater degree of subjectivity. Instead, the editing provides a visual analogy between the birds and the saint engaged in a common prayer of praise to the Creator, or perhaps the saint's praise of the Creator through His creatures, in accordance with the canto composed by Francis and sung at the beginning of the film. The approach to the text of *The Little Flowers* is not of simple adaptation but, at least in this sequence, an attempt to find some kind of equivalence between the text and the film. For a film that purports to communicate directly the ideals of the director, the response of the spectator is curiously distanced. The use of persuasive argument in the film is complex, and its formal pattern uses a series of rhetorical devices (especially what scholars of rhetoric call the enthymeme) which I shall explore further here.

Each of the episodes in *The Little Flowers* has a rubric which summarises the exemplary act of the saint and the message to be learned from the act; for example 'How he established the third order and preached to the birds and made the swallows keep their peace'. The film adopts a similar device by means of intertitles for each of the episodes, except the first, where a framing voice serves a similar function. In the film we are thereby presented with a 'how' before we see the narrative unfold. The use of intertitles is a convention made necessary by and usually associated with silent cinema. In this film, which for the most part is extremely verbose, the intertitles may either be considered redundant (they are apparently omitted from the version in the United States), or, as I would suggest, as serving further to distance the events and to support the didactic structure of the film. The use of the intertitles certainly offers a particular tension between the expectations of the spectator and the subsequent unfolding of the speech and actions within the narrative structure of the ensuing episode. The use of the 'how' in the intertitles suggests that whatever solution is shown in the actions of the narrative that follows, its greater importance is not be found in the result achieved, but in the way of achieving it.

I have suggested that the ingenuous statements about the film voiced by Rossellini in the course of interviews may have hindered rather than helped the critical response to it. Rossellini has spoken of the innocence and simplicity and humility of Francis and his companions and his desire to communicate the joy which he felt in the filming of their words and deeds. But surely it would be a mistake to suppose, as many critics seem to have done, that faith in simplicity can be made transparent by means of the film. A notorious but not unique instance of this disingenuous argument is to be found in the 1958 article by Marcel Oms, who argues that because the protagonist and his companions are simple-minded, the film itself is a 'monument to stupidity'; 'never before have Christianity and cretinism been so close to one another'.[12] Yet even if the film shows us a hero lacking in good sense and wisdom, we cannot assume that those qualities are neutrally transferred to the film itself (in fact the criticism, or abuse, settles upon what is not shown in the *mise-en-scène* and engages the fantasies of the critic: a carnal relationship between Francis and Clare). Oms's article is an extreme instance of the tendency to mistake the theme of simple and innocent joy associated with the protagonists for the formal strategies of the film. The faith in simplicity (which need not be the same as simple faith) is represented in an ambivalent way in the film, precisely because it is without equivocation. The homogeneity between the alleged foolishness and simplicity of Francis and his companions and the narrative strategies of the film cannot be taken for granted. These difficulties for the spectator have been described very well by Henri Agel: 'Most people who see the film once, or who are distracted by other spectators, come out complaining about the poverty of its style, its lack of rigour or unity, its occasional infantilism, and see nothing but buffoonery devoid of grandeur. But many who agree to see it a second time change their minds.'[13] A film which requires a second viewing for a proper reaction from the audience might be described as a failure. Alternatively, such a film may especially be seen to require further analysis on the part of the critics, even if they face the risk, if not of pedantry, then at least of an excess of piety towards the film and its subject.

Francis God's Jester (1950): the prologue.

For a historical film set in the Middle Ages, *Francis God's Jester* has a visually sparse and bare *mise-en-scène*. Usually, a historical film requires elaborate costumes and settings as a grounding for our suspended belief that the events have taken place during a specific period in the past. Yet most of this film was shot in a bare hillside landscape with few natural features, around the hovel which we see the friars construct in the second episode and whose form is so simple in design that it could be found in any region of Italy during any period in history. The repetition of middle-distance shots of the hovel which begin or end certain episodes, most notably as a setting for the assembly of Clare, Francis and their companions as if in a school photograph at the end of the fourth episode, is so apparent that it may be described as a formal motif of the film. Around and beyond this hovel the friars are often in movement, shot in deep focus and in long takes (again, the meeting between the Franciscans and St Clare is exceptional in the consistency with which this basic pattern of filming is used). This film style may suggest the interdependence of the community of friars for whom the location of the hovel serves as emotional focus, a communal interdependence which Rossellini has described with reference to his films as a choral quality, *coralità*. In the last episode, the taking leave of the hovel and its landscape setting by Francis and his companions is an important ritual that prepares us for their final departure and dispersal. Any deviation from this basic principle of shooting and any departure from this location, as we have seen with Francis preaching with the birds, serves a distinct function within the film. But this strategy does not primarily serve the purposes of historical veracity, the precise representation of what might have been true in a past epoch. And it is not necessary to identify this sparseness of setting and frequently stylised system of shooting with the lack of synthetic perspective found in medieval painting, as suggested by Peter Brunette.[14] Rather, for the most part, the friars seem distanced as well as isolated from both the medieval and the modern world.

The parts of St Francis and his companions are played in the film not only by non-professional actors but by contemporary Franciscans who are directed by Rossellini to act out the deeds of the founder of the order to which they belong. It is interesting to compare this specific use of non-professional actors with Rossellini's direction of the real partisans who are required to re-enact the rescue of the corpse of one of their comrades that floats down the river in the last episode of *Paisà*. The corpse bears a placard presumably placed by the Germans: *Partigiano* ('Partisan'). The partisans rescue the body which has been driven by the current of the water of the Po delta, and demonstrate how this was achieved by lighting explosives and using gunfire to distract the attention of the German guards. The body is retrieved and buried in a simple ritual; the placard bearing the name 'Partigiano', used in recrimination as a warning that other partisans will be killed, is placed on the grave by his comrades as a tribute to their victim. The rescue of the body has no pragmatic value. It is a collective act of piety for their comrade. The episode is especially poignant because the partisans are recapitulating the parts they played in the Resistance at a time before their roles in the film, and at a time when, as the dialogue puts it, they were 'fighting for their lives'. The formal strategy used in this sequence invites the spectator to follow the means, the procedure, whereby the body is rescued and buried. The value of its consequences is left to the response of the spectator. The pious motives behind Rossellini's employment of real partisans playing their previous roles in the war serve in part to give the film a guarantee of authenticity within the conventions of documentary realism. But their performance is also to show how things were done during a period of intense personal danger, and therefore the tacit contract with the director is aleatory and, as with their survival during the war, dependent upon uncertain contingencies. Of course, the acting out by the friars of the words and deeds of their founder is not overshadowed with the memory, or suspense, based upon the real threat of danger. The effect upon the audience nevertheless carries an element of risk, delicately poised between immanence and mental projection, between the trivia of the everyday events of their lives and the historical culture of Franciscan texts and biography, between religious faith and comedy. The suggestion made by Pio Baldelli in his various writings on *Francis* that the film takes an ambivalent position towards the conventions of the genre of historical films is pertinent. Not only is the setting sparse and devoid of historical features. The tunics, the religious habits of the real Franciscans in 1950, are based upon the costumes worn by the poor in the thirteenth century and adopted by St Francis and the early friars; they are a little more ragged than the modern Franciscan costume, perhaps, but basically the same. The modern friars also wear the tonsure worn by St Francis which materially designates Christ's crown of thorns. In 1952, Rossellini described the costumes of *Francis God's Jester* as serving the effect of realism of the film. 'The costumes . . . are part of the "reality". They are so true to life that you scarcely notice them.'[15] And again, Rossellini claims that the costumes are 'simple and timeless, in other words, costumes which don't look like costumes'.

The question that arises is whether the world of St Francis and his companions is represented in the film as effectively timeless. Rossellini's own statements are curiously ambivalent. In 1950 he said 'Historically speaking, the series of events narrated in the film rests between two fundamental moments: Francis's return from Rome after having received the permission to preach from the Pope, and the beginning of his preaching.'[16] From this account, the events of the film take place during a kind of lacuna, of suspended anticipation leading to the final dispersal of the friars to fulfil that vocation to preach defined at the beginning of the film. There is however a great deal of preaching within the film, which begins with a profusion of texts and voices, the meaning of which cannot be adequately grasped at a first viewing. The superabundant 'voices' are as follows:

1 While the title and the credits appear on the screen, a voice recites the 'Song of Praise for God's Creatures' ('Cantico delle creature'), which was composed by St Francis, against a background of music. (The song includes the lines: 'Be Thou praised my Lord through those who pardon for Thy love, and endure sickness and tribulations.')

2 The voice continues the recitation while a passage from St Paul's 'Epistle to the Corinthians' appears on the screen: 'God has chosen the foolish of the world to confound the wise, and the weak of the world to confound the mighty.'

3 A voice, in the manner usually used in documentary films, continues, 'And Francis became humble to confound the world . . . Pope Innocent III let him preach to the people his faith in humility and poverty.' Then the voice performs the function of telling us what will happen in this episode: the friars will journey to their hut and, after being turned away, they will find refuge at Santa Maria degli Angeli.

The friars appear from the distance in a long shot, struggling against the wind and rain. The camera remains static for the duration of their progress down the lane and towards the spectator. The dialogue begins with one of the friars saying: 'Were I to preach to the public, I would begin in this way . . .', whereupon the friars recite a pious homily, which defines the qualities of peace, joy, glory, divine love, and so on.

The film begins with a plethora of religious citations and pious oratory. Adriano Aprà has described Rossellini's polemical opposition between an 'oral culture' and a 'written culture' and the value of this opposition for a critical approach to the historical films made for television. In these films

> there is an 'oral' culture of a voice that was once written words, and that, in passing
> from writing to speech, has lost its immediacy, its dangerous emotionality. It's a
> 'dubbed' voice; other people's voices are imposed in a monotonous manner onto bodies
> that talk; and the characters 'quote' words that pre-exist in written form, in the source
> texts, and in the 'scenarios' in which Rossellini has transcribed them.[17]

Are we to suppose that the opening sequence of *Francis God's Jester* anticipates a general problem felt by Rossellini's commitment to an 'oral culture' within his project to make films set in a historical past? (A specimen of a 'voice that was once written words' and has passed 'from writing to speech' is that of the actor who plays Father Noel in *Blaise Pascal*, 1972, which cites a large part of an existing historical text which attempted to prove the impossibility of the existence of a vacuum.) I would suggest that there is a similar distancing of the sermon from the friars who 'preach' it, even though the actors who play their parts are presumably experts in the practice. The speech, rather than giving a historical authenticity to the film (as may be the effect of Father Noel's discourse), places the action of the film in a distant but not clearly determined past; a voice which has not lost its immediacy, nor what Aprà calls 'its dangerous emotionality'. The possibilities that arise from the dialogue which uses the proposition 'if' or 'were I' ('If I were to preach . . .') as an expression of desire, is found frequently in this film, as in other films by Rossellini. We may take an example from the Naples episode of *Paisà*. Seated upon a pile of rubble, the drunken American soldier dreams about his return home, while next to him squats a Neapolitan urchin who cannot understand his language and whose wish is to seize for himself the soldier's boots. The urchin gives a warning, which is also an expression of his desire: 'If you fall asleep, I'll steal your boots'. The next sequence begins with the soldier searching for the boy who has stolen his boots, and therefore we retrospectively infer that he had fallen asleep. This is, of course, another example of Rossellini's celebrated use of ellipsis in narrative, and also his concern for the consequences of any failure of communication between those caught up in the war, which is a constant feature of *Paisà*. But it also suggests that the boy's desires are mixed, and fall between friendship (he warns the soldier) and his own need for the boots, but the outcome is open to contingencies beyond his control. In a similar way, the characters that these modern friars are called upon to play, and the speeches they are required to deliver, create an aleatory effect, which is endorsed by the paradoxes (synecdoche) of the texts (for instance the humble will confound the world), which require not further explanation but an acting out in order to test their validity. In the first episode (based on an episode from *The Little Flowers*) there follows an ambivalent testimony to the obligation of 'holy' obedience that the friars owe to St Francis. Francis commands one of his companions to make an exemplary gesture of standing on his supine body and to pronounce a verbal formula which denounces his pride in inflicting pain upon his brothers. Again there is a paradox: Francis must appeal to a concept of obedience in order to command the humiliation of his pride. Whereas the paradox is resolved in the text *The Little Flowers* by our conviction that Francis is a saint, and that every act is exemplary, in the film the gesture of humiliation is either inadequate (it cannot resolve the paradox) or excessive (and hence foolish or comic).

The exposition at the beginning of the film does not set up a goal which will be unfolded in the narrative or plot that follows. It does not work to give a sense of authenticity to a specific period in history. The superabundant words and voices, the gestures, the austere setting, serve to distance the film into a series of visual and verbal compositions that may be described, with Rossellini, as 'primitive' (or primordial) 'Franciscanism'. All the characteristics, or 'thematics', of Francis's ideals (shared, it seems, by Rossellini at this time of crisis in his life) are included in the first episode of the film, but presented through controlled formal compositions, or, as Rossellini said about this episode, through imagination or fantasy (the power of the imagination or fantasy always played a part in Rossellini's broad project of realism). Having drawn the parameters of what he has called simple 'Franciscanism', a universal ideal, he can now take the risk along with the audience of exploring the consequences of this ideal through the action of the film, before the dispersal of the friars to preach to the world; for example, in the episode when Brother Juniper confronts the tyrant Nicolao (in which 'the humble confound the world') with a realisation that 'souls are saved through example, not words'.

Not all the episodes, I suggest, successfully work out the implications of an open interrogation of these universal (or 'essential') values intimately associated with the Franciscan ideal. In the episode in which Brother Leo and Francis submit to the trial of 'perfect joy',[18] the dialogue is little more than a quotation of the definition of joy in Chapter 8 of the *The Little Flowers* and the gestures remain wooden. The episode simply duplicates the opening episode of the film. On the other hand, the visit of Clare to Francis and his companions explores to the full, I suggest, the potentially heterogeneous elements that emerge from a scrutiny of the Franciscan ideal. This episode combines an episode from *The Little Flowers* (Chapter 15) with one from *The Life of Juniper* (Chapter 4). The sequence combines a masterful use of the movement of groups in long shot and long takes outside, against the landscape, with static medium-close shots within the chapel of Santa Maria degli Angeli. The episode begins with the mutual cooperation of the friars in their trivial activities of gathering blossoms, and shaving each other, in a rapt anticipation of Sister Clare's arrival, which at this stage may seem excessive in enthusiasm, and faintly comic. But Clare's arrival at Santa Maria degli Angeli prompts her reminiscences about the time when she professed her vows (including, one presumes, that of chastity) in this place. This recounted memory introduces a subjective element into the narration (which would create a quite different effect if a flashback had been introduced according to the requirements of classical Hollywood editing). There follows a commotion outside the church brought about by Brother Juniper returning without his tunic, given to him by Clare, which provokes the conjecture that he has disobeyed Francis's command that he should not give away his cloak to the poor. But the foolish Juniper, always logical, despite (or because of) his lack of common sense, has been able to reconcile his obedience to Francis with his desire to provide for the poor by the argument (again based upon an 'if') that if a poor man takes his tunic, he would not prevent it. Brother John complains when his cloak is given to Juniper, but one of the friars replies with a quotation from the gospel: 'he was naked and we clothed him'. Seated together outside the church, Juniper recounts to his fellow Franciscans and Clare how he prepares his heart against the entrance of the devil, by occupying it with holy meditations. As far as I know, it has escaped the attention of commentators of the film that Juniper's account of his Resistance to the devil has a textual source in *The Life of Juniper* (Chapter 7), with a rubric concerning the need to 'resist the temptations to carnal sin', and Juniper's strategy to defeat the devil forms a response to this specific temptation. Juniper's account of his victory over the devil is accompanied by a friar who, with two sticks, makes the gesture of playing a viola. Again, it seems to have escaped attention that this gesture imitates the music-making angel who, according to the text *Consideration of the Stigmata*, accompanied St Francis with the music of a viola during his rapturous participation in God's love.[19] But even an audience ignorant of these sources might recognise that the episode concludes with a rapt contemplation of God's love, or at least the desire for such, on the part of the mutually dependent friars and nuns. The conclusion of the episode is provided by a framing voice, which summarises a miracle from the text of *The Little Flowers*: 'And the people of Assisi saw the flame-red horizon. They thought Santa Maria degli Angeli was burning. The sky was alight with the flowing love of God by Clare and Francis.'

A single episode in the film can therefore investigate heterogeneous concerns, intimated in the 'voices' of the opening episode, in the form of a concentrated attention upon a kind of experiment, in this case the primitive society of friars. Their interdependence, their 'holy' obedience to the commands of the leader, Francis, the instinctive need for charity towards the poor, their shared love for Clare and her sisters and, despite the temptations of the devil, their desire to share in God's love are explored around this nucleus of attention. With such differing levels of discourse, it is not surprising that, within Rossellini's general programme of realism, the narrative shows many instances of ellipsis, especially around the different but complementary characters of Francis and Juniper. There emerges also the difficult and complex issue of whether the society of friars as represented in the film can be pushed in the direction of sociological or political realities. I will consider this issue at the end of this chapter. More obviously, how does Rossellini explore the possible religious issues in a film about a saint and his followers, especially through the complementary figures of Francis and Juniper?

In interviews, Rossellini's statements about his religious faith seem to me to be consistently evasive. And it is the nature of faith that it cannot be confirmed or denied by others. In his films, misfortunes and tribulations seem to come upon the victim unannounced and unexpected and undeserved, which often gives an emotional effect of overriding fear, notably *Rome Open City*. In *Francis God's Jester* this general fear of suffering or tribulation is resolved through the 'perfect joy' of the Franciscans, which, as we have seen, Rossellini wished to communicate to his audience. The fear of Juniper at the meeting with the tyrant, and his suffering in the hands of the camp followers is resolved by his pious saintly indifference to the tribulations that are inflicted upon him. If we use a religious language, we might say that what concerns him is a participation in the state of grace. From the evidence of the end sequences of both *Stromboli* and *Journey to Italy*, grace may be visited upon those characters who neither expect nor merit its intervention (this gratuitous and unmerited grace is called by theologians 'prevenient grace').

Saint Francis and the leper.

In *The Little Flowers*, the words and deeds of St Francis are exemplary because they imitate those of Christ. The most celebrated signs of this identification between St Francis and Christ are the stigmata: the signs of Christ's crucifixion materially imprinted upon the body of the saint. In the film, this central issue of grace through an identification with Christ's suffering is explored in the episode where Francis meets and embraces the leper.[20] The episode begins with the repeated motif of a middle-distance shot of the hovel, which is followed by a close shot of Francis's face while he utters the words, 'My God, my God ... Christ crucified.' In this atmosphere of suspended desire and expectation, we hear the sound of a bell which denotes the progress of a leper, and which should warn anyone from approaching. There is the song of a nightingale which, although not seen, causes both the leper and Francis who is following him to stop and listen. The spectator of the film is engaged with the 'look' or 'watching' of Francis through these movements and sounds, but without any appeal to Francis's individual subjectivity (there are no close shots and reverse shots which would establish subjective 'points of view' for Francis and the leper, although the whole sequence observes the 180-degree rule required by the conventions of Hollywood editing). Francis covers his face with his hands to contemplate within or to prevent him from seeing again the disfigured body of the leper. (We might be reminded of Karin's similar gesture when she is overwhelmed by the sight of the slaughter of the tuna in *Stromboli*, or Katherine's turning away from looking at the trace of the preserved lovers in Pompeii in *Journey to Italy*). With Francis, the horror of recognition does not defeat him; he withstands it and by his subsequent gesture of love, it is overcome. Francis makes a gesture of exorcism, and then approaches the leper and embraces him. The leper proceeds on his way accompanied by the sound of his bell, and then stops to look back at Francis and the viewer. Francis falls to the ground, and utters a prayer of thanks: 'God, God ...'. The camera moves upwards towards a night sky devoid of clouds. The screen is empty except for a featureless sky which cannot be distinguished from the substance of a blank exposed film. Whether any change has taken place and whether Francis's prayer or desire has been fulfilled will depend upon the opinions of the viewer. The visitation of grace cannot, by its very nature, be available for visual representation, especially in a film by Rossellini who, we can infer, seems to believe that it comes with risk, and is hazardous, and unmerited. However much the workings of grace may seem to be random, there is an extraordinary control over the formal composition of the sequence. Except for Francis's prayers, no words are spoken. There is no musical accompaniment. We hear only the diegetic sounds of the song of the nightingale and of the leper's bell. The movements, the pursuit, the enactment of a kind of 'hide and seek', the gestures of embrace, the prayers, evoke, I suggest, a general emotional response of suspended anticipation (of immanence) which is one of the defining features of this film.

The episode which is complementary to Francis's meeting with the leper is Juniper's confrontation with the tyrant Nicolao, in which the ideal whereby the humble will confound the mighty, intimated in the beginning of the film, is explored. Although Francis does not appear in this sequence, it is his response to Juniper's need to preach to the people which provokes the kind of apologetics that sanction Juniper's adventure. Francis commands Juniper to preach a seemingly meaningless sermon, 'Mbo Mbo Mbo, molto dico, poco fo' ('Bo Bo Bo, I say a lot and do little'), which seems to undermine the very purpose of preaching. As it turns out, his attempt to preach is frustrated by the resounding noise of the waterfall. But the episode begins with the longest tracking shot in the film, where the camera follows the little friar as he hastens down the paths, in eager anticipation of his task. The use of *temps mort* is characteristic of Rossellini's interest in the importance of the physiognomy of his non-professional actors for the action of his films. This frail and ungainly person walks into the locations of the waterfall, and the site of a military siege where he will suffer excessive physical torment, and walks out again, totally imperturbed. This impassivity and relative indifference to the effects that he has on others reminds us of the typical antics of the 'little man' in early Hollywood silent comedy. The physical torments to which his body is submitted are likewise represented with a form of aggression similar to that found in silent comedy. The confrontation between the little friar and the tyrant, Nicolao, whose body is entirely restrained by the elaborate armour, is entirely wordless. The tyrant is played by Aldo Fabrizi, who had a long experience in vaudeville as well as playing Don Pietro in *Rome Open City*. His silent grimaces and gestures, moving from threats which arouse no fear from Juniper, to interrogation and remorse, display a virtuoso performance from an experienced actor. Juniper's resilience has the impassivity of a non-professional actor who is not required to perform. This sequence is both comic and moving, partly as a result of the effects created by Rossellini's constant concern with the ontological problems that emerge from the use of non-professional or professional actors in his films. To put it in moral terms, Juniper possesses that kind of emotional accessibility which Rossellini seems to admire in his foolish heroes. Juniper has learned his lesson, which, he says, resides in the truth that 'souls are saved by example not by words'. This lesson was anticipated by Francis, in the formula given by him to Juniper. When Juniper confesses that he is a great sinner in the presence of Nicolao, the articulate Benedictine asks (with another 'if'): 'If this is Juniper, what must Francis be like?' Thereby the exemplary presence of Francis is felt in the episode, indeed throughout the film, even when he does not appear. I do not think that Juniper is set against Francis, as some critics have suggested.

The theme of the film seems to be the brotherhood of the friars but its formal strategies work to distance their words and actions from the spectator. The heterogeneity of the issues that make up the Franciscan ideal are explored through the episodes of the film and also anticipate the final dispersal of the friars: at the very end Francis gives a single command that the friars are required to 'preach peace throughout the world'. Are we to take this instruction as a pious sentiment, or a statement of a political and social commitment?

As Geoffrey Nowell-Smith argues in his chapter in this volume (Chapter 1), Rossellini was always aware of his political allegiances, which were broadly in line with the Christian Democrat party. The appeal to peace could be a general warning against the consequences of the increasing antagonism between the Communist bloc and the West. More specifically, in 1948, a major debate took place within the Christian Democrat party about the issue of Italy's entry into NATO. Although Italy entered the Atlantic alliance, there were certain prominent members of the party who withheld their full support. The most eminent Christian Democrat who pleaded for Italy to remain outside NATO was Giuseppe Dossetti, the party's vice-secretary, who argued that European countries should work within the Western ambit towards a peaceful union outside the power of military alliances. This ideal was shared by Giorgio La Pira, then the Christian Democrat mayor of Florence, who organised and presided over an international 'Conference of Christian Peace' there in 1952. Rossellini numbered La Pira among his friends and we can assume that he was broadly in sympathy with these aims at the time he made *Francis God's Jester*. Whatever his relations with the Catholic Church might have been, it is noticeable that he took little part in Catholic Action, the aims of which were described by Pius XI as 'the participation of the laity in the apostolate of the hierarchy of the Church'. From his Roman family background of secular liberalism, this is not surprising. He seems to have had few friends within the Curia, or among the bishops. *Francis God's Jester* was shown in October 1950 at the basilica at Assisi. This may have been not his decision but that of his friend Father Lisandrini, who delivered a spoken introduction to the film. Whatever the reason, Rossellini had friends among members of the religious orders. The importance of the religious orders within a Christian community was discussed throughout the 1950s among the group which may be broadly described as the Catholic left. When La Pira was mayor of Florence he regularly retired to the Dominican convent of St Mark in the city. The most dramatic event following this debate about the value of the religious orders in contemporary life was the decision made by Giuseppe Dossetti in 1956 to become founding member of a religious order, 'The Family of the Annunciation', which observes the rule of Benedict, but with the Franciscan vow of poverty. Perhaps anxious about its possible independence, the Curia placed the religious order under the direct jurisdiction of the bishop of Bologna. The vulnerable idealism of the film is thus not isolated from current events and debates. Many years later, Rossellini would explore the political role of De Gasperi in *Anno uno*. Dossetti's resignation from the government is marked by a letter written by him and read out by De Gasperi which reminds the leader of the need to remain faithful to an ideal of social justice. His wife remarks that many members of the party will still consider Dossetti as a source of moral authority. But Rossellini pursues his main concern in the film: De Gasperi's martyrdom in the service of the unity of the party and the country. Rossellini's preoccupation with the potential unity of human experience and search for a harmonious force in human affairs is apparent in both *Francis God's Jester* and *Anno uno*, made at a distance of nearly twenty-five years from one another. In this preoccupation, as with so many others, Rossellini remained resolutely consistent.

Notes

1 *Francis God's Jester* is the title of the film in Italian with English subtitles owned by the British Film Institute. All references to the film in this article are to this version. The version distributed in the United States, *Flowers of St Francis*, has an additional prologue featuring the frescoes of the life of St Francis, but omits the episode 'Perfect Happiness' and the intertitles between the episodes.

2 *La Rivista del Cinematografo*, no. 6, June 1954, pp. 16–18; reprinted in Roberto Rossellini, *Il mio metodo. Scritti e interviste*, edited by Adriano Aprà (Venice: Marsilio, 1987), pp. 104–7.

3 After the Concordat between the Vatican and the Fascist state (1929), St Francis of Assisi and St Catherine of Siena were pronounced the official patron saints of Italy. For Italians of Rossellini's generation, the dominant image of St Francis was probably filtered through the writings of the great poet of the ideological right, Gabriele d'Annunzio, as well as through the cult of Dante's *Divine Comedy* (*Paradise*, Canto XI). Rossellini and his collaborators must have been aware of and have chosen to ignore these traditions.

4 See André Bazin, 'Defence of Rossellini', this volume, pp. 157–61.

5 Jacques Rivette, 'Lettre sur Rossellini' in *Cahiers du Cinéma,* no. 46, April 1955, pp. 14–24; translated in Jim Hillier (ed.), *Cahiers du Cinéma*, vol. 1, *The 1950s: Neo-Realism, Hollywood, New Wave* (London: Routledge & Kegan Paul, 1985), pp. 192–204; also in Jonathan Rosenbaum (ed.), *Rivette: Texts and Interviews* (London: BFI, 1977), pp. 54–64; Maurice Schérer [Eric Rohmer], 'Stromboli' in *La Gazette du Cinéma*, no. 5, November 1950, and 'De trois films et d'une certaine école' in *Cahiers du Cinéma*, no. 26, August–September, 1953; both articles are reprinted in Eric Rohmer, *Le Gout de la beauté* (Paris: Cahiers du Cinéma/Editions de l'Etoile, 1984).

6 Roberto Rossellini, 'Il messaggio di *Francesco*', in *Epoca*, no. 6, November 1950, p. 4; reprinted in *Il mio metodo*, pp. 76–7; 'The Message of *The Flowers of St Francis*' in Roberto Rossellini, *My Method: Writings and Interviews*, edited by Adriano Aprà, translated by Annamaria Cancogni (New York: Marsilio, 1987), pp. 31–2.

7 Pio Baldelli, 'Falsificazione umana di un giullare di Dio', *Cinema*, no. 55, February 1951; 'Dibattito per *Francesco* di Rossellini', *Rivista del Cinema Italiano*, November 1954, pp. 55–69; *Roberto Rossellini* (Rome: Samonà e Savelli, 1972); Brunello Rondi, 'Per un riesame del *Francesco* di Rossellini', in *Rivista del Cinema Italiano*, January 1955, pp. 88–95; Brunello Rondi, 'La continua proposta del *Francesco* di Rossellini', *Filmcritica*, no. 147, July 1964, pp. 369–72.

8 'Francesco giullare di Dio', in *Inquadratura*, nos. 5–6, October 1958–September 1959, pp. 39–48.

9 *The Little Flowers of St Francis* is clearly by a different author from *The Life of Juniper*. The best translation of all the early lives of Francis is the Everyman's Library edition *The Little Flowers and The Life of St Francis with the Mirror of Perfection* (London and

Toronto: Dent, 1910). In Italian, both texts are published in *I fioretti di San Francesco*, edited by Guido Davico Bonino (Turin: Einaudi, 1964).

10 Rossellini, 'The Message of *The Flowers of St Francis*', p. 31.

11 See 'The Fourth Dimension in Cinema' [1929] in *The Eisenstein Reader*, edited by Richard Taylor (London: BFI, 1998), pp. 122–3.

12 Marcel Oms, 'Rossellini. Du fascisme à la démocratie chrétienne', *Positif*, no. 28, April 1958. The article is quoted from in Don Ranvaud (ed.), *Roberto Rossellini*, BFI Dossier, no. 8 (London: British Film Institute, 1981), p. 14. The use of the term 'cretinism' here implies a wilful misuse of the word *giullare* when applied to Francis. Rossellini's use seems to imply the joy and simplicity possessed by a holy 'fool'. In Italian, *giullare* (like the French *jongleur*) is not only a 'jester' but was, in the Middle Ages, also a 'minstrel', who sang the praises of the feudal lord. The term *giullare di Dio* was originally attributed to Francis insofar as he sang the praise (*laudes*) of God through the canticle of God's creatures which he composed and which is recited at the beginning of the film. Although the term 'cretin' (from Swiss-French dialect 'crestin'), which was first used of certain mentally handicapped persons living in the Swiss valleys, did originally mean 'Christian', in the sense this term possessed in various parts of Europe of 'poor creature' or 'mortal', Oms's association of it with Christianity is ill-judged.

13 Henri Agel, *Le Cinéma et le sacre*, 2nd edn (Paris: Editions du Cerf, 1961), p. 75.

14 Peter Brunette, *Roberto Rossellini* (New York: Oxford University Press, 1987), pp. 128–37.

15 Roberto Rossellini, 'Colloquio sul neorealismo', in *Bianco e Nero*, no. 2, February 1952, pp. 7–16; reprinted in *Il mio metodo*, p. 94; 'A Discussion of Neorealism', in *My Method*, p. 37.

16 Roberto Rossellini, 'Il messaggio di "Francesco" ', in *Il mio metodo*, pp. 76–7; 'The Message of *The Flowers of St Francis*', in *My Method*, pp. 31–2.

17 Adriano Aprà, 'Scrittura, lettura, voce', in Rossellini, *Il mio metodo*, pp. ix–xiii; 'Writing, Reading, Voice', in *My Method*, pp. xiv–xix.

18 The Italian version held by the BFI has a serious mistranslation in the subtitles. 'Perfetta letizia' ('perfect joy') is consistently translated as 'perfect grace', which is theological nonsense.

19 'The Considerations of the Stigmata' is frequently published as part of *The Little Flowers*. For the episode of the divine vision of the musical angel, see *The Little Flowers and the Life of Francis with The Mirror of Perfection*, p. 110. The vision is a frequent subject for seventeenth-century baroque painting.

20 There is an interesting account of this episode by Brunello Rondi, 'Un esempio dello stile di Rossellini. *Francesco giullare di Dio*. Il bacio del lebbroso, analisi della sequenza', in *Cinema e realtà* (Rome: Cinque Lune, 1957), pp. 239–43. This is not the only episode in which Francis covers his face with his hands. For a different interpretation, see Michel Serceau, *Roberto Rossellini* (Paris: Editions du Cerf, 1986).

7
Vesuvian Topographies: The Eruption of the Past in *Journey to Italy*

Laura Mulvey

The 'journey' in *Journey to Italy* (*Viaggio in Italia*) has, as its fictional skeleton, seven days that Katherine and Alex Joyce (Ingrid Bergman and George Sanders) spend in Naples and its environs.

Day 1: Alex and Katherine drive the last stage of their journey from London to Naples to sell the house belonging to their recently deceased uncle Homer.[1] In Naples, they meet some friends by chance in their hotel.

Day 2: Alex and Katherine are taken to uncle Homer's house in the country outside Naples by Tony, his manager. They meet Tony's wife Natalia. After lunch, they talk on the terrace. Katherine mentions the connection with the area of a former admirer of hers, Charles Lewington. Alex reacts badly.

Day 3: Katherine visits the Museo Archeologico Nazionale. She and Alex have dinner together at the house.

Day 4: After an evening party at the house of uncle Homer's friend, the Duke of Lipoli, Alex seems jealous and he and Katherine quarrel.

Day 5: Katherine visits Cumae (Alex has left a note to say he has gone to Capri).
On Capri, Alex pursues a flirtation with Marie, one of the group encountered on Day 1.

Day 6: Katherine visits the Phlegraean Fields. On Capri, Alex is rejected by Marie. Katherine talks to Natalia who tells her 'you have understood nothing about Naples'. Alex returns to Naples and is accosted by a prostitute. They go for a drive (note that dur-

Journey to Italy (1954): the beginning ...

... and the ends.

ing this sequence Alex is driving the Bentley: this is at odds with continuity). Alex returns to the house. Katherine pretends to sleep. They hardly speak.

Day 7: Natalia takes Katherine to the Fontanelle cemetery. On her return to the house, Alex and Katherine quarrel. They decide to divorce. Tony takes Alex and Katherine to visit the excavations at Pompeii. Katherine is upset. Driving back to Naples, they encounter a religious procession and get out of the car to watch. The crowd suddenly surges forward with the cry 'miracolo', sweeping Katherine with it. Alex struggles to reach her and, reunited, they acknowledge their love for each other. The film then finds its own ending.

Narrative lines, geographical space

In spite of the chaos that seemed to reign during its shooting, *Journey to Italy* has a clearly mapped narrative structure. The movement of Katherine and Alex's initial journey halts when they arrive in Naples and then, three days later, forks into divergent directions. On the last day, their paths reconverge leading towards the final 'halt' of reconciliation and 'the end'. The fictional journey opens up other dimensions. The journey has a metaphorical level to it as the space of transformative experience. Reaching back to the earliest forms of storytelling, the road along which the hero travels reflects his progress on other, metaphysical levels. Away from the safety of home and everyday life, he (and sometimes, she) has to struggle with monsters either literal or figurative in search of self-knowledge. Katherine and Alex's journey in Italy thus has both literal and metaphoric levels and Rossellini can graft the journey structure of self-discovery and closure on to this particular fictional trajectory. But Alex and Katherine's fictional journey is also, perhaps primarily, designed to take the film into a specific place, a real geography and geology that underpins the story like a map. Fiction leads to reality, in this Rossellini movie, rather than realism. *Journey to Italy* uses its fictional protagonists' tourism to draw the resonance of place into the plot and to give historical geography a presence on the screen. And these realities ultimately revolve around the presence of Vesuvius, and the cultures it had fostered throughout the ages.

But first of all, through Alex's character, Rossellini introduces a reflection on attitudes to time that emerge out of geographical difference, between northern and southern culture and *mores* (implicitly also between North and South Italy). The ordered clock time of the North bumps uneasily into the more leisured time of the South. It is the empty time, the forced waiting while a buyer is found for the house, that irritates Alex and precipitates his trip to Capri. Alex is infuriated by the invasion of *dolce far niente* into daily life, because he is also drawn to it, and this also, paradoxically, drives him to join his bohemian, pleasure-loving friends on Capri. It is as though the northern male were both more subjected to timetable and more vulnerable to its collapse. For Alex, there is something demasculinising about leisure, as though it threatened the coming of 'woman's time'. Through Katherine's sightseeing, Rossellini leads the film into Neapolitan culture and geology and opens up the story's present to the presence of the past. Then, on the last morning, the two strands come together. Alex and Katherine's decision to divorce is precipitated by her failure to bring the Bentley back 'on time'. Their quarrel is interrupted by another dimension of time, a journey back into the past. Their host, Tony, absolutely insists that they go with him to witness the excavation of a site at Pompeii in which bodies have been found preserved in the lava.

The visit to Pompeii is the last of the various smaller, branching, journeys into the past that the couple take inside the wider journey of the film. It is the only one they take together. At the Pompeii excavation, all other reflections on time are abruptly derailed by the actual presence, not just of the past, but of death. It is, furthermore, an image of death which is specific to the geography of the area. When Vesuvius erupted in AD 79, some of its victims were buried by the lava. Over time, the bodies disintegrated, leaving behind a void which preserved their shape as in the contours of a mould.[2] Through a 'lost wax' process, as a sculptor casts a statue, the figures could be retrieved in image. If an empty space was suspected in the excavation, which might signal the presence of a body, it would be carefully filled with liquid plaster. When hardened, the mould would be uncovered and the imprint of the figures revealed. It was the final stage of the process, the slow uncovering of the figures of a couple, that Alex and Katherine have been invited to witness. The sight of death preserved triggers Katherine's crisis and later her cry, during their long walk through the ruined streets and buildings of Pompeii: 'life's so short'.

'The ontology of the photographic image'

In a semiotic vocabulary, these retrieved Pompeii figures belong to the category of indexical signs which, unlike a realistic depiction, are formed by an imprint of the original.

Journey to Italy (1954): the appearance of life ...

Although there are other examples of Rossellini's interest in the most concrete, material manifestations of the past throughout *Journey*, the Pompeii episode is particularly relevant to its aesthetics. The indexical image has a direct bearing on the aesthetics and poetics of photography and film. Film, too, is an imprint. But while the images of the people of Pompeii were preserved at the moment of death, film is able to preserve the appearance of life. For Rossellini, in *Journey*, the inscription of the human figure onto celluloid is one more layer, one more trace, of the past fossilised in time. This is a step beyond realism, the accurate reconstruction, that is, of events for the cinema in their appropriate settings. Rossellini was, by this point in his career, more concerned to search for the continued presence of the past into the present and its translation into the reality of the celluloid image and thus into the future. But this final detour into the past, to a confrontation with the image of death itself, also affects the narrative trajectory of Alex and Katherine Joyce. Raymond Bellour describes both the narrative moment and its aesthetic implications:

> a distraught couple arrives in front of an excavation site in Pompeii from which, after an injection of plaster, there emerges the form of a couple clasped in an embrace, as a picture appears in a developer. Thus, a photograph is formed from the real itself.[3]

The plaster figures extend the indexical image beyond its material temporal dimension into its relation to death. *Journey to Italy* sets up a relation between materialism and the supernatural: the physical trace of the human figure meets the mystery of death, the point where religion and superstition become indeterminably entwined with human belief systems.

Journeys to Italy

Just before *Europe '51*, Rossellini had contributed an episode, *L'Envie* (*L'invidia/Envy*), based on the short story *La Chatte* by Colette, to the collaborative project *Les Sept Péchés capitaux*. Another Colette story, *Duo*, had been the project which had brought George Sanders to Italy from Hollywood to play opposite Ingrid Bergman. Once he failed to acquire the rights to this story of a marriage in crisis, Rossellini had quickly to find another film appropriate for Sanders. The story of Katherine and Alex's marriage in

... and the moment of death preserved.

Journey to Italy bears some, if only residual, traces of the Colette project. Certainly, *Journey* takes from *Duo* the sense of marriage as extreme intimacy of habit and familiarity of feeling, juxtaposed with the opacity of one human being for another. Such a complete lack of mutual understanding may only erupt at a moment of crisis when the rhythms of daily exchange, which keep the marriage moving along its normal lines, are disrupted.

Ingrid Bergman and George Sanders had already appeared on the screen together in 1941. In *Journey*, in 1953, they have to play an essentially English couple, whose insularity and complacency differ only in forms of expression. There are ironies here. Bergman and Sanders had both led unsettled, peripatetic lives. Bergman had uprooted herself twice, moving from Sweden to Hollywood and then from Hollywood to Italy. Playing an upper-class English woman, she makes no effort to conceal her Swedish accent. On the other hand, Sanders's performance of Englishness, the basis of his Hollywood persona, was always, perhaps, a little too perfect. He had been born and brought up in Russia where his Scottish family had lived for generations. His departure for school in England at the age of 12 coincided with the Revolution. He never went back to his idyllic childhood home in St Petersburg and stayed in England only long enough to perfect its upper-class mannerisms before leaving for Hollywood.

Both Bergman and Sanders have described Rossellini's invitation as a salvation. Just as Ingrid Bergman needed to get away from Hollywood in 1949, so George Sanders welcomed the chance to leave in 1953. In 1948, Bergman had ended her affair with the photographer Robert Capa. They had met in 1945 in liberated Paris and had toured war-torn Europe together, but when Capa followed Bergman to Hollywood he found himself bored and inactive.[4] It is possible to imagine that when Bergman saw *Rome Open City* and *Paisà* in New York and was inspired to write to Rossellini offering him her services, she envisaged a situation in which she would actually be able to collaborate with a great artist of war, realism and living human drama. She had also just endured the professional humiliation and financial loss incurred by her co-production *Joan of Arc*, a critical and box-office catastrophe, in which she had hoped to reproduce on screen her Broadway triumph in Maxwell Anderson's *Joan of Lorraine*. *Joan of Arc* was produced in collaboration with veteran Hollywood director (and Don Juan) Victor Fleming with whom she had had one of her very first Hollywood affairs. Not only was the attempt to rekindle the personal and professional relationship with Fleming a disaster; Bergman's many affairs were finally taking their toll on her relationship with her husband Petter Lindström. Her life had definitely reached a crisis when she left Hollywood for Rome and fell in love with Rossellini.

By 1953, the Bergman–Rossellini marriage was known to be in difficulties (George Sanders described her as 'the tearful, but bravely smiling, Ingrid'). She was, however, extremely familiar with Rossellini's highly secretive and idiosyncratic way of working. Sanders was not. He arrived in Italy keen to work with the director of *Rome Open City* and *Paisà*. Although his career was going well – he had recently won an Oscar for *All About Eve* – he too felt that he was at a turning point in his life, anxious to escape from his five-year stint as Zsa Zsa Gabor's third husband ('there came a time when I felt I simply had to get away').[5] But *Journey* was an unhappy and confusing experience for both its stars and their reactions have been exhaustively chronicled. Rossellini wanted both of them to be as confused and troubled during the process of production as their characters would be on the screen. In a perverse way, Rossellini has his cake and eats it in his relations with his stars. He needed their names, he truly appreciated the particular screen presence and performance they brought to his cinema. Personally, though, he was unwilling to risk his absolute control of every aspect of the film by allowing an actor to know the script and prepare a performance. And professionally he was looking for a spontaneity which, he felt, carefully prepared actors could not give. It also happened that neither Bergman nor Sanders was a natural improvisor and both depended on the security of an established script and the stable direction that they were used to under the studio system.

Ingrid Bergman and George Sanders's off-screen situations are relevant to, or rather, are part of, the *Journey to Italy* aesthetic, on a fundamental level that goes beyond naturalistic characterisation or a director's megalomania. Just as Rossellini precipitates Alex and Katherine towards Naples and towards the crisis of their marriage, so he dispatched two Hollywood stars, both facing crises in their real-life marriages, into unknown professional territory. But with *Journey to Italy*, out of a minimal plotline and two bewildered actors, he managed to create, in the words of many critics, the first modern film. It is, to paraphrase Deleuze, as though Rossellini uses Bergman and Sanders, in their off-screen and on-screen crises, to enact the crisis of the action image. The straightforward, linear, horizontal movement of the car had landed them in a cinematic world in which plot and character would no longer be the only determinants of what happened on the screen. The diegetic space they have entered is porous, blurred at the edges and, temporally, is held in suspense. The two stars' performances, under Rossellini's non-direction, slide between their own screen *personae*: Ingrid Bergman and George Sanders, and Alex and Katherine Joyce. It is as though the actors were being forced, as experienced professionals, to undergo and then endure a loss of power, a decentralising of the traditional unity of star and story. Out of this, Rossellini could disrupt their journey and revel in the weakness of the plot's 'motor-linkages'.[6] The presence of disorientated Hollywood stars in a European art film dramatises such a change in cinematic direction. Perhaps the only Hollywood stars who would have been prepared to participate in, and thus enable, this crisis in the narrative film would be these two semi-Europeans, both at crisis points in their own lives, both uncertain where their private and professional futures were leading.

In fact, the collapse of the *Duo* project allowed Rossellini to make a film about Naples. It is the history and geography of his chosen location that skews the film from its proper storyline and breaks open the cracks leading to a new kind of cinema. Ingrid Bergman, in her 1974 interview with Robin Wood, describes Rossellini's desire to use film as a teaching tool, but her actual words imply something more:

> In *Journey to Italy* it was to show Pompeii. He adored Pompeii. He knew everything about it. He was only looking for a story into which he could put Pompeii and the museums and Naples and all that Naples stands for which he was always fascinated with because the people of Naples are different from the people in Rome or Milano. He wanted to show all those grottoes with the relics and the bones and the museums and the laziness of all the statues. Hercules is always leaning on something instead of fighting something.[7]

Rossellini and the Bay of Naples

Almost like a refrain running throughout the film, Rossellini punctuates *Journey* with sweeping panning shots which take in the expanse of the Bay.[8] The first shot of this kind opens the second phase of the Joyces' journey, from their Naples hotel to uncle Homer's house. This shot is, as it were, semi-diegetic. Although relevant for locating the story, it is more like a small piece of directorial enunciation. The second pan is an explicit mapping of the whole area from uncle Homer's terrace. Tony shows Alex and Katherine the expanse of the Bay. The camera follows his indications:

> There's the Vesuvius. Ever since the eruption of 1944 there has been a period of calm, but the temperature is beginning to rise a little though. That point there, behind the hill, that first hill, is Pompeii. Then Castellammare, Torre Annunziata. Resina's over there, and Naples. There's Ischia, the Isle of Capri and that large strip down there is the Sorrento peninsula.

Throughout *Journey*, Vesuvius dominates the landscape, the geography of the area but also its history. The volcanic terrain created Naples's natural port, attracted settlers to its fertile soil and holidaymakers to its waters and climate, bringing wealth and culture to the area. Due to these outstanding natural conditions, the Greek colony of Parthenope and Neapolis, with its foundations at Cumae dating back to about 750 BC, became the most flourishing economic and intellectual community outside Greece. Later, Roman intellectuals were drawn to the Greek culture that continued to flourish in the city. The Roman Emperors Tiberius, Nero and Caligula built themselves luxurious villas on Capri and Ischia. The Roman rich, attracted to the sea bathing and the volcanic hot springs and mineral waters, turned the Bay area into the first European holiday resort during the first century AD. Then, in AD 79 came the eruption that destroyed Pompeii and Herculaneum and the volcano revealed its dark and destructive power. It was because of the perpetual fear of Vesuvius that a vast array of cults and superstitions were always rife in its environs. This tradition, already characteristic of the daily life of Pompeii, continued in the semi-pagan, semi-Catholic religion, with its ritual processions and statues of saints, that particularly appealed to Rossellini. If he could bring vividly together, towards the end of *Journey*, two kinds of image that were important for his cinema, the material and the supernatural, it was due to Vesuvius. The two figures excavated in Pompeii, killed by the volcano and then preserved in its lava, represent the indexical image and the real of cinema. And then, at the end, the statue of the Madonna, which ultimately only signifies the human mind's imaginative powers, its propensity both to need and to enjoy belief in the supernatural and the magic powers of the cinema.

A fascinating document is reproduced in Tag Gallagher's recent biography of Rossellini.[9] On four and a half pages of notebook, Rossellini wrote an outline of *Journey to Italy* for his production manager. Rather than a summary of plot events, it is a list of the film's main locations, concentrating particularly on the tourist sites, indicating how important these locations were for his conception of the film. Three locations on the list are not in the final film; the most important of these is the Cappella di San Gennaro, in Naples cathedral. Since the fourteenth century, San Gennaro (Saint Januarius) has been the Neapolitan antidote to Vesuvius. Three times a year his blood miraculously liquefies, defending Naples from all kinds of harm, but most particularly from the volcano. There is a kind of poetic symmetry in the way that the reanimation of the saint's blood should keep the volcano in quiescence, or, if the worst comes to the worst, at least ward off invasion by the flow of molten lava. Discussing his fascination with Neapolitan popular culture in a *Cahiers du Cinéma* interview in 1954, Rossellini mentions San Gennaro, saying:

> Besides, you must remember that Naples is the only place in the world where a miracle takes place on a fixed date, September 19th, the miracle of San Gennaro. And San Gennaro look out! If the miracle doesn't happen, he gets into trouble. And all kinds of dreadful things start to happen! [10]

Alex's journey

Both Alex and Katherine's divergent journeys are the product of tourism or, at least, the 'liminal' space of a holiday. Alex's expedition to Capri confirms his sensual side, his readiness to pursue sexual adventure, while Rossellini tends to depict Katherine as a caricature English lady tourist, cluttered with camera, umbrella, dark glasses and *Blue Guide*. Alex's visit to Capri in search of 'fun' reflects the island's ancient associations with pleasure. It was also Rossellini's own preferred holiday place and the home, for many years, of his mistress, Roswitha Schmidt. Alex's pursuit of Marie in Capri's relaxed bohemian setting is unsuccessful and, according to Tag Gallagher, Rossellini felt this section of the film suffered from the lack of sexual rapport between Sanders and Marie Mauban.[11]

Alex's next, near-sexual, encounter, takes place in Naples itself. The figure of the young prostitute who accosts Alex outside the Excelsior Hotel takes the film into another story of sexuality. But, in contrast to the bourgeois, pleasure-loving atmosphere of Capri, this story is dark and sad and invokes the city's sufferings during the Allied occupation of 1944. Rossellini had visited Naples during the war and also during the appalling days of 1944 when the whole population was faced with starvation and many did starve. The American army, its institutional corruption and its GIs, provided the only available means of survival and Naples was almost immediately overwhelmed in prostitution, the black market and systematic theft. The Naples episode of *Paisà*, an encounter between the GI and the child who steals his boots, shows the desperate state of the city and celebrates the culture and language of its street boys, whose traditional amoral ingenuity had now become a matter of life or death. The Rome episode of *Paisà*, which traces the transformation of an ordinary young woman into a prostitute, could better refer to the notorious fate of the women of Naples. *Journey* was shot in 1953, only eight years after the Allies' traumatic occupation. Alex's encounter with the desperate young woman obliquely reinscribes the relations between the foreign armies and the women of Naples. Her command of English forges a link to the Allied occupation.

Katherine's journeys

Katherine's sightseeing expeditions literally lead the film to the heart of the ancient history and the geography of the Bay of Naples. Although she is an instinctive tourist, she is also inspired by the lines 'Temple of the Spirit' written by Charles Lewington, her former admirer, when he landed in the area as a soldier in 1944. Her three principal sightseeing trips take place on successive days (ignoring the actual proximity of the Phlegraean Fields to Cumae). Their order follows a series of archaeological strata: Katherine moves from the classical Greek and Roman statues of the museum, back in time to the extremely ancient site of the Cumaean Sibyl, to the geological formations, the volcanic substructure, which made the area both so appealing and so deadly to ancient civilisations.

Each expedition is preceded by a 'montage' sequence of people and scenes in the streets of Naples, which have an autonomous life. Although intercut with Katherine's (supposed) point of view and her voice-over, each has a sketchy internal structure. Themes of interest to Rossellini lie behind Katherine's condescending curiosity and touch aspects of life that he found both difficult and interesting. The first montage includes a juxtaposition between the Church and politics. After shots of workers mix with shots of priests and nuns, the camera picks out a priest walking past an election poster for the PCI, placing the two opposites within the same frame. The second montage which shows an elaborate, typically Neapolitan, funeral procession is followed by a series of shots of pregnant women, bringing together the oppositions: birth and death, womb and coffin, the first home and the last. The final montage juxtaposes courting couples, men and women in love, with shots of babies in prams. This particular irreconcilable – love and sex on the one hand and family responsibility on the other – was one Rossellini quite often mentioned in relation to his own life.

Museo Archeologico Nazionale

Rossellini only filmed the statues in the Museo Archeologico. Perhaps because it was the first sequence he shot, taking what seemed to his waiting stars a disproportionate week over the filming, it dominates the film rather as the giant Farnese statues dominate the museum.[12] It was one of the few times in the film that Rossellini used a crane, which was necessary not only to film in proportion to the size of the statues but also to give the sequence its distinctive style. Although Ingrid Bergman looks at the statues in wonder, she does not provide the sequence with a viewing position or a point of view. The camera movements acquire an autonomy that is enhanced by the first appearance of Renzo Rossellini's music. Stylistically, the sequence builds up gradually, starting with small panning movements across and around the statues. The director was clearly fascinated by these objects, and the autonomous self-sufficient world of the fiction seems to collapse under their weight. That is to say, the combination of camera with music and editing that gives the sequence its aesthetic unity overwhelms Katherine and her fictional subjectivity. The camera is liberated from its subordination to her movements. As Katherine and the guide reach the Farnese Hercules, the camera moves higher with sweeping movements, defying gravity as it transcends the limitations of the human eye and its earth-bound perspective. Throughout the sequence, the music, with its eerie, other-worldly quality, is mixed in ironic juxtaposition to the guide's patter, in which his heavy clichés are interposed with guidebook-style, but important, information about the statues and their origins.

Rossellini begins the sequence with a dissolve that brings Katherine into the museum as it were through the huge stone base of a pillar. Movement emerges out of stasis, setting the scene for the rest of the sequence. It is as though Rossellini imagined bringing life to those blocks of stone and that his camera could provide the magic means of doing so. Some of the statues are poised in mid-gesture: the discus thrower with his eyes looking straight into and challenging the camera, the drunken poet, caught at the moment he falls backwards into a stupor. It is as though the gaze of the Medusa, or some other malign magician, had turned living movement into stone. The aesthetic of classical Greek sculpture, later copied by the Romans, aspired to create the illusion that living movement had been frozen at a given moment. This illusion was, of course, to be ultimately transformed into reality by photography. For André Bazin, the photograph's ability to capture and freeze a moment is indicative of transcendence of time and of death itself. In *Journey*, however, the camera brings the cinema's movement to the statues and attempts to revitalise their stillness, reaching a crescendo with the gigantic Farnese Bull group. Here, movement stilled finds an even more complex relation with camera mobility. The brothers, Zethus and Amphion, struggle to hold the huge bull on which Dirce, who lies at their feet, will be tied. This violent scene of brute force and dramatic violence is completed by the presence of a little dog barking at its edge. The sculptor seems to have tried to give the impression that he had caught the action and then, at that split second, left it forever in suspended animation. The museum sequence revolves around a variety of reflections on movement and stillness, the relation between the animate and the inanimate, the living and the dead, that importantly not only recur in *Journey to Italy* but are intrinsic to Rossellini's conception of cinema in general.

Towards the beginning of the sequence, the guide takes Katherine to a series of busts of the Roman Emperors, not caught in action, but calm methodical portraits of actual men. Here the significance is in their relation between a 'now' and a 'then' which Katherine tries to collapse when she describes the statues to Alex. She says:

> To think that these men lived thousands of years ago and you feel they're just like the men of today. It's amazing. It is as if Nero or Caracalla, Caesar [sic] or Tiberius, would suddenly tell you what they felt and you could understand exactly what they were like.

Katherine has left out the guide's dramatic stories of the Emperors' cruelty, so that history blurs and her point underlines, once again, the legacy left by the past and its visible materialisation in the present that so interested Rossellini.

Cumae

Katherine's visit to Cumae presents a sharp contrast to the museum sequence. The statues belong to a comparatively short and historically coherent period of ancient history. Cumae's history is layered with different epochs, different cultures, different religions and mythologies. The oldest of the Greek settlements, with massive walls, supposedly in Minoan style, the site of the Sibyl's cave, Cumae stretches back into prehistory. After the decline of Rome, the site had been used as catacombs by the Christians and a fortress by the Saracens. In contrast to the museum, the sequence is organised around Katherine's emotion and her subjective responses to the scene. The guide, bracketing the long history of the site, says: 'After abandoning Troy, Aeneas landed here on this very beach. In the last war, the British troops landed here.' The subsequent shot shows Katherine's reaction as it dawns on her that Charles Lewington might have been camped in that very spot. The ghostliness already associated with Charles then finds a kind of uncanny presence as the guide demonstrates the echo that resounds through the huge passage. Rossellini holds the shot of Katherine and the guide walking, with light and shadow falling across their path, with the echoes resounding around them, until they reach a chamber of Christian remains. The music then changes the feeling of the scene, linking it back to the museum and its uncanniness. The lines of Charles's poem begin to run through Katherine's head. Her reverie is abruptly disrupted by the guide who draws her attention to two marks in the wall where, he claims, the Saracens chained their prisoners. 'This is how they would have tied a beautiful woman like you.'

Although its uncanniness is, by and large, refracted through Katherine's thoughts and Charles's ghostly presence, Cumae brings with it an accumulation of resonance, trace and relic. It is also a place of mystery, or rather of 'the mysteries', the secrets of the religion, whether of the oracle or of early Christianity, that their devotees believed in. The echo, which takes on a life of its own as it reverberates, belongs to that aura of dematerialised mystery. At the same time, it is also a material link with the past, in continuity with all the previous echoes, stretching back across the centuries to when, as the guide explains, it was much louder because the walls were covered in bronze. And, bringing the atmosphere of the scene out of its other-worldliness, Rossellini uses the marks on the wall as a material sign of the presence of the past, its indexical inscription.

The Phlegraean Fields

Katherine's third journey takes her to the Phlegraean Fields, where she witnesses the live volcanic activity of the 'little Vesuvius' and the 'mystery' of ionisation. Here the film reaches the area's geological substructure, that seethes under the ground occasionally reaching the surface, as in these sulphur pits or in the actual eruptions of Vesuvius. The sequence is organised visually in two contrasting ways. On the one hand, there is Katherine's delight in the natural phenomena she is witnessing. She photographs the smoking pits, experiments with the ionisation mystery, exclaiming as the whole area responds in unison to one lighted paper or cigarette. She recognises in the 'pocket Vesuvius' the ash and cinders that had buried Pompeii in AD 79. But, meanwhile, the camera finds its own independent relation with the movement of the smoke. As the volume of smoke increases, the camera follows as it drifts away until it fills the screen. There is a stark contrast between the camera's relation to the hard-edged, exquisitely worked bodies in the museum and this insubstantial flow without shape or form, beginning or end. As the

Journey to Italy (1954): movement in inanimate matter.

Inanimate matter in movement.

smoke drifts across the screen and the camera drifts with it, once again, even if on a less formally evolved level, the image moves away from its fictional frame of reference. Film turns into something beyond its usual subservience to iconic representation, dissolving into wispy grey tones. But, there is a thematic link back to the two previous expeditions. The volcanic activity and the smoke from the ionisation process have a flow and a movement which animates an inanimate material, the earth itself. Of course, this 'coming to life' of the earth brings death to man and the landscape of *Journey to Italy* is constantly haunted by the distant presence of Vesuvius.

Katherine leads the film slightly to one side of her own fictional story, standing back, as it were, to allow the cinema to find its own dialogue with the history and geography of the area. Then Rossellini's primary aesthetic preoccupation can be focused on the visible presence of the past, its material legacy in the images he was filming. The statues in the museum, although sanctified as art, although they have lost their original settings, are there 'now', images of the human body 'then'. Cumae, on the other hand, is topography. Selected as a sacred site in prehistory due to its intrinsic geomantic qualities, subsequently overlaid by layers of other histories which add to the power of the place itself, it exists across time. While the statues are like snapshots, moments of frozen time, Cumae is a palimpsest. As a place that has been sanctified by human belief in the supernatural, it leads logically to the sulphur pits, where a natural phenomenon assumes the appearance of mystery. The theme that unifies the three sites, on a second level, is the relation between inanimate matter and its animation. From this perspective, all three relate to the mysteriousness of the cinema in which inanimate photogrammes come alive in projection, giving frozen moments of time a semblance of movement.

The Dead

When Alex and Katherine are sitting on the terrace after their first lunch in uncle Homer's house, their ways part for the first time. While Alex goes in search of mineral water and confronts the concepts of time and its organisation that separate north from south, Katherine daydreams and resurrects the ghost of Charles Lewington. The ensuing dialogue is loosely based on James Joyce's short story 'The Dead'. Katherine's story of the young poet echoes Gretta's story of Michael Furey. Both women had been loved hopelessly by a young, sensitive and frail man, one a singer, the other a poet, who then died prematurely. In both cases, chance contributes to the way this young, doomed, long dead lover returns in memory to disrupt the present. But once felt, his presence haunts both husbands. In 'The Dead', jealousy and irritation give way to an intimation of universal mortality; in *Journey*, Alex cannot escape from the jealousy and irritation which continue to haunt him, as Charles Lewington does, throughout the film. Although so little is known about the conception and development of the script which became *Journey to Italy*, the couple's name, Joyce, suggests a reference back to James Joyce's story.[13] Charles Lewington haunts Katherine, Alex and the film itself. The lines of his poetry, which return like a refrain into Katherine's mind and for which she seems to be searching for a meaning, finally find their significance outside her consciousness in the image of death that pervades the film:

> Temple of the Spirit. No longer bodies
> But pure ascetic images.

Katherine had hoped to find these images in the sculptures at the museum. Rather, the resonance of Charles Lewington's words is found in the images of death which the movie finds towards its end, in the figures at Pompeii and the skeletons in the Fontanelle cemetery.

Katherine's last expedition is suggested to her by Natalia in their conversation on the afternoon of Day 6 and which they take on the morning of Day 7. Katherine makes her last drive through the streets of Naples. This time she has Natalia with her to comment on her observations and, once again, the focus is on the number of pregnant women in the street. These images of new life, however, lead to the dead, the heaps of skulls and the skeletons collected in the Fontanelle. This expedition is not suggested by the *Blue Guide* but by a native Neapolitan; it closely follows Rossellini's anecdote in his autobiography about the Neopolitan attitude to the dead. He describes the way that the influx of people into the city in the nineteenth century displaced the dead from the graveyards which were then deconsecrated and the bones thrown into the Roman catacombs. During the Second World War, the poor hid in the catacombs and began to adopt the skeletons:

Astonished by this practice, I asked what its origin was. They replied: 'We have lost so many sons on the other side of the sea. No one knows where they're buried, dispersed by the wind and the sand or burnt by the scorching sun. We have nothing, not a tomb, not a cross to pray over. We want to make up for this.'

They adopted what were presumably skulls of young people because it was likely that they had sinned less. These skulls fulfilled the same role for them, in their relation to God, as satellites have now in intercontinental communication. They were satellites of love.[14]

Natalia tells Katherine about her brother who was killed in Greece and whom she mourns in the Fontanelle and then, once again joining death to new life, about her hope for a child. This sequence is disorientating for Katherine. For the first time in her journeys, she is outside the tourist route, mingling with Neapolitans, disturbed by the skulls and skeletons piled high against the walls. She watches Natalia from a distance as she makes the strange gestures of the Catholic religion, but their childlessness also links the two women across their cultures. For Katherine, this strange experience at the Fontanelle leads directly to her quarrel with Alex, to Pompeii and the emotional crisis which she later tries, ineffectually, to explain to him.

In *Journey to Italy* reality intrudes into the fictional lives of its protagonists and their story. This reality is a materialisation of time itself, a constant reiteration of the past, as history, memory or relic, into the texture of the film. The dead play an important part in these returns. Not only do they haunt the passage between one life and another but they condense the passing of time with their insistent presence in the present. And just as Rossellini's reality is penetrated by irrationality, religion and mystery, so are the rational northern Europeans surrounded by the past and its ghosts. Alex and Katherine's journey in Italy has been precipitated by uncle Homer's death. In the elaborate sequence in which Tony and Natalia take Alex and Katherine on a guided tour of uncle Homer's house, they make his presence felt through his collection of objects, through the rooms he loved. At the Duke of Lipoli's party, Homer's friends not only joke about his death but talk easily about meeting him 'up there'. As the story of the skeletons adopted at the Fontanelle indicates, Rossellini is interested in the continued presence of the dead among the living.

Film

The film itself is the final layer in the process which extends the materiality of the index into its relation with time, the preservation of the past and the image of the living after death. Questions of cinema and questions of time begin to bounce off each other. From the present perspective, nearly fifty years later, the relation between cinema and history in *Journey* has acquired another dimension that seems to collapse the space between fiction and reality even further. With the coming of death and the passing of time, Ingrid Bergman and George Sanders, as well as the passers-by in the streets of Naples, are now themselves the dead. In *Journey to Italy* they are images fossilised on celluloid just as the figures in Pompeii were cast in plaster. The juxtapositions of life and death that pervade the film and the ghosts of the past that haunt it indicate that, for Rossellini, celluloid was yet another, more creative, more sophisticated, means of setting up a dialogue with a reality that was always in the process of becoming history. The images of Ingrid

Bergman and George Sanders preserved on film become, over time, more pure presence and less the record of performance. If the film had already blurred boundaries between George Sanders and Alex, Ingrid Bergman and Katherine, the actors' gestures and movements on the screen now seem to detach themselves from the artifice. Now Ingrid Bergman sits at the mirror brushing her hair, displacing Katherine. Now George Sanders plays the piano, displacing Alex.

The tension between the power of the fiction and its disruption by non-fiction in *Journey* reaches a crisis with the question of how the film ends. Rossellini gives his two Hollywood stars their aesthetically appropriate ending: the couple's reconciliation and their embrace, in a gesture to the conventions of narrative closure. These tensions condense in the crowded street of a small town when Alex and Katherine find their car's progress blocked by the press of people. Just as the film had opened with the visual equivalent of a play on the word 'drive', so narrative closure also finds a visualisation, a graphic form, in the car's gradual loss of speed, for the word 'stop'. There is an application of the brakes, a blocked passage. The linear structure of the narrative, searching for an appropriate form of closure, marks its own shift of gear, winding down towards the final stillness of 'the end'. In an inverse symmetry, the forward drive of the journey, which has twisted and turned with subordinate movements on its way, now comes to a complete halt.

But this ending, which satisfies the conventions of fiction and its structure's desire for stillness, does not fit with Rossellini's cinema. He then caps it with another ending that overrides the fiction. The camera turns away from the couple and their ending. A crane shot is carried forward, as it were, by the people now streaming along the street; and then the camera finds its own ending in this renewed flow of movement, not of narrative but of reality. The film then simply fades away, as the local brass band plays and people drift past. Life goes on. One ending halts, the other flows. One is a concentration focused on the stars' role in producing the fiction and its coherence, and the other is a distraction, the film's tendency to wander off in search of another kind of cinema. This is the 'continuance of time' that, for Jacques Rivette, is the essential element in Rossellini's mode of storytelling:

> For there are films which begin and end, which have a beginning and an ending, which conduct their story from an initial premise until everything has been restored to peace and order, and there have been deaths, a marriage or a revelation; there is Hawks, Hitchcock, Murnau, Ray, Griffith. And there are films quite unlike this, which recede into time like rivers to the sea; and which offer us only the most banal of closing images: rivers flowing, crowds, armies, shadows passing, curtains falling in perpetuity, a girl dancing till the end of time; there is Renoir and Rossellini.[15]

Ending

In 1998, Chris Petit made *Negative Images*, a videotape of his journey to meet the American critic and artist Manny Farber. Petit describes Farber's ability to see through the surface of a film ('he saw stuff you didn't') to find moments of inconsequence, or arbitrary gestures ('not the main item ... the movie's about something else'). These are 'defining moments which then stick in the mind long after the rest of the movie has been

forgotten'. Appropriately, *Journey to Italy* figures in the tape, in Manny Farber's observations and Chris Petit's thoughts. First of all, Farber describes the scene in which Alex
and Katherine are just sitting down to dinner (Day 3). Their attention is drawn to the
window by the sound of a quarrel outside. Natalia shouts up in explanation: 'They are
getting married in a week and already they are fighting. It's jealousy.' Apart from the displacement of Alex and Katherine's problems to the fiancés, the scene simply registers the
presence of life outside the main line of the story. It has no material bearing on the plot.
Perhaps this is the kind of moment that David Rodowick refers to as an 'aleatory stroll'
when describing the importance of Rossellini's cinema for the Deleuzian transition from
movement image to time image.[16] The scene has an extra, striking, beauty. Katherine is
poaching eggs at the dining-room table when the sound of the quarrel takes her and
Alex to the window. She suddenly turns away from the window with a start when she
remembers the eggs. Alex then closes the window and follows her. Although the shot is
clearly not constructed in real time, the constraints of real time, the time the eggs take
to cook, is written into its formal pattern and, of course, Katherine's fictional train of
thought.

Later, the tape slows down the sequence of Alex and Katherine driving through the
crowd in the streets of Maiori. While Ingrid Bergman's intricate changes of expression
are in the foreground, outside the car, three of the children running alongside it are suddenly made visible in detail, rather than lost in the swift movement of twenty-four
frames per second. The ability to slow down film and make the incidental and the arbitrary visible, Chris Petit implies, has an equivalence to Rossellini's ability to include the
incidental and the arbitrary as a counter-current to the narrative drive of his film. And
as film gains a new transparency with new technologies, Manny Farber's special ability
to see through the surface of the cinema can now be spread more widely. Chris Petit uses
Journey to Italy to carry his most elegiac thoughts on the cinema. Rather than resur-
recting *Journey's* contribution, in its own time, to the transformation of cinema, Petit
uses it to think about the cinema and death, which are, after all, ideas that are central to
Rossellini. In his voice-over, across the driving sequence, Petit says:

> Cinema, whose flickering dreams always carried with them a sense of departure,
> increasingly becomes a long list of the dead. And now as the century ends, it's
> fashionable to talk of the death of the cinema as though this were pre-empting the
> forces of wider technological revolution.

The sequence ends with the death of the movie's stars, George Sanders (1906–72) and
Ingrid Bergman (1915–82). 'Cinema becomes increasingly about what is past. It
becomes a mausoleum as much as a palace of dreams.' This is a fitting final reflection
on the complex interweaving of the continuous presence of the past in the present and
the appearance of life after death in Rossellini's *Journey to Italy*.

Notes

1   There is some ambiguity about whose uncle Homer is, probably due to the film's
    production circumstances (no fixed script, improvisation etc.).
2   The method was devised by Giuseppe Fiorelli, archaeologist and former supporter of

the carbonari movement for a united Italy, who was put in charge of the excavations in the 1860s by Victor Emmanuel II.

3 Raymond Bellour, 'The Film Stilled', *Camera Obscura*, no. 24, September 1990, p. 110.

4 The Bergman–Capa relationship is said to have inspired that between Jeff (James Stewart) and Lisa (Grace Kelly) in Hitchcock's *Rear Window*: see Gaby Wood, 'Robert Capa', *The Observer*, 31 May 1998.

5 George Sanders, *Memoirs of a Professional Cad* (New York: Putnam, 1960), p. 120.

6 Jacques Deleuze, *Cinema 2: The Time Image* (Minneapolis: University of Minnesota Press, 1989), p. 18.

7 Robin Wood, 'Ingrid Bergman on Roberto Rossellini', *Film Comment*, no. 10, July–August 1974, p. 14.

8 'Attention to panoramas, exterior views and landscape is traditionally an important component of the visual culture of Naples ... This is reflected in its artistic tradition: landscapes and 'vedute' ['views'] predominate in Neapolitan art from painting to photography.' Giuliana Bruno, *Streetwalking on a Ruined Map: Cultural Theory and the City Films of Elvira Notari* (Princeton, NJ: Princeton University Press, 1993), p. 210.

9 Tag Gallagher, *The Adventures of Roberto Rossellini: His Life and Films* (New York: Da Capo, 1998), pp. 398–9.

10 Maurice Schérer [Eric Rohmer] and François Truffaut, 'Entretien avec Roberto Rossellini', *Cahiers du Cinéma*, no. 37, July 1954, p. 10; the interview is translated in full in Roberto Rossellini, *My Method*, edited by Adriano Aprà (New York: Marsilio, 1992), pp. 47–57 and partially (excluding this passage) in Jim Hillier (ed.), *Cahiers du Cinéma*, vol. 1, *The 1950s: Neo-Realism, Hollywood, New Wave* (London: Routledge & Kegan Paul, 1985), pp. 209–12.

11 Gallagher, *Adventures*, p. 402.

12 These giant sculptures had been originally made to stand in the Baths of Caracalla in Rome as spectacular decorative features. They were brought to Naples by Charles, founder of the Bourbon dynasty, in the eighteenth century.

13 The sudden disruption of a relationship between husband and wife by a slight detail which provokes the husband's jealousy is common to 'The Dead' and Colette's *Duo*. For discussion of the relation between Joyce's story and *Journey to Italy* see: Luciana Bohme, 'A Variation on a Theme by Joyce', *Film Criticism*, vol. 3 no. 2, Winter 1979; James Naremore, 'The Return of the Living Dead', *Journal of Literary Studies*, Spring 1991; and G. Elisa Bussi, 'From The Dead to *Viaggio in Italia*. Joyce's Story into Rossellini's Picture?' in G. Elisa Bussi and Laura Salmon Kovarski (eds), *Letteratura e Cinema. La Trasposizione* (Cooperativa Libreria Universitaria Edizione: Bologna, 1996).

14 Roberto Rossellini, *Quasi un'autobiografia*, edited by Stefano Roncoroni (Milan: Mondadori, 1987), p. 63.

15 Jacques Rivette, 'Letter on Rossellini', in Hillier, *Cahiers du Cinéma*, vol. 1, p. 194 (originally in *Cahiers du Cinéma*, no. 46, April 1955, pp. 14–24).

16 '[A]ccording to Deleuze, the appearance of neo-realism represents a crisis in the cinema of action and movement. Especially in Rossellini's films, such as *Germania anno zero* (1947), *Stromboli* (1949) or *Viaggio in Italia* (1953) narrative situations appear where reality is represented as lacunary and dispersive. Linear actions dissolve into the form of aleatory strolls.' D.N. Rodowick, *Gilles Deleuze's Time Machine* (Durham, NC: Duke University Press, 1997), p. 13.

8
India

Sam Rohdie

'I am not a film-maker ... the cinema is not my profession.'[1]

In December 1956 Rossellini went to India where he spent nearly a year travelling and filming. He made two films from the material he gathered. The first, made for French television and broadcast in ten episodes over three months at the beginning of 1958, was called *J'ai fait un beau voyage* (*I Had a Good Trip*). In it, Rossellini discussed with a French critic his experience of India against the backdrop of the footage he shot there. An Italian version, *L'India vista da Rossellini* (*India as Seen by Rossellini*), had the same material but with an Italian interviewer. Both transmissions were original and spontaneous, with different interlocutors; nevertheless, Rossellini said the same things with the same words related to the same images projected in the same sequence in both films.

The second film, which used footage from the first, and with which this essay is principally concerned, was entitled *India* or *India Matri Bhumi* (*India Mother Land*). Rossellini defined the relation between the film he made for television and *India* as that between a documentary and a work of poetry. The first film had the status of notes and of a document, the second was an elaboration and fictionalisation of that 'documentary'. *India* is made up of four fictional episodes. Each is introduced by an external narrator who discusses the physical and geographical setting for the events which take place. In each, the role of the external narrator is taken over by the principal character who then becomes the narrator of that episode. In the fourth episode, whose principal character is a monkey, the narration remains exterior and 'objective'. There is no fictional connection between the episodes nor continuity of events or characters between them. In three of the episodes the 'natural' is predominantly represented by animals: elephants in the first, a tiger and a monkey in the third and fourth respectively. In the second, the role of a natural exteriority is taken by a hydro-electric dam. Though the animals and the dam belong within the fiction, they also exist outside it as a reality which the fictional characters must face, or as a reality which disrupts the fiction. In either case, the animals and the dam are not background to a fiction but protagonists within it. The film overall – that is, the set of four episodes – is introduced by a documentary-like introduction to India (in Bombay), which also closes the film.

'It is the country of realism more than any other ... India lives only in the concrete.'[2]

The introduction

India begins on the streets of Bombay: crowds, people in movement, at work or at
leisure. The voice-over narration stresses the density of people in India, as well as their
variety: of race, religion, profession, class. The narrator remarks on the differences that
compose India and the tolerance that binds these differences. The introduction is noisy.
The soundtrack is composed of rhythmic, syncopated loud drumming. The introduction is organised by a series of rapidly cut and joined scenes. The spectator is given
'glimpses'. The general sense is one of movement, a hurrying.

Episode one

The first episode begins quietly and smoothly. The camera tracks through a rural India
of fields and rivers. The narrator speaks of the 580,000 villages that compose rural India,
its most authentic part, he says. The film moves from villages to temples to a sacred city
to an elephant, painted and bedecked, swaying down a street in the sacred city beside a
temple. We are told that the elephant has been brought from the jungle to take part in
a religious ceremony. The film enters the jungle. There is a lengthy sequence, filled with
natural sounds, of elephants working: pushing down trees, hauling logs, lifting them
onto lorries.

 The narration shifts to one of the elephant handlers. He describes the hard work,
the habits of the elephants, how much they eat, and how it is he who serves the elephant, more than the elephant who serves him. There is a sequence of elephants in the
river, on their sides, being scrubbed and bathed by their handlers. At lunchtime, a bus
arrives in the village. From it alight travelling puppeteers, come to provide entertainment. It was one of the most important days of my life, the narrator says. He falls in

India (1957–9).

love, at first sight, with the daughter of the head of the troupe. She shyly responds. He and the girl are framed alternately in close-up. There is a puppet show. The handler complains that he, at that time, must attend to his elephant, whom he feeds and caresses. He sees his 'love' come to the riverside for water as he is scrubbing his elephant. The male and female elephants in his charge fall in love, so he hopes. It will relieve him, he says, of the burden of some of his work. He talks about the shyness of male elephants. We see backstage during an evening performance of the puppet show. His 'love' is singing and helping to provide sound effects. Each morning he takes his elephant to feed on a tree which overlooks the compound of his 'love'. The tree comes to be stripped bare because he constantly returns to it. He goes to the schoolmaster to ask him to write a proposal letter on his behalf. The schoolmaster then acts as an intermediary between the fathers of the two lovers. A marriage is agreed. The lovers marry. Ten months later, the elephant cow is pregnant and must separate from the company of the bull elephant who bellows at the separation. The cow goes off with another female elephant. The wife of the elephant handler is pregnant. She departs for her own village accompanied by her mother.

The episode is reminiscent of *Francis God's Jester* (1950).

Episode two

The episode begins in the foothills and valleys formed by the Himalayas. The narration speaks of the Himalayas as the source of the rivers of India. We are in the holy city of Benares with its steps down to the Ganges where people are cremated and their ashes delivered to the river. The narration speaks of the continuity of life and death in India and says that all men are brothers. It then moves to a river system parallel to the Ganges where a hydroelectric dam is nearing completion. Various facts about its construction are provided, with images of the dam being built, more with hand power than machine power: armies of half-naked workers carry baskets of earth and stone on their heads.

The narration shifts to the character narrator who is an engineer on the Hirakud Dam project. He continues with factual details of the dam's construction. He (and his wife and child) are in the office of the Hirakud administration. He receives his final payment. He exits with his wife. He hails a jeep and waves to his wife to carry on home. He is taken to the dam site where he walks around, for a last look, to say farewell. He talks with pride of the work, the immensity of the project, its benefits in electricity, irrigation. He celebrates knowledge, science, reason. He watches a cremation scene and reflects on the happiness of being at one with nature as the body is put to flame.

It is dusk. With a piece of chalk, by a temple that will be flooded, beside a sacred lake that will also be flooded, he inscribes his history: how he and his wife were refugees from West Bengal at the time of the Partition, arrived to work on the dam, made a home, had a child, and now they must leave with the work completed. He takes a ritual bath in the dam. His wife finds him there. They brusquely exchange words as he brushes past her. There is a final banquet with friends. When the banquet is over, his wife nags him concerning her distress at departure. He shouts at her and roughly pushes her away. The next morning they are on the road with their things leaving Hirakud. She is upset. He walks in front of her at a distance, each separate and alone. He stops and calls to her gently and they walk away together with their child.

The entire episode is reminiscent of *Journey to Italy* (1953) (and thereby of Jean-Luc Godard's *Tout va bien* (1971)).

Episode three

The camera tracks beside ordered fields of rice cultivation with an appropriate voice-over. The narration shifts to a character. He is an 80-year-old man who has lived beside the forest, alongside the animals, at one with both, for his entire life. He especially mentions the tigers, of whom he is fond. He wakes in the morning beside his wife in their hut in joy and in tranquillity. He mentions their unquestioned solidarity, and closeness, an unspoken, accustomed intimacy and peace. He remarks upon, and we see, her religious devotion to the traditional gods. He says he is too old to work. It is time now for his children to work. There is a scene of women drawing water at a well. He leads a contemplative life now, he says. Each day he takes his two cows to the forest, smokes a cigarette and finds his closeness to nature. We see a tiger. The tiger is part of this nature and close to him.

There is a noisy disturbance. Three vehicles come into the village. They belong to mineral prospectors. They set up their machinery. The noise frightens the birds and animals of the forest, and the men as well. The old man finds blood traces of a wounded tiger in the forest. He knows that a wounded tiger can be dangerous to humans. That night a man is killed by a tiger. There is a meeting of the village and it is planned to hunt the tiger. The old man, early in the morning, races to the forest, squats down before some twigs, lights them. There is a forest fire. It chases away the animals including the tiger to another forest where the animals might be safe. The old man comments: 'The world is large. There is room in it for everyone.'

Episode four

The narrator is external to the entire episode. It begins with the presence of a terrible heat and its effect on animals and people. A man and his monkey are walking through the parched land. There are vultures circling overhead. The 'couple', man and monkey, are travelling fairground performers. The man collapses from the heat and dies. The distraught monkey buries himself under the blouse of his dead master. The monkey is alone, frightened. He finally runs off. The vultures circle the dead man. The monkey arrives in a village where there is a circus.

There is a scene of a bullock and cart race. The monkey does his accustomed act and begs for money. The narrator points out that the monkey has no use for money. The monkey seeks to make contact with wild monkeys but they reject him. They smell the scent of the human in him. He is equally rejected by the world of men. He goes to a temple and lies there at dusk, alone and separate. The narrator indicates that he has been adopted by a circus person. He will once again become a performing monkey. We see a trapeze performance of a monkey in a tent. When the performance is over the audience exits.

The episode is reminiscent of *Stromboli, terra di Dio* (1949).

Close

The audience, which exits from the theatre, merges with the crowds in Bombay with which the film began. With that same crowd the film ends.

'I begin with the documentary, because it is from that reality that I proceed, in order to penetrate into the interior of things.'[3]

The co-presence of documentary and fictional elements is a commonplace in the cinema. Indeed, it is a central aspect of most films due to the photographic realistic nature of film. No matter how fictionalised or fantastic a film may be, it is composed of real elements photographically reproduced and projected. What you see, or at least what you saw until the recent manufacture of virtualised images, is what had been there at the moment it was photographed. The fictional, narrative cinema has exploited the realism of the photographic image, and beyond it, the realism of documentary material, to enhance a reality effect in fiction. The verisimilitude of the fiction is made more convincing by the truthfulness and real presence of the document.

In the 1950s, at the time that Rossellini made his cycle of Bergman films and *India*, the 'documentary', as a film genre, increasingly strove for a realism in which fictional and subjective impulses, including the tendency to transform the real into poetry and the beautiful, were, among some film-makers, resisted and opposed, in order to create a documentary of cinema truth which would be as objective and unmanipulated as possible, that is, as close as one could get to reality, a *cinéma vérité*. This did not exactly nor always mean that the ideal was one of complete transparency between film and the real. Many of these documentary films had a narrative core. The narrative, however, arose from out of a documentary reality rather than the story simply being made up from real elements. Some of the procedures of *cinéma verité*, particularly in the work of Jean Rouch, played with, and were aware of, the role of filming and the presence of the film-maker in provoking stories and performances, making things happen and causing the people in the films to 'act' as the one means to find their authentic truth.

Cinéma verité exemplified a consciousness, or perhaps better, a vigilance, regarding the instability of the truth and the objectivity of documentary film images. It sought to guard against this truth of things being compromised. It either stripped the image, and through it, the documentary film, of tendencies to stray outside the real towards fiction, story and aestheticisation, or it acknowledged, as Rouch did, a fictional impulse in all film-making, a fictional inevitability, which Rouch incorporated among the 'real' elements of his films and often as their essential truths. For example, in his *Jaguar* (1954–67) and *Moi, un noir* (1958), reality consists in part of the act of fabulation by the character-actors and their enactment of the story they tell. This approach is evident also in the film Rouch made with Edgar Morin, *Chronique d'un été* (1961). Chris Marker and Godard, in different ways, would play with similar ideas.

While some documentary film-makers sought a *cinéma vérité* by limiting fictionalisation, some fictional film-makers, in the mainstream of the cinema, sought a *vérité* and realism in their films by the addition to them of documentary material and the integration of documentary material into fictional structures. This had always been true of film, but in the 1940s, with *film noir*, with war films, and to some extent with the western in the 1950s, atmosphere, setting, real locations, were no longer simply background and context for the fiction, but protagonists within it: the city, the rain, shabbiness, empty streets, night, dusk or dawn, the grit and mud of the trenches, the openness and barrenness of the landscape of the West.

The most distinctive feature of the development in Italian cinema of the 1940s and 1950s usually referred to as neo-realism (if we exclude from it, for the moment, the films of Rossellini) was the combination of fiction and documentary, of the invented and the real. The approach to reality in neo-realist cinema and its almost direct incorporation in neo-realist films was stimulated by the conditions of war and a social commitment and populism, which characterised the Italian Resistance and the culture of the immediate postwar period, particularly that of the Italian left. The actuality of the postwar situation, of poverty, unemployment, exploitation and the sight of the presumed 'real' Italy on the screen, as opposed to the idealised Italy presented in the films of the 1930s during Fascism, was the material from which the dramas and spectacles of neo-realist films were composed.

Consider Vittorio De Sica. *Ladri di biciclette* (*Bicycle Thieves*) (1948) is structured by an alternation between hope and despair, which are connected to the possession or loss of a bicycle. In turn, the bicycle becomes a sign of an entire social, historical situation. As the film plays with, and escalates, the drama of the bicycle and the significance of its loss and recovery, it traverses Rome and a series of 'real' social situations and locations: political clubs, the markets, the streets of the city, a restaurant, a charitable shelter, the employment office. The film simultaneously, in these places and by these incidents, dramatises and personalises a social reality and lends to the personal drama, that is, to the fiction, a heightened effect of the real.

Thus, though fiction and documentary may be appropriate terms for describing the elements of this and other neo-realist films, it is the levelling of both, and the inclusion of each within the other, that was most important to neo-realism and most characteristic of it. The formula was that of social reality plus fiction. Just as hope and despair alternate in *Bicycle Thieves*, the film alternates between the real and the fictional, heightening the fictional drama by its documentary social–realist setting while giving the setting the real emotions of fiction. Each intensifies the charge of the other and the believability of the other. Together they lead to the ecstasy of the finale where reality teaches a lesson to the boy and to his father and where they fill reality with heart-rending sentiment. The film closes down, perfectly unified.

De Sica might have secured Hollywood backing for *Bicycle Thieves* had he been willing to accept a Hollywood star in the lead. Cary Grant was suggested, but De Sica rejected the idea. The presence of Cary Grant in his film would have destroyed, he believed (and he was right), its realistic coherence. Some Italian neo-realist directors, like Pietro Germi and Giuseppe De Santis, had less trouble with the presence of 'stars' in their socially realistic films because they felt they could mix the unreality of stardom and the reality of social issues successfully to the benefit of both. The star was brought into the universe of the real and the real in turn profited from the spectacle and appeal of the star. Commercial motives and aesthetic ones were in accord. This is true, for example, of De Santis's *Riso amaro* (*Bitter Rice*) 1949. The aims of De Santis and De Sica were similar, even if their means differed. Both wanted to create a dramatic spectacle where the real and the fictional would be, if not seamlessly joined, certainly complementary.

Leaving to one side the content of social realism and the politics of postwar commitment exemplified in Italian neo-realist films, the treatment of different levels of reality in Italian neo-realism was relatively conventional and familiar. That is to say, what mattered was not 'reality', but an undisturbed appearance of reality, a scenic realism where the levels of reality were integrated and combined to give an illusory effect of the real: in short, verisimilitude as homogeneity. One might say, with regard to *Ladri di bici-clette*, that the social reality presented by the film was disturbing (poverty and its fictional dramatisation as desperation), but it is not possible to say that 'reality' was a disturbance in the film since reality had been smoothed over and integrated into the fiction. The classical film, for example, the Hollywood film, particularly of the 1940s, had already moved in the direction of making the reality of its fictions more acute by the admixture of elements of social and physical reality. You could find comfort in these films. They touched your social conscience without disturbing your sense of reality. The poverty or social distress you saw was presented within traditional forms and familiar perspectives of seeing.

It seemed, certainly with *Rome Open City* (1945) and *Paisà* (1946), at first sight at least, that Rossellini belonged to this same Italian school of realism. These early post-war films were immensely appreciated, not only in Italy but all over the world. Ingrid Bergman, on seeing *Rome Open City*, wrote a letter to 'Mr Rossellini' saying how wonderful she found the film and offering to work for him – see Chapter 5 in this volume, p. 65. They became lovers and married. Bergman became Rossellini's principal 'star' in six of his films between 1949 and 1954 (he made nine films in all during the period), after which the marriage disintegrated. In 1956, Bergman returned to Hollywood to work, making *Anastasia* (1956) under the direction of Anatole Litvak. Rossellini found this intolerable ('The idea of becoming the husband of a star, I absolutely cannot swallow … I am leaving for India … You, you can do what you want').[4]

Bergman was constructed by Rossellini in his films as an unsympathetic and disturbing presence. The films concentrated on her out-of-placeness as a character, as a woman, and as a Hollywood actress. (In addition to male pride and self-assertion, Rossellini's refusal to accept Bergman's return to Hollywood had an aesthetic dimension.) In Rossellini's 'realism', the relation between documentary reality and fiction, rather than being complementary, as it was in neo-realist films, appeared as irreconcilable. This was a new consciousness in cinema. The fiction, in the Bergman films, is essentially centred on 'the couple'. Reality is outside the couple. Rather than these terms (or locations), and their differences, becoming integrated, reality provokes a scandal, a crisis in the couple. The couple is forced to face reality and the difference it represents, including the reality of their relation and the illusions which constitute it. This is *the* theme of the three principal Bergman films: *Stromboli, Europe '51*(1952) and *Journey to Italy*. Reality, rather than being a dramatic support easily blended into the fiction, became uncomfortable and troubling, like an alien presence. This represented a radical difference, even though this notion of reality needs to be pluralised, as we shall see. It shattered the conventions of a scenic realism which had characterised the films of neo-realism and indeed of films more generally of a classical tradition *to which the films of neo-realism essentially belonged*. In *Stromboli*, for example, the island is not a backdrop to Bergman's personal drama, but a physical presence that constitutes her drama. The same is true for the presence of Naples for the Bergman–Sanders couple in *Journey to Italy*.

At this point, and correctly I think, Italian critics, especially on the left, condemned Rossellini for what they felt was his betrayal of neo-realist principles, the most important of which to them was an evident (and conventionalised) social commitment. Rossellini never had such principles. Or, at least, he never had them as the critics defined them. Italian critics thought neo-realism had been 'betrayed' by Rossellini and Antonioni, the two most modern and innovative Italian postwar film directors. Their betrayal – the accusation was essentially political and thereby ethical – was in fact the positive sign of their modernity. What they betrayed were conventions of conformity dressed up as social protest. French critics, on the other hand, particularly André Bazin and those with him on *Cahiers du Cinéma*, like Eric Rohmer, Jacques Rivette, Godard and Fereydoun Hoveyda (who worked with Rossellini on *India*), recognised the Bergman films for their modernity and radical newness. These critics were responsive to, and supportive of, a new cinema. They would become the film-makers of the new wave, within which Rossellini was a crucial and frequent point of reference. Italian critics, with few exceptions, were still too attached to the provincialism and conservatism of the social realism of neo-realist cinema, and to the Resistance political culture of social commitment which had given rise to it, to be able to appreciate fully the importance of Rossellini's films.

India is composed of a collage of heterogeneous elements which do not cohere. Their non-coherence governs the structure of the episodes and the relations between them. The heterogeneity and irreconcilability are also the theme and drama of the film, as if the form of the film is what primarily is being staged. I want to indicate some instances of this heterogeneity. My immediate purpose in doing so is to suggest the absence of a scenic realism in the film and the presence instead of a pluralised reality. Because there is a plurality of realities in the film, and because these do not cohere, the presence of each as different from any other gives to each an unaccustomed force and clarity. It is as if in order to make one aware of reality – and this is, I think, the Rossellinian lesson – you need to unveil it and uncover the illusions which mask it, the primary one of which is the convention of homogeneity which obtains in scenic verisimilitude and which was

India (1957–9).

the rule in the socially directed films of Italian neo-realism. That is, reality is a matter of approach, a way of filming, of structuring, narratively and visually. Whatever Rossellini may have said about 'reality', what he spoke about were the cinematic images of reality. What he recognised, and what neo-realism evaded, was the problematic relation between reality and the presentation of it. It is when reality seems strange that it is most true and that you can begin to see it.

Each of the episodes in *India* is marked by a separation. In the first, the male and female of the elephant couple must separate after the cow becomes pregnant and the elephant handler and his wife also separate when she becomes pregnant. In the second, the couple from the Hirakud Dam worksite must leave the dam, which had been their home and the place of their unity. In the third, the old man is forced to chase away the animals, and especially the tigers he loves, when he feels them threatened by the disruption of the new reality posed by the mineral prospectors. Finally, in the last episode, the monkey is set adrift in a hostile world by the death of his master. In each episode, reality is not a thing or essence to be defined, but a relationship of levels, and of different types of reality, which come into conflict or open out into each other. These levels are not reducible to the clichés of fiction and documentary, nor are they reducible to each other. It is the separation, the difference that is disrupting, even scandalous and thereby becomes revealing. Men and animals are compared in different ways in the episodes. Their similarities are made to point to their differences and within those differences, the further difference of men to women is made evident in the couple (elephant or human, animal and human). Other film-makers proceeded by erasing lines; Rossellini worked to re-establish them.

Whatever is taken for granted, and thus not usually seen, becomes in his films visible by a confrontation of differences which cannot be avoided. Not only are the old man's harmony and contemplative life placed at risk by the arrival of the alien prospectors; as a consequence, also, he must act to drive away the animals and the forest he is close to, in fact, all that is central to his existence, to his happiness, to what he treasures, and even more, assumes. Similarly, the structure of the relation of the couple in the Hirakud Dam episode (as in *Journey to Italy*) is revealed when the context in which the couple has lived is taken from them and they must leave Hirakud (in *Journey to Italy* the couple arrives in Naples after having left their familiar 'north', a change which initiates a disturbance). The couple is thrown back on itself, forced to rethink, even to think for the first time, where they are, who they are, the nature of their relationship. The monkey must do the same when he is stripped of supports, and the old man must do the same when his home and security are threatened.

Schematically, the couple can be thought of as the fictional centre of the episodes, at least the most contrived element of them, whereas the landscape, the animals, the dam, belong to the document and to reality. Insofar as this is true, Rossellini makes the documentary aspect of the film not the background to the fiction, but the primary element of it which the fictional couple must face, that is, the documentary is included in the fiction, becomes part of it, but as a difference (as in the dam episode, and in the episode with the old man and the tiger, and the final episode involving the monkey) which cannot be reconciled. It is this difference, and the force of it, that is opened up by 'reality'.

The cinema, for Rossellini, is an instrument for creating a confrontation with reality and then observing, as you might through a microscope, the consequences of that con-

frontation. Rossellini's reality has the effect of stripping away supports, comforts, ratio-
nalisations. It acts on the couple, or on individuals, to force them to see that reality and
thereby themselves, and their condition. In this way, and by these means, the couple
enters the real, or is opened, like a wound is opened, to the force of the real. The fiction,
which belongs to the couple, or to the character, is opened to history, to the document,
that which needs unavoidably to be faced and which cannot be reconciled or ignored.
It is difficult to define reality in Rossellini's films except as this relation of discomfort,
separation, awareness, and scandal (*Europe '51*).

Rossellinian cinema is not, strictly speaking, representational in its ends, that is, it is
not concerned to create a world, certainly not a consistent one, but rather to use the
mechanisms of cinema as a provocative, investigative tool, to make reality appear as it
does appear to the characters in his films, suddenly and without warning, and which
turns their lives around, by turning their consciousness around. It is a reality obdurately,
concretely 'present', almost like an obstacle to what is accustomed and unrecognised.
This turning of consciousness before the presence of the real is a direct consequence of
the plurality and heterogeneity of reality in Rossellini's films. His cinema does not bring
a message, does not state this or that, still less constructs a lifelike world, but rather shows
a way of thinking, a structure of cognition and consciousness and a way toward understanding. This path is not exactly intellectual nor reducible or transferable to anything
else but the cinema in which it is realised. Rossellini spoke of the 'idea', but the idea as
concrete images, not as illustration.

Rossellinian reality is phenomenological (and Catholic) in the sense it was for Bazin
and for many of those of the new wave. It allowed Bazin to be sensitive to the mechanisms of the cinema in his criticism and enabled the directors of the new wave to be
sensitive to the possibilities of cinema. Rossellinian cinema is intent on showing things
as they are ('Things are there … why manipulate them?'),[5] not as a matter of transparency, but as a matter of stripping from things what prevents us from seeing them,
laying them bare. The uniform, homogeneous scenic reality that dominated the cinema
and to which Rossellini objected in practice and which Bazin opposed in theory was not
a way to see, but a substitution of illusions for sight, that is a masking of sight. It was
precisely Rossellini's almost uncinematic, certainly humanist, and often naïve search for
reality, which he equated with truth, that resulted in a cinema that dismantled many of
the procedures that had constituted the existing cinema.

To 'show' – the aim of his cinema – was, for him, not to explain. To 'show' was not to
create false relations (illusions). To 'show' was to set the conditions in which true
relations might appear (suddenly, without warning). To 'show' was to make films in the
name of a reality which was not interpretative, which did not reach conclusions, which
did not align, which did not signify, which was seemingly, impossibly, reality 'before'
meaning and 'before' interpretation and thus before the verbal, or at least reality not
illustrative of the verbal; in short, a cinema which did not 'demonstrate'. Reality could
only be found in the cinema, in the medium of photographic duplication which would
'show'. Rossellini's reality was divorced from the explication of a verbal or written text
(the script), from prior meanings, from imposed narratives, and made instead a tool for
investigating and revealing the real as the not-yet-signified, therefore of reality as still
open, still true, as yet free from illusions, including ideology. The effort to keep reality
and its images so open in the face of traditions to close it down was considerable.

'In his article on *Voyage to Italy* Rivette compared me to Matisse. It struck me and made me aware of this spareness. A spareness that represents a new effort for me, but when I manage to achieve it my satisfaction is boundless.'[6]

The two films usually considered to be the founding films of Italian neo-realism are Rossellini's *Rome Open City* and Luchino Visconti's *Ossessione* (1943). It is evident, when you see the films, that, aesthetically speaking, they share almost nothing in common. The *osteria* (inn) in which much of the action and passion of *Ossessione* takes place is carefully wrought by Visconti in three ways. First, as a *mise-en-scène* it is inclusive of precise and abundant realistic details. It has everything an *osteria* should have in the Po valley and even more than it should have. No detail of its authenticity is left out. There are no loose ends, there is no out-of-placeness, no openings, either in the location and accumulation of objects or in the movements and gestures of characters in the *osteria*, including in its kitchen and in its bedrooms. Second, Visconti's camera is careful to record this space and its objects with the same precision with which he created that space before filming and to similar ends of authenticity. The strategies are overwhelmingly 'realistic'. Third, just as the setting is intent on connecting everything and just as that everything is abundant (overwhelming even), and just as the filming demonstrates these connections and underlines them in the overall structure of *Ossessione*, the *osteria* functions as a connective place of return, of integration, a sticky narrative glue where all dramatic movement and all else in the film, all of its scenes and the emotions they evoke, and to extravagance, come together, cohere. This way of filming is interpretative, closed, complete. The details and the precision constitute a consistent whole. There may be a plurality of objects and things, but they belong within a singular, gathered reality. (In Rossellini's films, objects are few, even minimal, but they rub against the grains and textures of each other.) In *Ossessione*, accumulation, as in a collection, is made possible by the likenesses and shared reality of all things. Visconti's emphasis is on filling in, filling up, on accretions, aggregation, additions, not, as with Rossellini, on subtraction, the ellipse, the sketch, spareness, to the point of abstraction. 'A film is always a sketch.'[7]

In *Rome Open City*, perhaps the most dramatic and certainly one of the lengthier sequences of the film is the torture and death of Manfredi. It involves three main spaces: the torture chamber, the office of Gestapo chief Bergmann, and the recreation room of the SS officers, directly opposite the room in which Manfredi is being tortured. The décor of these three spaces is minimal, certainly sketchy, summary, even careless. Rossellini provides only enough décor to give you the 'idea' of what these spaces constitute rather than actually constituting them in a coherent and consistent realistic manner, in the sense of completeness and detail, of being lifelike. Rossellini's reality does not belong to verisimilitude, is more often not lifelike. It is 'unreal', like a sketch might be, or sits uneasily beside the lifelike, making it strange, as in *Paisà*. 'I know what it is I want and I find the most direct means to achieve it. That's it, I don't worry myself too much over it.'[8] What we are given is an elliptical setting, a visual ellipse. It abstracts the idea without the detail or specifics of a lifelike reality. These rooms are the reverse of the scenically realistic, certainly the reverse of everything Visconti did. The camera, which with Visconti lingers over the surfaces he has so carefully filled, in *Rome Open City*, only stays long enough in any space or with any action to render what is happening, *and no more*, and then it moves on. The sense of Rossellini's filming is one of constant speed, almost headlong but without a predestined end.

The Rossellinian camera then moves to film another instance in a similar manner. It is not a question of editing or not, of a sequence shot or not, but simply of establishing an action, just as the décor of a room establishes that it is the room of the Gestapo chief or a room designed for torture. Whatever manner suits Rossellini best to realise this 'idea' is the one he chooses. The manner of his filming lies in this concision and clarity, not in the particular use of this or that technique which some writers have falsely attributed to him, for example, the use of the sequence-shot to keep reality 'whole'. The relation between the spaces which make up the sequence are relations of separateness and irreconcilability, and also of incomprehension, that is, what Rossellini stages in the sequence are different realities which confront each other as different ideas and it is this confrontation that reveals the differences. What needs to be stressed is that each space, by elliptical means, has been brought to a level of abstraction and idea so that the confrontation of realities effectively is a confrontation of these ideas and the display of ideas as something which is not explained but rather shown, and principally by stripping down each reality to its core or essence, that is, by abstracting it. Abstraction renders the clarity of the Rossellinian image. The image is clear because it has been minimalised, sharp because it is not interpreted. It is as if it is no more than what it is. This is not realistic transparency, realism in an ordinary sense, but an uncovering and dissolution of reality to an unheard of, and as yet unseen, level of abstraction in the cinema and confronts us with the presence of emptiness.

Bazin remarked, when first writing about Rossellini, that the logic of a Rossellini narrative is retrospective, not prospective. You cannot see, and the characters cannot see, and to an extent Rossellini cannot see, where an action or actions will lead, what their consequences might be, when and how the consequences will be manifest. It is only after they occur that you can see how they occurred in the way they did, but nothing 'before' leads you to this 'after'. Jean Narboni wrote of 'pas de trace' ('no trace', or 'without trace') of the 'trace de pas' ('footstep') in *Germany Year Zero* (1947), which might be considered the paradigm film of this procedure.[9] Narboni, beautifully, and with great concision, points out that Edmund's flight forward to what will be his suicide in *Germany Year Zero* is not a logically cumulative sequence of steps, each leading to the other, but rather a movement in which each step erases the one that preceded it, not as a displacement of causes and consequences, but rather as the removal and effacement of causes and consequences. That is why Edmund's leap to his death occurs so suddenly for us and for Edmund, as if it is only when, at the precise moment of the discovery of a truth, which is not a process of logic, or not exactly that, but an experience as an experience of the working inside one of reality, that the logic of an action and the necessity of that action appears in all its simplicity and becomes evident, and only then, and only at that moment, does one leap, 'pas de trace', which reveals a logic, not as illustration but as an action of comprehension which has to be seen to be believed. Literally, Edmund meets his death as the experience of an idea, as an act of consciousness *which we see* in action. No writing, no ordinary discursive logic can lead you to this place.

Each episode of *India* is structurally similar. The lighting of the forest fire by the old man in the third episode and more especially, of the return of the monkey to his 'profession' as fairground performer in the fourth, are instances of the elliptical procedures of Rossellini, temporally, in the organisation of the sequence of narrative events and, visually, in the images of events which constitute the sequence. As with *Rome Open City*, there is a variety of locations, each of which is summarily drawn or sketched. In the fourth episode, there is, in quick succession, the space of the wild monkeys, the human spaces, and then the space of the temple where the monkey is alone and separated. In the third episode, there is the village and the prospecting team, the old man lighting his fire, and the space of the animals and of the tiger. To go to the essence of things, for Rossellini, which also, abstractly, is the idea of them, is to remove from things all that is not pertinent to them. One reason for doing this is to be able to resist an interpretation, to halt interpretation. For Rossellini, interpretation is not reality but what we add to it and what must be removed before we can see it again.

In what sense can one say that the scene of the desolation of the monkey or, similarly, of the desolation of the old man is not interpreted by the film, not provided with a sense? Certainly, there is a view in place. Even if Rossellini believes that this view is what is there in reality, not one that he has provided or imposed, his words seem hardly credible. What Rossellini does in these sequences, and by a double movement, is to take from the old man, and from the monkey, all that supports them in their existences and all that they rely on for what they are and who they are. It is a double movement, because it occurs narratively in the dissolution of ties and of identities for the characters, and it occurs visually because it is the state of that dissolution, and only that state, that is displayed, as if there is no reason for further details or elaboration. Stripped bare, in both senses, in the fictive space in which the monkey and old man are caught and where their own fictions are faced with a reality they had not expected, nor could calculate, and, in the filmic space in which the images of them are reduced to this separation and desperate isolation, Rossellini wants to know what will happen, what will be the consequences of this double meeting with 'reality', what will occur, and in what manner it will occur as they face the void.

Reality for Rossellini is what is left when all that is superimposed upon it, all that is irrelevant but has accrued to it, is taken away, a removal then of traces, 'pas de trace', of steps, literally a laying bare, and this laying bare *is* reality. When the moment of reality comes, which can never be known in advance, when Edmund leaps, when the old man lights the match, it is a moment which must be waited for and experienced, including the experience of waiting. It requires our attention and our vigilance. When reality appears, it allows us to see the film not as its representation but as the instrument to make reality appear and to display the act and moment of its appearance, almost as a miracle, which is the sense of Rossellini's remark 'things as they are', 'things in their reality',[10] and which becomes in his films, something that no one has ever seen before until that revelation of it. In that sense, that revelatory sense, Rossellini believed his films were the instruments for revealing reality as it is. And what is reality as it is? It is the difference to what one supposes it is, it is the scandal of reality. It is decentred, blank. It gives no comfort.

For Godard, *India* 'is the creation of the world'.[11]

Notes

1 Roberto Rossellini, *Fragments d'une autobiographie* (Paris: Ramsay, 1987), p. 19.

2 Ibid., p. 164.

3 Fereydoun Hoveyda and Jacques Rivette, 'Entretien avec Roberto Rossellini', *Cahiers du Cinéma*, no. 94, April 1959, pp. 2–3; translation in Roberto Rossellini, *My Method: Writings and Interviews*, (ed.) Adriano Aprà, translated by Annapaola Cancogni (New York: Marsilio, 1992), p. 101.

4 Rossellini, *Fragments*, p. 154.

5 Hoveyda and Rivette, 'Entretien', p. 6 ('Les choses sont là – et surtout dans ce film [*India*]. Pourquoi les manipuler?'); this translation is an abridged version of the interview in Jim Hillier (ed.), *Cahiers du Cinéma*, vol. 1, *The 1950s: Neo-Realism, Hollywood, New Wave* (London: Routledge & Kegan Paul, 1985), p. 212; an alternative translation is in Rossellini, *My Method*, p. 106.

6 Hoveyda and Rivette, 'Entretien', p. 6; *My Method*, pp. 105–6

7 'Who Were You?' An Interview with Dacia Maraini', in *My Method*, p. 7.

8 Hoveyda and Rivette, 'Entretien', p. 7; *My Method*, p. 107.

9 Jean Narboni, '*Allemagne Année Zero*', in *Cahiers du Cinéma*, nos. 290–2, July–August 1978, p. 47.

10 'Who Were You?', p. 14; Hoveyda and Rivette, 'Entretien', pp. 3–4.

11 Jean Luc-Godard, '*India*', *Cahiers du Cinéma*, no. 96, June 1959, p. 41.

9
Rossellini's Historical Encyclopedia

Adriano Aprà

The adventure of educational film[1]

In terms of running time, half of Rossellini's work – a bit more or a bit less, depending on the criteria one uses to subdivide it – is historical. The majority of this historical work was produced for television between 1963 and 1974, from *The Iron Age* (*L'età del ferro*) to *Cartesius* (*Descartes*). This was an extremely active period for Rossellini. As well as making these films, he developed a number of projects, many of which survive as scripts, and he wrote numerous essays and books, some of which remain unpublished. Yet this phase of his activity has been relatively neglected, even more so in Italy than abroad, for various reasons: copies of the films are hard to find, many film scholars remain biased against television, and, above all, the evident switch of stylistic register has disconcerted them. The only exception has been the one television film to have also had a theatrical release, *La Prise de pouvoir par Louis XIV* ('The Taking of Power by Louis XIV') (1966).[2]

Rossellini gave many reasons for his break with the cinema, and with his own cinema. In the title card which opens 'Illibatezza' ('Chastity'), his episode in *RoGoPaG* (1962), he quotes the Austrian psychoanalyst Alfred Adler:

> Man today is often oppressed by an indefinable anguish. And amidst his daily travail, the unconscious proposes a refuge to him where he can be protected and nourished: the maternal womb. For the man of today, henceforth deprived of himself, even love becomes the whimpering search for the protecting womb.

When one sees the film, one realises that the protecting maternal womb is the cinematic apparatus, with all its emotive and illusory power, its processes of identification and projection, its 'allusive' language.

The trip to India, from December 1956 to September 1957, was without doubt a turning point for Rossellini in his search for a different kind of cinema. The last film he completed before leaving, *Fear* (*Angst/La paura*) (1954), may be considered the furthest point of a search in an opposite direction, the one on which 'Illibatezza' had reflected critically: a cinema of 'illusion' and 'allusion', in which the theme of the couple is transposed from the essay style of *Journey to Italy* to a style reminiscent of Lang or Hitchcock. In India, Rossellini made two complementary works: an ethnographic feature film, *India Matri Bhumi* (*India Mother Land*) (1959), part-documentary, part-fiction, in four episodes, shot on 35 mm in colour, and a television series in ten parts of approximately thirty minutes each, broadcast in France as *J'ai fait un beau voyage* and in Italy as *L'India vista da Rossellini* (1959). The series was a visual travelogue, a film diary, with Rossellini's reflections and comments, to different interviewers in the two versions, over documentary images on 16 mm shot originally in colour, but broadcast, and unfortunately also conserved, in black and white.

In 1958, Rossellini planned to continue this type of documentary work with a film based on *The Geography of Hunger* by the Brazilian ethnographer Josué de Castro. In August, he went to Rio de Janeiro to try to make it but was unsuccessful. The idea, however, according to his son Renzo, formed the basis for a later project, *La straordinaria storia della nostra alimentazione* (*The Extraordinary History of Our Food*) (c. 1964), the script of which has been conserved. This project, in turn, would be carried over into the television series *Man's Struggle for Survival* (*La lotta dell'uomo per la sua sopravvivenza*) (1967–71).[3]

The encyclopedic historical project on which Rossellini's energies were concentrated in the 1960s and 1970s was thus preceded by a *geographical* project. In India, he had however already intuited the main nucleus of the historical project, as is shown in a fascinating letter which I published in the journal *Trafic* (no. 1, Winter 1991). In it, Rossellini starts with some reflections on Indian cooking, then embarks on a lengthy digression from ancient Rome to a comparison of southern and northern civilisations by type of clothing – he calls the former 'draped' (*drappeggiate*), the latter 'stitched' (*cucite*) – before returning to the present. We can see here in embryo his subsequent films: a re-examination of the past through elements of its everyday life (cooking, clothing) in order to draw lessons for the present. From 1959 to 1961 he made four films about Italian history, recent (*General Della Rovere*, 1959; *Era notte a Roma*, 1960) and not so recent (*Viva l'Italia*, 1960; *Vanina Vanini*, 1961), which may be taken as rehearsals for his definitive move to an educational type of historical cinema and to the techniques (zoom and trick shots) he required to achieve it. In these films, we find elements of his earlier cinema (carried to novelistic extremes in *Vanina Vanini*) and anticipations of his imminent project (in *Viva l'Italia*).

Ideas for a new cinema

Alongside these films and film projects, Rossellini produced, from the early 1960s until his death in 1977, a series of essays and books in which, with unusual insistence, he made explicit the main outlines of his historical project (although, as was his way, he was extremely sparing even in interviews in his remarks about his individual films).[4] What follows is a necessarily schematic synthesis of his arguments.

History, for Rossellini (as for Vico and Croce before him), is the teacher of life. 'We are, in all ways, the product of our history. To be conscious of what we have become we need to know our history in its *architecture*: not as a series of dates, names, alliances, treaties, betrayals, wars, conquests, but following *the thread of the transformations of thought*.'[5] 'We must use history not to celebrate the past but to judge ourselves and guide ourselves better towards the future.' [6]

What have we become? What awaits us in the future? Rossellini's diagnosis is implacable: 'Our civilisation is plunging into an abyss, as did that of ancient Rome and other great civilisations.'[7] Human beings, he argues, faced with the epochal challenge of the extraordinary evolution of the last centuries – from scientific to electronic civilisation, the highest stage of the industrial revolution – need increasingly to use their own intelligence (the faculty they obtain from the cerebral cortex) to understand what is happening and orientate themselves. However – and this is the reason for the present crisis – humans, overwhelmed by fear, draw back from the responsibilities they have as thinking, rational creatures and retreat to the sub-cortex of the brain – its original, instinctive, animal part.

The regression of humans to an animal state, in the sense of a triumph of propaganda and persuasion over knowledge, of rhetoric over dialogue, of entertainment and seduction over reasoning, is manifested not only in human behaviour but also in artistic expression and in the means of communication in general. Art, which comes to interest Rossellini ever less, and the media of communication, which interest him more and more, have become the main channels by which our civilisation is infected and through which the pathology of our behaviour is celebrated. And yet:

> the powerful voices of radio, television, cinema and the press should, according to my dream, become the means through which one should disseminate not only recreation but also knowledge, and, through the invention of new formulas, they should be used to reestablish a dialogue of each with all. If we were able to attain this goal it would be intoxicating to take part in this vast dialogue.[8]

Through television, Rossellini believes he can achieve this 'intoxicating adventure of thinking' and establish a dialogic relationship between people, because television is an art in its infancy, not conditioned, like cinema, by a codified language and a mass public but directed at millions of viewers who are millions of individuals. The television he has in mind is educational. 'The principal aim of teaching and education has always (or nearly always) been to maintain the status quo', as he put it in *Un Esprit libre ne doit rien apprendre en esclave* (*A Free Mind Must Learn Nothing as a Slave*) (1977). This system prevents each individual from developing his or her potential. 'In order to save ourselves, to enable us to get back our ability to reason and improve ourselves, we must invent a new system of education: free, simple, pleasurable, integral', to which we can devote an ever-increasing portion of our free time. This new system must be permanent, in other words not restricted to the period of full-time education, it must be made available to all, adults as well as children, and it must be able to draw together and synthesise the sum of knowledge accumulated over the centuries. Rossellini's model here was the great seventeenth-century educationalist Comenius (Jan Ámos Komenský) with his concept of pansophy: a science which could draw together all the sciences in order to teach everything to everyone. But it was not just a matter of finding a method through a new audiovisual language and producing works which could put it into practice; 'the problem facing us now is political, because it is a problem of how to develop and disseminate this integral means of education.'[9]

From Comenius, Rossellini took the concepts of 'direct sight' (or 'autopsy', which originally meant 'seeing with one's own eyes') and the 'essential image'. 'A large part of the difficulty of learning', wrote Comenius, as quoted by Rossellini, in the former's *Pansophiae Prodromus* (1637), 'comes from the fact that things are not taught to pupils by direct sight but by tedious descriptions, by which means it is very hard for the images of things to be imprinted on the understanding; they therefore inhere so weakly in the memory that they fade away easily or become confused with other things.'[10] The symbolic character of the word has engendered its power of demonstration, changed probabilities into certainties, magnified dissension and suspicion, leading us astray. Since our mental processes are, by habit, verbal ones, the images we produce end up becoming subordinate to words, mere illustrations. If only we could return to the image as it was before the development of verbal language it would acquire a very different value. An illustration *demonstrates* a thing, whereas 'direct sight' *shows* it. We must rediscover the ability to show, to state; we must rediscover the pure image:

> the essential, fundamental image, in which we can condense all necessary information. When we have attained it there will be no more need to proceed by argumentation; we shall proceed, rather, by indications, by essential and complete proofs of things as they are. When we have rediscovered the image we will be able to accumulate within it, contextually, a huge amount of information.[11]

The ultimate aim of this new educative process through the audiovisual media is to overcome the crisis that threatens us:

> When the created world and our lives are able to appear to us in a more correct perspective we will have taken a decisive step towards a greater equilibrium, towards harmony. To take part together in the adventure of knowledge will console us and give us courage. To be better orientated will give us tranquillity and calm. In this way we will lay the essential basis for a humanly constructive existence.[12]

Rossellini's project was avowedly Utopian. It started from a recognition, with which one can largely agree, of the crisis of our civilisation, which has lost its sense of fundamental human values in the name of a sullying commodification of everything and a blunting of reason, produced by those same mass media in which Rossellini, in the 1960s and 1970s, still saw a chance of salvation. Never, more than today, might his project appear more out of key with the present. But, never, more than today, does his courage in translating words into actions point a way forward, which it is worth taking seriously, to counteract the domination of a form of cinema and television which celebrate their unconditional surrender to commodification and defend destruction.

A chronology

It may be useful to begin by summarising Rossellini's historical films, using the chronological schema he himself drafted at various times as a framework but enlarging it to include not just his television films but also those he made before and after, and the main unfilmed projects with tentative dates.[13] In the timechart below I have separated, in the left-hand column, the various parts of *The Iron Age* and *Man's Struggle for Survival* (abbreviated hereafter to '*Struggle*'), which Rossellini himself described as the two 'backbones' of his project, and I have indicated in the second column the points where the other films slot chronologically into these (the unrealised projects are in square brackets). I have excluded the films set in the twentieth century, even though these themselves could also be seen in retrospect as another encyclopedic project, combining a historical perspective (on the Second World War, principally) with a geographical one (from Italy to the rest of Europe to India) and one on 'the emotions' and 'morality', of which a number of titles are emblematic: *Desiderio* (*Desire*), *L'Amore* (*Love*), 'Envy' ('L'invidia'), *Dov'è la libertà ...?* (*Where is Freedom ...?*), *Fear*, *Anima nera* (*Dark Soul*), 'Illibatezza' ('Chastity').

Timechart of Rossellini's historical encyclopedia

Relevant parts of *Iron Age* and *Struggle*	Other films/projects in relation to these		
Struggle (Part 1a)		c. 7000 BCE	Neolithic Period (Stone Age) Rise of matriarchy
Struggle (Pt 2)		c. 2600–2500	Egypt. Fourth Dynasty. Building of the pyramids
Struggle (Pt 1b)		c. 2100	Bronze Age. Arrival of Hellenes in the Mediterranean. Transition to a patriarchal society
Struggle (Pt 3a)		c. 1500–1300	Egypt. Dynasties of the Theban period
	The Messiah	1150–1050	Arrival of Samuel in the land of Canaan. Election of King Saul
	(Prologue)		
Iron Age (Pt 1a)		8th–7th cent.	The Etruscans
	Socrates	404–399	Athens: trial and death of Socrates
Struggle (Pt 3b)		c. 370	Greece. Hippocratic medicine
Iron Age (Pt 1b)		3rd cent. 202	Roman conquest of Etruria Scipio and the battle of Zama (from Carmine Gallone's *Scipione l'africano*, 1937)
Struggle (Pt 3c)		c. 20 BCE–14 CE	Augustan Rome. Persistence of ancient rites and myths
	The Messiah	1–33 CE	Birth and death of Jesus Christ
	[*Caligula*] (c. 1970)	31–41	Rome
Struggle (Pt 3d)		30–40	Jerusalem
	Acts of the Apostles (Pts 1–5)	31–60	Peter and Paul: Palestine, Syria, Pisidia (part of modern-day Turkey), Greece, Rome
	Augustine	395–413	Hippo, Calama and Carthage in Numidia (modern-day Algeria)

Relevant parts of *Iron Age* and *Struggle*	Other films/projects in relation to these		
Struggle (Pt 3e)		c. 410	Rome under the barbarian occupation
Struggle (Pt 4a)		c. 500	Subsequent barbarian invasions of Italy
		c. 529	Work of the Benedictine monks
		751	Paper invented by the Arabs
		c. 786	The Arab world in the period of Haroun al-Rashid
Struggle (Pt 5)		11th cent.	First Crusade (1096) Troubadour movement
Struggle (Pt 6)		11th–12th cent.	Use of water mills Third Crusade Founding of University of Bologna
	Francis God's Jester	1210–18	Saint Francis of Assisi, Italy (Umbria)
	[*Catherine of Siena*] (1960s)	14th cent.	
Iron Age (Pt 1c)		c. 1380	Invention of gunpowder
	Cosimo de'Medici (Pt 1)	1429–33	Cosimo I de' Medici (the Elder): Florence, London, Venice
	Giovanna d'Arco al rogo	1431	Rouen: trial and execution of Joan of Arc
	Cosimo de'Medici (Pt 2)	1434–5	Cosimo de' Medici and Leon Battista Alberti: Venice, Florence
	Cosimo de'Medici (Pt 3)	1435–71	Cosimo and Alberti: Florence, Rimini, Rome
Iron Age (Pt 1d)		1471	Alberti
Struggle (Pt 4b)		15th cent.	The monk Basilio Valentino experiments unsuccessfully with the powers of antimony[14]
Struggle (Pt 7)		15th cent.	Candlemaking Working of copper and iron
		1447	Paper manufacture in Mainz, Germany
		1455	Gutenberg
		1485–92	Christopher Columbus
Iron Age (Pt 2a)		16th cent.	Manufacture of arms and armour

Relevant parts of *Iron Age* and *Struggle*			Other films/projects in relation to these
			Meeting between mathematician Niccolò Tartaglia and the Duke of Urbino
		17th cent.	Rifles. Use of saltpetre for gunpowder
Struggle (Pt 8)		16th–17th cent.	Alchemists
			Medicine: Paracelsus (c. 1527) and Rabelais (c. 1534)
		c. 1609–10	Galileo
		c. 1651	Followers of William Harvey's new theories of anatomy
	[*Comenius*] (1970s)	17th cent.	
	Cartesius	1613–41	France, Netherlands
	Blaise Pascal	1639–62	Rouen, Paris
	[*Pulcinella*] (drafted c. 1962, reworked 1974)	1647–97	Michelangelo Fracanzani: Naples, Rome; journey from Rome to France; Lyons, Paris
	Louis XIV	1661–82	Paris, Versailles
Iron Age (Pt 2b)		1742	English clockmaker Benjamin Huntsman invents a new kind of steel
		18th cent.	Other uses of metal in medicine and war
Struggle (Pt 9a)		18th cent.	Developments in chemistry (Lavoisier) and electricity (Abbé Mollet's demonstrations in the Paris salons)
		1752	Benjamin Franklin's experiments
		1765	James Watt's experiments with steam engines
		1780	Luigi Galvani's experiments on frogs
	[*Diderot*] (c. 1972)	1751–2	*L'Encyclopédie*
	[*American Revolution*] (c. 1970)	1775–87	Thomas Jefferson and George Washington
Struggle (Pt 9b)		1800	Alessandro Volta demonstrates electricity

Relevant parts of *Iron Age* and *Struggle*	Other films/projects relation to these		
Iron Age (Pt 2c)		18th–19th cent.	Manufacture of swords
		1805	Battle of Austerlitz (from Abel Gance's *Austerlitz*, 1960)
	[*Niepce and Daguerre*] (c. 1972)	1822–39	Photography
	Vanina Vanini	1824	Rome and the Papal States
	[*Lavorare per l'umanità*] (1976)	1835–48	Karl Marx and Frederick Engels
Struggle (Pt 9c)		1829	George Stephenson's locomotive
		1845	First uses of the telegraph
		1857	Louis Pasteur's experiments
	Viva l'Italia	1860	Giuseppe Garibaldi and the exploit of the Thousand
Struggle (Pt 9d)		1895	Guglielmo Marconi's wireless telegraph
Iron Age (Pt 2d)		turn of the 20th cent.	Rapid progress of communications (archive film)

The third, fourth and fifth parts of *Iron Age* and the tenth, eleventh and twelfth parts of *Struggle* all cover the twentieth century (the eleventh also deals in part with nineteenth-century painting) and (apart from the fourth part of *Iron Age* and the start of the fifth, which tell the story of the efforts of a steelworker from the Ilva plant in Piombino, Tuscany, to save the machinery from requisition by the Germans and retrieve it after the war) they are all based on archive film.

Other projects for which script materials exist, and which may also be considered 'backbones' covering various historical periods, are *The Extraordinary History of Our Food* which was to be in two parts, respectively from prehistoric times to the nineteenth century and the present and future; *Islam* (c. 1973), from Mohammed (seventh century) to the present; *The Civilisation of the Conquistadores* (*La civiltà dei conquistadores*) (c. 1970), set in the Americas from 1498 to 1826; *The Industrial Revolution* (*La rivoluzione industriale*) (c. 1965), in three parts (12 hours), from the eighteenth century to 1859, 1860–1939, and 1940 to the present; *Science* (c. 1970; 10 hours), dealing mainly with the current state and future prospects of the various sciences. Several hours' worth of material, in the form of filmed locations, working notes and documentary footage, was filmed for *History of Our Food* and *Science*.

A new language

In abandoning, or indeed rejecting, fiction cinema – which he saw as still too bound both to the processes of fascination and illusion of the darkened screening room and to the dictates of producers – in favour of televisual and educational cinema, Rossellini embarked on a search not only for new types of content but also for new means of expression. He outlined these between 1957 and 1962 and then realised them in full in his television period.

In *Viva l'Italia* (1960), in other respects the most deliberately educational of the films of this intermediate period, one still finds the taste for the capturing of the live event, as in a war documentary, which makes it a sort of costume *Paisà*. From *The Iron Age* onwards, these residues of a realism of immediacy, which allow the spectator to empathise with the events narrated, disappear or at any rate appear only very sporadically. A realism of facts (a notion which has given rise to many misunderstandings, above all in Italy, in the 'neo-realist' interpretation of Rossellini) gives way to a realism of documents, in other words to an authenticity of the historical sources which Rossellini uses, or claims to use, in reconstructing events. The spectator no longer looks at a lifelike reality, as through a window on the world (assuming this was true of the earlier films) but, in a much more mediated way, at a cinema screen or television screen whose edges, as it were, are clearly visible and upon which images and sounds appear in all their artificiality, with their concreteness removed and their power of abstraction emphasised. What Godard said about *India* is even more true of the television films: 'L'image n'est que le complément de l'idée qui la provoque' ('The image is only the complement of the idea that provokes it').

Rossellini reached this point by stripping everything that was still typically cinematic out of his language. In entrusting the direction of *Iron Age* and *Struggle* to his son Renzo, he was not so much delegating creativity as renouncing all temptations of creativity, all claims to being artistic. His 'art' is that of a highly skilled craftsman, thoroughly familiar with the tools of his trade and able to use them in a way that is both economical (also in a financial sense) and effective. Those who have criticised the 'woodenness' of Rossellini's television films, and his earlier films, have not realised not only how considerable his technical knowledge was but also how he made a constant effort to save money, and thereby to resolve to his own advantage the contradiction of cinema as both a means of expression and an industrial medium. Reducing costs by a shrewd use of the technical means available meant gaining the opportunity to express himself freely. The fact that his encyclopedic historical project inevitably entailed higher costs than his earlier films (costumes, props, sets, but also longer running times than the standard ninety minutes) drove him to perfect or invent technical processes, most notably the zoom and optical tricks. But there were many other technical-economic devices which were at the same time an inseparable part of Rossellini's mode of expression, such as the use of sequence-shots, of little-known or non-professional actors who, if they were unable to memorise long stretches of dialogue could read them from prompters placed off camera, of filming no more than two or three takes of each shot, and the skilful transformation of real locations into credible historical settings.

'Show, don't demonstrate' ('Mostrare e non dimostrare') was the formula Rossellini frequently used to define what he sought to achieve with his educational cinema. To 'demonstrate' for him meant to give undue emphasis to one's intended meaning and thus to deceive the audience, to delude them with all the means the cinema had developed in the course of its history, which had now become the 'standard' language of the fiction film. Rossellini wanted to limit himself to 'showing' because he believed that only in this way could the image express the truth or, more precisely, the idea of the truth.

This conception of a 'showing' cinema has some interesting analogies with the theories developed by Noël Burch and others about early cinema. Perhaps because television was still a young medium (regular transmissions had begun in Italy in January 1954) Rossellini approached it as if it did not have the whole history of cinema behind it, still less a specific language of its own (such as the 'live broadcast'). By making his films for television, Rossellini felt he was addressing an audience whose gaze was not yet polluted by the 'aestheticisms' of cinema, or who at any rate looked at the television screen with a detachment which allowed them to accept naturally his quest for linguistic simplicity and essentialism, his 'primitivism'. Like early cinema, Rossellini's educational cinema rediscovered the values and strengths of a 'theatrical' conception of audiovisual language, a conception historically prior to cinema, or at any rate to what Burch called the institutional mode of representation. The rejection of forms of drama based on suspense, in the broad sense, the absence of action as such, the reduction to a minimum of cause-effect links between scenes in favour of a series of more or less self-standing, if not quite self-sufficient, 'tableaux', reinforces this impression of an 'expository', 'presentational', 'theatrical' cinema.

Acting

Various other elements contributed to this return to origins of Rossellini's language. I have already mentioned the use of prompt cards to help the actors (who in any case were always dubbed, except in *Louis XIV*). This is an expedient typical both of theatre (the prompter) and television (the newsreader's autocue), but in these cases one generally makes every effort to hide it. Rossellini uses it not only for practical reasons but also to prevent the actors from 'acting', from immersing themselves in a role, appearing natural and lifelike. Since they are often reading their lines off camera they cannot look each other in the eye and this contributes to that sense of almost puppet-like rigidity he imposes on them in front of the camera. In fact they do not act, they 'recite', they read, they talk like a book, they are not individualised voices but mouthpieces. They do not give us the illusion that they incarnate Louis XIV, Pascal or Descartes. Rather, they 'stand for' these characters, as if they were walking around with placards with their names written on them. They appear in order to convey information to the audience in unnatural monologues or in dialogues where the other speakers utter a few words at most, since the latters' real function is to stand in for the audience.

Another typically 'theatrical' device used by Rossellini is the 'aside' in which secondary characters introduce or comment on the main action, with a function similar to the voice-over in traditional television documentaries. Examples of this include the openings of *Acts of the Apostles* (an unusually long instance), *Augustine* (*Agostino d'Ippona*) and *The Age of Cosimo de' Medici* (*L'età di Cosimo de' Medici*). Whereas in the theatre the aside is addressed directly to the audience, in Rossellini's films the characters talk to one another, but the aim is clearly to provide the audience with succinct information. Their looks are looks to camera in disguise.

This disembodiment of the actors, this process of abstraction which relegates their function to that of 'showing', of being emotionless conveyors of information, is then perfected by dubbing, which detaches them from their own natural voices and completes their de-individualisation.

One sometimes notices (though much less often than Rossellini's rapid working methods would lead one to expect) 'mistakes' in the acting of those with walk-on parts and even in some leading players. As Rossellini put it in an interview of 1973:

> I never look at the daily rushes because I deny myself the need to be perfect, to iron out the rough spots. Imperfection and chance are a vital part of the fabric of history, and by neglecting them we increase our alienation, our inability to get *inside* things. This is also why I use nonprofessional actors. Most of them are too terrified to act when the camera is rolling, so they give me what I want: not the creation of a *role*, but the recreation of a historical character – with all the warts and weaknesses left in.[15]

The imperfection and chance he refers to here are those of the set, not of the reality being represented, as they are in *Paisà* or *Viva l'Italia* or in direct cinema. Ultimately, this too makes it impossible for the spectators to merge with the film. They can only 'see at a distance' (the etymological meaning of 'television') something which is plainly artificial, staged, 'false'.

Less justifiable are the moments (also rare) when one of the actors gives vent to an 'expressive' mode of acting. An example of this is Anne Caprile's performance, reminiscent of Anna Magnani, as Xanthippe in *Socrates*. One might say that her manner of acting here serves to contrast her with the sobriety of Socrates himself ('Xanthippe represents the devil', Rossellini said gnomically as early as 1952)[16] but it seems undeniable that it is in fact a throwback to the forms of aesthetic preciosity which Rossellini had by now put behind him. Much more interesting is the way he manages to repress to his own advantage the attempts at performance of certain actors, such as Ugo Cardea in the role of Descartes (somewhat similar to his handling of George Sanders in *Journey to Italy*).

All this might lead one to think that Rossellini was uninterested in acting, but this is

Descartes (Ugo Cardea, right) in *Cartesius* (1973). (Adriano Aprà Collection.)

not true. One need consider only his two explorations of the actor's true-false dilemma, 'Una voce umana' (1948) and *General Della Rovere* (1959), using those virtuoso actors Anna Magnani and Vittorio De Sica. What is true is that he was generally interested not in the performance of the actor but in the 'being in the world' of the human person and, by contrast, in the television films, in an opaque kind of acting, 'obtuse' as Barthes might say.

Mise-en-scène

Rossellini's 'educational' style of framing tends to be frontal, eye-level, showing the whole figure. Two-dimensional elements prevail over three-dimensional ones. Generally, one or two actors stand on the set as if they were facing an audience and the space behind them is like a backdrop. Here too one can see a connection with early cinema. Off-screen space is absent. The surface of the frame absorbs the camera's and the spectator's interest. Tricks of perspective and depth of field play a minimal part. One might say that Rossellini's model was medieval painting, not that of the Quattrocento inventors of perspective. The 'geometry' he is interested in is not that of the illusionistic technique of visual representation but the order to be imposed on the chaos of the representable world.

Camera movements are used to follow characters or, in some cases, to ensure the continuity of the sequence-shot. They are 'invisible', though sometimes refined, movements. The forward and backward tracking shots in the dinner scene in *Louis XIV* (filmed in any case by his son Renzo) are a rare exception, though here they help to underscore the ceremonial character of this film about the spectacle of power. The use of the zoom is different. As is well known, Rossellini invented a remote-control device which allowed him to move the zoom without looking through the camera (another demonstration of his command of cinematic techniques). In most cases he used the zoom, like the pan and the dolly, to follow moving actors or to adjust the field of the shot with minimal movements. He used it less frequently, but very expressively, to make forward or backward movements, as if the eye were singling out a portion of the shot, generally a close-up, or were absorbing that portion back into the initial long shot, because of a momentary arousal of interest. The effect of this is very different from a dolly in or out, both because the optical movement of the zoom maintains the tendential flatness of the image whereas a dolly generally heightens the sense of three-dimensionality, and because it appears to be almost a natural extension of the spectator's gaze.

The tendency to film sequence-shots, or at any rate to cut as little as possible within individual sequences, is a constant feature of Rossellini's work and it becomes systematic in his television films. The zoom, used a few times in *General Della Rovere* and then regularly from *Era notte a Roma* (1960), not only provided a way of making long shots technically easier but also represented a new way of looking. Previously the shot-reverse shot, particularly the alternation between subjective and objective shots, had marked an opposition, a conflict, a 'wounding' of the eye. Reality was a reality in action, it was captured in its unfolding and its totality, its duration, in expectation of an event which might transform it, or was cut up to insert points of conflict. In his television films, Rossellini is much more reconciled with what he sees, the eye of the zoom moves harmoniously around a place or penetrates with positive interest into an ideally unitary representation. The length of the shots is a means not of producing tension, still less of displaying technical bravura, but of transmitting a calm breathing. Everything has already taken place, we are watching a repeat performance, a repetition in which real time has been suspended. By limiting himself to 'showing', Rossellini is inviting us to adopt a gaze of detachment, contemplation, meditation.

The systematic use of the sequence-shot is not taken to obsessive extremes by Rossellini. There are various cuts within spatio-temporal continuity, motivated either by a change of setting, as when a character moves into another room, or by the need to insert a clarificatory detail. Although the reaction shots sometimes give the impression of being used to cover up an imperfection or to join two different takes of the same shot, they are more often used (or so it seems to me) to indicate a contrast, in which case they are amplified by an alternation of shots, which, however, never assumes the clear oppositional function it had in Rossellini's earlier films. The contrast is always contained within a dialectic of points of view and the historical distance makes it less violent.

The space represented is a homogeneous space which the camera can capture in its entirety. When editing intervenes, it follows almost elementary principles, and this too is reminiscent of early cinema. Even the device of opposition, where separate shots are occupied by separate characters expressing different opinions, seems to me to be a figure of silent cinema which the sound film subsequently reduced to a cliché but which Rossellini restores to its original expressiveness precisely because he uses it discreetly.

Set design, props and costumes inhabit this space without being obtrusive. They do not violate verisimilitude and yet they stand at the opposite pole from the obsessively detailed reconstructions of a Visconti. Only when Rossellini needs to include objects or machines that directly serve his educational purpose does the reconstruction become impeccable and the object acquire an absolutely concrete presence, like the armour in *The Iron Age* and *Struggle*, the clothes in *Louis XIV*, the workers' tools in *Acts of the Apostles* and, above all, the numerous extraordinary machines in *Struggle*, *Pascal* and *Cosimo de'*

Glass shot of Jerusalem in *Acts of the Apostles* (1968). (Adriano Aprà Collection.)

Rossellini preparing the glass shot of Jerusalem. (Adriano Aprà Collection.)

Medici. In a cinema with little action of a traditional kind, these everyday working actions are the ones which really fascinate Rossellini, the moments where the concrete intervenes to enliven the dominant abstraction.

Rossellini tended to film everything in real settings, as much as was necessary to ensure verisimilitude without letting himself be seduced by the charms of ancient places. He rarely filmed in studios and when he did one can, in my view, detect a dislike of doing so which comes across in the film, as in many of the scenes in *Socrates* and all the scenes with Herod in *The Messiah* (*Il Messia*). These are among the least good things he did and possibly the only cases in which he did not manage to exploit production constraints to his advantage.

The 'glass shot' is a different matter. This was a variant he developed of a trick shot that had been used in the silent era in which a painted background placed behind the camera is reflected in a plate of glass and joined in the viewfinder to the real set in front. Rossellini adapted the device in order to make simple camera or zoom movements without the real and the reflected portions of the set slipping out of register. He had already tried out the glass shot in *Giovanna d'Arco al rogo* (*Joan of Arc at the Stake*). He began to vary it in *Vanina Vanini* and then used it in its definitive form in his television films, particularly in certain shots in *Louis XIV*, *Struggle*, *Acts*, *Socrates*, *Augustine* and *Cosimo*. It is a trick shot that 'shows', but for this very reason it contributes to the effect of disbelief which pervades Rossellini's historical cinema. It is not the illusion of reality which interests him but the idea lying behind reality.

Sound

All Rossellini's television films apart from *Louis XIV*, filmed in France, are dubbed, nearly always by voices different from those of the actors. This was standard practice in

Italy, at least from 1945 to 1970 (to his credit, Rossellini recorded live sound for part of *Paisà* and of the English-language version of *Stromboli*, the German-language versions of *Germany Year Zero* and *Fear*, 'Una voce umana' and *Giovanna d'Arco al rogo*). Dubbing, as I have mentioned, helped to make the characters into 'mouthpieces' rather than individuals. The abstraction was further accentuated by the reduction of ambient noise to a minimum. The effect is like being inside an aquarium.

The use of music is radically different from that of the cinema films. Rossellini's brother Renzo was replaced by Mario Nascimbene (with the exception of *The Iron Age* and *Cosimo de' Medici*, although in the last of these, Manuel De Sica seems to follow in his predecessor's footsteps). Renzo Rossellini's scores worked in contrast, one might say in counterpoint, to the images. Against visual restraint he placed musical emphasis. What the images suggested, the music exhibited. I do not believe Rossellini gave his brother a free hand without realising that this contrast allowed him to tie his own modernity to classical models, to rediscover the archetype of tradition in the apparent cliché of this type of music. Ultimately, Renzo's music works to suggest that Roberto's new style is a way of 'putting back in place' (as Straub wrote, quoting Charles Péguy, in the introduction to the published screenplay of *The Chronicle of Anna Magdalena Bach*) 'very ancient but forgotten things'. At the point when Rossellini, in the television films, moves away from modernity and identifies with classicism, with an idea of the total person whose models for him are the Greece of Socrates and the Renaissance of Alberti, the music can afford to become 'modern' and once again to work in counterpoint to the images. Nascimbene's music is reduced to essentials. It does not comment on the action. It tends to blend into an almost inaudible, electronically generated, 'tuneless' evocative sonority. In *Atti*, a flute and the voice of Sonali, Rossellini's Indian companion, are woven in. It is a way of discreetly emphasising the warmth of this film, the least 'cold' of his works for television, of lifting it slightly out of its Judaeo-Graeco-Roman historical context and opening it to a more universal dimension.

Narrative typologies

It was Rossellini himself who distinguished *The Iron Age* and *Struggle* from the other films of his historical encyclopedia, and not just because he got his son Renzo to direct them. He called them 'backbones' because they covered a long time period and because he could graft onto them (as I have tried to show in the timechart – see pp. 130–3) the films, or projects, in which he analysed specific periods. These two works, however, are distinct from the others above all because they use very different narrative models. In both of them, Rossellini appears in person at the beginning, and at times during the programmes themselves, to introduce in very general terms what is about to follow. A voice-over then takes over, providing more detailed information on some, but not all, of the episodes narrated. This voice is reduced to a bare minimum, except when the programmes are based on archive footage. The subdivision into episodes does not follow a single model: some episodes effectively consist of a single sequence while others have a greater narrative range. The latter include the first (Etruscan) part of *Iron Age* and that of the worker from the Ilva plant, virtually a film in itself (Part 4 and the beginning of Part 5), and, in *Struggle*, Part 1 (primitive humans), Parts 2 and the beginning of Part 3 (the Egyptians), Part 4 (the monks) and Part 7 (Columbus).[17]

In both series this alternation between episodes of different lengths makes the educational presentation flexible. The impression is that of an oral, anti-academic narrative, with pauses, rapid summaries and moments of detail. It is almost as if Rossellini were handing the audience his notebook and inviting them to develop the notes for themselves. The inclusion alongside the fictional material of reconstructions based on archive film (documentaries, newsreels, industrial films, films on art, even short extracts from his own and others' fiction films) also helps to liberate these films from the standard model of programmes for schools. With the chronological framework securely in place, Rossellini can move around inside it in a refreshingly casual way, putting the spectator at ease with a relaxed narrative rhythm.

The choice of episodes to narrate is often surprising. Rossellini seems deliberately to foreground, even when famous characters are present, apparently secondary but revealing moments. *Iron Age* shows urine being used to temper steel and work saltpetre. *Struggle* shows Columbus's attempts to convince his financiers that his project is well founded but does not show the result; it has Rabelais appear as a doctor but not as a writer; it shows Volta demonstrating the battery he has invented (known as the Voltaic pile) not to his fellow scientists but to an intrigued customs officer he meets by chance. Equally surprising is the way Augustan Rome is represented through obscure episodes showing the persistence of ancient rites and myths without any attention being paid to the cultural developments of the period. Indeed, in the other films where ancient Rome appears, including *Acts* and *Augustine,* as well as the *Caligula* (*Caligola*) project, it is depicted above all as a decadent civilisation, a place of barbarism.

In reconstructing the overall encyclopedia project, one needs to keep in mind not just the gaps in the series filled by the various films (or projects) but also the cross-references between them: the reference to Jerusalem in *Struggle* (which also incorporates several

Leon Battista Alberti (Virginio Gazzolo, second from left) demonstrating the camera obscura he has invented, in *The Age of Cosimo de' Medici* (1972). (Adriano Aprà Collection.)

shots from *Acts*) is inserted between *The Messiah* and *Acts*; the Benedictine monks are an extension of the friars in *Francis God's Jester*); Alberti's monologue in *Iron Age* is the same as in Part 3 of *Cosimo*; Joan of Arc is mentioned at the beginning of *Cosimo* and Galileo at the beginning of *Cartesius*; Descartes had already appeared in *Blaise Pascal* and Father Mersenne also appears in both films; Pulcinella (Michelangelo Fracanzani) goes to Louis XIV's court; Niepce and Daguerre are mentioned in Part 9 of *Struggle*.

The other historical films may be divided into two narrative typologies: 'portraits of individuals' (*Louis XIV, Socrates, Pascal, Augustine, Cartesius, The Messiah*) and 'portraits of an age' (*Acts* and *Cosimo*). The last two differ from the others not just in running time (340 and 246 minutes respectively) and their subdivision into parts (five and three) but also because they explore in much more depth the age in which the protagonists are immersed. Each of them has two main characters – Peter and Paul; Cosimo I de' Medici and Leon Battista Alberti – who take turns, as it were, as protagonists, coming together in the middle parts. In other respects, the two films are reversals of one another like two faces of a coin: *Acts* is a film of movement, it is about the dissemination of an idea through a process of religious and spiritual quest in a conflictual political context (Judaic, Greek, Roman); *Cosimo* is a more static film, it registers the almost unopposed rise of a new political and artistic idea. *Acts* is dominated by dialogue, *Cosimo* by monologue.

The 'portraits of individuals' are not really biographical films. They follow the trajectory not of a life so much as of an idea. It is significant that there are few or no signs of the characters becoming old. With the exception of Socrates and, in part, Cosimo, whose story is over in just a few years, the period shown for most of the protagonists is between twenty and thirty years of their lives. Yet even when chronological elements are given in the dialogue (these have helped me place events in the timechart – see pp. 130–3) the impression is that of an immobility of time and also, with the exception of *Acts* and *The Messiah*, of space. It therefore does not make much sense to criticise Rossellini for not having recounted this or that episode of the period he was examining. The historical fidelity he wanted was fidelity to his personal interpretation of the dominant idea of a philosophical movement or a historical period. What interested him in dealing with the past was not to show what actually happened, but to take from it an idea that could help us to reorientate ourselves in the present. Like Croce, he saw all history as 'contemporary history'.

Towards an essayistic cinema

Jacques Rivette wrote in 1955 in his 'Letter on Rossellini': 'There was *The River* [Jean Renoir, 1951], the first didactic poem: now there is *Journey to Italy* which, with absolute lucidity, at last offers the cinema, hitherto condemned to narrative, the possibility of the essay.'[18] This perceptive remark, made about a fiction film, may be applied even more logically not just to *India* and *J'ai fait un beau voyage*, to *The Iron Age* and *Struggle*, where fiction and documentary intertwine, but also to Rossellini's entire television output, which one can classify as fictional but which, beyond its educational intentions, is conceived in formal terms as an attempt to overcome illusionism and convey abstract ideas by audiovisual means.

A modern conception of essayistic cinema should not be confused with traditional forms of documentary, even though its models are normally found outside fiction cinema. A conceptual type of essayistic cinema is represented by Vertov, Hurwitz, Jennings, Marker and Godard: film-makers concerned with overcoming the boundaries between fiction and documentary. Rossellini does not really belong in this tradition, but it may be useful nevertheless to try to compare him with film-makers who throw the dominant notions both of fiction and of documentary into crisis: Griffith, Marker, Godard and Straub above all, but also, for less obvious reasons, Guitry and Warhol (not to mention the serial 'catalogues', which are particular sorts of encyclopedia, such as the 'catalogues of views' produced by the Lumière brothers or Albert Kahn or 'the catalogues of tricks' made by Méliès or Segundo de Chomón).

Of course, neither Godard nor Warhol ever made historical films and Marker has done so only – though in the spirit of Rossellini – in his television series *L'Héritage de la chouette* (1989). The formal rigour of Godard and Straub seems at the opposite pole from Rossellini's simplifications; Griffith and Guitry treat the problem of actors in a radically different way from him. And yet there is a certain affinity with Rossellini in Straub and Warhol's 'primitivism', in early Griffith or in Guitry's theatrical 'two-dimensionality' as well as in the casual educational manner of films like *Les Perles de la couronne* (1937) and *Remontons les Champs-Elysées* (1938). There is something of Griffith, too, in Rossellini's educational mission and something of Marker and the later Godard in his wish to draw the cinema away from fiction and tie it to the essay by various means, including television (if Rossellini had still been alive he would, like Marker, have been excited by the potential of digital technologies such as CD and DVD).[19] Rossellini's television films do not appear modern, yet I believe that with his idea of a historical encyclopedia going beyond the narrative and documentary traditions of the cinema he had 'already set off', as Godard said of *India*, 'from the point which others will reach perhaps only twenty years from now'.

Some notes on the films

In his cinematic period, Rossellini, while maintaining a basic thematic consistency, changed stylistic tack virtually from one film to the next: the novel-like plot structure of *Rome Open City* is followed by the documentary manner of *Paisà*, the microscopic investigation of 'Una voce umana' by the ascetic detachment of *Francis*, the essay-fiction *Journey to Italy* by the ascetic 'expressionism' of *Fear*. In the television films, on the other hand, the coherence of the encyclopedic project is reflected in a stylistic coherence, as if the various films were merely facets of a single film. This does not mean that Rossellini's method in these films, as I have attempted to outline it here, is without changes of tone, exceptions or detours from film to film, or that one cannot detect a progressive improvement in the method. Its culminating moments, in the different narrative typologies, may be identified in *Struggle, The Age of Cosimo de' Medici* and *Cartesius*.

The Iron Age is, in this respect, still an experimental film, where Rossellini tries out a number of solutions that partly build on earlier works and partly anticipate later ones. The long episode of the Ilva worker is like the third part of a trilogy of return to the Second World War whose first two parts were *General Della Rovere* and *Era notte a Roma*. The scene of the knight shopping in an armour store anticipates the costumes of *Louis XIV*. The scene with Leon Battista Alberti is a 'rehearsal' for Part 3 of *The Age of Cosimo de' Medici*. The use of archive footage is repeated and developed in the final parts of

Struggle. The fascination of this work lies also in its being a draft, a scale drawing for the subsequent frescoes.

Man's Struggle for Survival – the least-well known of Rossellini's little-known television films – already has a more coherent and compact structure, which unfortunately he will not manage to take further. Its alternation between short scenes and longer episodes, its ability both to synthesise and analyse, its casual manner of drawing exemplary teachings from apparently minor events are all fascinating. The episodes on the Egyptians, the Benedictine monks and Columbus, although directed mainly by Renzo, deserve a place in an ideal anthology of the best of Rossellini.

La Prise de pouvoir par Louis XIV received critical acclaim not just because it was the only one of the television films to have been shown in cinemas but also because it adopted a typically cinematic, and in this sense traditional, solution to the visualisation of power – that of ceremony, ritual, *mise-en-scène*, spectacle – and because, more than any of the later works, it fitted easily into the contemporary interest (for instance in the *Annales* school of historians) in the history of 'everyday life'. The absence or diminished presence of these elements in the later films partly explains the critical reticence towards them.

Acts of the Apostles is, in my opinion, alongside *The Age of Cosimo de' Medici* and *Cartesius*, the best of Rossellini's television films. It is also the 'hottest', the one where the emotional involvement he renounces elsewhere is most visible. There is a broad sweep: the film starts from a centre, Jerusalem, and a community of brothers, the apostles, then gradually the circle widens. The apostles set out on their journey (like the friars at the end of *Francesco*); the conflict between Jews, Greeks and Romans, initially contained within the city, echoes along the route which takes the apostles and later Paul to Palestine, Syria, Pisidia, Athens and Rome, where the last scene in the film opens with the same invocation as the first ('Jerusalem! Jerusalem!') and the circle is closed. *Acts* is the film of harmonic totality. The itinerary of the abstract idea is a concrete journey where the characters are cocooned by the surrounding space; the male community of the brothers is constantly given warmth by the silent activity of the women, who are frequently highlighted by the zoom; the dialogue, more than in the other films, is used to establish contact between people and to try to overcome differences. Rossellini takes liberties with the text of the apostle Luke, synthesising, expanding, cutting and inventing to good effect. This is no longer the case in *The Messiah*, where he too often seems intimidated and restrained by the gospel text.

Socrates is, along with *Augustine* and *The Messiah*, in my opinion, the least successful of the films of this period. Production difficulties may have been partly responsible (disagreements with the RAI, requirements imposed by the Spanish co-producers) but I suspect that a deeper reason is that Rossellini had wanted to make it for too long (he spoke about the project as far back as 1952) and by the time he came to direct it his motivation had gone cold. In the first part, in particular, the scenes seem hurriedly filmed, just enough to sketch in a context for Socrates, who has difficulty establishing a convincing dialogue either with his disciples or his opponents. Only towards the end, when he is preparing to die, does the rhythm relax. Despite this, Socrates was, with Alberti, the historical figure with whom Rossellini most readily identified, and certain precepts of Socratic thought ('I know that I know nothing', 'In my own way, without formally pursuing it, I am seeking only the truth', maieutics as the art of bringing forth thought from others without imposing it) continue to haunt him in his writings of the period.

Blaise Pascal (more convincing in the French-dubbed version than the Italian one) moves from scene to scene with extraordinary fluidity. The method of the sequence-shot, which began to be established here, seems to transform the film into an ideal single sequence-shot, which gives compactness to the philosopher's thought beyond his momentary doubts. Rossellini manages to maintain the right distance from the character, drawing out his ideas without erasing the individual.

Augustine was probably put together too hurriedly. The itinerant narrative structure makes it appear similar to *Acts* and *The Messiah* (there are journeys in *Cartesius* too, but it is as if one were returning always to the same place) and yet the progression of scenes does not correspond to a progression of ideas. It is not clear where Rossellini's main interest lies. His attention seems to switch randomly from Augustine to the secondary characters, from the conflict between Christians and Donatists to that between Christians loyal to the idea of Rome and Christians who proclaim it obsolescent. There are a few fine scenes (the baths, the inn, the meetings with Marcellinus) but there are too many others where Rossellini seems uncomfortable.

The Age of Cosimo de' Medici – in three parts dealing respectively with Cosimo in exile (*L'esilio di Cosimo*), in power (*Potere di Cosimo*) and with Alberti and Humanism (*Leon Battista Alberti: l'Umanesimo*) – is the film where the sequence-shot becomes stabilised as 'tableau' and where each successive scene preserves its own autonomy. It is significant that Rossellini here, as in his subsequent films, does without the dissolves (lap dissolves, fades in and out) which in his previous television films (though already less frequently in *Augustine*) had been used to mark out blocks of sequences and accentuate their fluidity. Characters become mouthpieces of ideas, sacrificing their individuality (thus Cosimo's wife or Alberti's brother both have marginal roles). The ideal of harmony, Rossellini's model for the contemporary world, whose spiritual solution is *Acts of the Apostles*, here has its most perfect secular counterpart.

Cartesius is the most distilled, pared-down film of this period, the one in which Rossellini carries furthest the consequences of his method. Nothing is allowed to stand in the way of the exposition of Descartes's thought, not even the anomalous presence of a fine female character, Hélène, whose function perhaps is to balance with her warmth the otherwise dominant coldness. It is here that Rossellini demonstrates stylistically the fundamental importance of a rationality from which all traces of the irrational have been filtered out, something he repeatedly stressed in his writings and interviews. His gaze implacably and rigorously surveys a character who hesitates to come to maturity, who is inclined to laziness, sleep and dreaming, to think more than to write, and who only at the end accepts adulthood by writing and publishing, marrying and becoming a father.

After this 'absolute' film, *The Messiah* tries a different tack. Perhaps because he made it for the cinema, Rossellini gives up his rigorous sequence-shots and harmonious zooms for a more segmented *découpage*, as if, frightened by the majestic slowness of *Cartesius*, which he only rediscovers here occasionally and in the final part, he were anxious to quicken the pace. One senses a rather deliberate desire to avoid clichés, to secularise (albeit not heavy-handedly) a narrative everyone knows by heart, to emphasise the everyday, almost as if the film were a report on Jesus's life (it is symptomatic here that the film leaves out not only the miracles but also the stations of the cross). The rhythm of speech, which in the preceding films Rossellini had no qualms about letting fill as much space as necessary, is here artificially speeded up, as if he were frightened of the rhetoric of over-familiar speeches and wanted to get through them as fast as possible.

In this chapter I have attempted, by offering some general reflections both on Rossellini's historical–encyclopedic project as a whole and on the individual films, to contribute towards rescuing this fundamental part of his work from the neglect into which it has unjustly fallen. I hope these reflections may stimulate more detailed research, especially in the following areas: the relation between Rossellini's historical project and similar projects, recent or not, whether in film and television or in other disciplines; the project's ideological value in terms of modern theories of philosophy, history and education; the practical applicability of these films for the purposes of teaching, outside the traditional film and television circuits; a comparison between the historical and documentary sources of the films and the use Rossellini actually made of them; a detailed analysis of the style and content of the individual films.

Notes

1   'Education' and 'educational' are used throughout this chapter to translate 'didattica' and 'didattico', which in Italian do not have the generally pejorative connotations 'didactic' has in English. It should be noted, however, that Rossellini himself disliked the word 'educazione', which, on the other hand, does have a number of inappropriate or negative connotations in an Italian context, including a meaning of 'good manners' and associations with the Fascist period, when the term 'Educazione Nazionale' replaced 'Pubblica Istruzione' as the name of the ministry responsible for schools. Rossellini himself also saw 'ducere'/'duce' in the term as well as a (spurious) etymological derivation from 'castration' (see below). The essential point is that, for Rossellini, the educational project (*progetto didattico*) he pursued through television involved a freeing of the mind, a teaching to understand by seeing for oneself. [Translator's note]

2   The books which give adequate coverage to Rossellini's television period include José-Luis Guarner, *Roberto Rossellini* (Valencia: Fundació Municipal de Cine-Mostra de Valencia, 1996) (1st edn, up to *Socrates*: London: Studio Vista, 1970); Pio Baldelli, *Roberto Rossellini* (Rome: Samonà e Savelli, 1972) (critically hostile); Sergio Trasatti, *Rossellini e la televisione* (Rome: La Rassegna, 1978) (includes anthology of writings and interviews); Peter Brunette, *Roberto Rossellini* (New York: Oxford University Press, 1987); Gianni Rondolino, *Rossellini* (Turin: UTET, 1989); Ángel Quintana, *Roberto Rossellini* (Madrid: Cátedra, 1995); Nicole Brenez, 'L'etre humain dans son intégrité', *De la figure en général et du corps en particulier: L'invention figurative au cinéma* (De Boeck Université, Paris/Bruxelles, 1998), pp. 407–13; Tag Gallagher, *The Adventures of Roberto Rossellini: His Life and Films* (New York: Da Capo, 1998) (the best); Raymond Bellour, 'Le cinéma, au-delà', *L'entre-images 2: Mots, Images* (POL, Paris, 1999), pp. 103–112. Essays on the television films include John Hughes, 'Recent Rossellini', *Film Comment*, July–August 1974; Louis Norman, 'Rossellini's Case Histories for Moral Education', *Film Quarterly*, Summer 1974; Michael Silverman, 'Rossellini and Leon Battista Alberti: the Centring Power of Perspective', *Yale Italian Studies*, no. 1, 1977; Nuccio Lodato, 'Rossellini: cinepalinodia o telepalingenesi?', *Cinema & Cinema*, no. 15, April–June

1978; Harry Lawton, 'Rossellini's Didactic Cinema', *Sight and Sound*, Autumn 1978; Virgilio Fantuzzi, seven essays collected in his *Cinema sacro e profano* (Rome: La Civiltà Cattolica, 1983); Roger McNiven, 'Rossellini's Alberti: Architecture and the Perspective System Versus the Invention of the Cinema', *Iris*, no. 12, December 1991 (the best).

3 The documentary *A Question of People* (16 mm, colour, 125 minutes, 1974), made for the United Nations for World Population Year, may be considered an appendix to the geographical project. It alternates interviews by Rossellini with population specialists with documentary materials, accompanied by a voice-over commentary, filmed by his colleagues in Brazil and Africa and by Rossellini himself in India in 1957, as well as with films from NASA and Soviet archives. On the other hand, several of Rossellini's documentaries may be considered part of his historical project: *Torino nei cent'anni* (Turin in its Hundred Years [since Italy's Unification]) (1961), a sort of appendix to *Viva l'Italia*; *Idea di un'isola* (*The Sicily of Roberto Rossellini*) (1967–8); *Concerto per Michelangelo* (1977).

4 See Roberto Rossellini, *Utopia, autopsia, 10¹⁰* (Rome: Armando, 1974); *Un esprit libre ne doit rien apprendre en esclave* (Paris: Fayard, 1977); *Fragments d'une autobiographie* (Paris: Ramsay, 1987); the writings and interviews collected in Trasatti, *Rossellini e la televisione*; *R.R. Roberto Rossellini*, edited by Edoardo Bruno (Rome: Bulzoni, 1979); *Il mio metodo*, edited by Adriano Aprà (Venice: Marsilio, 1987) (2nd edn, 1997): a selection has been translated in English as *My Method* (New York: Marsilio, 1992). Among Rossellini's papers, acquired by the Scuola Nazionale di Cinema-Cineteca Nazionale, Rome, there is the typescript of an unpublished book, probably written before *Utopia: La comunicazione dall'anno uno all'anno zero* [*Communication from Year One to Year Zero*].

5 'Perché faccio film storici' ['Why I Make Historical Films'], *La Stampa*, 6 May 1971 (translated as 'Roberto Rossellini by Roberto Rossellini', *Cinema* (Beverly Hills), vol. 7, no.1, Autumn 1971) (my emphasis).

6 Rossellini, *Utopia, autopsia*, p. 14.

7 Ibid., p. 21.

8 Ibid., p. 16.

9 *Un esprit libre*, pp. 77, 111, 110–11.

10 Ibid., p. 101. There is a striking similarity between Comenius's (and Rossellini's) programme here and that of the film pioneer Boleslaw Matuszewski, even though the latter was writing about the documentary character of the cinema: 'Animated photography will cease to be a way of killing time and it will become an agreeable method of investigating the past and, above all, by offering a direct vision, it will remove – at least in some cases not devoid of importance – the necessity of tiresome studies. Furthermore it could become a particularly effective means of education. How many ambiguous descriptions can be removed from books for the youth the moment it is possible, with the help of a moving picture, to show the students in schools [documents of actual events]', 'A New Source of History' (originally published in French in 1898), in Boleslaw Matuszewski, *A New Source of History; Animated Photography, What It Is, What It Should Be* (Warsaw: Filmoteka Narodowa, 1999) (two texts published in Warsaw in English, translated from the original French).

11 *Utopia, autopsia*, pp. 207–8.

12 *Un esprit libre*, p. 105.

13 Various script materials of the historical films have been published (in Italian unless
    otherwise indicated): dialogue transcripts plus descriptions of scenes (but not a shot
    breakdown) of *Acts of the Apostles, Socrates, Blaise Pascal, Augustine, The Age of Cosimo
    de' Medici, Cartesius,* edited by Luciano Scaffa and Marcella Mariani Rossellini
    (Rossellini's sister, screenwriter for many of his TV films and script assistant) (Turin:
    ERI, 1980); treatments for *Francis God's Jester* (in *Inquadrature,* nos. 5–6, October
    1958–September 1959) and *The Iron Age* (in *Filmcritica,* nos. 139–40,
    November–December 1963); large extracts from the shooting script of *The Messiah* (in
    Rivista del Cinematografo, July–August 1977) and documents or scripts for various
    projects that never went into production: *Caligola* (reproduced in Baldelli, *Roberto
    Rossellini*), *Pulcinella* (in *Filmcritica,* nos. 374–5, May–June 1987), *American Revolution*
    (*Rivoluzione americana*) (in Italian and English) and *Science* (*Scienza*) (only in
    English), both in *Roberto Rossellini* (Rome: EAGC, 1987), and, lastly, *Lavorare per
    l'umanità* (*Working for Humanity*) (in *Filmcritica,* nos. 289–90, November–December
    1978). The SNC-Cineteca Nazionale now possesses the shooting scripts (often very
    different from the completed films) of *La Prise de pouvoir par Louis XIV* (only the
    beginning, roughly the first quarter of the film), *Socrates, Blaise Pascal* (incomplete),
    Augustine, Leon Battista Alberti (namely the second and third parts of *The Age of
    Cosimo de' Medici*), *Cartesius* and *The Messiah,* as well as the originals of the
    aforementioned published scripts (*Caligula, Pulcinella, American Revolution, Science,
    Lavorare per l'umanità*) and script materials, not yet published, for the projects *The
    Extraordinary History of Our Food, The Industrial Revolution, The Civilization of the
    Conquistadores* and *Islam.* It has not yet been possible to trace, among the television
    films, complete shooting scripts of *Louis XIV* or *Blaise Pascal,* the first part of *The Age
    of Cosimo de' Medici* or *Struggle,* or (assuming they exist) any materials on the projects
    for *Catherine of Siena, Diderot, Niepce and Daguerre* and *Comenius.*
14 Although the voice-over correctly places this scene in the fifteenth century, it follows
    straight on from the other scenes of Benedictine monks in the fourth part of *Struggle.*
15 Quoted in John Hughes, 'In Search of the "Essential Image"', *The Village Voice,* 10 May
    1973.
16 'A Discussion of Neo-Realism: Rossellini Interviewed by Mario Verdone', *Screen,* vol. 14,
    no. 4, Winter 1973/4, p. 77 (originally in *Bianco e Nero,* no. 2, 1952, pp. 7–16),
    reproduced below, pp. 149–55.
17 The longer duration of some episodes of *Struggle* is explained by the fact that – as
    Renzo told me – they initially considered distributing them as separate films, perhaps
    filming further scenes later.
18 Jacques Rivette, 'Letter on Rossellini', in Jim Hillier (ed.), *Cahiers du Cinéma,* vol. 1, *The
    1950s: Neo-Realism, Hollywood, New Wave* (London: Routledge & Kegan Paul, 1985),
    p. 199 (originally in *Cahiers du Cinéma,* no. 46, April 1955).
19 Jay Leyda recounts that Maxim Gorky began working in 1919 on an educational
    project which, according to an American journalist who interviewed him, was to
    consist of 'a series of motion-picture scenarios, composed with scientific historical
    exactness, showing the history of man from the Stone Age down through the Middle
    Ages to the time of Louis XVI of France, and finally to the present day'. *Kino: A History
    of the Russian and Soviet Film* (London: Allen & Unwin, 1960), p. 141. The similarity
    with Rossellini's historical encyclopedia is striking.

Documents

The following selection of writings by and on Rossellini concentrates on two periods in his career: the early 1950s and the 1970s. The interview he gave to Mario Verdone in 1951 (Document A) contains his fullest statement in the first period of his views on realism and neo-realism and his own film-making practice, while the exchange (B) between Guido Aristarco and André Bazin eloquently illustrates what was at stake in the critical debates over his work in the early 1950s. The second period is represented by three texts in which Rossellini explains his conception of educational film: a letter of 1972 to the historian Peter H. Wood outlining his cycle of television films (C), a statement from the same year on the death of cinema and the importance of television (D) and his introductory notes for a film about Marx that was never made (E). The recollection by Federico Fellini (F), published three years after Rossellini's death, is included as a tailpiece. For a more comprehensive selection of writings see the Select Bibliography in this volume.

A   A discussion of neo-realism: Rossellini interviewed by Mario Verdone (1952)

I met Roberto Rossellini in a break in the making of *Europe '51* at the studios in Via della Vasca Navale. A dialogue writer was at work on the lines Ingrid Bergman was about to speak. The walls of the set were freshly painted: it was not long since they had been made, as Rossellini had changed his original idea of shooting in a real interior. No one knew what scenes would be shot the next day. Rossellini himself had not decided. The producer was not there – he might well never appear throughout the making of the film. Ingrid Bergman was sitting to one side on a wooden bench, wearing a fur coat and knitting. When the order to shoot came her expression changed effortlessly, spontaneously and with complete conviction, and she threw herself into the part as only a great actor can. The scene was a hospital ward, and on the director's instructions his assistant had arranged movements for white-clad extras, but when Rossellini arrived he had everything changed, in one of those sudden decisions with which he characteristically throws out every plan or arrangement. A technician who was waiting to speak to him pointed out to me that however bewildering these preparations seemed, they were in a sense quite normal: 'It is one of those films in which only the director, his authority and his improvisation, counts; our logic has no value. That's what makes a Rossellini film really a Rossellini film'.

I had already gathered enough elements to make a first attempt to sum up the man who had made *Rome Open City*. But I was able to form a clearer idea of him, as a director and as a man, after the discussions we had that day and later on. Though I knew him only through his films, he answered my questions with complete sincerity, as if confiding in a friend.

The subject I intended to write about was 'The poetic world of Rossellini', piecing it together through question-and-answer and observation. Rossellini cordially agreed to take part in this exercise in criticism and self-criticism, an exercise I proposed to base on authentic and concrete facts.

Would you claim to be the father of Italian neo-realism?

I leave it to other people to judge whether what is called neo-realism made a greater impression on the world through *Rome Open City*. I myself would place the birth of neo-realism further back, especially in some fictionalised war documentaries, which I contributed to with *La nave bianca*, and in some war films proper on which I worked on the scenario, like *Luciano Serra pilota*, or which I directed, like *L'uomo dalla croce*; but above all there were some minor films like *Avanti c'è posto*, *L'ultima carrozzella* and *Campo de' Fiori*, in which what might be called the formula of neo-realism began to emerge through the spontaneous creations of the actors, especially Anna Magnani and Aldo Fabrizi. It's undeniably the case that these actors were the first to bring neo-realism to life and that the variety acts invented by Magnani, with strong men or Roman ballads, performed on a mat and to the accompaniment of a single guitar, or the figure Fabrizi cut on the boards of some local theatre, already gave a foretaste of certain films of the neo-realist period. Neo-realism arose unconsciously as film spoken in dialect, and then it acquired a conscious life in the heat of the human and social problems of wartime and the postwar years. On the subject of films in dialect, we should mention, historically, our less immediate predecessors, namely Blasetti with his film using character 'types', *1860*, and Camerini with films like *Gli uomini, che mascalzoni!*

But historical precedents aside, Italian postwar films have a certain air of realism which would have been quite inconceivable before the war. Can you give a definition of it?

I'm a film-maker, not an aesthete, and I don't think I can give an exact definition of realism. All I can say is what I feel about it and what ideas I've formed about it. Perhaps someone else would be able to explain it better.

It involves a greater interest in individuals. Modern man feels a need to tell of things as they are, to take account of reality in an uncompromisingly concrete way, which goes with today's interest in statistics and scientific results. Neo-realism is also a response to the genuine need to see human beings for what they are, with humility and without recourse to fabricating the exceptional; it means an awareness that the exceptional is arrived at through the investigation of reality. Lastly, it's an urge for self-clarification, an urge not to ignore reality, whatever it may be.

This is why I have tried in my films to reach an understanding of things, and give them their true value. It's not something easy or lightly undertaken, but an ambitious project, because to give anything its true value means grasping its authentic universal meaning.

You give a clear meaning for the term neo-realism – or more simply realism – but do you think it is as clear for everyone who discusses it or represents it?

I think there is still some confusion about the term 'realism' even after all these years of realist films. Some people still think of realism as something external, as a matter of going out into the open air, as a contemplation of poverty and suffering. To me realism is simply the artistic form of truth. When truth is reconstituted, expression is achieved. If it's a fake truth you can feel its falsity and expression is not achieved. With these views of course I cannot believe in the 'entertainment' film, as the term is understood in certain industrial circles, outside Europe too, except as a partially acceptable film, in that it is partially capable of achieving truth.

What object does a realist film have that you would contrast with the usual kind of 'entertainment' films?

The realist film has the 'world' as its living object, not the story, the narrative. It does not have preconceived arguments: these arise of their own accord. It has no love for the superfluous and the spectacular, and rejects these, going instead to the root of things. It does not stop at surface appearances, but seeks out the most subtle strands of the soul. It rejects formulas and doesn't pander to its audience, but seeks out the inner motives in each of us.

What other characteristics do you think a realist film has?

To put it briefly, it poses problems and poses them to itself. An American paper wrote an attack on my film 'The Miracle' saying that 'since cinema is an entertainment it ought not to raise problems'. But for me a realist film is precisely one which tries to make people think.

At the end of the war we set ourselves this task, and none of us wanted to make what you might call an 'entertainment' film. What mattered to us was the investigation of reality, the correspondence to reality. For the first Italian directors who came to be called neo-realist it was a genuine act of courage. Then after the real innovators came the popularisers – who were perhaps even more important, as they spread neo-realism everywhere, and perhaps even with greater clarity. They didn't have to change anything and were perhaps better able to express themselves, making neo-realism more widely understood. But then, inevitably, deviations and distortions crept in. But by this time neo-realism had completed most of its journey.

Do you think you have remained faithful in all your films to this concept of realism as you've now spelled it out?

If I have been faithful to it it has been spontaneously and without effort on my part. I don't think that one should preserve one's consistency at any price. Anyone who does so is close to madness. In so far as I have respected certain principles in which I firmly believe, and which are very deep-rooted in me, then you can say that I have been consistent. And I think perhaps I have, since there is a single line you can trace through all my various works – the documentaries, the early war films, the postwar films and the ones I am making now. For example, it's undeniable that you find the same spirituality in *La nave bianca*, *L'uomo dalla croce*, *Paisà*, *Francis God's Jester*, the episode 'The Miracle' and the ending of *Stromboli*.

Do you regard Francis, God's Jester *as a realistic film?*

Of course, even in imagining what Francis might be like as a man, I never abandoned reality, either as regards the events, which are strictly historical, or in any other visual aspect. The costumes, for example, are part of the 'reality'. They are so true to life that you scarcely notice them.

What I tried to do in this film was show a new side of Francis, but not one which lies outside reality: to show a Francis who is at least humanly and artistically valid.

What do you think have been the constant elements in your films?

I don't go by formulas and preconceptions. But looking back on my films, I certainly do find that there are things which have been constant features, recurring not in a planned way but, as I said, quite naturally. First of all, their *chorality*. The realist film in itself is choral. The sailors in *La nave bianca* count as much as the people hiding in the hut at the end of *L'uomo dalla croce*, as much as the population in *Rome Open City*, the partisans in *Paisà* and the friars in *Francis God's Jester*.

La nave bianca is an example of a choral film – from the first scene, with the sailors' letters to their 'godmothers', to the battle itself and then the wounded going to Mass or playing or singing. It also shows the pitiless cruelty of the machine towards human beings; and the unheroic side of men living on a battleship, acting almost in the dark, surrounded by measuring instruments, protractors and steering wheels – a side of them which appears unlyrical and unheroic, and yet is frighteningly heroic.

Then there is the *documentary* manner of observing and analysing, which I learned in my first shorts – *Fantasia sottomarina*, *Il ruscello di Ripasottile*, *Prélude à l'après-midi d'un faune* – and took up again in *Paisà* and in *Germany Year Zero* and *Stromboli*.

Then there is the continual return, even in the strictest documentation, to *fantasy*, because one part of man tends towards the concrete and the other pushes towards imagination, and the former must not be allowed to suffocate the latter. This is why you find fantasy elements in 'The Miracle', *La macchina ammazzacattivi*, and in *Paisà* too if you like, as well as in *Francis God's Jester*, with the rain at the beginning, the young friar being beaten up by the soldiers, and Saint Clare standing by the hut. Even the ending, here, in the snow was meant to have an appearance of fantasy.

Finally there is the *religious* quality – I don't mean so much the invocation of divine authority by the woman at the end of *Stromboli* as the themes I was dealing with even ten years ago.

Do you think then that you have maintained the chorality which you say is a characteristic of your work?

I definitely began by aiming at chorality above all. It was the war which pushed me towards it: war is choral in itself. If then I moved on from chorality to the discovery of the character, a deeper study of the protagonist, as with the boy in *Germany Year Zero* or the refugee in *Stromboli*; this was part of my natural evolution as a director.

Is it true to say that in your films there is often a break between a particularly good episode, like for example the boy walking through the city in Germany Year Zero, *and other parts which are inexplicably left incomplete or at least much more hastily sketched in?*

That's right. As a matter of fact every film I make interests me for a particular scene, perhaps for an ending I already have in mind. In every film I see on the one hand the narrative episode – such as the first part of *Germany Year Zero*, or the shot from *Europe '51* that you just saw me filming – and on the other the *fact*. My sole concern is to reach that *fact*. In the others, the narrative episodes, I feel myself hesitating, alienated, absent.

I don't deny that this is a weakness on my part, but I must confess that an episode which is not of key importance irritates me, tires me, makes me feel quite powerless. I only feel sure of myself at the decisive moment. *Germany Year Zero*, to tell the truth, was conceived specifically for the scene with the boy wandering on his own through the ruins. The whole of the preceding part held no interest at all for me. 'The Miracle' too stemmed from the episode of the tin containers. And when I filmed the last episode of *Paisà* I had an image in my head of those dead bodies floating by on the water, being carried slowly down the Po, with placards bearing the word 'Partisan'. The river carried those corpses for months. You were likely to come across several on a single day.

Do you get inspiration when you're writing the script or when you're making the film? Do you believe in having a 'rigid script' that cannot be altered or rejected?

In the case of a film purely for entertainment it may be right to have a rigid script. For realistic cinema of the kind Italy has produced, which poses problems and seeks the truth, you cannot use the same criteria. Here inspiration plays the main part – it's not the rigid script that counts, but the film itself. An author writes a paragraph or a page, then crosses it out. A painter uses red, then paints over it with green. Why shouldn't I be able to cross things out too, to remake and replace? This is why for me the script cannot be rigid. If I thought it was, I would consider myself a scriptwriter, not a director. But I'm not a scriptwriter. I make films.

I study and reflect for a long time on the subject of every film I make. The script is written, because it would be absurd to try to improvise everything at the last minute. But the scenes, the dialogue, and the sets are adjusted from day to day. This is the place of inspiration in the pre-arranged design of the film. Finally you arrive at an exact layout of the scene that is to be shot. The

Paisà: the opening shot of the final episode.

preparations are completed. Everything is prearranged and foreseen: at this point, if I may say so, begins the most annoying part of the making a film, the terrible part.

What contribution do you think is made by the people who make up the company on a film?

They are the means to an end. A director has them at his disposal like the books in a library. It's up to him to judge what's of use and what's not. The very act of choosing is a part of expressing himself. When a director knows his collaborators thoroughly, and knows what he can get out of them, it's as if he expresses himself through them.

From the time of my first documentaries I have been lucky enough to have a composer I get along with exceptionally well: my brother. I discussed my first attempts at film-making with him and we tried to bring the picture and the music together in the most harmonious way possible.

As for actors, I have had very valuable collaborators: Marcello Pagliero and Anna Magnani, Aldo Fabrizi and Ingrid Bergman, but also real sailors and real partisans, real friars and real fishermen. It is to them, the actors and the 'chorus', that a large part of the success of my films is due. And since I've mentioned Fabrizi, I must make it clear that it was I who wanted him to play that controversial grotesque character in *Francis God's Jester* and I therefore assume full responsibility for it.

Do you admit that you like films with short episodes, like those in Paisà *or* Francis, *the two in* L'Amore *('A Human Voice' and 'The Miracle'), or 'L'invidia' ['Envy'] (from Colette's 'La Chatte', forming a section of* The Seven Deadly Sins) *and even the episodes in* La nave bianca *(in the bunk room, the battle, the hospital ship),* Germany Year Zero *(the boy hurrying through the ruins) and* Stromboli *(the tuna fishing and the escape), which are all self-contained episodes?*

It's true. It's because I hate a story once it begins to constrain me. I hate the logical nexus of a story. The narrative passages are necessary for getting to the fact: but my natural inclination is to skip them and not bother with them. This is, I admit, one of my limitations: the incompleteness of my language. To be honest, I would be happy making only such episodes as you've mentioned. When

I feel that the scene I'm shooting is important only for the logical nexus, and not what I'm most anxious to say, then you see how powerless I am, I don't know what to do. But when the scene is important, when it's essential, then everything becomes simple and easy.

Are you saying that it's natural that you prefer to film short episodes, or is this an excuse for avoiding making a film with a complete story?

I've made films in episodes because I feel more at ease like that. It's enabled me to avoid passages which, as I say, are useful in a continuous narrative, but precisely because they are *useful* rather than *decisive*, are, God knows why, extremely tiresome to me. I am only at ease where I can avoid the logical nexus. Staying within the limits laid down by the story is really what I find most difficult.

What do you think is essential in film narrative?

As I see it, *waiting*. Every solution arises from waiting. It is waiting that brings things alive, waiting that unleashes reality, waiting that – after preparation – brings liberation. Take for example the fishing scene in *Stromboli*. It's an episode born out of waiting. The spectator's curiosity is aroused about what is going to happen: then comes the explosion of the slaughter of the shoal of tuna.

Waiting is the force of every event in our lives: and so it is in cinema.

Can you now tell me how you began your film career?

By chance. I had been struck by Vidor's films: *The Crowd, Hallelujah*, etc.; they were perhaps the only 'classic' films I had then seen. I often went to see films because my father was the owner of the Cinema Corso. My first attempts at film-making were documentaries, made in consultation with my brother. *Prélude à l'après-midi d'un faune* is not a film of a ballet, as one might think if one had not seen it. It's a documentary about nature, as are *Il ruscello di Ripasottile* and *Fantasia sottomarina*. I was struck by the water with the grass snake slithering about in it and the dragonfly overhead. It's a sensitivity to little things, if you want, like the puppies on the main deck in *La nave bianca* or the flower hooked by the sailor about to disembark.

How much is autobiographical in your films?

It's certainly no accident that you should touch on this. There is a lot that's autobiographical in my films. In the documentaries you can find my youthful daydreams – a hornet buzzing, leaping fish mirrored in the water. Then came the war and the occupation: episodes recalled to memory, those we would like to have experienced. *Rome Open City* is the film of 'fear': the fear felt by us all but by me in particular. I too had to go into hiding, I too was on the run, I too had friends who were captured or killed. It was real fear: I lost thirty-four kilos, perhaps through hunger, perhaps because of the terror I described in *Open City*.

Then there's *Paisà*. It's been said that the best episode is the last: the mouths of the Po, the water, the reeds. People expressed astonishment that I had understood that part of Italy so well. But I'd spent years of my childhood there. My mother was from there – I used to go hunting and fishing there.

With 'The Miracle' and 'A Human Voice' Anna Magnani enters my world. In *Stromboli* a stranger enters the life of a simple man, the fisherman Antonio. And the feelings of the woman in *Stromboli*, brutalised by reality and returning to her dreams: why should this not be autobiographical too? The desire to expand, to embrace everyone without letting go of reality, finding inner liberation in the call to God which is the final thrust of the film. She looks at the problem for the first time, almost unconsciously. It is only in the presence of nature, of her own self, and of God, that she has come to understand.

La macchina ammazzacattivi shows my wanderings on the Amalfi coast, places where I'd been happy, places I love, where some poor devils are convinced they have seen Satan. One of them told me one day, 'I've met the werewolf, I ran over him on my bicycle last night'. They are mad, crazed by the sun. But they have a power few of us possess – the power of fantasy.

In this film – which like *L'Amore* represents a search and a crisis – I had another aim as well: to get closer to commedia dell'arte.

Francis God's Jester and *Europe '51* are also autobiographical in that they express feelings I have observed in myself and in people around me. In each of us there's the jester side and its opposite; there is the tendency toward concreteness and the tendency toward fantasy. Today one tends brutally to suppress the second of these. The world is more and more divided in two, between those who want to kill fantasy and those who want to save it, those who want to die and those who want to live. This is the problem I confront in *Europe '51*. There is a danger of forgetting the second tendency, the tendency toward fantasy, and killing every feeling of humanity left in us, creating robot man, who must think in only one way, the concrete way. In *Europe '51* this inhuman threat is openly and violently denounced. I wanted to state my own opinion quite frankly, in my own interest and in my children's. That is the goal I have tried to achieve in this latest film.

The ability to see both sides of man, to look at him charitably, seems to me to be a supremely Latin and Italian attitude. It results from a degree of civility which has been our custom from very ancient times – the habit of seeing every side of man. For me it is extraordinarily important to have been born into such a civilisation. I believe that what has saved us from the disasters of the war, and other equally terrible scourges, has been this view of life we have, which is unmistakably Catholic. Christianity does not pretend that everything is good and perfect: it recognises sin and error, but it also admits the possibility of salvation. It is the opposing camp which only allows man to be perfectly consistent and infallible. To me that is monstrous and nonsensical. The only possibility I see for getting nearer to the truth is to try to understand sin and be tolerant of it.

What are your plans for the future?

I have a great many, but I think most about *Socrates: Life and Trial*. Socrates is a man of today. Xanthippe represents the devil. The story should be shown in three sections: an introduction, the trial, the death scene. The introduction will be set in Athens. I picture a city strung out, as the story has it, all along a road, with a landscape of infinite perspectives. Life here is simple and primitive. The houses look like some of the Etruscan tombs I saw at Cerveteri, with weasels scuttling round inside, cauldrons hanging from the beams, goats sharing houses with humans and leaving the signs of their animal existence. Under the sandals of the inhabitants the name of their city is written, and so it is stamped into the earth they tread. As in *Francis God's Jester* the costumes will be simple and timeless, in other words, costumes which don't look like costumes.

As in *Francis*, too, the events must correspond to reality. Socrates is bound to reach the same conclusions as Francis, though Francis came to them under the impulse of his dreams and hopes, and Socrates by logic. In Francis it is instinct: in Socrates reasoning.

In our civilisation – Latin and Christian – we don't accept truth as given. We are full of irony and scepticism, and constantly in search of truth. We don't look at things with a materialist eye, or see only the façade: we look at things in perspective. This is how Francis saw things. This is how Socrates saw things.

'Colloquio sul neorealismo', first published in *Bianco e Nero*, no. 2, 1952, pp. 7–16; this is a slightly modified version of the translation by Judith White first published in *Screen*, vol. 14, no. 4, Winter 1973–4, subsequently reprinted in Don Ranvaud (ed.), *Roberto Rossellini*, BFI Dossier No. 8 (London: BFI, 1981), pp. 70–4 and in Roberto Rossellini, *My Method: Writings and Interviews*, edited by Adriano Aprà (New York: Marsilio, 1992), pp. 33–43.

B   The Aristarco–Bazin debate

The Italian Marxist critic Guido Aristarco reviewed *Europe '51* in the first issue of his new magazine *Cinema Nuovo* on 15 December 1952. After that, the magazine more or less ignored Rossellini
for a couple of years. The combination of Aristarco's hostile review of *Europe '51* and the magazine's subsequent silence prompted the French critic André Bazin to write an open letter to
Aristarco, which was published in Italian in *Cinema Nuovo* on 25 August 1955. Bazin's letter was
later published in French in *Qu'est-ce que le cinéma?*, vol. 4, *Une esthéthique de la réalité: le néo-
realisme* (Paris: Editions du Cerf, 1962), pp. 150–60.

1   Guido Aristarco on *Europe '51* (1952)

The title reveals the nature of the director's intentions: *Europe '51*, that is to say, mid-century, its
problems and its dramas. Rossellini had set out on the search for God with films which have the
name of God in them but basically only in the title: *Francesco, giullare di Dio* and *Stromboli, terra
di Dio*. The idea for *Europe '51* came to him while working on the former and it can be said that
the new film is in a sense a continuation or, if you like, an attempted development of the latter.

Irene has many features in common with Karin. Both are complex women, egoistical, egocen-
tric even (before their crisis, of course). Both are foreigners and designed to represent a form of
suffering humanity: a world without faith, atheistic, in search not of good but of well-being. To
both can be applied the epigraph from Isaiah (with which *Stromboli* opens): 'I am sought of them
that asked not for me; I am found of them that sought me not' (Isaiah, 65: 1).[1] And Irene, like Karin
before her, is touched by grace at the end. If Karin calls out to God 'give me the strength, the understanding and the courage', Irene, behind the bars of her cell in the asylum, seems more resigned, in
the spirit of the gospel, so much so that someone shouts out 'She's a saint!', just as they do during
the passion of Joan of Arc.

But here, in *Europe '51*, the ideological enterprise is more wide-ranging. Irene is the wife of a
rich foreign diplomat and has a 13-year-old son who kills himself because she neglects him. Her
crisis is used to open up the issue dividing humanity, no less: the hand-to-hand battle between two
conceptions of the world, Marxism and Catholicism. Irene at first is attracted to both. Then she
rejects the left intellectual and the priest, and even the law in the person of the judge charged with
her case. According to her (and to Rossellini), they are conformists. The whole world is conformist:
'idolators of the rule, we live in continual terror of becoming the exception'.

Irene, Rossellini concludes, is guilty of the sin of non-conformism. In the truth she has found
in the gospel, there is no room for hypocrisy. Therefore she is mad. The judge asks her 'Are you a
Communist?'. 'No.' 'Do you want to be a missionary?' 'No.' The representative of the law concludes
'She is insane'. There is a lot in the film that isn't clear. Indeed much is ambiguous, contradictory,
confused. The dialogue purports to be the demonstration of a theorem; but the reasoning is often
faulty, the proposition whose truth is meant to be demonstrated by deduction gets complicated
and lost *en route* – whether looked at scientifically or emotionally and psychologically. In the same
way, the priest, the judge and the Communist are superficial and schematic (it is already schematic
to have divided the world into Marxism and Catholicism and even to have included idealism in
Catholicism). The Communist is ditched by the woman with no justification when she claims to
discover that work is a penal sentence: 'I have seen them work. It's monstrous'. The problem of
work, of which we only see the alienating aspect, is thus swept aside in a totally crazy way. Irene
takes refuge in love, charity, evangelical brotherhood – in 'sanctity'. (The words she pronounces are
from the gospel, though not the interpretation put upon them.) And the conclusion at the end: 'It
is easier for a camel . . .'. With Irene locked up in the asylum, her family leaves, leaving behind the
poor she has befriended who cry out 'She is a saint'. (The priest, interestingly, is with them, but does
not call her a saint.)

But if the condition and way of life of the bourgeoisie (or a section of it) are well depicted (particularly in the first part, up to the time the boy kills himself, which is full of honestly observed and

lifelike detail), the poor by contrast are portrayed in a one-sided manner. Among them are to be found a degenerate and murderous young man, a woman interested only in having children by various fathers, street-walkers. And yet even in the presentation of the working-class district from time to time you see flashes of the sincere, authentic, artistic Rossellini of *Paisà* – particularly the children on the river bank and the kiss Irene gives to one of them.

These are moments which, given their context, leave one open-mouthed. They arouse the suspicion that, with his accusations of 'moral deafness' and conformism, Rossellini is holding out his hands with the gesture of someone who, knowing he is the guilty party, is accusing others of his crime.

(Translated from the Italian by Geoffrey Nowell-Smith)

2   André Bazin: Defence of Rossellini (1955)

My dear Aristarco,

I have been meaning to write this article for quite some time but month after month I keep putting it off in the face of the importance and complexity of the problem. I am also aware of my own lack of theoretical background compared with the seriousness and persistence with which Italian left criticism continues to advance the study of neo-realism. Although I greeted neo-realism immediately on its arrival in France and have not ceased ever since to devote to it my most scrupulous attention as a critic, I cannot claim to be able to oppose to yours a coherent theory of my own or to situate as completely as you do the neo-realist phenomenon in the history of Italian culture. Add to this the risk of appearing ridiculous in purporting to give the Italians a lesson in their own cinema and you have the main reasons why I have not replied earlier to your invitation for a discussion, in the columns of *Cinema Nuovo*, of the critical position taken by you and your group on certain recent works.

I should also remind you, before getting into the debate proper, that international differences of opinion are quite common, even among critics of the same generation who in most respects might be expected to agree. We found this on *Cahiers du Cinéma* with the *Sight and Sound* group and I am not ashamed to admit that it was partly because of Lindsay Anderson's high regard for Jacques Becker's *Casque d'or* – a film which was a failure in France – that I was prompted to revise my own opinion and discover in the film hidden virtues that had escaped me. It is true that foreign opinion can go wrong because of ignorance of the production context. For example the success outside France of Duvivier or Pagnol is certainly based on a misunderstanding. What is admired is a certain interpretation of France which foreigners find marvellously typical and this exoticism is confused with the aesthetic value of the film. I admit that differences of this type are sterile and I imagine that the success abroad of some of the Italian films that you rightly despise is due to the same misunderstanding. However, I do not think that this is basically the case with the films that find us on opposing sides, nor with neo-realism in general. For a start, you would admit that French critics were not wrong at the outset to be more enthusiastic than their Italian counterparts on the subject of films which today are your uncontested glory on both sides of the Alps. I also flatter myself that I was one of the few French critics who always identified the renaissance of Italian cinema with 'neo-realism' even at a time when it was fashionable to say that the phrase was meaningless, and I persist today in thinking that the word remains the most appropriate designation for what is best and most fertile about the Italian school.

But that is also the reason why I am concerned about the way you defend it. Dare I suggest, dear Aristarco, that the severity displayed by *Cinema Nuovo* towards certain tendencies which you describe as involutions of neo-realism makes me fear that you are hacking away, without realising it, at the richest and most alive part of your cinema? For my part I admire Italian cinema in a fairly eclectic way but I would expect Italian critics to be more severe. I can quite see why you are annoyed by the success in France of *Pane, amore e gelosia*; it's the same way as I feel towards Duvivier's films about Paris. However when I see you nitpicking at the tousled hair of Gelsomina[2] or treating Rossellini's latest film as less than nothing, I have to conclude that, under cover of theoretical integrity, you are doing your bit to sterilise the liveliest and most promising branches of what I persist in calling neo-realism.

You tell me you are astonished at the relative success of *Journey to Italy* in Paris and especially at the near unanimous enthusiasm of the French critics. As for *La strada*, you know how well it has done. These two films rekindled the interest not just of the public but of the intellectuals in Italian cinema, an interest which had been flagging for a year or two. The cases of these two films, for a number of reasons, are not the same. But I still maintain that, far from being regarded here as a break with neo-realism, still less an involution, they gave us a feeling of creative invention in the best tradition of the Italian school. I shall try to explain why.

First, however, I must express my distaste for the idea of a neo-realism defined exclusively in relation to one of its present components and a priori limiting the potential of its future evolution. Perhaps I do not have enough of a head for theory. But I prefer to think it is out of a wish to grant to art its natural freedom. In sterile periods, theory is useful to analyse the reasons for the drought and organise the conditions for a revival; but when one is lucky enough to be sharing in the admirable flourishing of Italian cinema which has been going on for ten years, is it not more dangerous than helpful to be pronouncing theoretical vetos? Not that it is wrong to be severe. On the contrary, I think that to be demanding and critically rigorous is as necessary as ever; but the reason these qualities are required is to denounce commercial compromises, demagogy, or a lowering of ambition, not in order to impose a priori aesthetic patterns on creators. I personally think that a film-maker whose ideal is close to your own conceptions but who admits from the outset that he only puts ten to twenty per cent of it into the commercial scripts he can make is less deserving than someone who shoots his films as best he can but rigorously in accordance with his ideal, even if his conception of neo-realism is not your own. Now, when it comes to the former, you limit yourself to recording objectively the part which escapes compromise while giving him just two stars in your critique, whereas you relegate the second without appeal straight to your aesthetic hell.

Rossellini would undoubtedly be less guilty in your eyes if he had shot the equivalent of *Stazione Termini* or *La spiaggia* rather than *Giovanna d'Arco al rogo* or *Fear*.[3] It is not my purpose to defend the author of *Europe '51* at the expense of Lattuada or De Sica: the politics of compromise can be defended up to a point, though what point this is is not for me to say; but it seems to me that Rossellini's independence gives his work – whatever else one may think about it – an integrity of style and a moral unity which is all too rare in the cinema and which demand respect even more than admiration.

But it is not on the methodological level that I want to defend him. My defence submission will address the heart of the debate. Was Rossellini truly a neo-realist and is he still? It seems to me you concede that he was. Indeed who could argue with the role played by *Rome Open City* or *Paisà* in establishing and developing neo-realism? But you find his 'involution' perceptible already in *Germany Year Zero*, decisive by the time of *Stromboli* and *Francis*, and catastrophic in *Europe '51* and *Journey to Italy*. What is the real complaint against this aesthetic itinerary? That of having more or less overtly abandoned a concern with social realism, with the chronicle of contemporary events, in favour, it must be said, of an increasingly visible moral message and one which one might, if maliciously inclined, assimilate to one of the major Italian political tendencies.

I refuse flat out to let the debate descend to this far too contingent level. Supposing Rossellini has Christian Democrat sympathies (and I have no evidence, either public or private, of this), he would not a priori be excluded as an artist from being called a neo-realist, so we can lay this objection aside. It remains true, however, that one can legitimately reject the moral or spiritual postulate that is emerging more and more clearly in his work. But this would not imply rejecting the aesthetic in which the message is realised unless Rossellini's films were *films à thèse* – that is, films which limited themselves to a dramatisation of a priori ideas. Now there is no Italian director whose intentions are harder to separate from his chosen form, and it is on this basis that I should like to define his neo-realism.

If the word has any meaning, and whatever disagreements there might be in its interpretation, it seems to me as a minimum that neo-realism is essentially and from the outset opposed to traditional dramatic systems including certain well-known features of realism – both in literature and in cinema – by virtue of its affirmation of a certain globality of the real. I borrow this definition, which seems to me correct and appropriate, from Abbé Amédée Ayfre (see *Cahiers du Cinéma*, no. 17).[4] Neo-realism is a global description of reality by a global consciousness. I mean by this that neo-realism is opposed to the realist aesthetics that preceded it, and specifically naturalism and verism, in that its realism is directed not at the choice of subject-matter but at the process of awareness. If you like, what is realist in *Paisà* is the Italian Resistance; but what is neo-realist is Rossellini's *mise-en-scène* and his elliptical and at the same time synthesising presentation of events. To express it in yet another way, neo-realism by definition rejects analysis (whether political, moral, psychological, logical, social or whatever kind you like) of the characters and their actions. It considers reality as a bloc, not incomprehensible but indivisible. This is why neo-realism is, if not necessarily anti-spectacular (although spectacle is on the whole foreign to it) then at least radically anti-theatrical to the extent that the performance of the theatrical actor supposes a psychological analysis of feelings and a physical expressionism, symbolising a whole series of moral categories.

This does not mean – indeed, far from it – that neo-realism can be reduced to some form of objective documentarism. Rossellini likes to say that the starting point of his *mise-en-scène* is love not just for his characters but for the real itself, and it is precisely this love which prevents him from separating what reality has joined: character and setting. Neo-realism therefore does not mark out a refusal to take a position towards the world, or to judge it, but it does suppose a mental attitude: it is always reality seen by an artist, refracted through his consciousness – but by the whole of that consciousness and not just his reason or passion or beliefs and then put together again from separate bits. I would suggest that the traditional realist artist (Zola for example) analyses reality and then resynthesises it in conformity with his moral conception of the world, whereas the consciousness of the neo-realist director filters it. No doubt his consciousness, like anyone else's, does not let the whole of reality through, but the choice operated is neither logical nor psychological: it is ontological in the sense that the image of reality returned to us remains global, in the same way, if you will allow the metaphor, that a black and white photograph is not an image of reality taken apart and put together again 'without colour', but a true imprint of the real, a sort of luminous cast in which colour does not appear. There is an ontological identity between the object and its photograph. An example will make this clearer, and I shall take it from *Journey to Italy* itself. The audience is often disappointed by the film to the extent that Naples only appears in it in an incomplete and fragmentary fashion. This reality is in fact only a thousandth part of what one could show, but the little bits one sees – some statues in a museum, some pregnant women, an excavation at Pompeii, the end of a San Gennaro procession – nevertheless possess this global character which seems to me essential. It is Naples 'filtered' by the consciousness of the heroine, and if the landscape is poor and limited, it is because the consciousness of this mediocre upper-middle-class woman is itself of a rare spiritual poverty. The Naples of the film is not, however, false (which on the other hand a three-hour documentary could be); it is a mental landscape which is both objective like a pure photograph and subjective like a pure consciousness. It is clear that Rossellini's attitude towards his characters and their geographical and social environment is a second-degree reflection of that of his heroine when faced with Naples, with the difference that his consciousness is that of an artist of considerable culture and, in my opinion, a rare spiritual vitality.

I apologise for proceeding by metaphor, but this is because I am not a philosopher and cannot express myself more directly. I shall therefore attempt another comparison. I would assert of the forms of classic art and traditional realism that they construct works like one builds houses, with

bricks or cut stone. It is not a question of arguing against the usefulness of houses, or their possible beauty, or the perfect adaptation of bricks to this use, but it can be agreed that the reality of
the brick lies less in its composition than in its shape and its resistance. It would not occur to one
to define it as a piece of clay; its specificity as a mineral is of little importance: what matters is the
convenience of its volume. A brick is an element of a house. So much is clear in appearance itself.
One could say the same about the cut stones which form a bridge. They are perfectly shaped to
form an arch. But the blocks of stone scattered in a river bed are and remain rocks; their reality as
stone is not affected if, jumping from one to the next, I take advantage of them to cross the river.
If they have provisionally made that use possible for me it is because I have been able to contribute
to the accident of their layout my own touch of invention, adding the movement which, without
changing their nature or appearance, has given them a provisional meaning and use.

In the same way the neo-realist film has a meaning, but a posteriori, to the extent that it allows
our consciousness to pass from one fact to another, from one fragment of reality to the next,
whereas meaning is given a priori in classical artistic composition: the house is already there in the
brick.

If my analysis is correct, it follows that the term neo-realism should never be used as a noun,
except to designate the ensemble of neo-realist directors. Neo-realism does not exist in itself: there
are only neo-realist directors, whether they are materialist, Christian, Communist, or what have
you. Visconti is neo-realist in *La terra trema*, which calls for social revolt, and Rossellini is neo-
realist in *Francis*, which illustrates a purely spiritual reality. I would refuse the term only to
someone who set out to convince me by dividing what reality had joined.

I maintain therefore that *Journey to Italy* is neo-realist and considerably more so than for
example [De Sica's] *L'oro di Napoli*, which I admire a lot but which is based on a psychological and
subtly theatrical kind of realism, in spite of all the realistic details which try to fool us. I would go
further and say that of all Italian directors it is Rossellini who seems to me to have pushed furthest
the aesthetic of neo-realism. As I have said, there is no pure neo-realism. The neo-realist attitude
is an ideal that one can get more or less close to. In all so-called neo-realist films, there are still
residues of traditional spectacular, dramatic or psychological realism. One could analyse them thus:
documentary reality plus something else, that something else being variously the plastic beauty of
the images, social feeling, poetry, comedy, etc. One would look in vain in Rossellini for this separation of the event from the effect sought after. There is nothing literary or poetic in his work, not
even anything 'beautiful' in the superficial sense. His characters seem haunted by the demon of
mobility; the little friars of Saint Francis have no other way of rendering glory to God than by running a race. And that haunting march to his death of the boy in *Germany Year Zero*! Gesture, change,
physical movement are for Rossellini the very essence of human reality. One moves through physical settings which themselves at times move through the character. The Rossellinian universe is a
universe of pure acts, insignificant in themselves, but preparing almost behind God's back, as it
were, the sudden dazzling revelation of their meaning. This is the case with the miracle in *Journey
to Italy*, invisible to the characters and almost invisible to the camera, and also quite ambiguous
(for Rossellini does not claim that there has been a miracle, just the shouting and jostling that
accompany one) but whose jolt to the characters' consciousness unexpectedly releases their love.
No one, in my opinion, has succeeded better than the author of *Europe '51* in filming events with
a firmer, more integral aesthetic structure or with a more perfect transparency where it is less possible to see anything other than the event itself. Like a body which can present itself in either
amorphous or crystallised form. Rossellini's art lies in being able to give to facts simultaneously
their densest and their most elegant structure; not the most gracious but the sharpest, the most
direct, and the most penetrating. With him, neo-realism finds its way naturally towards the style
and materials of abstraction. Respecting the real does not mean piling up appearances; on the contrary it means stripping it of everything except the essential, it means attaining totality in simplicity.
Rossellini's art is linear and melodic. It is true that many of his films seem like sketches, their strokes

indicating more than they paint. But should this sureness of line be mistaken for poverty or laziness? No more than with Matisse. Perhaps Rossellini is, in fact, more a draftsman than a painter, a story-writer rather than a novelist. But hierarchy is not between genres but between artists.

I do not expect, my dear Aristarco, to have convinced you. Arguments never convince anybody. The conviction put into them often counts for more. I would be quite happy if my conviction, behind which lies that of some other critics who are friends of mine, could at least give yours a shake.

(Translated from the French version by Geoffrey Nowell-Smith)

C   Letter from Rossellini to Peter H. Wood (1972)

Peter H. Wood, a professor of history at Duke University and author of *Black Majority* (1974), had met Rossellini in New York in the early 1970s when the director was seeking advice and support for a film on the American Revolution. The film never got funded but Rossellini and Wood remained in contact. This letter is published here unabridged for the first time.

July 20, 1972

Dear Dr Wood

Your letter of June 12, mailed to Houston, was forwarded to Rome, and has caught up with me here in Fiesole. I'm very actively working on the science programs, in addition to the two films I am shooting here; one on Leon Battista Alberti, and another on Cosimo de' Medici. I do not have the treatment of *The American Revolution* here with me, but I shall have it sent to me from Rome, and then will forward it to you.

However, meanwhile in this letter, perhaps I can explain the substance of my ideas, and explain where they (like the science program) fit into the general scheme of my programs. Let me begin with this point: I believe we men are advancing at breakneck speed toward the time when we will have to constantly reshape the habits, behavior, and instincts we have developed over the course of our history. We should already have done this, but are absolutely not ready to face our problems at the necessary pace.

Man's knowledge is expanding at a giddy speed, and to keep up with it, individuals must multiply their present capabilities. Only new methods of education and communication can help us achieve this. And that is what I am trying to do. I have abandoned commercial, traditional cinema, and have dedicated myself to developing new educational methods through the use of visual images.

The etymological meaning of 'education' is, as we know: to castrate, or to conduct, or (a later meaning) to make bloom. Traditional educational methods almost always establish models, and in so doing invite imitation. In fact, this castrates the potential of human personality – which would conduct us toward the very 'best' of goals. The past is what we are most certain of; so traditional educational methods – superimposed on one of our most primitive impulses, that is, fear – induce us to copy, and to root ourselves in the past.

Yet we know that the past shows us only the historic road we have already traveled in search of perfection and wisdom. Therefore, if we take the past as a model, we go backwards. When progress was slow, when new ideas and discoveries appeared in moments greatly separated in time, educational methods rooted in the past did little harm. The fact is, we needed many centuries, many thousands of years to complete our first revolution: that of articulating (after mentally perceiving, examining and cataloguing) a language which communicates.

Language gave a new and powerful impetus to our intellectual faculties. Since then, revolutionary periods have taken place at an ever more accelerated tempo. The homo sapiens, after some thousands of years, reached the agricultural revolution. Then, in briefer and briefer time spans – always gaining more awareness – he advanced to other upheavals which shattered his past and pushed him, with increasing speed, toward the future. The revolutions which followed – first over the space of millenniums, then centuries, and finally, decades – are (after that of agriculture): axial scientific technology, and now, electronics.

Where are we heading now? Are we ready to confront the problems in the vast future which awaits us? No, we are not ready. All the bewilderment in the world today proves this.

Bacon, using the experimental method, contributed to scientific development, and also to the formation of a society of specialists. And through specialisation, we have accumulated enormous knowledge, scattered here and there like sheaves of wheat which we cannot gather up in a harvest of knowledge.

Now I shall tell you what I am trying to do toward exactly this end. I know that you Anglo-Saxons raise your eyebrows at those of us Latins who always speak in generalities. And you are right, in part. I have learned from you that action is (almost) all. So I shall tell you what I have done up to now, and what I plan to do. I'll explain why I have chosen the visual image as a means of education.

As I've told you, I have spent my professional life as a film producer/director. And I have learned that visual images are a most efficient means of saying something, and having it remembered.

Comenius, the great seventeenth-century Moravian pedagogue, said teaching is the queen of the arts, and the teaching method is as necessary as maps are to the navigator. But he admitted the inefficiency of the (then) available methods, because one could not teach with direct, visual images, but only through discourses which often became long and obscure. For 'direct vision', Comenius used the word 'autopsy', in its original meaning (which lasted until the end of the eighteenth century) 'to see with one's own eyes'.

Having established this point, I asked myself which images one should propose. Even those who are not professionals in film and television know the difference between the images of what are called 'documentary' films and those of the entertainment film. 'Documentary' images often fail to arouse the spectator's interest, perhaps because they are too basically demonstrative, because they too clearly are didactic and informative. Also because, over the millennium, even the most unprepared and ordinary works of man used dialectic procedures which were much more subtle and complex.

An educational method must be attractive. Visual images have accustomed us to expect entertainment. So images used for education must have the appeal of the entertainment film, yet maintain the rigor of the documentary. But if they are to be truly effective, one more thing must be kept in mind. I do not know if you are familiar with Dr Omar Moore's work with children. Well, besides traditional findings, he has identified a third basic impulse, in addition to the two elementary ones we already know: desire and fear. The third impulse is: pretending to know.

And think how true this is. We can observe it every day of our life. It is the major obstacle whenever one tries to establish a dialogue or convey information. So one must take this into account and invent a way that makes the didactic element seem a nod between 'those who know'.

The films I have made (and those I have been making ever since I was seized by the mania to create educational information) do take this into account. I believe you know one or two of my works. In these films, I show the customs, prejudices, fears, aspirations, ideas and agonies of an epoch and a place. I show a man – an innovator – confront these. And I have a drama equal to any other drama ever conceived, or ever to be conceived. I always avoid the temptation to exalt this personality; I limit myself to observing him. Confronting a man with his age gives me enough material to construct action and incite curiosity. Shakespeare said, 'Action is eloquence. The eyes of the ignorant are more learned than their ears'.

Following these concepts, I have produced the following programs, which were destined primarily for television: *Man's Struggle for Survival* (12 hours); *The Iron Age* (5 hours); *The Acts of the Apostles* (6 hours); *Blaise Pascal* (2 hours); *The Rise of Louis XIV* (1 hour, 35 minutes). I am now in production with *Leon Battista Alberti* and *Cosimo De' Medici* (4 hours). I have already prepared, and will this year produce *Descartes* (2 hours). Next year, I will produce *Denis Diderot* (2 hours); *Niepce and Daguerre* (2 hours) and *The American Revolution* (2 hours). I have one television series

The Iron Age (1964): the smelting process.

in production on *The Industrial Revolution* (12 hours), and another on *Science* (10 hours). When all of these programs are in release, I believe I will have completed a work which, in its entirety, will give a cultural orientation, in a general way, to vast masses of the public. From my point of view, each of these programs is complementary to the others. The entire body of work should serve to trace a good part of the history of human progress. The human 'I' develops step by step as man gains new experience, and shapes these experiences with his intelligence.

With *Man's Struggle for Survival*, I tried to delineate a general historic picture from the caveman to the man of our time. I showed the passage of the hunting, fishing, and fruit-picking epoch to the agricultural civilisation, which is matriarchal. It is man's first step toward living from nature, rather than in nature. Then I describe, with the arrival of the Hellenists in the Mediterranean, the change to a patriarchal society. I tell of the development of the Egyptian civilisation, the fall of Rome, the transformation of predatory, barbaric tribes into farmers. The monastic movement with its ideal of prayer and work. The formation of the feudal society. The crusades. The advent of the artisans, inhabitants of boroughs; the bourgeoisie. The formation of communal society. The troubadour movement. The foundation of the university. The development of alchemy, the yearning for science. The diffusion of the machine. Christopher Columbus. The beginnings of the scientific era: Galileo, Rabelais, Harvey, Lavoisier, Franklin, Galvani, Volta, Pasteur. Then Watt's steam engine, Stephenson's locomotive, Morse's telegraph, Marconi's wireless. Finally, the contemporary age: the space adventure, student revolution, the hippies, the bewilderment in which we writhe.

The images from each age demonstrate the development of technology, medicine, of a growing scientific rationalism, and of religious ideas. I also show machines, manufacturing procedures, experiments, philosophic debates, and enthusiasms and fears. It is an educational series incorporating the ingredients of the entertainment film, with characters, actions, dialogue, dramatic and comic situations, accurate reconstruction of ambients which are difficult to describe in a letter (even in one as long as this one). I have put all of these elements into this program of cultural orientation. This television series was conceived and produced by me, and directed by my son Renzo. I intended *Man's Struggle for Survival* to be sort of a spinal cord to which I would attach the other productions.

The Iron Age, also directed by my son, follows more or less the same concept of programming already described, but deals with a period of history more specific than this age is usually considered to be.

The Acts of the Apostles is the story of Luke the Evangelist, but also of the change in ethics in our history when the Hebrew idea of nature – a gift of God which man must use to distinguish himself from the animals – spreads, thanks to Christianity, through the Greek–Roman pagan world, which had regarded nature as something inviolable which men, through rite and ritual, tried to render benign.

Socrates is based on Plato, but is also indebted to Diogenes Laertius and Xenophon. It represents, with all historic reality, the Athens of that time. The age, with its sophists and its rhetoricians, was developing methods of persuasion, and with Socrates' character, we show his method of developing logic and intelligence.

Augustine of Hippo shows us Saint Augustine and the history of the fall of the Roman Empire; the end of one civilisation and the birth of another.

Leon Battista Alberti takes place at the beginning of the Age of Humanism, following the degeneration of the pedantic scholasticism which had paralysed intelligence. Humanism brings a fresh wind of knowledge and enthusiasm, after the sad, cramped medieval mysticism. It stands for order and intellectual synthesis, after the confusion of an ever more specialised dialectic; minute, vain and obscure.

Cosimo De' Medici gives great impetus to mercantilism, to the commerce in money, to bank organisation. He lends vigor and new spirit to taste, and to the joy of adventure. *Cosimo De' Medici* also follows the development of an economic system which, with certain variations, still exists today.

Blaise Pascal shows us the drama of a man who develops scientific thought which is in conflict with the dogmatism of his deep religious faith.

Descartes represents, among other things, the advent of a method in which human thought becomes more rational and definitively moves toward the age of technical and scientific development.

The American Revolution is perhaps the only true social–political revolution achieved by man since the time of Babylon. Other revolutions (for example, the French and the Russian) brought to power a new social class which crushed and cancelled out the one which had held power before. The American Revolution determined the success of new ideas. Power and obedience have always characterised social order. The American Revolution brings a new concept to the idea of power. Thomas Paine, who well expressed the opinion of his world and his time, conveyed this concept, saying: the state is a necessary evil. Instead of institutionalising the most modern ideas of its time – from Locke to Rousseau, etc. – the American Revolution was concerned with reducing the 'evil' of the state to a minimum. It strained to reduce the state's power to a guarantee which respected a few fundamental rules of social organisation. The audience will see what a profound difference there is between the idea of democracy left by the American Revolution, and the Greek ideal, accurately described in *Socrates*. In *The American Revolution*, Jefferson is my hero.

Denis Diderot and his encyclopedia bring further order to general knowledge. Their contribution is toward making men more rational, and therefore enabling them to advance.

The Industrial Revolution shows, of course, technical and scientific development, but also the new urban and social organisation built up around the factories and machines, and the arrival of all the new political and social ideas: liberalism, socialism, Fascism, Marxism.

Niepce and Daguerre, with the invention of photography, usher in a new age of communication and also an immense change in the figurative arts. Up to the time of Niepce and Daguerre, as we have seen in other programs – particularly in *Leon Battista Alberti* – the figurative arts and other human activities have searched, over the centuries, for truth. After the advent of photography – which is the truth as it appears to our eyes – figurative art pulls away from accurate depiction with enormous rapidity, and reaches every form of abstraction. And in this movement, many other intellectual activities are implicated.

As we know, from the origins of human life, men have been regulated by two main inclinations: that of Prometheus and that of Orpheus; the techno-scientific and the artistic; the constructive and the expressive. And these have taken different roads toward the same goal: truth. Today, it seems to me, our goal does not seem to be a singular one. We seem to be searching for more than one truth.

The *Science* series I am producing is just a statement of what we know. Science, which defines our time, appears ever more mysterious and menacing. Perhaps if we understand it, we will no longer fear it.

All that I have written here may seem presumptuous, and perhaps it is. But I believe that we men of today have an enormous need to orient ourselves in the new reality we have discovered. Even though a work be imperfect, it is always better than nothing.

If one thinks for a moment of the enormous investment of money made, after the scholastic age, in improving 'taste' (the museums, exhibits, concerts, art academies, etc.) and then of the little – the very little – spent (outside the professions) to realise a return from the enormous capital of intelligence of men, one is astonished. I do not have money, and therefore, with the help of some few friends, I invest all my talents and capabilities in this direction. If additional means were available, I would do more, and do it better. As you know, I am also trying to bring young people in the schools of cinema in which I am active into [sic] this same direction.

Unfortunately, we know that it is considered a poor investment to spend money on improving the quality of men. Without doubt, men can be with or without culture: yet culture, like economy, forms a basic part of any human society. We know that in the present economic system, one sector and then another declines, or risks ruin. Or – and this has already taken place in agriculture, and now is occurring in industry – technical advances increase productive capabilities to such an extent that the need for manpower is reduced. Individuals will react better – much better – to these changes, to this mobility, if they have a vaster culture to aid them in their general orientation. For example, it has been noted that the longer one's education lasts, the more open one is to change and innovation.

In the near future, it is possible that other phenomenal changes will occur more frequently, on a larger scale, and in ever briefer periods of time. We need to be ready to face these changes, and their new implications. That is why every investment made in spreading knowledge, through visual and audio means, would be excellent. One could then plan a rhythm of production and distribution adequate to the goal of 'permanent education', which has been discussed for so long, but which has never been confronted or resolved.

I believe we can resolve the problems of the future which are dizzily speeding toward us only if we learn how to multiply man's capacities, how to crush specialisation, and how to acquire vast knowledge. I believe in this.

Forgive me for this extremely long letter. It is the price you must pay for being a man I found intelligent, and capable of true interest.

Reproduced, with minor corrections, from the typescript in English in the Pacific Film Archive, Berkeley. A shortened version was published, with an introduction by Peter H. Wood, as 'I Believe in This: A Letter from Roberto Rossellini', in *The New Republic*, 2 July 1977, pp. 27–30.

D   Seeing with our own eyes (1972)

I have faith in everything, except cinema. I have faith in man, in history, in the future of the world, in the coexistence of ideologies, but not in the future of the cinema. I'm convinced that if it's not dead, it's on the point of dying. I don't know how many times I have reiterated this notion during the past ten years, but every time that for one reason or another I reaffirm it I feel more and more convinced of its truth. Cinema as traditionally understood, in its structures of production, but even more in its structures of distribution, has today been superseded by television. With the transmission of pictures via cable, a project which even a few years ago seemed to come straight out of science fiction (namely the system which would enable one to project the same film in many cinemas simultaneously, overtaking the antiquated system in which many copies had to be sent out, stored and were therefore liable to deteriorate) will be reality. But if cinema is to have a social function it must be educative, it must teach people something, it must speak about humans to other humans. In other words, the public must not simply have a few hours for recreation, but must also participate in historical and human events through a form of immediate spectacle, conducted in a new and dynamic way. Is it not television that plays this role? I recently noted that technological specialisations have fragmented knowledge and society, creating many little sub-groups. So human society has become atomised and has lost the capacity to develop any kind of choral life and an integral unity of thought. To mend this damage we must now try patiently to sew up again, to mend the vast lacerations we have caused. How can we do this? Can television help solve this problem? To answer these questions we must go back to the notion of 'free time', and to the space that, in the free time of every human being, is covered by television programmes.

We must thus take advantage of what the French call 'loisir', which means the opportunity and comfort that free time offers us to relax and enjoy ourselves, to organise and fuse together the countless forms of knowledge which swarm chaotically around us as random atoms, and make a solid body of them, so that we can at last, on that basis, develop our human personality, which is mainly based on intelligence. To grasp this point we should re-examine our notions about education. We must go back to what the director-general of UNESCO said about education – no longer understood as an education for life, but as a coordinate of life itself such that it enables us to follow and assimilate daily new knowledge which happens with an ever faster rhythm, and inevitably changes our general view of things. Let us therefore make use of television which is capable of transmitting ever new forms of knowledge to us.

The image, as we know, is a very valuable source of information. Shakespeare said that the eyes of the ignorant are more intelligent than their ears. But Comenius, the eminent Moravian pedagogue, also said about 300 years before television was invented that education, queen of arts, encountered many difficulties because traditional teaching methods, by not allowing one to learn through direct sight, forced one to remember long speeches which often ended in apparent confusion. For 'direct sight' he used the word 'autopsy' in its etymological sense of 'seeing with one's own eyes'. Television enables us to see with our own eyes. Today our reasonable irrationality has hurled us into chaos, but fortunately we are still managing to float on this ocean of confusion, shaken by the gusts of new experiences, and images, with their naked purity and their demonstrative directness, can show us the route we must follow to orientate ourselves in knowledge.

Originally published in the pamphlet *Film della TV* produced to accompany the second season of RAI television films at the Museum of Modern Art, New York, 30 November–28 December 1972; reproduced in *Rossellini e la televisione*, edited by Sergio Trasatti (Rome: La Rassegna, 1978), pp. 201–3; this translation was previously published in Ranvaud (ed.), *Roberto Rossellini*, p. 84.

E   Ideas towards a film about Marx (1976)

Marxism has divided the world in two. One side considers Karl Marx the leader who will guide humanity towards a better future; the other side regards him as a demon – the enemy of civilisation. Some celebrate his genius as the herald of revenge and freedom; others damn him as a pernicious freedom-killing tyrant.

This division is responsible for the proliferation of hatred and violence. Why this disunion? Marx is considered heretical by his adversaries because he introduced and developed a new vision of the world; an overall version of the nature of man with all its consequences. This new idea of the world forms a 'theory' that implies *action*. In the Marxist conception of the world action must be defined 'rationally' and be responsible for the foundation of a new political programme. Marx has aroused indignation and anger to match the furore which surrounded Galileo when he affirmed and demonstrated the precise and accurate nature of the Copernican theories that placed the sun at the centre of a number of planets, one of which (being the earth) could no longer be conceived as the centre of the universe. These 'scandals' are not a novelty in the history of mankind: we were indignant and angry when it was said that the earth was round and not flat; when the physiologist Harvey revolutionised the laws of blood circulation; when we lifted the seat of feelings from the heart to the brain; and so on. Marxist conceptions have exasperated many, but, what is worse, they have precipitated others into a world of 'fantastic' hopes. But these flights of fancy, as Marx clearly stated, do not bring salvation in themselves.

At the meeting of the 'correspondence' committee, held in Brussels on 30 March 1846, he said:

> To arouse the masses without founding their activities simultaneously on solid bases is deceitful. To turn to the workers without having precise scientific ideas and a concrete doctrine is to transform propaganda into a meaningless game without scruples, one which relies on the assumption that what is needed is an ardent apostle of enthusiasm faced with donkeys who listen open-mouthed. In a civilised country one cannot pretend to realise any political goal without a definite and concrete didactic programme. Without this, we have so far achieved nothing but a great deal of noise, an inauspicious flurry of excitement, and the disarray of the cause we wish to defend.

On the same occasion he added: 'Until now ignorance has never been of any use to anyone'.

On 15 September 1850, four years later, during the meeting of the Communist League which ratified Willich's dissent, he confirmed:

> The minority replaces the notion of criticism with that of dogmatism, the materialist with the idealist. While we say to the workers 'You must embark on fifteen, twenty, twenty-five years of civil and international wars not only to transform the present situation but also to transform yourselves and be ready to seize political power', you say to them: 'We must seize power immediately, otherwise we might as well go to sleep'.

> In the same way that the 'democrats' hail the word *masses* as a sacrosanct entity, you sanctify another 'deity', the word *proletariat*!

In the *Introduction to the Critique of Political Economy* of 1857, Marx wrote: 'We can establish that something is concrete by the synthesis of the interaction between given determinations containing in themselves multiple permutations'.

For him history is the history of man from his discovery of knowledge and his development through the ages.

Marx has also identified the historical and logical reality of contradictions: 'The world would precipitate into absurdity if we did not focus our preoccupations on the study of contradictions and their solutions'.

Marxism indicates a methodology that allows man to become himself authentically, and thus be rescued from absurdity.

Metaphysicians attempt to assess and determine mankind in relation to reason, refusing to take into consideration its vices which are to relegated to the realism of the devil. Marx conversely stresses that the 'non-human' is a real fact to be treated in the same way as the 'human'. The human element is essentially positive; the non-human element is by the same token negative: it marks the alienation of the human.

Capitalism gave rise to the Industrial Revolution, the overturning of traditional modes of production, with all the enormous consequences.

It fostered the extraordinary development of all technologies, and yet so far it has proved incapable of satisfying many material requirements of life; on the contrary it has generated an increase of artificial need, thereby locating the fetishistic concern for money solely as an end, and no longer a means.

The relationship of a human being to his fetishes exiles man from himself and makes him lose touch with his sense of identity, fostering alienation.

The fetish-world is falsely human; human history demonstrates clearly the endless interpenetration and interaction of three elements:
– the spontaneous element (biological, physiological, natural);
– the element of thought (rising consciousness);
– the illusory element (part of the fetishistic alienation).
Only a dialectical analysis can allow us to discern and distinguish these elements in the perpetual struggle characteristic of real movement in history.

For Karl Marx, what counts is the formulation of a thought that synthesises, connects and unifies all the permutations of the available data: in this context the deductions arrived at will never be atrophied or present themselves as final resolutions.

Dialectical materialism is, in this sense, a product of thought bent on developing a rational knowledge of the world which can never be fulfilled by its findings – it must constantly sharpen itself and overcome the procedural stages achieved.

Marx is never dogmatic.

There are many societies, associations, political coalitions, economic and state foundations aimed at supporting or destroying Marxism that operate according to highly dogmatic principles. But the masses that move or are moved for or against his ideas have very little, if any, first-hand experience of his writings. Furthermore, he has been instrumentalised by so-called 'political' groups to an absurd degree.

In his intellectual elaboration Marx has developed a methodology capable of analysing human society in great detail: a truly anatomical practice of the social corpus. His aim was to provide the slave as well as the tyrant with the means of encouraging the surfacing of authentic human qualities on which a human society composed of free and equal people could be founded.

The confusion which surrounds Marx's ideas finds further fuel in the political events that have taken place in the world on account of political forces that are or have been labelled 'Marxist'.

The labels were certainly correct, but as Marx points out, 'the methods by which changes are achieved will be profoundly different in each country' (Amsterdam, 8 September 1872):

> We have never claimed that to arrive at the given end (the proletarian revolution) the means have to be identical in every country of the world. We are well aware of the importance that institutions, customs and tradition have in various countries such as the United States, Britain, and, if I were more familiar wfth your institutions, I would have added the Netherlands, in which your workers may be able to reach their goal by peaceful means.

But in everyday practice greater confusion on Marxism is derived from the meaning(s) given to certain words. One such word is 'revolution'. It has commonly assumed the stereotyped meaning of a *coup* that shatters all in its path in a gigantic carnival of violence.

Yet those who will be able to or want to *know* Marx will understand whether he claims that it is necessary to engage in revolution in order to change men or whether we should concentrate on man in order to revolutionise everything.

He claims that the revolutionary struggle presupposes a self-aware proletariat capable of becoming a class through its own thoughts, its own intellectual groups, its own 'values', its own 'cultural models' set in opposition to those of the bourgeoisie. Communism, for Marx, must not become a generalisation and a glorification of the proletarian condition, but the abolition of this condition precisely because its goal is the *abolition of classes*: 'an association in which each individual's free development is the basis for the free development of the social corpus' (From the Manifesto of the Communist Party).

Another terrifying term is 'dictatorship of the proletariat'.

Marx states that the bourgeoisie with its relationship between production and commerce gives birth to a juridicial and political superstructure: one state. But each state however much it may flaunt its apparent 'independence' in relation to 'society' is always the state of the dominant class.

There is no need for capital punishment, concentration camps, deportations: in practice a class dictatorship may also be realised with other political forms: the Republic, bourgeois Democracy are probably the best forms adopted by the 'dictatorship of the bourgeoisie'.

Therefore to counterpose this dictatorship, as a means of achieving a transition, it is possible to establish the dictatorship of the proletariat in the sense given by Marx – see his writings on the Paris Commune – as the utmost condition of democracy. It is important, however, to arrive at the goal of the dismantlement of classes, that the proletariat, when it has constituted its own thought, can achieve hegemony.

Preface to treatment for the unrealised film *Lavorare per l'umanità*, 1976, translated by Don Ranvaud in *Framework*, no. 11, Autumn 1979, republished in Ranvaud (ed.), *Roberto Rossellini*, pp. 75–6 (originally published as 'Il mio Marx', *Paese Sera*, 5 June 1977, then in *Filmcritica*, nos. 289–90, November–December 1978, pp. 364–6).

F   Fellini on Rossellini (1980)

I felt more comfortable [than in the studio] making films outside, in the open air. In this Rossellini was the pioneer. My experience with Rossellini, the journey of *Paisà*, represented for me the discovery of Italy. Until then I hadn't seen much: Rimini, Florence, Rome and some little places in the South which I got a glimpse of when touring in variety – villages and little townships hidden away in a medieval darkness rather like the places I had known as a child except that the dialect was different. I liked Rossellini's way of making films as a pleasant trip, a day out with friends. [...]

Following Rossellini around when he was shooting *Paisà* provided me with the sudden joyous revelation that you could make a film with the same freedom, the same lightness of spirit, with which you might draw or write, enjoying it and suffering with it day by day, hour by hour, without agonising too much about the final result; and having the same, secret, anxious and exciting relationship with it that one has with one's own neuroses; I realised too that the blockages, the doubts, the second thoughts, the dramas, the travails were not that different from those suffered by the painter trying to fix a tint on the canvas or a writer crossing out, rewriting, correcting and starting again, looking for a mode of expression hidden, impalpable and elusive, as one possibility among a thousand. Rossellini searched, he pursued his film through the streets, with the Allied armoured cars rumbling past a couple of feet behind his back, folk at the windows shouting and singing, hundreds of people trying to sell us something or steal something from us, in that incandescent hell, that teeming anthill which is Naples, and then again in Florence and Rome and in the countless channels of the Po delta, with every imaginable problem, permits withdrawn at the last minute, schedules scrapped, money mysteriously disappearing, and a constant succession of producers, each greedier, more childish, more of a liar and even more fly-by-night than the last.

So it seems to me that from Rossellini I learnt – a lesson never translated into words, never expressed, never transformed into a programme – the possibility of staying on one's feet in the midst of the most adverse, the most hostile conditions and with this the ability to turn these adversities and hostilities to advantage, to convert them into artistic feeling, into emotional values, into a point of view. This is what Rossellini did. He lived the life of a film like a marvellous adventure to be experienced and recounted at the same time. His abandonment in the face of reality, while remaining attentive, clear-headed, engaged, his natural ability to place himself at an imaginary but exact point in between indifferent detachment and clumsy identification, enabled him to pinpoint and to capture reality in all its dimensions, to look at things from inside and outside at the same time, to photograph the air around things, to uncover the intangible, arcane, magical aspects of life. Is this not what neo-realism is all about? Therefore when talking about neo-realism one can only refer to Rossellini. The others did realism, or naturalism, or tried to translate a talent, a vocation, into a formula, a recipe.

And in the more recent films, those that he made because he had been paid an advance or because the idea had appealed to him only to be instantly forgotten, in these films which are sometimes embarrassing and have been made without any real drive – even in these films you will always find a moment which reveals his eye, his feeling for a reality caught in the moment of its inevitability, its tragic potential intact. These moments in Rossellini have an almost sacred quality, lurking precisely in the excessive familiarity of the all too banal gesture, the tritest habit, the cliché. It was as if the apparently casual and distracted eye that Rossellini cast over the most appalling situations allowed them to preserve untouched their terrible power, and the shock they created seemed to be the product of the transparent unawareness of the onlooking eye. This look, this way of observing things, coincided with a moment in time when everything that happened was instant history, was already narration, character, dialectic. So long as reality continued to be the painful, fragmented, tragic, elusive reality of the post-war years, there was a miraculous coincidence between this reality and the detached eye of Rossellini observing it.

Later, when times changed and this style and this way of seeing needed to be pursued in more depth because reality was becoming more complex, more concealed, less external, less outwardly dramatised, Rossellini, who was deeply in love with life and who liked to live life adventurously, totally, without restraint, probably thought it was not worth the sacrifice to have to stand outside of life and look at it and think and reflect on it so that he could represent it with an eye that retained its original purity and intensity. Perhaps he thought that it was more worthwhile to live life than to stand on the outside perfecting and keeping intact his perceptual talent, protecting it from losing its clarity, and from the short-sightedness of passions, desires, greed. But he didn't do this, and got into a fight with that part of himself, distancing it from himself, denying it, maintaining that it was an immature part, infantile, spoilt, aristocratic, and he didn't need it.

But in his eagerness to affirm, as he did for a number of years, his disagreement with and contempt for everything that was not avowedly educational, I think one can see traces of the nostalgia, the bitterness and the embarrassment of someone who knows he has denied and betrayed something. But perhaps this is just a whimsical interpretation of my own, an equally nostalgic and embarrassed projection foisted on him by someone who has not had the skill or the strength to be different.

(From Federico Fellini, *Fare un film* (Turin: Einaudi 1980), pp. 44–7; translated by GeoffreyNowell-Smith)

Notes

1   In fact (at least in the English-language version) the quotation is a slightly different one, not from Isaiah but from the Epistle to the Romans, 10: 20: 'I was found of them that sought me not. I was made manifest unto them that asked not after me'.

2   The character played by Giulietta Masina in Federico Fellini's *La strada* (1954). The film was reviewed by Aristarco in *Cinema Nuovo*, vol. 3, no. 46, 10 November 1954.

3   Vittorio De Sica's *Stazione Termini* (English title: *Indiscretion of an American Wife*), funded by David Selznick and starring his protégée Jennifer Jones, was reviewed by Aristarco in *Cinema*

Nuovo, vol. 2, no. 9, 15 April 1953, respectfully but not as favourably as Bazin implies later in his letter. Alberto Lattuada's *La spiaggia* ('The Beach'), aka *La Pensionnaire*, was another 'commercial' production by a former neo-realist director.

4   Amédée Ayfre, 'Néo-réalisme et phénoménologie', *Cahiers du Cinéma*, vol. 3, no. 17, 1952, pp. 6–18; translated in Jim Hillier (ed.), *Cahiers du Cinéma*, vol. 1: *The 1950s: Neo-Realism, Hollywood, New Wave* (London: Routledge & Kegan Paul, 1985), pp. 182–91.

Filmography

Adriano Aprà, Sarah Lutton

Except where otherwise specified, original language and production is Italian and films are black and white, 35 mm, 1:1.37, at 24 fps. English-language translations of titles are in brackets; English-language titles under which films were released are in italics. Square brackets indicate uncredited contributors. Asterisks indicate films to which Rossellini made only a minor contribution. All data have been checked on extant prints except where otherwise specified.

1935 *Dafne*. Short film directed by Rossellini.
Subject: possibly inspired by the classical characters Daphnis and Chloë.
No known print exists.
(Two images from this film were published in *Lo Schermo*, November 1935, which show a young man and woman in costumes like fauns. This film may in fact be the same as the later *Prélude à l'après-midi d'un faune*).

1937 (?) *Prélude à l'après-midi d'un faune* (Prelude to the Afternoon of a Faun)
Director: Roberto Rossellini.
Subject: possibly from Stéphane Mallarmé's eclogue 'L'après-midi d'un faune' (1876) and/or Claude Debussy's *Prélude à l'après-midi d'un faune* (1894).
Unreleased, possibly unfinished. No known print exists.
As stated above, possibly the same film as *Dafne*.

*1937 *La fossa degli angeli* (The Quarry of the Angels)
Director: Carlo Ludovico Bragaglia. [Assistant director: Roberto Rossellini].
Production Company: Diorama Film.
Subject: Cesare Vico Lodovici.
Script: Curt Alexander, Carlo Ludovico Bragaglia, [Roberto Rossellini].
Director of Photography: Piero Pupilli, Mario Albertelli.
Editor: Ferdinando M. Poggioli.
Music: Enzo Masetti.
Cast includes: Amedeo Nazzari (Pietro), Luisa Ferida (Luisa), Antonio Gradoli (Domenico).
Length: 88 minutes.
No known print exists.

*1938 *Luciano Serra pilota* (Luciano Serra, Pilot)
Director: Goffredo Alessandrini. [Supervisor: Vittorio Mussolini]. Assistant: Umberto Scarpelli.
Producer: Angelo Monti.
Production Company: Aquila Film SA (Milan)
Production Manager: Franco Riganti.
Subject: Based on a story by F[ilippo] Masoero and Goffredo Alessandrini adapted by Fulvio Palmieri, Ivo Perilli.
Script: Roberto Rossellini, Goffredo Alessandrini.
Dialogue: Cesare Giulio Viola.
Director of Photography: Ubaldo Arata.
Editor: Giorgio C. Simonelli.
Music: Giulio Cesare Sonzogno, conducted by Edoardo De Risi.
Cast includes: Amedeo Nazzari (Luciano Serra), Germana Paolieri (his wife, Sandra), Roberto Villa (their son, Aldo), Mario Ferrari (Colonel Franco Morelli).
First screened: August 1938, Venice Film Festival.
Length: 105 minutes (no known print of this length exists).

1940 *Fantasia sottomarina* (Undersea Fantasy)
Director: Roberto Rossellini.
[Producer: Roberto Rossellini].
[Production Company (for post-production): INCOM].
[Production Manager: Domenico Paolella (for INCOM)].
Subject: Roberto Rossellini.
[Narrator: Guido Notari].
Director of Photography: Rodolfo Lombardi.
Music: Edoardo Micucci.
Released: 12 April 1940, Rome. (Shot 1938, post-production 1939.)
Length: 10 minutes.

1940 *Il tacchino prepotente* (The Bullying Turkey)
Director: Roberto Rossellini.
[Production Company: Scalera].
Director of Photography: Mario Bava.
Music: Maria Strino.
Released: No record of any release, although there may have been a limited postwar release.
Length: 5 minutes.

1940 *La vispa Teresa* (Lively Teresa)
Director: Roberto Rossellini.
Production Company: Scalera.
Director of Photography: Mario Bava.
Music: Simone Cuccia.
[Cast includes: Adriana Ceriani (Teresa)]
Released: No record of any release.
Length: 7 minutes.

1941 *Il ruscello di Ripasottile* (The Brook of Ripasottile)
Director: Roberto Rossellini.
Production Company: Excelsior-Saci.
Executive Producer: Franco Riganti.
Commentary: Elisabetta Riganti.
Director of Photography: Rodolfo Lombardi.
Music: Ugo Filippini.
Released: 4(?) May 1941, Rome.
Length: *c.* 10 minutes.
No known print exists.

1941 *La nave bianca* (The White Ship)
[Director: Roberto Rossellini (with the supervision of Francesco De Robertis)].
Production Company: Centro Cinematografico del Ministero della Marina, for Scalera.
[Subject: Francesco De Robertis].
[Script: Francesco De Robertis, Roberto Rossellini].
[Director of Photography: Giuseppe Caracciolo].
[Editor: Eraldo Da Roma].
Music: Renzo Rossellini.
Cast includes: Non-professionals, officers and men of the navy, and nurses of the
voluntary corps (Corpo Volontario).
First screened: 14 September 1941, Venice Film Festival.
Released: 4 October 1941, Rome.
Length: Release print 84 minutes, existing print 71 minutes.
No names, apart from Renzo Rossellini, are mentioned in the titles.

1942 *Un pilota ritorna* (A Pilot Returns)
Director: Roberto Rossellini.
Production Company: Anonima Cinematografica Italiana (ACI).
Executive Producer: Franco Riganti.
Production Manager: Luigi Giacosi.
Subject: Tito Silvio Mursino [alias Vittorio Mussolini].
Script: Rosario Leone, Michelangelo Antonioni, Massimo Mida, Margherita Maglione,
Roberto Rossellini.
[Dialogue: Ugo Betti, Gherardo Gherardi].
Director of Photography: Vincenzo Seratrice.
Editor: Eraldo Da Roma.
Music: Renzo Rossellini, conducted by Pietro Sassòli.
Cast includes: Massimo Girotti (Lieutenant Gino Rossati), Michela Belmonte (Anna),
Gaetano Masier (Lieutenant Trisotti), [Elvira Betrone (Gino's Mother)].
Released: 8 April 1942, Rome.
Length: Release print 85 minutes, existing print 81 minutes.

*1942 *I 3 aquilotti* (Three Pilots in Training)
Director: Mario Mattòli.
Production Company: Anonima Cinematografica Italiana (ACI).

Production Manager: Luigi Giacosi.

[Script: Mario Mattòli, Alessandro De Stefani, Roberto Rossellini].

Director of Photography: Anchise Brizzi.

Editor: Fernando Tropea.

Music: Ezio Carabella, [Renzo Rossellini, Giovanni D'Anzi].

Cast includes: Leonardo Cortese (Marco Massi), Michela Belmonte (Adriana Terrazzani), Carlo Minello (Mario Terrazzani, her brother), Alberto Sordi (Filippo Nardini).

Released: 30 August 1942.

Length: 77 minutes.

*1943–9 *L'invasore* (The Invader)

Director: Nino Giannini, with the supervision of Roberto Rossellini.

Producer: Federico D'Avack.

Production Company: Imperator/Sovrania and/or Produttori Associati.

Subject: Nino Giannini.

Script: Gherardo Gherardi, Nino Giannini, Alberto Consiglio.

Dialogue: Giovanni Del Lungo.

Director of Photography: Tony Frenguelli.

Editor: Nino Giannini.

Music: Edoardo Micucci.

Cast includes: Miria di San Servolo (Diana di Valfreda), Amedeo Nazzari (Count Carlo di Valfreda), Osvaldo Valenti (Roger de la Fierté), Olga Solbelli (Countess di Valfreda).

Released: 16 December 1949.

Length: 85 minutes.

Credits not checked on print.

1943 *L'uomo dalla croce* (The Man with the Cross)

Director: Roberto Rossellini, supervised by Asvero Gravelli. Assistants: Mariano Cafiero, Franco Pompili.

Production Company: Continentalcine [in collaboration with Cines].

Production Manager: Giuseppe Sylos.

Subject: Asvero Gravelli.

Script: Asvero Gravelli, Alberto Consiglio, Giovanni D'Alicandro, Roberto Rossellini.

Director of Photography: Guglielmo Lombardi.

Editor: Eraldo Da Roma.

Music: Renzo Rossellini conducted by Pietro Sassòli.

Cast includes: Alberto Tavazzi (Military Chaplain), Roswitha Schmidt (Irina), Attilio Dottesio (wounded tank driver), Antonio Marietti (Sergei).

Released: 9 June 1943, Rome.

Length: 74 minutes.

1943–6 *Desiderio* (Desire) (*Woman*, USA).

Directors: Roberto Rossellini, Marcello Pagliero.

[Production Companies: Sovrania Film (with Rossellini), SAFIR – Società Anonima Film Italiani Roma (with Pagliero)].

Subject: Anna Benvenuti.
[Script: Rosario Leone, Giuseppe De Santis, Diego Calcagno, Roberto Rossellini (for Rossellini section), Guglielmo Santangelo, Marcello Pagliero (for Pagliero section)].
Director of Photography: Rodolfo Lombardi (with Rossellini), Ugo Lombardi (with Pagliero).
[Editor: Marcello Pagliero].
Music: Renzo Rossellini.
Cast includes: Elli Parvo (Paola Previtali), Massimo Girotti (Nando Mancini), Roswitha Schmidt (Anna Previtali Mancini), Carlo Ninchi (Giovanni Mirelli).
Released: 9 August 1946, Rome.
Length: Release print 85 minutes (according to censorship visa, possibly incorrect), existing print 79 minutes (nude shots were removed from original release print before general release, but are included in the existing print). Announced as *Scalo merci*, started in July 1943 as *Rinuncia*, interrupted in September 1943, completed by Pagliero in October 1945 as *Desiderio*.

1945 *Roma città aperta* (*Rome Open City*, UK; *Open City*, USA).
Director: Roberto Rossellini. Assistants: Sergio Amidei, [Federico Fellini, Mario Chiari, Alberto Manni, Bruno Todini].
[Producers: Chiara Politi, Giuseppe Amato (briefly), Aldo Venturini].
Production Company: Excelsa Film.
Production Managers: [Carlo Civallero, Angelo Besozzi, Ermanno Donati, Luigi Carpentieri (initially)], Ferruccio De Martino.
Subject: Sergio Amidei, [Alberto Consiglio].
Script: Sergio Amidei, with the collaboration of Federico Fellini.
Director of Photography: Ubaldo Arata.
Editor: Eraldo Da Roma.
Music: Renzo Rossellini, conducted by Luigi Ricci.
Cast includes: Anna Magnani (Pina), Aldo Fabrizi (Don Pietro Pellegrini), Marcello Pagliero (Manfredi), Maria Michi (Marina), Francesco Grandjacquet (Francesco), Harry Feist (Major Bergmann), Vito Annicchiarico (Marcello).
First screened: 28 August 1945 by the US Information Agency at the Italian Ministry for Press and Entertainment; 24 September 1945, Rome, Teatro Quirino, first Festival internazionale della musica, del teatro e del cinematografo (with the title *Città aperta*).
Released: 8 October 1945, Rome.
Length: 104 minutes.

1946 *Paisà* (released under original title in all territories except USA, where released as *Paisan*).
Director: Roberto Rossellini. Assistants: Federico Fellini, Massimo Mida, Eugenia Handamir, Annalena Limentani, [Renzo Avanzo, Vercours, Basilio Franchina].
Producers: Roberto Rossellini, [Mario Conti, Renato Campos] (OFI), Rod E. Geiger, [Robert Lawrence] (FFP).
Production Companies: Organizzazione Film Internazionale(OFI), Foreign Film Productions (FFP).

Production Manager: Ugo Lombardi.
Subject: Sergio Amidei, with the collaboration of Klaus Mann, Federico Fellini, Marcello Pagliero, Alfred Hayes, Roberto Rossellini.
Script: Sergio Amidei, Federico Fellini, Roberto Rossellini (adaptation and English translation, Annalena Limentani).
Director of Photography: Otello Martelli.
Editor: Eraldo Da Roma.
Music: Renzo Rossellini.
Cast includes: Sicily Episode: Carmela Sazio (Carmela), Robert van Loon (Joe).
Naples Episode: Alfonsino [Bovino] (Pasquale), Dotts M. Johnson (Joe).
Rome Episode: Maria Michi (Francesca), Gar Moore (Fred).
Florence Episode: Harriet White (Harriet), Renzo Avanzo (Massimo).
Romagna Episode: Bill Tubbs (Father Bill Martin), [Captain Owen Jones (Protestant Chaplain), Sergeant Elmer Feldman (Jewish Chaplain)].
Po Delta Episode: Dale Edmonds (Dale), [Achille Siviero] (Cigolani).
First screened: 18 September 1946, Venice Film Festival.
Released: 10 December 1946, Turin.
Length: 126 minutes (Venice version 134 minutes).

1947 *Deutschland im Jahre Null* (original version shot and spoken in German); *Germania anno zero* (*Germany in Year Zero*, UK; *Germany Year Zero*, USA).
Director: Roberto Rossellini. Assistants: Carlo Lizzani, Max Colpet, [Franz Treuberg].
Producers: Roberto Rossellini, [Alfredo Guarini].
Production Companies: Tevere Film, in collaboration with Salvo D'Angelo Produzione (Rome), [Sadfi (Berlin)] and Union Générale Cinématographique (Paris).
Subject: Roberto Rossellini, [Basilio Franchina].
Script: Roberto Rossellini, Max Colpet, [Carlo Lizzani, Franz Treuberg], Sergio Amidei (for Italian translation of dialogue only).
Director of Photography: Robert Juillard.
Editor: Eraldo Da Roma (Italian version), Anne-Marie Findeisen (German version),
Music: Renzo Rossellini, conducted by Edoardo Micucci.
Cast includes: Edmund Meschke (Edmund Koehler), Ernst Pittschau (Edmund's father), Ingetraud Hinze (Eva, Edmund's sister), Franz Krüger (Karl-Heinz, Edmund's brother), Erich Gühne (Enning, the teacher).
First screened: 11 April 1948, Circolo Romano del Cinema, Rome (Italian version); 9 July 1948, Locarno Film Festival (German version).
Released: 1 December 1948, Milan.
Length: 72 minutes (Italian and German versions) (first screening print of Italian version: 79 minutes).

1947–8. *L'Amore. Due storie d'amore* (*Love. Two Love Stories*).
Director: Roberto Rossellini [Assistant: Basilio Franchina].
Producer: Roberto Rossellini.
Production Company: Tevere Film.
Episode One: 'Una voce umana' ('A Human Voice').
Subject: *La Voix humaine*, one-act play by Jean Cocteau (1930).

[Script: Roberto Rossellini. Italian translation: Basilio Franchina].
Director of Photography: Robert Juillard.
Editor: Eraldo Da Roma.
Music: Renzo Rossellini.
Cast: Anna Magnani (the woman).
Episode Two: 'Il miracolo' ('The Miracle').
Assistant: Federico Fellini.
Subject: Federico Fellini [from a story by Ramón María del Valle-Inclán].
Screenplay: Tullio Pinelli, Roberto Rossellini.
Director of Photography: Aldo Tonti.
Editor: Eraldo Da Roma.
Music: Renzo Rossellini.
Cast includes: Anna Magnani (Nannina), Federico Fellini ('Saint Joseph', the vagabond).
First screened: 21 August 1948, Venice Film Festival.
Released: 2 November 1948, Rome.
Length: 78 minutes (35 minutes and 43 minutes). A few final shots of 'Il miracolo'
were cut after first private screenings.

1948–52 *La macchina ammazzacattivi* (*The Machine to Kill Bad People*).
Director: Roberto Rossellini. Assistants: Massimo Mida, Renzo Avanzo.
[Additional material shot under the direction of Luciano Emmer. Post-production
directed by Ettore Giannini].
Producers: Roberto Rossellini, Luigi Rovere, Salvo D'Angelo (for Universalia).
Production Companies: Universalia, Tevere Film.
Production Manager: Alberto Manni.
Subject: Eduardo De Filippo, Fabrizio Sarazani.
Script: Sergio Amidei, Franco Brusati, Liana Ferri, Giancarlo Vigorelli, [Roberto
Rossellini].
Directors of Photography: Tino Santoni, Enrico Betti.
Editor: Jolanda Benvenuti.
Music: Renzo Rossellini (also conductor).
Cast includes: Gennaro Pisano [= Alfonso Della Mura] (Celestino Esposito), Giovanni
Amato [=Domenico Fusco?] (devil/saint), William Tubbs (American man), Marilyn
Buferd (his daughter).
Released: 20 May 1952, Milan.
Length: 83 minutes.

1949–50 *Stromboli* (English version), *Stromboli terra di Dio* (Italian version [Stromboli
Land of God]).
Director: Roberto Rossellini. Assistant: Marcello Caracciolo.
Producers: Roberto Rossellini, [Ingrid Bergman] (for Berit), [Howard Hughes (for RKO)].
Production Companies: Berit (Rossellini and Bergman), RKO.
[Production Managers: Luigi Giacosi, Ed Killy, Harold Lewis].
Subject: Roberto Rossellini, [Sergio Amidei].
Script: Sergio Amidei, Gian Paolo Callegari, Renzo Cesana, Art Cohn, religious theme
inspired by Father Félix Morlion, O.P.

Director of Photography: Otello Martelli.

Editor: Jolanda Benvenuti.

Music: Renzo Rossellini, conducted by C. Bakaleinikoff.

Cast includes: Ingrid Bergman (Karin Bjorsen), Mario Vitale (Antonio Mastrostefano), Renzo Cesana (the priest), Mario Sponza (lighthouse keeper).

At RKO's insistence the original version of this film was reduced (by Roland Gross and Alfred Werker) from 106 minutes to 84 minutes and some voice-over was inserted for the American release.

Released: 15 February 1950, USA (RKO version); 9 March 1951, Milan (Italian version) [dubbed in Italian by Ingrid Bergman]. Also screened at Prix Rome, March 1950, and Venice Film Festival, 26 August 1950 (English-language version).

Length: 106 minutes (English-language version), 100 minutes (Italian version), 84 minutes (RKO version).

1950 *Francesco giullare di Dio* (*Francis God's Jester*, UK; alternative UK release title *The Adventures of St Francis; Flowers of St Francis* (USA).

Director: Roberto Rossellini. Assistant: Brunello Rondi.

Production Company: Rizzoli Film.

Associate Producer: Giuseppe Amato.

Production Manager: Luigi Giacosi.

Subject: Roberto Rossellini from *The Little Flowers of Saint Francis* [and *The Life of Brother Juniper*].

Script: [Roberto Rossellini], Federico Fellini, Father Félix Morlion, O.P., Father Antonio Lisandrini, O.F.M.

Director of Photography: Otello Martelli.

Editor: Jolanda Benvenuti.

Music: Renzo Rossellini, liturgical chants by Father Enrico Buondonno.

Cast includes: Franciscan friars [including Brother Nazario Gerardi (Saint Francis), Brother Severino Pisacane (Brother Juniper)], [Esposito Bonaventura aka Peparuolo (John the simpleton)], Aldo Fabrizi (Nicolaio the tyrant), Arabella Lemaître (Saint Clare).

First screened: 26 August 1950, Venice Film Festival (93 minutes).

Released: 15 December 1950, Milan (86 minutes).

Length: Italian version and *The Adventures of St Francis* 86 minutes; *Flowers of St. Francis* 79 minutes, including an introduction, cut after Venice on other prints, but missing one episode.

1951 *Santa Brigida* (Saint Bridget).

Director: Roberto Rossellini.

Director of Photography: Aldo Tonti.

Cast includes: Ingrid Bergman.

An unfinished documentary commissioned by the Swedish Red Cross for victims of the Po valley flood of November 1951, charting the work of the Swedish sisters of the Saint Bridget convent, Rome. 10 minutes of outtakes are preserved by the Cinemateket Svenska Filminstitutet. Some of this material was later incorporated in a Swedish documentary, *För Barnens Skull* (1953, 22 minutes).

1952 *I sette peccati capitali/Les Sept Péchés capitaux* (*The Seven Deadly Sins*)
French-Italian co-production.
Episode five: 'L'invidia'/'L'Envie' ['Envy'].
Director: Roberto Rossellini. Assistant: Antonio Pietrangeli.
Producer: Turi Vasile, [Henry Deutschmeister].
Production Companies: Film Costellazione (Rome), Franco-London Film (Paris).
Subject: Roberto Rossellini from the short story 'La Chatte' by Colette (1933).
Script: Roberto Rossellini, Diego Fabbri, Liana Ferri, Turi Vasile, Antonio Pietrangeli.
Director of Photography: Enzo Serafin.
Editor: Louisette Hautecoeur.
Music: Yves Baudrier.
Each episode is introduced by Gérard Philipe. Cast includes: Andrée Debar (Camilla),
Orfeo Tamburi (Orfeo).
Released: 3 May 1952, Milan.
Length: Rossellini's episode 21 minutes; total running time 140 minutes.
Other episodes: 'L'avarizia e la collera' (Eduardo De Filippo), 'La gola' (Carlo-Rim),
'La lussuria' (Yves Allégret), 'L'orgoglio' (Claude Autant-Lara); 'La pigrizia' (Jean
Dréville), 'L'ottavo peccato' (Georges Lacombe).

1952 *Europe '51*, English (aka *The Greatest Love*) (*Europa '51*, dubbed Italian version).
Director: Roberto Rossellini. Assistants: Marcello Caracciolo, Marcello Girosi, Antonio
Pietrangeli, William Demby.
Producers: Carlo Ponti, Dino De Laurentiis.
Production Company: Lux Film
Executive Producer: Bruno Todini.
Production Manager: Nando Pisani.
Subject: Roberto Rossellini [a previous subject, set in Paris, was written with Massimo
Mida and Antonello Trombadori].
Script: [Roberto Rossellini], Sandro De Feo, Mario Pannunzio, Ivo Perilli, Brunello
Rondi, [Diego Fabbri, Antonio Pietrangeli].
Director of Photography: Aldo Tonti.
Editor: Jolanda Benvenuti.
Music: Renzo Rossellini (also conductor).
Cast includes: Ingrid Bergman (Irene Gerard), Alexander Knox (George Gerard),
Sandro Franchina (Michel, their son), Ettore Giannini (Andrea Casati), Giulietta
Masina ('Passerotto'), Teresa Pellati (Ines, the prostitute).
First screened: 12 September 1952, Venice Film Festival (118 minutes Italian version).
Released: 8 January 1953, Rome.
Length: English version 109 minutes, Italian released version 114 minutes.

*1952 *Rivalità (Medico condotto)* (Rivalry (Community Doctor)).
Director: Giuliano Biagetti. Assistant: Vittorio Taviani, Amasi Damiani.
Production Company: Liburnia Film (Livorno).
Subject: Roberto Rossellini, Antonio Pietrangeli.
Script: Antonio Pietrangeli, Gaspare Cataldo, Vittorio Taviani.

Director of Photography: Giuseppe Caracciolo.
Editor: Giancarlo Cappelli.
Music: Mario Zafred.
Cast includes: Marco Vicario (Roberto Ferrero), Franca Marzi (Franca Jacopetti), Giovanna Ralli (Luisa), Saro Urzì (Giovanni Fauci).
Released: 18 July 1953.
Length: 90 minutes.

1952–4 *Dov'è la libertà*, re-released as *Dov'è la libertà...?* (Where is Freedom?).
Director: Roberto Rossellini [additional scenes directed by Federico Fellini].
Assistants: Marcello Caracciolo, Luigi Giacosi.
Producers: Carlo Ponti, Dino De Laurentiis (Lux Film), [Giovanni Amati (Golden Film)].
Production Companies: Lux Film, Golden Film.
Production Manager: Nando Pisani.
Subject: Roberto Rossellini.
Script: Vitaliano Brancati, Ennio Flaiano, Antonio Pietrangeli, Vincenzo Talarico.
Director of Photography: Aldo Tonti, [Tonino Delli Colli, for Fellini scenes].
Editor: Jolanda Benvenuti.
Music: Renzo Rossellini, conducted by Giuseppe Morelli.
Cast includes: Totò (Salvatore Lojacono), Vera Molnar (Agnesina), Nyta Dover (the marathon girl), Franca Faldini (Maria), Giacomo Rondinella (the prisoner singer), Leopoldo Trieste (Abramo Piperno).
Released: 26 March 1954, Rome.
Length: 91 minutes.

1952–3 *Siamo donne* (Italian version)/*We, the Women* (English version).
Episode: 'Ingrid Bergman' (Italian version); 'The Chicken' (English version).
Director: Roberto Rossellini. Assistant: Niccolò Ferrari.
Production Companies: Titanus, Film Costellazione, Guarini.
Executive Producer: Alfredo Guarini.
Production Manager: Marcello d'Amico, with Giancarlo Campidori for Rossellini's episode.
Subject: Cesare Zavattini.
Script: Cesare Zavattini, Luigi Chiarini, [Roberto Rossellini].
Director of Photography: Otello Martelli.
Editor: Jolanda Benvenuti.
Music: Alessandro Cicognini.
Cast includes: Ingrid Bergman (as herself), [Albamaria Setaccioli (Signora Annovazzi), Franco, Renzo, Robertino Rossellini as themselves].
Released: 27 October 1953, Milan.
Length: Rossellini's episode 17 minutes; total running time 100 minutes.
Other episodes directed by Alfredo Guarini ('Concorso 4 attrici 1 speranza'), Gianni Franciolini ('Isa Miranda'), Luigi Zampa ('Alida Valli'), Luchino Visconti ('Anna Magnani').

1953–4 *Journey to Italy* (UK, France subtitled); aka *The Lonely Woman* (UK), *Strangers* (USA), *Viaggio in Italia* (Italy).
Director: Roberto Rossellini. Assistants: Marcello Caracciolo, Vladimiro Cecchi.
Producers: Roberto Rossellini (Sveva Film), [Adolfo Fossataro (Junior Film), Alfredo Guarini (Italia Film)].
Production Companies: Sveva Film, Junior Film, Italia Film (Rome), SGC, [Ariane Film, Francinex] (Paris).
Production Managers: Mario Del Papa, Marcello d'Amico.
Subject: Vitaliano Brancati, Roberto Rossellini.
Script: Vitaliano Brancati, Roberto Rossellini, [Antonio Pietrangeli, Ugo Pirro].
Director of Photography: Enzo Serafin.
Editor: Jolanda Benvenuti.
Music: Renzo Rossellini (also conductor).
Cast includes: Ingrid Bergman (Katherine Joyce), George Sanders (Alexander Joyce), Marie Mauban (Marie), [Tony La Penna (Tony Burton)], Natalia Rai [= Ray] (Natalia Burton), Anna Proclemer (the prostitute).
Released: 7 September 1954, Milan (Italian version).
Length: English version 84 minutes, Italian dubbed version 81 minutes.

1953 *Amori di mezzo secolo* (Mid-century Loves).
Episode four: 'Napoli '43' (not written in the titles of extant prints).
Director: Roberto Rossellini. Assistant: Marcello Caracciolo.
Producer: Carlo Infascelli.
Production Companies: Excelsa, Roma Film.
Production Manager: Silvio Clementelli.
Script: Roberto Rossellini.
Director of Photography: Tonino Delli Colli (Ferraniacolor).
Editors: Rolando Benedetti, Dolores Tamburini.
Music: Carlo Rustichelli, conducted by Alberto Paoletti.
Cast includes: Antonella Lualdi (Carla), Franco Pastorino (Renato).
Released: 18 February 1954, Milan.
Length: Rossellini's episode 14 minutes; total running time 100 minutes.
Other episodes: 'L'amore romantico' (Glauco Pellegrini), 'Guerra 1915–18' (Pietro Germi), 'Epoca fascista' (Mario Chiari), 'Girandola 1910' (Antonio Pietrangeli), scenes between each episode ('intermezzi') directed by Vinicio Marinucci.

*1954 *Orient Express*
Director: Carlo Ludovico Bragaglia. Supervision: Roberto Rossellini (nominal).
Production Companies: Fonoroma (Rome), Les Films Sirius CICC (Paris), Meteor Films (Wiesbaden).
Subject: Jacques Companeez.
Script: Aldo De Benedetti, Vitaliano Brancati, Agenore Incrocci, Furio Scarpelli, Vittorio Nino Novarese. For French version: Paul Andréota. For German version: Joseph Than, Kurt Henser.
Director of Photography: Aldo Tonti (Gevacolor).
Editor: Roberto Cinquini.

Music: Renzo Rossellini.

Cast includes: Silvana Pampanini (Beatrice), Henri Vidal (Jacques Ferrand), Folco Lulli (Filippo Dal Pozzo), Michael Lenz (Giovanni).

Released: 8 October 1954.

Length: 100 minutes.

Credits not checked on print.

1954 *Giovanna d'Arco al rogo* (Italian version); *Jeanne au bûcher* (French version) (Joan of Arc at the Stake)

Director: Roberto Rossellini. Assistants: Marcello Caracciolo, Leonardo Picconi.

Producers: Giorgio Criscuolo and Franco Francese for PCA.

Production Companies: Produzioni Cinematografiche Associate (PCA) (Rome), Franco London Film (Paris).

Production Manager: Raffaello Teti.

Subject: From the dramatic oratorio *Jeanne d'Arc au bûcher* by Paul Claudel (text) and Arthur Honegger (music) (1938).

[Script: Adaptation by Roberto Rossellini].

Director of Photography: Gabor Pogany (Gevacolor).

Editors: (Italian version) Jolanda Benvenuti, (French version, dubbed by Claude Nollier) Robert Audenet.

Music: Arthur Honegger. Italian version: orchestra, conducted by Angelo Spagnolo, chorus and ballet of Teatro San Carlo, Naples; French version (dubbed by Claude Nollier): Chorus of Théâtre National de l'Opéra de Paris, conducted by René Duclos.

Cast includes: Ingrid Bergman (Joan of Arc), Tullio Carminati (Brother Domenico).

Released: 29 January 1955, Rome.

Length: 73 minutes.

A French version dubbed by Ingrid Bergman was completed, but no known prints of this version now exist.

The oratorio was staged by Rossellini, with Bergman, in Naples (December 1953, with Carminati as Brother Domenico), Milan (April 1954), Paris (June), London (October–November), Barcelona (December), Stockholm (January–February 1955), Palermo (April).

1954 *Angst* (German version); *Fear* (English version); *La paura* (Italian-dubbed version)

Director: Roberto Rossellini. Assistants: Franz Treuberg, Pietro Servedio.

Producer: Roberto Rossellini.

Production Companies: Aniene Film (Rome), Ariston Films (Munich).

Production Managers: Jochen Genzow, Mario Del Papa.

Subject: *Die Angst*, novel by Stefan Zweig (1913–20).

Script: Sergio Amidei, Franz Treuberg, [Roberto Rossellini].

Director of Photography: Carlo Carlini. Assistant for German version: Heinz Schnackertz.

Editor: Jolanda Benvenuti (Italian version), Walter Boos (German version) (both credited on English version).

Music: Renzo Rossellini, conducted by Franco Ferrara.

Cast includes: Ingrid Bergman (Irene Wagner), Mathias Wieman (Professor Albert Wagner), Renate Mannhardt (Johanna Schultze, alias Luise Vidor), Kurt Kreuger (Heinrich Stoltz).

The film was shot simultaneously in German, with direct sound, and in English, dubbed, with different shots and scenes at many points; the Italian version is based on the English one.

Released: 5 November 1954, Germany (German version); 21 February 1955, Milan (Italian version); no record of a public release of the English version has been found.

Length: *Angst* 81 minutes; *La paura* 82 minutes; *Fear* 83 minutes.

Re-released in Italy in 1958 as *Non credo più all'amore* (I No Longer Believe in Love) with distributors' cuts and changes, 75 minutes.

1956 *Le Psychodrame*, French
Director: Roberto Rossellini.
Production Company: ORTF, Service de la Recherche (directed by Pierre Schaeffer).
Unfinished project recording a psychodrama directed by Jacob Levi Moreno and Anne Ancelin-Schützenberger. Filmed during a congress on psychodrama in Paris.

*1957 *Seawife*, English
Director: Bob McNaught.
Producer: André Hakim.
Production Companies: Suma Productions, 20th Century-Fox (Spyros Skouras).
Script: George K. Burke. [First script: Roberto Rossellini, Bruce Marshall].
Photography: Ted Scaife (CinemaScope, DeLuxe Colour).
Music: Kenneth V. Jones, Leonardo Salzedo.
Cast: Joan Collins (Seawife), Richard Burton (Biscuit).
Length: 82 minutes.
Rossellini went to Jamaica in June 1956 to begin shooting but left after a few days because of disagreement with producers about script changes. Joan Collins was chosen by Rossellini.
Credits not checked on print.

1957–8 *L'India vista da Rossellini* (India as seen by Rossellini) (For RAI TV series *I viaggi del telegiornale*)
Director: Roberto Rossellini.
Director of television interviews: Franco Morabito.
[Producer: Roberto Rossellini].
Production Company: RAI.
Production Manager: Giuseppe Sala.
Director of Photography: Aldo Tonti (Kodachrome 16 mm, broadcast in b/w).
Music: Traditional Indian music.
Editors: Adriana Alberti, Jenner Menghi.
Cast includes: Roberto Rossellini and Marco Cesarini Sforza in discussion while watching footage shot by Rossellini in India.
Broadcast: Ten episodes on Italian television between 7 January and 11 March 1959.
Length: 250 minutes at 25 fps.

1957–8 *J'ai fait un beau voyage* (I Had a Good Trip), French
Director: Roberto Rossellini.
Director of television interviews: Jean L'Hôte. Assistant: Pierre Robin.
[Producer: Roberto Rossellini].
Production Company: ORTF TV (France).
Director of Photography: Aldo Tonti (film; Kodachrome 16 mm, broadcast in b/w).
Music: 'Sound illustration' by Pierre Poulteau.
Cast includes: Roberto Rossellini and Etienne Lalou in discussion while watching
footage shot by Rossellini in India. (The same footage as in the Italian version.)
Broadcast: Ten episodes on French television between 11 January and 6 August
1959.
Length: 276 minutes at 25 fps.

1957–9 *India Matri Bhumi*, French/Italian (India Mother Land/India)
Director: Roberto Rossellini. Assistants: Jean Herman (India), Giovanni (Tinto) Brass
(post-production, Rome).
[Producer: Roberto Rossellini].
Production Companies: Aniene Film (Rome), Union Générale Cinématographique
(Paris) [with help from Indian Films Development (Jean Bhownagari)].
Subject: Roberto Rossellini.
Script: Roberto Rossellini, Sonali Senroy Das Gupta, Fereydoun Hoveyda.
Commentary: Jean L'Hôte (French version), Vincenzo Talarico (Italian version).
Director of Photography: Aldo Tonti (Gevacolor, Ferraniacolor, Kodachrome).
Editor: Cesare Cavagna.
Music: Philippe Arthuys, traditional Indian music elaborated by Alain Danielou.
Cast includes: Non-professional actors from local Indian communities.
First screened: 9 May 1959, Cannes Film Festival (French version).
Released: 12 March 1960, Milan (Italian version).
Length: French version 95 minutes, Italian version 89 minutes, Italian restored version from
incomplete prints 87 minutes (the original negative of both versions appears to be lost).

1959 *Il generale Della Rovere* (*General Della Rovere*)
Director: Roberto Rossellini. Assistants: Philippe Arthuys, Renzo Rossellini, Giovanni
(Tinto) Brass.
Producer: Moris Ergas (Zebra Film).
Production Companies: Zebra Film (Rome), Société Nouvelle des Etablissements
Gaumont (Paris).
Production Manager: Paolo Frascà.
Subject: From a story by Indro Montanelli (1950).
Script: Sergio Amidei, Diego Fabbri, Indro Montanelli.
Director of Photography: Carlo Carlini.
Editor: Cesare Cavagna.
Music: Renzo Rossellini.
Cast includes: Vittorio De Sica (Giovanni Bertone aka Colonel Grimaldi, General
Giovanni Braccioforte Della Rovere), Hannes Messemer (Colonel Müller), Sandra
Milo (Olga), Giovanna Ralli (Valeria).

First screened: 31 August 1959, Venice Film Festival (137 minutes).
Released: 7 October 1959, Milan.
Length: 132 minutes (Italian release print).

1960 *Era notte a Roma* (It was Night in Rome/*Blackout in Rome*)
Director: Roberto Rossellini. Assistants: Renzo Rossellini Jr, Franco Rossellini.
Producer: Giovan Battista Romanengo (International Golden Star).
Production Companies: International Golden Star (Genova), Dismage Film (Paris).
Executive Producer: Franco Magli.
Production Manager: Oscar Brazzi.
Subject: Sergio Amidei.
Script: Sergio Amidei, Diego Fabbri, Brunello Rondi, Roberto Rossellini. English
dialogue: Mario Del Papa.
Director of Photography: Carlo Carlini (1:1.66).
Editor: Roberto Cinquini.
Music: Renzo Rossellini, conducted by Edgardo Micucci. Sound effects: Philippe
Arthuys.
Cast includes: Leo Genn (Major Michael Pemberton), Giovanna Ralli (Esperia Belli),
Sergei Bondarchuk (Sergeant Fyodor Natzukov), Peter Baldwin (Lieutenant Peter
Bradley), Hannes Messemer (Colonel Baron von Kleist), Renato Salvatori (Renato
Balducci).
First screened: 13 May 1960, Cannes Film Festival (157 minutes).
Released: 7 October 1960, Milan.
Length: 157 minutes (Italian shortened version 114 minutes).

1960 *Viva l'Italia* (Long Live Italy) (90-minute English-dubbed version released in
USA as *Garibaldi*)
Director: Roberto Rossellini. Assistants: Renzo Rossellini Jr, Ruggero Deodato, Franco
Rossellini.
[Producers: Arturo Tofanelli (Tempo Film), Lionello Santi (Galatea), Roberto Dandi
(Cinematografica Rire)].
Production Companies: [Tempo Film, Galatea], Cinematografica Rire (Rome),
[Francinex (Paris)].
Production Manager: Oscar Brazzi.
Subject: Sergio Amidei, Antonio Petrucci, Luigi Chiarini, Carlo Alianello.
Script: Sergio Amidei, Diego Fabbri, Antonio Petrucci, Roberto Rossellini, Antonello
Trombadori.
Director of Photography: Luciano Trasatti (1:1.66, Eastman Color).
Editor: Roberto Cinquini.
Music: Renzo Rossellini, conducted by Pier Luigi Urbini.
Cast includes: Renzo Ricci (Giuseppe Garibaldi), Paolo Stoppa (Nino Bixio), Franco
Interlenghi (Giuseppe Bandi), Giovanna Ralli (Rosa).
First screened: 27 January 1961, Rome Opera (to an audience including the President
of Italy).
Released: 2 February 1961, Rome.
Length: 129 minutes.

1961 *Torino nei cent'anni* (Turin in its Hundred Years [since Italy's unification])
Director: Roberto Rossellini. Assistants: Enzo Leonardo, Gilberto Casini.
Producer: Federigo Valli.
Production Company: Produttori Associati (PROA) for RAI.
Executive Producer: Piero Valli.
Production Manager: Ugo De Lucia.
Script: Valentino Orsini.
Historical consultants: Carlo Casalegno, Enrico Gianeri.
Commentary: Vittorio Gorresio.
Directors of Photography: Leopoldo Piccinelli, Mario Vulpiani, Mario Volpi (16 mm).
Editor: Vasco Micucci.
Broadcast: 10 September 1961, RAI.
Length: 47 minutes at 25 fps.

1961 *Torino tra due secoli* (Turin Across Two Centuries)
Director: Roberto Rossellini. Assistant: Enzo Leonardo.
Production Company: PROA.
Executive Producer: Federigo Valli.
Script: Valentino Orsini.
Commentary: Vittorio Gorresio.
Director of Photography: Leopoldo Piccinelli (Colour).
Length: 12 minutes.

1961 *Vanina Vanini* (*The Betrayer,* edited UK release version)
Director: Roberto Rossellini. Assistants: Franco Rossellini, Renzo Rossellini Jr,
Philippe Arthuys.
Producer: Moris Ergas (Zebra Film).
Production Companies: Zebra Film (Rome), Orsay Films (Paris).
Production Manager: Manolo Bolognini.
Subject: *Vanina Vanini,* short story by Stendhal (1829), adapted by Franco Solinas,
Antonello Trombadori.
Script: Diego Fabbri, Monique Lange (nominal), Roberto Rossellini, Franco Solinas,
Antonello Trombadori, [Jean Gruault].
Director of Photography: Luciano Trasatti (1:1.66, Technicolor).
Editors: Daniele Alabiso, supervised by Mario Serandrei.
Music: Renzo Rossellini, conducted by Pier Luigi Urbini.
Cast includes: Sandra Milo (Vanina Vanini), Laurent Terzieff (Pietro Missirilli),
Martine Carol (Countess Vitelleschi), Paolo Stoppa (Prince Asdrubale Vanini).
First screened: 27 August 1961, Venice Film Festival.
Released: 12 October 1961, Milan.
Length: 113 minutes (the print was c. 125 minutes before producers' cuts).

*1961 *Benito Mussolini*
Director: Pasquale Prunas. Supervision: Roberto Rossellini.
Production Companies: Etrusca Cinematografica, Galatea (Rome).
Script: Giovan Battista Cavallaro, Ernesto G. Laura.

Commentary: Enzo Biagi, Sergio Zavoli.
Editor: Romeo Ciatti. Supervision: Mario Serandrei.
Music: Roberto Nicolosi, conducted by Pier Luigi Urbini.
Released: 18 January 1962.
Length: 112 minutes.
Credits not checked on print.

1962 *Anima nera* (Black Soul)
Director: Roberto Rossellini. Assistants: Franco Rossellini, Ruggero Deodato, Gerardo Giuliano.
Producer: Gianni Hecht Lucari (Documento Film).
Production Companies: Documento Film (Rome), Le Louvre Film (Paris).
Production Manager: Piero Lazzari.
Story: Based on the play *Anima nera* by Giuseppe Patroni Griffi (1960).
Script: Roberto Rossellini, Alfio Valdarnini.
Director of Photography: Luciano Trasatti (1:1.85).
Editor: Daniele Alabiso.
Music: Piero Piccioni.
Cast includes: Vittorio Gassman (Adriano Zucchelli), Nadja Tiller (Mimosa), Annette Stroyberg (Marcella), Eleonora Rossi Drago (Alessandra), Yvonne Sanson (Olga Manfredi).
Released: 5 September 1962, Milan.
Length: 97 minutes.

1962 *RoGoPaG*; re-released as *Laviamoci il cervello* (Let's Have a Brainwash)
Episode One: 'Illibatezza' ('Chastity').
Director: Roberto Rossellini. Assistant: Renzo Rossellini Jr
Producer: Alfredo Bini (Arco Film).
Production Companies: Arco Film (Rome), Société Cinématographique Lyre (Paris).
Executive Producer: Manolo Bolognini.
Production Manager: Eliseo Boschi.
Story: Roberto Rossellini.
Script: Roberto Rossellini.
Director of Photography: Luciano Trasatti (1:1.85).
Editor: Daniele Alabiso.
Music: Carlo Rustichelli.
Cast includes: Rosanna Schiaffino (Anna Maria), Bruce Balaban (Joe).
Other episodes: 'Il nuovo mondo', Jean-Luc Godard; 'La ricotta', Pier Paolo Pasolini; 'Il pollo ruspante', Ugo Gregoretti.
Released: 21 February 1963, Milan.
Length: Rossellini's episode 33 minutes; total running time 128 minutes.

*1963 *Les Carabiniers* (The Carabiniers)
Director: Jean-Luc Godard.
Production Companies: Rome–Paris Films (Paris), Laetitia (Rome).
Producer: Georges de Beauregard.

Story: *Les Carabiniers*, play by Beniamino Joppolo.
Script: Jean Gruault, [Jean-Luc Godard], Roberto Rossellini (who resumed for
Gruault the play he staged at Spoleto in June 1962).
Director of Photography: Raoul Coutard.
Editor: Agnès Guillemot.
Music: Philippe Arthuys.
Cast includes: Marino Masè (Ulysse), Albert Juross (Michelange), Geneviève Galéa
(Vénus), Catherine Ribeiro (Cléopâtre).
Released: 31 May 1963, Paris.
Length: 80 minutes.

1964 *L'età del ferro* (The Iron Age); *L'âge du fer* (French-dubbed version)
Director: Renzo Rossellini Jr Supervision: Roberto Rossellini. Assistant: Ruggero
Deodato.
Production Companies: Istituto Luce, Italsider for RAI.
Executive Producer: Alberto Soffientini.
Production Manager: Alfonso Donati.
Story: Roberto Rossellini.
Script: Roberto Rossellini.
Director of Photography: Carlo Carlini.
Editor: Daniele Alabiso.
Music: Carmine Rizzo.
Cast includes (with each episode introduced by Rossellini): Episode One: [Nino Fruscella
(Lysis)], Evar Maran (Leon Battista Alberti). Episode Two: Alberto Barberito, Pasquale
Campagnola, Walter Maestosi (Niccolò Tartaglia), Osvaldo Ruggeri (Duke of Urbino).
Episodes Four and Five: Arnolfo Dominici (Montagnani).
Broadcast: Five episodes on RAI 2, 19 February–19 March 1965 (Italian version); four
episodes on ORTF 2, 7 December 1966–25 January 1967 (French-dubbed version);
eight episodes on TVE (Spain), 19 April–7 June 1971.
An edited one-hour version was dubbed into French in 1966, and subsequently into
English, apparently for private exhibition.
Length: 278 minutes (267 minutes at 25 fps).

1966 *La Prise de pouvoir par Louis XIV*, French (The Taking of Power by Louis XIV;
English-subtitled version released as *The Rise to Power of Louis XIV*)
Director: Roberto Rossellini. Assistants: Yves Kovacs, [Egérie Mavraki] (Banquet and
sections of the hunt sequences directed by Renzo Rossellini Jr).
Producer: Pierre Gout.
Production Company: ORTF.
Story: Philippe Erlanger.
Script: Philippe Erlanger. Dialogue and adaptation: Jean Gruault.
Artistic Consultant: Jean-Dominique de la Rochefoucauld.
Director of Photography: Georges Leclerc, Jean-Louis Picavet [for a few shots]
(Eastman Color).
Editor: Armand Ridel.
Sound: Jacques Gayet. 'Sound Illustration': Betty Willemetz.

Cast includes: Jean-Marie Patte (Louis XIV), Raymond Jourdan (Colbert), Giulio Cesare Silvani (Mazarin), Katharina Renn (Ann of Austria), Pierre Barat (Fouquet). First screened: 10 September 1966, Venice Film Festival.
Broadcast: ORTF (France), 8 October 1966; released on film in France 9 November 1966; broadcast by RAI 1 (Italy), 23 April 1967; released on film in Italy January 1969 (as *La presa di potere di Luigi XIV*).
Length: 94 minutes (90 minutes at 25 fps).

1967–8 *Idea di un'isola* (Idea of an Island/*The Sicily of Roberto Rossellini*)
Director: Roberto Rossellini. First Assistant: Renzo Rossellini Jr Assistants: Roberto Capanna, Paolo Poeti.
Producer: Roberto Rossellini.
Production Companies: Orizzonte 2000 in collaboration with RAI (Rome).
Production Manager: Francesco Orefici.
Story: Roberto Rossellini.
Script: Roberto Rossellini.
Narrator: Corrado Gaipa.
Director of Photography: Mario Fioretti (Eastman Color).
Editor: Maria Rosada.
Music: Mario Nascimbene.
Introduced by Roberto Rossellini.
Broadcast: NBC (USA), 29 December 1968; RAI 2, 3 February 1970.
Length: 52 minutes at 25 fps.

1967–9 *La lotta dell'uomo per la sua sopravvivenza* (*Man's Struggle for Survival*)
Director: Renzo Rossellini Jr Assistants: Pitt Popesco, Roberto Capanna, Paolo Poeti, Emiliano Giannino, Ilie Sterian.
Production Companies: Orizzonte 2000, RAI (Rome), Logos Films (Paris), Romania Film (Bucharest), Copro Film (Cairo).
Executive Producer: Michele Bini.
Production Managers: Francesco Orefici, Adrian Caracas.
Story: Roberto Rossellini.
Script: Roberto Rossellini.
Director of Photography: Mario Fioretti (Eastman Color).
Editor: Daniele Alabiso, Gabriele Alessandro, Alfredo Muschietti.
Music: Mario Nascimbene.
Cast includes (with each episode introduced by Rossellini): [Shadi Abdes-Salam (Pharaoh, Episode Two), Emiliano Giannino (young Benedectin monk, Episode Four)], Vitaliano Elia (Basilio Valentino, Episode Four), Marzio Margine (troubadour, Episode Five), Conrad Andersen (Columbus, Episode Seven), Massimo Sarchielli (Lavoisier, Episode Nine), Bepy Mannaiuolo (Guglielmo Marconi, Episode Nine).
Broadcast: Twelve episodes (across two series) on RAI 1, 7 August–11 September 1970 and on RAI 2, 4 September–16 October 1971. Also broadcast in twelve episodes on TVE (Spain), 14 April–30 June 1972. A shortened version dubbed into English for non-commercial distribution was also released (c. 105 minutes, *Man's Struggle for Survival*).
Length: 655 minutes (629 minutes at 25 fps).

1968 *Atti degli apostoli*; *Les Actes des Apôtres* (Acts of the Apostles) (simultaneous production for Italian, French and Spanish television)
Director: Roberto Rossellini. Assistants: Maurizio Brass, Roberto Capanna, Hedi Besbes, Abeljalil el Bahi, Mahamed Naceur al Ktârî.
Producer: Renzo Rossellini Jr
Production Companies: Orizzonte 2000, RAI (Rome), ORTF (Paris), Televisión Española (TVE) (Madrid), Studio Hamburg, Les Films de Carthage (Tunis).
Production Manager: Francesco Orefici.
Story: Based on *The Acts of the Apostles* and other books of the New Testament.
Script: Jean-Dominique de la Rochefoucauld, Vittorio Bonicelli, Luciano Scaffa, Roberto Rossellini.
Director of Photography: Mario Fioretti (Eastman Color).
Editor: Jolanda Benvenuti.
Music: Mario Nascimbene. Flute: Severino Gazzelloni. Voice: Sonali Senroy Das Gupta.
Cast includes: Jacques Dumur (Peter), Edoardo Torricella (Paul), Mohamed Kouka (John), Bradai Ridha (Matthew), Renzo Rossi (Zacharias), Enrico Ostermann (Caiphas).
Broadcast: Five episodes on RAI 1, 6 April–4 May 1969; five episodes daily on TVE (Spain) 23–27 March 1969; five episodes on ORTF 2 (France), 7 October–4 November 1970.
Length: 354 minutes (340 minutes at 25 fps).

1970 *Socrate*, French (*Socrates*); dubbed Italian version *Socrate* also produced
Director: Roberto Rossellini. Assistants: Juan García Atienza, José Luis Guarner.
[French adaptation and artistic direction: Jean-Dominique de la Rochefoucauld].
Producer: Renzo Rossellini Jr
Production Companies: Orizzonte 2000, RAI (Rome), TVE (Madrid), ORTF (France).
Production Managers: Francesco Orefici, Antonio Matilla.
Story: Based on Plato's Dialogues and other works.
Script: Roberto Rossellini, Marcella Mariani.
Dialogue: Jean-Dominique de la Rochefoucauld.
Director of Photography: Jorge Herrero Martin (Eastman Color).
Editor: Alfredo Muschietti.
Music: Mario Nascimbene.
Cast includes: Jean Sylvère (Socrates), Anne Caprile (Xanthippe), Ricardo Palacios (Criton), Bepy Mannaiuolo (Apollodorus).
First screened: 19 August 1970, Venice Film Festival.
Broadcast: In two parts on RAI 2 on 17 and 20 June 1971; in France on ORTF 1 in two parts on 28 and 29 October 1974.
Length: 119 minutes (115 minutes at 25 fps).

1971 *La forza e la ragione. Intervista con Salvatore Allende* (Strength and Reason: Interview with Salvador Allende)
Director: Emidio Greco, [Helvio Soto].
Producer: Renzo Rossellini Jr
Production Companies: Orizzonte 2000, San Diego Cinematografica.
[Photography: Roberto Girometti (16 mm, colour)].

Cast includes: Salvador Allende, Roberto Rossellini.
Broadcast: Interview took place in May 1971 and was first broadcast in Italy on RAI 1 on 15 September 1973 after Allende's death (as *La forza e la ragione*).
Length: 36 minutes at 25 fps. Re-edited for television from a previous 16mm colour version of 45 minutes (*Intervista con Salvatore Allende*). Original dialogue in Italian (Rossellini) and Spanish (Allende); Italian version has oversound in Italian.

1971–2 *Blaise Pascal*, French
Director: Roberto Rossellini. Assistants: Gabriele Polverosi, Andrea Ferendeles.
Producer: Roberto Rossellini.
Production Companies: Orizzonte 2000, RAI, ORTF.
Production Manager: Sergio Iacobis.
Script: Marcella Mariani, Luciano Scaffa, Jean-Dominique de la Rochefoucauld, Roberto Rossellini. (French dubbing under the direction of Jean-Dominique de la Rochefoucauld.)
Director of Photography: Mario Fioretti (Eastman Color).
Editor: Jolanda Benvenuti.
Music: Mario Nascimbene.
Cast includes: Pierre Arditi (Blaise Pascal), Giuseppe Addobbati (Etienne Pascal), Rita Forzano (Jacqueline Pascal), Teresa Ricci (Gilberte Pascal), Livio Galassi (Jacques, the servant), Claude Baks (Descartes).
Broadcast: In two parts on RAI 1 on 16 and 17 May 1972; in France complete on ORTF 1 on 29 May 1974.
Length: 135 minutes (129 minutes at 25 fps).

1972 *Agostino d'Ippona* (Augustine of Hippo)
Director: Roberto Rossellini. Assistants: Andrea Ferendeles, Claudio Bondì, Claudio Amati.
[Producer: Roberto Rossellini].
Production Companies: Orizzonte 2000, RAI.
Executive Producer: Sergio Iacobis.
Production Manager: Francesco Orefici.
Script: Roberto Rossellini, Marcella Mariani, Luciano Scaffa. Dialogue: Jean-Dominique de la Rochefoucauld.
Director of Photography: Mario Fioretti (Eastman Color).
Editor: Jolanda Benvenuti.
Music: Mario Nascimbene.
Cast includes: Dary Berkani (Augustine), Fabio Garriba (Marcellino), Virginio Gazzolo (Alipio), Cesare Barbetti (Volusiano), Bruno Cattaneo (Massimo).
First screened: September 1972, RAI Auditorium, Turin.
Broadcast: In two parts on RAI 1, 25 October and 1 November 1972.
Length: 122 minutes (117 minutes at 25 fps).

1972 *L'età di Cosimo de' Medici* (*The Age of the Medici*) (The Age of Cosimo de' Medici [originally shot in English])
Director: Roberto Rossellini. Assistants: Claudio Bondì, Beppe Cino, Claudio Amati.
Producer: Roberto Rossellini.
Production Companies: Orizzonte 2000, RAI.

Executive Producer: Sergio Iacobis.

Production Manager: Francesco Orefici.

Script: Roberto Rossellini, Marcella Mariani, Luciano Scaffa.

Director of Photography: Mario Montuori (Eastman Color).

Editor: Jolanda Benvenuti.

Music: Composed and directed by Manuel De Sica.

Cast includes: Marcello Di Falco (Cosimo de' Medici), Virginio Gazzolo (Leon Battista Alberti), Tom Felleghy (Rinaldo degli Albizzi), Mario Erpichini (Totto Machiavelli), John Stacy (Ilarione de' Bardi), Goffredo Matassi (Bernardo Guadagni), Sergio Nicolai (Francesco Soderini), Dario Michaelis (Carlo Marsuppini), Piero Gerlini (Poggio Bracciolini), Ugo Cardea (Nicolò Niccoli).

Shown in three episodes: 'L'esilio di Cosimo' (Cosimo's Exile, aka Cosimo de' Medici), 'Potere di Cosimo' (Cosimo's Power), and 'Leon Battista Alberti: l'Umanesimo' (Leon Battista Alberti: Humanism).

Broadcast: Three episodes on RAI 1, 26 December 1972–10 January 1973.

Length: 256 minutes (82', 82', 92') (246 minutes at 25 fps (79', 79', 88')).

1973 *Cartesius* (Descartes)

Director: Roberto Rossellini. Assistants: [Beppe Cino], Claudio Amati.

Producer: Roberto Rossellini.

Production Companies: Orizzonte 2000, RAI, ORTF.

Executive Producer: Sergio Iacobis.

Production Manager: Francesco Orefici.

Script: Roberto Rossellini, Marcella Mariani, Luciano Scaffa, [Jean-Dominique de la Rochefoucauld].

Director of Photography: Mario Montuori (Eastman Color).

Editor: Jolanda Benvenuti.

Music: Mario Nascimbene.

Cast includes: Ugo Cardea (René Descartes), Anne Pouchie (Helena Jans), Gabriele Banchero (Bretagne, the servant), Kenneth Belton (Isaac Beeckman), Renato Montalbano (Constantijn Huygens), Vernon Dobtcheff (the astronomer Cyprus).

Broadcast: Two parts on RAI 1 (with Italian dubbing), 20 and 27 February 1974. Never broadcast on French television.

Length: 161 minutes (154 minutes at 25 fps).

1973 *Rice University*, English (aka *Roberto Rossellini at Rice University, Houston*)

Director: Beppe Cino.

Director of Photography: William Colville (colour, 16 mm).

Editor: Beppe Cino.

A series of conversations and discussions between Rossellini and various scientists at Rice University which was to form part of the proposed *Science* series.

Length: c. 120 minutes.

This version was bought but never broadcast on Italian television; extracts were used in Angelo d'Alessandro's *Roberto Rossellini: un ricordo* (*Roberto Rossellini: A Recollection*, RAI, 1977) with oversound spoken by Rossellini. The print sold to RAI was apparently lost after the extracts were taken.

1974 *A Question of People*, English
Director: Roberto Rossellini. Assistant: Beppe Cino.
Production Company: UNESCO (United Nations Fund for Population Activities).
Post-production and Editor: Beppe Cino.
Photography: Colour, 16 mm.
Length: 125 minutes.
Screened at the 1974 United Nations Conference on World Population, Bucharest, and
at the Festival del Film di Montagna, Trento, in April–May 1975 (in Italian version, *La
popolazione mondiale*).

1974 *Anno uno* (Year One)
Director: Roberto Rossellini. Assistant: Beppe Cino.
Production Company: Rusconi Film.
Executive Producer: Silvia d'Amico Bendicò.
Production Manager: Sergio Iacobis.
Story and Script: Roberto Rossellini, Marcella Mariani, Luciano Scaffa.
Director of Photography: Mario Montuori (Eastman Color).
Editor: Jolanda Benvenuti.
Music: Mario Nascimbene.
Cast includes: Luigi Vannucchi (Alcide De Gasperi), Dominique Darel (Maria
Romana De Gasperi), Valeria Sabel (Francesca De Gasperi), Rita Forzano (Lucia De
Gasperi).
Released: 15 November 1974, Rome.
Length: 123 minutes.

1975 *Il Messia* (The Messiah) (originally mostly shot in English and later dubbed into
Italian; an English-language dubbing was never undertaken). French dubbed version
Le Messie
Director: Roberto Rossellini. Assistants: Beppe Cino, Carlos de Carvalho, Abdellatif
Ben Ammar (in Tunisia).
Production Companies: Orizzonte 2000, Procinex, FR3, Téléfilm Productions (Paris).
Executive Producer: Silvia d'Amico Bendicò (with, in Tunisia, Tarak Ben Ammar).
Production Manager: Enzo Provenzale (with, in Tunisia, Aloulou Cherif).
Story and Script: Roberto Rossellini, Silvia d'Amico Bendicò.
Director of Photography: Mario Montuori (Eastman Color).
Editor: Jolanda Benvenuti.
Music: Mario Nascimbene.
Cast includes: Pier Maria Rossi (Jesus Christ), Mita Ungaro (Mary), Carlos de
Carvalho (John the Baptist), Jean Martin (Pontius Pilate), Toni Ucci (Herod Antipas),
Vittorio Caprioli (Herod the Great).
First screened: 25 October 1975 during the Assemblea del Sindacato Nazionale Critici
Cinematografici Italiani in Montecatini.
Released: 18 February 1976, Paris (with French dubbing) and 30 September 1976,
Rome (with Italian dubbing).
Length: 144 minutes.

1977 *Concerto per Michelangelo* (Concert for Michelangelo)
Director: Roberto Rossellini. Assistant: Laura Basile.
Production Company: RAI 2.
Production Manager: Guido Sacerdote.
Director of Photography: [Mario Montuori (film)], Giorgio Ojetti (video). Colour
35 mm and video (final version on video).
Music: Choir of the Pontifical Musical Chapel, conducted by Monsignor Domenico
Bartolucci.
Narrator: Alberto Lori.
Broadcast: 9 April 1977 on RAI 2.
Length: 43 minutes at 25 fps.

1977 *Le Centre Georges Pompidou*, French (The Georges Pompidou Centre)
Director: Roberto Rossellini. Assistants: Christian Ledieu, Pascal Judelewicz.
Producer: Jacques Grandclaude.
Production Company: Création 9 Information (Paris).
Director of Photography: Nestor Almendros (Eastman Color).
Editors: Véritable Silve, Colette Le Tallec, Dominique Taysse.
Broadcast: 4 June 1977 in France on ORTF, and 1 October 1983 in Italy on RAI 3 (as
Il Centro Georges Pompidou). No voice-over or spoken dialogue.
Length: 56 minutes at 25 fps.

Select Bibliography

Compiled by Sarah Lutton and Adriano Aprà

A Works in English

Scripts

1 'Interview with Salvator Allende by Roberto Rossellini', *Take One*, January–February 1973 (published in May 1974), vol. 4 no. 3; republished in item 10 below, pp. 65–70 (transcript of the dialogue of *Intervista a Salvatore Allende*, 1971).
2 (With Federico Fellini), '*Paisà*, Sixth Episode – Scenario and Dialogue', *Film Culture*, Winter 1963–4, no. 31.
3 *The War Trilogy: Open City, Paisan, Germany – Year Zero*, translated by Judith Green (New York: Grossman; London: Lorrimer, 1973) (translation of item 96 below).

Books and pamphlets about Rossellini

4 Adriano Aprà, *Rossellini. India 1957* (Rome: Cinecittà International, 1991) (In English and French.)
5 Bondanella, Peter, *The Films of Roberto Rossellini* (New York: Cambridge University Press, 1993).
6 Brunette, Peter, *Roberto Rossellini* (New York: Oxford University Press, 1987).
7 Degener, David, *Sighting Rossellini* (Berkeley: University Art Museum, University of California Press, undated, but 1973).
8 Forgacs, David, *Rome Open City (Roma città aperta)* (London: BFI Publishing, 2000).
9 Guarner, José Luis, *Roberto Rossellini*, translated by Elisabeth Cameron (London: Studio Vista, 1970) (an updated edition of this text was published in Spanish in 1996: see item 117).
10 Ranvaud, Don (ed.), *Roberto Rossellini*, BFI Dossier, no. 8 (London: British Film Institute, 1981).
11 *Roberto Rossellini* (Rome: EAGC, 1987) (In Italian and English; no editor indicated.)
12 Rossi, Patrizio, *Roberto Rossellini: A Guide to References and Resources* (Boston: Hall, 1988).

Biography

13 Gallagher, Tag, *The Adventures of Roberto Rossellini: His Life and Films* (New York: Da Capo, 1998).

Articles on Rossellini

14 Belton, John and Tector, Lyle, 'The Bionic Eye: The Aesthetics of the Zoom', *Film*

Comment, September–October 1980, vol. 16 (includes discussion of Rossellini's development of the Pancinor zoom).

15 Bergman, Ingrid, 'Ingrid Bergman on Rossellini: Interviewed by Robin Wood', *Film Comment*, July–August 1974, vol. 10, no. 4.

16 Brunette, Peter, 'Just How Brechtian is Rossellini?', *Film Criticism*, 1979, vol. 3, no. 2.

17 Brunette, Peter, 'Unity and Difference in *Paisan*', *Studies in the Literary Imagination*, 1983 vol. 1.

18 Brunette, Peter, 'Rossellini and Cinematic Realism', *Cinema Journal*, Autumn 1985, vol. 25, no. 1.

19 Bruno, Edoardo, 'Rossellini's *Acts of the Apostles*', *Screen*, Spring 1974, vol. 15, no. 1. Reprinted and translated from *Filmcritica*, March–April 1968.

20 Bruno, Edoardo, 'Rossellini 3', *Framework*, Spring 1979, no. 10 (translated from text in item 115 below.

21 Burgoyne, Robert, 'The Imaginary and the Neo-Real' (on *Rome Open City*), *Enclitic*, vol. 3, no. 1, Spring 1979, pp. 16–34.

22 Casty, Alan, 'The Achievement of Roberto Rossellini', *Film Comment*, Autumn 1964.

23 Damico, J., 'Ingrid from Lorraine to Stromboli: Analysing the Public's Perception of a Film Star' (also about Rossellini), *Journal of Popular Film*, vol. 4, no. 1.

24 Dorr, John H., 'Roberto Rossellini in 1974', *Take One*, January–February 1973 (published May 1974), vol. 4, no. 3.

25 Gallagher, Tag, 'Roberto Rossellini and Historical Neorealism', *Artforum*, Summer 1975.

26 Gallagher, Tag, 'The "Essential" Roberto Rossellini', *Changes*, 1974, vol. 87.

27 Gallagher, Tag and Hughes, John W., 'Where are We Going?', *Changes*, April 1974, no. 87.

28 Gilliat, Penelope, 'The Current Cinema: Perpetuum Mobile', *New Yorker*, 13 May 1974, vol. 50, no. 12; republished in Penelope Gilliat, *Three-Quarter Face: Reports & Reflections* (London: Secker & Warburg, 1980).

29 Grant, Michael, 'Heidegger's Poetic: On Anthony Barnett and Roberto Rossellini', *Arts Quarterly*, 1991, vol. 1, no. 2.

30 Halliday, Jon, 'Roberto Rossellini', *Monogram*, Summer 1972, no. 2.

31 Harcourt-Smith, Simon, 'The Stature of Rossellini', *Sight and Sound*, 1950, vol. 19, no. 2.

32 Hughes, John W., 'Film: Rossellini on Rossellini: In Search of the "Essential Image"', *The Village Voice*, 10 May 1973 (includes an interview).

33 Hughes, John W., 'Rossellini and His Contradictions', *Changes*, April 1974, no. 87.

34 Hughes, John W. 'Recent Rossellini', *Film Comment*, July–August 1974, vol. 10, no. 4.

35 Hughes, John W., 'In Memoriam: Roberto Rossellini', *Film Comment*, 1977, vol. 13, no. 4.

36 Joannides, Paul, 'The Aesthetics of the Zoom Lens', *Sight and Sound*, Summer 1970, vol. 40, no. 1 (on Rossellini and the Pancinor zoom).

37 Kelman, Ken, 'Rossellini's Tragedy of Manners', *Film Culture*, Summer 1969, no. 47.

38 Kent, Leticia, 'Roberto Rossellini – Arrivederci Roma and Hello, Yale', *New York Times*, 10 March 1974, no. 123, section D, 9 (includes an interview).

39 Lawton, Harry, 'Rossellini's Didactic Cinema', *Sight and Sound*, Autumn 1978, vol. 47, no. 4.

40 Lennon, Peter, 'Away with Neo-realism' (with excerpts from an interview with Rossellini), the *Guardian*, 3 March 1966.

41 MacBean, James Roy, 'Rossellini's Materialist *mise-en-scène* of *La Prise de pouvoir par Louis XIV*', *Film Quarterly*, vol. 25, no. 2, Winter 1971–2.

42 McNiven, Roger, 'Rossellini's Alberti: Architecture and the Perspective System Versus the Invention of the Cinema', *Iris*, no. 12, December 1991.

43 Norman, Louis, 'Rossellini's Case Histories for Moral Education', *Film Quarterly*, Summer 1974, vol. 27, no. 4.

44 Nowell-Smith, Geoffrey, 'Rossellini 2', *Framework*, Spring 1979, no. 10 (in Italian in item 115 below).

45 Ordway, Peter, 'Prophet With Honour', *Theatre Arts*, January 1949, no. 33.

46 Ranvaud, Don, 'Rossellini 1', *Framework*, Spring 1979, no. 10.

47 Ranvaud, Don, 'Documentary and Dullness: Rossellini according to the British critic', *Monthly Film Bulletin*, February 1981, vol. 48, no. 565 (also in item 10 above).

48 Ranvaud, Don, 'Neo-realism – the Second Coming', *Monthly Film Bulletin*, March 1981, vol. 48 no. 566.

49 Russell, Lee [Peter Wollen], 'Roberto Rossellini', *New Left Review*, March–April 1967, no. 42 (longer version in item 10 above).

50 Sarris, Andrew, 'Rossellini Rediscovered', *Film Culture*, Spring 1964, no. 32.

51 Sherman, E. and Dorr, John H., 'Roberto Rossellini', *East West Journal*, February 1974.

52 Silverman, Michael, 'Rossellini and Leon Battista Alberti: The Centering Power of Perspective', *Yale Italian Studies*, Winter 1977, vol. 1, no. 1.

53 Sinclair, Michael, 'Ellipsis in Rossellini's *Paisà*: The Privileging of the Invisible', *Spectator*, Autumn 1988, vol. 9, no. 1.

54 Strick, Philip, 'Rossellini in '76' (includes a brief interview with Rossellini), *Sight and Sound*, Spring 1976, vol. 45, no. 2.

55 Walsh, Martin, '*Rome, Open City; The Rise to Power of Louis* XIV: Re-evaluating Rossellini', *Jump Cut*, July 1977, no. 15.

56 Wood, Peter H., 'I Believe in This: A Letter from Roberto Rossellini' (includes abridged transcript of letter from Rossellini to Wood – also reproduced in the Documents section of this volume: see pp. 161–5), *New Republic*, 2 July 1977, vol. 177.

57 Wood, Robin, 'Rossellini', *Film Comment*, July–August 1974, vol. 10, no. 4.

58 Žižek, Slavoj, 'Rossellini: Woman as Symptom of Man', *October*, Autumn 1990, vol. 54; republished as 'Why Is *Woman* a Symptom of Man?' in *Enjoy Your Symptom! Jacques Lacan in Hollywood and Out* (London & New York: Routledge, 1992).

Books and articles by Rossellini

59 'A Few Words about Neo-realism' (translation of 'Due parole sul neorealismo' in *Retrospettive*, no. 4, April 1953), in David Overbey (ed.), *Springtime in Italy: A Reader on Neo-Realism* (London: Talisman, 1978). This article is simply an edited extract from the interview with Mario Verdone (item 69 below and reproduced in this volume: see Documents section, pp. 149–55).

60 'Manifesto', *Screen*, vol. 14, no. 4, Winter 1973–4 (also in French in *Cahiers du Cinéma*, no. 171, October 1965).

61 'Man's Well-Being, Behaviour and the Spread of Knowledge', *Film Culture*, Spring 1973, vol. 7 nos. 56–7 (translation of 'Verso il futuro come ciechi', *La Stampa*, 24 August 1971).

62 *My Method: Writings and Interviews*, edited by Adriano Aprà, translated by Anna-paola Cancogni, introduction by Tag Gallagher (New York: Marsilio, 1992) (a selection of 21 of the 62 texts in item 140 below, plus item 66).

63 'Neapolitan Note in a Director's Diary', *New York Times*, 30 May 1948 (on the making of *Paisà*).

64 'Roberto Rossellini by Roberto Rossellini', *Cinema* (Beverly Hills), vol. 7, no. 1, Autumn 1971 (translation of 'Perché faccio film storici', *La Stampa*, 6 May 1971).

65 'Rossellini on Rossellini (1960)', *Screen*, vol. 14 no. 4, Winter 1973–4 (reprinted and translated from *La Table Ronde*, May 1960).

66 'Ten Years of Cinema' (translation of item 142), in Overbey, *Springtime in Italy* (see 59), and in *My Method* (item 62).

Interviews

67 'Letter from Rome: A Meeting with Rossellini', *World Review*, January 1949 (interview by Derek Monsey).

68 'Interview with Roberto Rossellini by Francis Koval', *Sight and Sound*, 1951, vol. 19, no. 10.

69 'A Discussion of Neo-Realism: Rossellini Interviewed by Mario Verdone (1952)', *Screen*, vol. 14, no. 4, Winter 1973–4 (reprinted and translated from *Bianco e Nero*, 1952, no. 2 (reproduced in this volume: see Documents section, pp. 149–55); also in *My Method* (item 62).

70 'Interview with Roberto Rossellini by Maurice Schérer and François Truffaut (1954)', *Film Culture*, March–April 1955, vol. 1, no. 2; partially in item 149 below; in full in *My Method* (item 62).

71 Parker, P., 'Rossellini Talks', *Photoplay*, September 1957 (interview in India).

72 Bazin, André, 'Cinema and Television: Jean Renoir and Roberto Rossellini Interviewed by André Bazin', *Sight and Sound*, Winter 1958–9, vol. 28, no. 1.

73 'Me: by Rossellini' (interviewed by E. Frank), *New Chronicle*, 15 March 1960.

74 'An Interview with Roberto Rossellini by Adriano Aprà and Maurizio Ponzi (1965)', *Screen*, Winter 1973–4, vol. 14, no. 4 (reprinted and translated from *Filmcritica*, April–May 1965, nos. 156–7); also in *My Method* (item 62).

75 'Rossellini on *The Rise of Louis XIV*' (interview with Jonas Mekas), *The Village Voice*, 5 October 1967.

76 'Interview with Roberto Rossellini' (with J. Soltero and T. Mussman), *Medium*, Winter 1967–8, no. 2.

77 'Rossellini on Neo-realist Method', *Faux-Raccord*, November 1969, no. 1.

78 'A Panorama of History: Interview with Rossellini by Francisco Llinas and Miguel Marias with Antonio Drove and Jos Oliver, Madrid, January 1970', *Screen*, Winter 1973–4, vol. 14, no. 4; also in *My Method* (item 62).

79 'Inter/VIEW with Roberto Rossellini' (with J. Keller and G. O'Brien), *Inter/VIEW*, 1970, no. 2.

80 Thomas, K., 'Roberto Rossellini, Once Forgotten Man, Now Back in Style', *Los Angeles Times*, 1 February 1971.

81 Thomas, K., 'Rossellini and an Educated Camera', *Chicago Sun-Times*, 21 February 1971.

82 'Interview with Roberto Rossellini, February 22–5, 1971 in Houston, Texas by Victoria Schultz', *Film Culture*, Spring 1971, no. 52.

83 Gussow, M., 'Rossellini Caps a Quest with Filming of "Science"', *New York Times*, 21 June 1971.

84 'An Interview with Rossellini' (at Rice University, Houston, 1972 with James Blue), in pamphlet, *May 1–20 1979*, published on the occasion of a retrospective season at the Public Theater, New York; also in *My Method* (item 62).

85 Stein, S., 'World's Population Stars in Rossellini Film', *The Demographic Express*, November 1973.

86 Bordas, J., 'Rossellini Looks to Future in TV', *The News* (Mexico City), 15 November 1973.

87 Gilliatt, P., 'Dialogue', *New Yorker*, 4 March 1974 (reports statements by Rossellini at the New School for Social Research).

88 'Interview with Roberto Rossellini' (with E. Sherman and John Dorr), *Take One*, June 1974.

89 Oakes, P., 'A Point without a View', *Sunday Times*, 23 November 1975.

90 'Roberto Rossellini Talks About Marx, Freud and Jesus: An Interview by Giovanna Di Bernardo (1976)', *Cineaste*, Summer 1977, vol. 8, no. 1.

B Works in other languages

Scripts, transcripts, story materials, treatments

91 *Francesco giullare di Dio*, Inquadrature, nos. 5–6, October 1958–September 1959 (integral treatment).

92 Rossellini, Roberto, 'L'India tra il vecchio e il nuovo', *Il Contemporaneo*, 11 January 1958 (six stories for *India*, presented by Antonello Trombadori).

93 Montanelli, Indro, *Il generale Della Rovere* (Milan: Rizzoli, 1959) (novelisation of treatment for film).

94 *Era notte a Roma*, edited by Renzo Renzi (Bologna: Cappelli, 1960) (script).

95 '*Il ferro*', Filmcritica, nos. 139–40, November–December 1963 (script of *L'età del ferro*).

96 *La trilogia della guerra: Roma, città aperta, Paisà, Germania anno zero*, edited by Stefano Roncoroni (Bologna: Cappelli, 1972) (dialogue transcript with shot breakdown).

97 '*Il Messia*', Rivista del Cinematografo, nos 7–8, July–August 1977 (script).

98 '*Voyage en Italie*', L'Avant-Scène du Cinéma, no. 361, June 1987 (dialogue transcript).

99 '*India*', Trafic, no. 28, Winter 1998 (transcript of voice-over, by Rossellini and Jean l'Hôte).

100 '*Stromboli*', Trafic, no. 33, Spring 2000 (story).

101 *La TV di Rossellini: Socrate, Pascal, Agostino d'Ippona* (Rome: Coines, 1972) (dialogue transcripts).

102 *La TV di Rossellini: Cartesius* (Rome: Coines, 1974) (dialogue transcript).

103 *Atti degli Apostoli, Socrate, Blaise Pascal, Agostino d'Ippona, L'età dei Medici, Cartesius,*

edited by Luciano Scaffa and Marcella Mariani Rossellini (Turin: ERI, 1980) (dia-logue transcripts and other materials).

Critical studies and resource books

104 Anile, Alberto and Giannice, Maria Gabriella *La guerra dei vulcani* (Recco, Genova: Le Mani, 2000).

105 Aprà, Adriano (ed.), *Il dopoguerra di Rossellini* (Rome: Cinecittà International, 1995). (Illustrated resource book on *Rome Open City, Paisà* and *Germany Year Zero*, including script material on *Paisà* and *Germania anno zero* and an international selection of early reviews of the three films.)

106 Aprà, Adriano (ed.), *Roberto Rossellini. India* (Rome: Cinecittà Estero, 1991) (in French).

107 Aprà, Adriano (ed.), *Roma città aperta di Rossellini* (Rome: Comune di Roma, Assessorato alla Cultura, 1994). (Detailed book on the film, including documents, testimonies, studies and a wide selection of early reviews.)

108 Aprà, Adriano (ed.), *Rosselliniana. Bibliografia internazionale. Dossier Paisà* (Rome: Di Giacomo, 1987). (Contains extensive bibliography up to 1987 and materials on the making of *Paisà*.)

109 Aprà, Adriano and Semeraro, Giovanni Andrea, *Roberto Rossellini, l'uomo, la parola, l'immagine* (Rome: La Camera Verde, 2000).

110 Baldelli, Pio, *Roberto Rossellini* (Rome: La Nuova Sinistra-Samonà e Savelli, 1972).

111 Bergala, Alain, *Voyage en Italie de Roberto Rossellini* (Crisnée, Belgium: Editions Yellow Now, 1990).

112 Bergala, Alain and Narboni, Jean (eds), *Roberto Rossellini* (Paris: Editions de l'Etoile/ Cahiers du Cinéma, 1990).

113 Bourgeois, Nathalie, Bénoliel, Bernard with Bergala, Alain (eds), *India. Rossellini et les animaux* (Paris: Cinémathèque Française, 1997).

114 Bruno, Edoardo (ed.), *R.R. Roberto Rossellini* (Rome: Bulzoni, 1979) (contains interviews with Rossellini from a range of sources).

115 Bruno, Edoardo (ed.), *Roberto Rossellini. Il cinema, la televisione, la storia, la critica* (Sanremo: Città di Sanremo, 1980). Proceedings of the conference held in Sanremo, 16–23 September 1978.

116 Di Giammatteo, Fernaldo, *Roberto Rossellini* (Florence: La Nuova Italia, 1990).

117 Guarner, José-Luis, *Roberto Rossellini* (Valencia: Fundació Municipal de Cine-Mostra de Valencia, 1996) (updated edition of text first published in English in 1970: see item 9).

118 Hovald, P.G., *Roberto Rossellini* (Brussels: Club du Livre de Cinéma, 1958).

119 Masi, S. and Lancia, E., *I film di Roberto Rossellini* (Rome: Gremese, 1987).

120 Meder, Thomas, *Vom Sichtbarmachen der Geschichte: der italienisch 'Neorealismus', Rossellinis Paisà und Klaus Mann* (Munich: Trickster, 1993).

121 Menon, Gianni (ed.), *Dibattito su Rossellini* (Rome: Partisan, 1972) (transcript of a seminar in Pisa, 23–6 May 1969).

122 Michelone, Guido, *Invito al cinema di Rossellini* (Milan: Mursia, 1996).

123 Mida, Massimo, *Roberto Rossellini* (Parma: Guanda, 1953).

124 Quintana, Ángel, *Roberto Rossellini* (Madrid: Cátedra, 1995).

125 *Roberto Rossellini* (Munich–Vienna: Carl Hanser Verlag/Reihe Film 36, 1987).

126 Rondolino, Gianni, *Roberto Rossellini* (Florence: La Nuova Italia, 1974, in the series Il Castoro Cinema). Contains select filmography.

127 Serceau, Michel, *Roberto Rossellini* (Paris: Cerf, 1986).

128 Trasatti, Sergio, *Rossellini e la televisione* (Rome: La Rassegna, 1978). Includes an anthology of writings by and interviews with Rossellini.

129 Verdone, Mario, *Roberto Rossellini* (Paris: Seghers, 1963).

Biography

130 Rondolino, Gianni, *Roberto Rossellini* (Turin: UTET, 1989).

Articles on Rossellini

131 *Bianco e Nero*, February 1952, no. 2. Contains two articles on Rossellini's film-making, filmography and lengthy interview with Rossellini by Mario Verdone (item 69).

132 Bruno, Edoardo, '*Atti degli Apostoli* di Rossellini', *Filmcritica*, March–April 1968.

133 Ferendeles, Andrea, 'Il *Pascal* di Roberto Rossellini', *Filmcritica*, September–October 1971.

134 Seknadje-Askénazi, Enrique, 'Il realismo di Rossellini. La prima trilogia. La guerra fascista', *Il Nuovo Spettatore*, no. 97, 1998.

135 Seknadje-Askénazi, Enrique, 'Il realismo di Rossellini. La seconda trilogia. Il "dopoguerra" di Rossellini', *Il Nuovo Spettatore*, no. 98, 1998.

Works by Rossellini

Books

136 *Le Cinéma révélé*, edited by Alain Bergala (Paris: Cahiers du Cinéma/Editions de l'Etoile, 1984). Contains articles and materials written by Rossellini on film-making.

137 *Un Esprit libre ne doit rien apprendre en esclave* (Paris: Fayard, 1977).

138 *Fragments d'une autobiographie* (Paris: Ramsay, 1987) (French edition of item 139).

139 *Quasi un'autobiografia*, edited by Stefano Roncoroni (Milan: Mondadori, 1987). (Rossellini interviewed by Roncoroni on different phases of his life.)

140 *Il mio metodo. Scritti e interviste*, edited by Adriano Aprà (Venice: Marsilio, 1987; second edition 1997). Collection of texts by and interviews with Rossellini.

141 *Utopia, autopsia, 10^{10}* (Rome: Armando, 1974).

Articles

142 'Dix ans du cinéma', *Cahiers du Cinéma* (article in three parts): no. 50, August–September 1955; no. 52, November 1955; no. 54, January 1956 (for English translation see item 66).

143 'Cinema e televisione (1977)', *Filmcritica*, December 1989.

144 'Roberto Rossellini, une lettre', *Trafic*, no. 1, Winter 1991.

145 Truffaut, François, 'Rossellini 55', *Arts*, 19 January 1955, no. 499 (interview in French).

C Other relevant texts

146 Bazin, André, *Qu'est-ce que le cinéma?* (Paris: Editions du Cerf, 1981). Definitive

edition, contains all four volumes. Abridged and translated by Hugh Gray as *What is Cinema?*, 2 vols (Berkeley and Los Angeles: University of California Press, 1967 and 1971).

147 Bergman, Ingrid and Burgess, Alan, *Ingrid Bergman: My Story* (London: Sphere, 1981). First published in Great Britain by Michael Joseph, 1980. Includes detailed information on Rossellini and Bergman's professional and personal relationship.

148 De Marchis Rossellini, Marcella, *Un matrimonio riuscito. Autobiografia* (Milan: Il Castoro, 1996).

149 Hillier, Jim (ed.), *Cahiers du Cinéma*, vol. 1, *The 1950s: Neo-Realism, Hollywood, New Wave* (London: Routledge & Kegan Paul, 1985). Both this and the next volume in the series (item 150) contain important articles in translation on critical responses to neo-realism and the development of postwar European film culture.

150 Hillier, Jim (ed.), *Cahiers du Cinéma*, vol. 2, *1960–8: New Wave, New Cinema, Re-evaluating Hollywood* (London: Routledge & Keagan Paul, 1986).

151 Pirro, Ugo, *Celluloide* (Milan: Rizzoli, 1983; republished Turin: Einaudi, 1995) (novelised reconstruction of the making of *Rome Open City*).

152 Toscan du Plantier, Daniel, *Les Enfants d'Al Capone et de Rossellini* (Paris: Mazarine, 1981).

153 Wagner, Jon, 'Lost Aura: Benjamin, Bazin and the Realist Paradox', *Spectator*, Autumn 1988, vol. 9, no. 1.

154 Williams, Christopher, 'Bazin on Neo-Realism', *Screen*, Winter 1973–4, vol. 14, no. 4.

Index

Numbers in italics refer to pictures

Acts of the Apostles, 130, 135,
 138, 139, 141, 142, 144,
 145, 162
Adam Had Four Sons, 69
Adler, Alfred, 126
Aeneid, The, 58
Age of Cosimo de' Medici, The,
 see *Cosimo de' Medici*
Agostino d'Ippona see
 Augustine
Alessandrini, Goffredo, 2, 21
All about Eve, 100
American Revolution, The,
 132, 162
Amiche, Le, 41
Amidei, Sergio, 46
Amore, L', 3, 7, 8, 10, 59–60,
 130
Anastasia, 76, 118
Anderson, Lindsay, 157
Anderson, Maxwell, 99
Andreotti, Giulio, 38, 40
Angst (Zweig), 14 – see also
 Fear
Anima nera, 5, 130
Anno uno, 1, 14, *14*, 82, 92–3
Antonioni, Michelangelo, 38,
 40, 118
Aprà, Adriano, 87
Arata, Ubaldo, 37
Arch of Triumph, 69
Arendt, Hannah, 51
Aristarco, Guido, 4, 8, 9, 25,
 50, 74, 156–7
Augustine, 1, 5, 82, 130, 135,
 139, 141, 142, 144, 145
Avventura, L', 38, 41
Ayfre, Amédée, 159
Balázs, Béla, 57
Baldelli, Pio, 81–2
Battleship Potemkin, The, 54

Bazin, André, 4, 7, 8, 9, 11,
 36, 44, 50, 104, 119, 121,
 156, 157–61
Becker, Jacques, 157
Bellissima, 38
Bellour, Raymond, 98
Bells of St Mary's, The, 69
Benjamin, Walter, 50, 51, 54
Bergala, Alain, 58
Bergman cycle, 3, 5, 7, 8,
 12–15, 119
Bergman, Ingrid, 3, 12, 13,
 14, 64–, *67*, 95, *96*,
 98–100, *98*, 103, 108–9,
 110, 118, 153
Berkany, Dary, 17
Berlin: Symphony of a City, 22
Bicycle Thieves, *37*, 38, *41*,
 42–3, 117–18
Bidone, Il, 41
Bitter Rice, 38, 117
Blaise Pascal, 11, 132, 138,
 142, 145, 162
Blasetti, Alessandro, 150
Bragaglia, Carlo Ludovico, 20
Breen, Joseph, 66, 70
Brignone, Guido, 22
Brunette, Peter, 75, 85
Burgess, Alan, 71
Cahiers du Cinéma, 4, 7, 8,
 102, 119, 157
Caligula, 17, 130, 141
Calvino, Italo, 39
Camerini, Mario, 150
Cammino degli eroi, Il, 22
Canetti, Elias, 51
Capa, Robert, 99
Capacci, Aldo, 30
Capra, Frank, 65
Caprile, Anna, 136
Carabiniers, Les, 8
Cardea, Anna, 136
Cartesius, 132, 142, 143, 144,
 145, 162

Caruso, Pietro, 48
Casablanca, 65, 69
Casiraghi, Ugo, 74
Casque d'or, 157
Castro, Josué de, 127
Catherine of Siena, 131
Catholicism, 28–9, 155
Catholic Church 71–3
Cavalcanti, Alberto, 22
Centro Sperimentale di
 Cinematografia, 20
Chaplin, Charles, 2, 69
Chatte, La, 98, 153
Chiaretti, Tommaso, 74
Chinigo, Mike, 70
Chomon, Segundo de, 143
Christ Stopped at Eboli, 40
Christian Democracy, 3, 9,
 15–16, 73, 92–3
christianity, 21, 28 – see also
 Catholicism
Christian, Linda, 72
*Chronicle of Anna Magdalena
 Bach, The*, 140
Chronique d'un été, 116
Ciano, Galeazzo, 21
Cine–GUF – see Gruppi
 Universitari Fascisti
Cinecittà, 28
Cinema (magazine), 27
Cinema Nuovo, 8, 156
cinéma verité, 116
Cinémathèque Française, 41
*Civilisation of the
 Conquistadores*, 133
Claudel, Paul, 14, 75
Cocteau, Jacques, 10
Colette, 14, 98–9, 153
Comenius (Jan Ámos
 Komenský), 128, 162
Comenius, 132
Communism, 9, 28–30, 73,
 92, 168

Consideration of the Stigmata,
    89
Contempt – see *Mépris*
Cosimo de' Medici, 131, 135,
    138, 139, *141,* 142, 143,
    144, 145, 162
Cristo si è fermato a Eboli, 40
Croce, Benedetto, 127
Crowd, The, 154
Crowther, Bosley, 68
Davidson, Bill, 64
Damico, James, 69
De Chirico, Giorgio, 55
De Gasperi, Alcide, 16, 82,
    92–3
De Gaulle, General, 15,
De Laurentiis, Dino, 10,
De Robertis, Francesco,
    22–25, 28
De Santis, Giuseppe, 27, 38,
    40, 48, 117
De Sica, Manuel, 140
De Sica, Vittorio, 10, 38, 117,
    137, 158
'Dead, The', 107
Deleuze, Gilles, 100
Delmar, Rosalind, 18
Descartes, René, 17
Desiderio, 30, 130
Diderot, 132, 162
Dieterle, William, 70
documentary, 22–4, 75, 115–7
Dolce vita, La, 41, 72, 77
Dossetti, Giuseppe, 92
Dottesio, Attilio, 29
Dov'è la libertà…?, 1, 10, 130
Dr Jeykll and Mr Hyde, 69
Duo, 98, 101
1860 (Blasetti), 150
Eisenstein, Sergei, 25, 54
Eliade, Mircea, 50
Eluard, Paul, 54
'Envy', 3, 14, 98, 153
Era notte a Roma, 5, 127, 137,
    143
Esilio di Cosimo de' Medici, L',
    145; see also *Cosimo
    de'Medici*
Età del ferro,L', see *Iron Age*
Ethiopia, Invasion of, 21, 22
Europe '51, 7, 8, 10, 12–13,
    14, 38, 41, 57–8, 74, 75,
    80, 81, 118, 121, 152, 155,
    156–7, 158, 160

*Extraordinary History of our
    Food, The,* 127, 133
Fabrizi, Aldo, 91, 150,
Fantasia sottomarina, 151,
    154
Farber, Manny, 109–10
Farmer, Frances, 37
Fascism, 39, 40
Fascist war trilogy, 20–31
Fear (Angst/La paura), 7, 8,
    12, 14, 76, 126, 130, 140,
    143, 158
Feist, Harry, *47*
Fellini, Federico, 5, 38, 39–40,
    59, 72, 169–70
Films in Review, 68
Fioretti di San Francesco see
    Little Flowers of St Francis
Fleming, Victor, 69, 99–100
Flynn, Errol, 69
For Whom the Bell Tolls, 65
Forzano, Giovacchino, 22
Fossa degli angeli, La, 20
Francesco giullare di Dio, –
    see *Francis God's Jester*
Francis God's Jester, 3, 14,
    56–7, 73, 80–93, *84,* 114,
    131, 143, 151, 152, 155,
    156, 158
Franciscans, 82, 88 – see also
    St Francis
Gabor, Zsa Zsa, 100
Galileo, 167
Gallagher, Tag, 72, 102
Gargan, William, 37
Gaslight, 69
Geiger, Rod, 37
General Della Rovere, 1, 5, 7,
    127, 137, 143
Genina, Augusto, 22
Geography of Hunger, The, 127
Germany Year Zero, 3, 4, 5, 7,
    8, 10, 11, 13–14, 40, 54–5,
    54, 66, 81, 123, 140, 151,
    152, 153, 160
Germi, Pietro, 40
Giorni di gloria, 48
Giovanna d'Arco al rogo, 14,
    131, 139, 140, 158
Girotti, Massimo, 25, *26,*
Godard, Jean-Luc, 4, 7, 8, 60,
    114, 119, 134 143
Goethe, J. W. von, 50, 58
Goldwyn, Samuel, 66

Gramsci, Antonio, 15,
Grant, Cary, 117
Gravelli, Asvero, 27–8
Greece, War in, 25–7, 28
Grido, Il, 38
Griffith, D. W., 2, 109, 143
Gruppi Universitari Fascisti, 20
Gualino, Riccardo, 10
Guitry, Sacha, 143
Halleujah, 154
Hawks, Howard, 109
Hayworth, Rita, 67
Hearst, W. Randolph, 70
Hegel, G. W. F., 51
Hinerman, Stephen, 68, 69
*History of Our Food and
    Science,* 133
Hitchcock, Alfred, 126
Hölderlin, Friedrich, 61
Hollywood, 3, 10, 12, 13, 15,
    25, 46, 64, 66, 68–70,
    72–77, 88, 90, 92, 98–100,
    110, 117, 118, 124
Honegger, Arthur, 75
Hopper, Hedda, 70
Hoveyda, Fereydoun, 4, 119
Hughes, Howard, 66, 70
'Human voice, The' see
    'Voce umana'
'Illibatezza' ('Chastity'), 3,
    126, 130
India Matri Bhumi – see *India*
India, 4, 16, 60–2, 76, 112–24,
    113, 126, 134, 142
India vista da Rossellini, L',
    112, 126
Industrial Revolution, The,
    133, 162
Innocent III, 86
Intermezzo, 69
'Invidia, L' see 'Envy'
Iron Age, The, 16, 129, 130–3,
    134, 138, 140–2, 143,
    162–3
Islam, 133
Istituto LUCE, 22, 25
J'ai fait un beau voyage, 112,
    142
Jaguar, 116
Jeanne au bûcher
    (Claudel/Honegger), 75;
    see also *Giovanna d'Arco
    al rogo,*
Joan of Arc, 69, 142

Joan of Arc (Fleming), 65, 99
Joan of Lorraine, 99
Johnson, Edwin (Senator),
    67, 73
Journey to Italy, 4, 7, 8, 12–14,
    15, 41, 51, 58–60, 68, 81,
    89, 90, 95–110, *95, 96, 98,*
    99, 106, 158–61
Joyce, James, 58, 107
Kafka, Franz, 60
Kahn, Albert, 60, 143
Kazan, Elia, 65
Knox, Alexander, 12
La Pira, Giorgio, 92
Lang, Fritz, 8, 126
Lattuada, Alberto, 158
Lavorare per l'umanità, 133
Lee, Canada, 37
Leon Battista Alberti:
    l'Umanesimo, 145, 162
Leone, Rosario, 27
Leopardi, Giacomo, 55
Leprohon, Pierre,
Levi, Carlo, 40
Lévy-Bruhl, Lucien, 50
Life magazine, 66, 72
Life of Brother Juniper, The,
    14, 56, 82, 88, 89
Lindström, Petter, 13, 66, 71, 100
Lisandrini, Father Antonio
    O.F.M., 82, 92
Little Flowers of St Francis,
    The, 14, 56, 82–3, 87–8
Litvak, Anatol, 118
Lombardo, Goffredo, 10,
Lotta dell'uomo per la sua
    sopravvivenza, La, see
    Man's Struggle for
    Survival.
Louis XIV, see *Prise de*
    pouvoir par Louis XIV
Luciano Serra pilota, 2, 21
Lukacs, George, 9,
Lull, James, 68, 69
Lumière, Louis and Auguste,
    59, 60, 143
Macchina ammazzacattivi, La,
    3, 10, 152, 155
Machine to Kill Bad People,
    The, see *Macchina*
    ammazzacattivi
Magnani, Anna, 7, 66, 70,
    73–4, 136, 137, 150, 153,
    154

Man's Struggle for Survival,
    127, 129–33, 134, 138,
    139, 140–4, 162–3
March, Fredric, 65
Marker, Chris, 143
Marshall Plan, 9, 15,
Marx, Karl, 9, 166–9
Matarazzo, Raffaello, 22
Matisse, Henri, 161
Mauban, Marie, 102
McCormick, Miron, 37
Mediterranean, The, 13, 16, 58
Méliès, Georges, 59, 143
Mépris, Le, 4, 8,
Meredith, Burgess,
Messia, Il, 130, 142, 144,
    145–6
Mida, Massimo, 74
1860 (Blasetti), 150
Miller, Randall, 70
'Miracolo, Il', 10, 59, 73,
    151–2, 153, 154
Miranda, Isa,
Moi, un noir, 116
Moore, Dr Omar, 162
Morin, Edgar, 116
Morlion, Father Félix O.P., 73
Murnau, F. W., 109
Mussolini, Benito, 25
Mussolini, Vittorio, 21, 25, 27
Naples, 13, 42–5, 101–9, 118,
    159
Narboni, Jean, 123
Nascimbene, Mario, 140
Nave bianca, La, 3, 20, 23–5,
    28, 30, 54, 151, 153
Nazzari, Amedeo, 21
Negative Images, 109–10
nékya, 58
neo-realism, 9–10, 37–, 81,
    116–20, 149–51 (see also
    realism)
New Wave, The, 119, 121
New York Herald Tribune, 68
New York Times, 68
Niepce and Daguerre, 133
Notorious, 65, 69
Notti di Cabiria, Le, 41
Odyssey, The, 58
Oms, Marcel, 84
Onorevole Angelina, l', 73
Oro di Napoli, L', 160
Ore, Le, 72
Ossessione, 122

Pagliero, Marcello, *47,* 153
Paisà, 1, 3, 5, 7, 8, 10, 11–12,
    13, 15, 30, 36, 37, 38–9,
    40, 41–6, *43,* 51–4, *52,* 65,
    80, 85–6, 87, 99, 100, 103,
    122, 134, 136, 140, 143,
    151, 152, *153,* 154, 158,
    169–70
Pancinor – see zoom
Pansophiae Prodromus, 128
Parsons, Louella, 70
Pascal, Blaise, 17
Pasolini, Pier Paolo, 56, 57
Pavese, Cesare, 39
Péguy, Charles, 140
Peirce, C.S., 36
Perles de la couronne, la, 143
Petit, Chris, 109–10
Pilota ritorna, Un, 3, 20, 21,
    25, *26,* 28
Pius XI, 80, 92
Ponti, Carlo, 10
Potere di Cosimo, Il, 145
Power, Tyrone, 72
Prélude à l'après-midi d'un
    faune, 151, 154
Prise de pouvoir par Louis
    XIV, La, 1, 7, 126, 132,
    135, *137,* 138, 139, 142,
    144, 162
Promio, Giuseppe, 60
Production Code
    Administration, 66
Pulcinella, 132
Quatre cents coups, Les, 4
Rage in Heaven, 69
Ray, Nicholas, 109
realism, 10–11, 21–2, 50, 116,
    150–1 (see also neo-
    realism)
religion – see Catholicism,
    Christianity, sacredness
Remontons les Champs-
    Elysées, 143
Renoir, Jean, 4
Rien que les heures, 22
Riso amaro, see *Bitter Rice*
River, The (Renoir), 142
Rivette, Jacques, 4, 7, 50, 109,
    119, 142
Rivista del Cinematografo, La,
    80
RKO, 4, 7, 10,
RoGoPaG, 126

Rohmer, Eric, 4, 7, 55, 60, 119
Rome Open City, 1, 3, 7, 10, 11, 28, 29, 30–1, 37, 40, 42, 46–8, *47*, 73, 91, 99, 100, 122, 123, 154, 158
Rondi, Brunello, 82
Rooney, Mickey, 69
Rossellini, Isabella, 68
Rossellini, Isotta, 68
Rossellini, Renzo Jr., 17, 137
Rossellini, Renzo, 26, 103, 140
Rossellini, Robertino, *67*, 68, 75
Rouch, Jean, 116
Ruscello di Ripasottile, Il, 151, 154
Ruttmann, Walter, 22
sacredness, 50, 56, 61
Sanders, George, 12, 95, *96*, 98–9, *98*, 100, 108–9, 110, 136
Saratoga Trunk, 69
Scalfaro, Luigi, 38, 40
Scalo merci, see *Desiderio*
Schmidt, Roswitha, 29, 102
Second World War, 21, 23
Selznick, David O., 65, 69
Selznick, Irene, 65
Senroy Das Gupta, Sonali, 76, 140
Sentiero dei nidi di ragno, Il, 39
Sept Péchés capitaux, Les (*The Seven Deadly Sins*, 1952), 13, 98, 153
Serandrei, Mario, 48
Settimana Incom, La, 68, *67*, 73
Seven Deadly Sins – see *Sept Péchés capitaux*
Shakespeare, William, 162
Sieg im Osten, 22
Sight and Sound, 157

Socrates, 17
Socrates, 130, 136, 139, 142, 144–5
Soldati, Mario, 20
Sole sorge ancora, Il , 38
Sorrentino, Lamberti, 72, 73
sound, 139–40
Spiaggia, La, 158
Specchio, Lo, 72
Spellbound, 69
Spellman, Cardinal, 73
Spoto, Donald, 69, 71
St Augustine, 17
St Clare (Santa Chiara), 84, 85, 88, 89, 152
St Francis, 1, 56–7, 81
St Paul, 17,
Stazione Termini, 158
Steele, Joseph, 7
Strada, La, 38, 41, 158
Straordinaria storia della nostra alimentazione, La, see *Extraordinary History of our Food*
Straub, Jean-Marie, 140, 143
Stroheim, Erich von, 2,
Stromboli terra di Dio – see *Stromboli*
Stromboli, 7, 8, 10, 13–14, 38, 42, 55–6, 66, 70, 73, 74, 75, 80–1, 89, 90, 115, 118, 140, 151, 156, 158
Swanson, Gloria, 68
Tavazzi, Alberto, 28
television, 4, 5, 126–46
Tempo, 72
Terra trema, La, 38
Time magazine, 70
Tomlinson, John, 71, 78
Tout va bien, 114
Trafic (journal), 127
Truffaut, Francois, 4
Turner, Lana, 69

2001 – A Space Odyssey, 61
Umberto D, 41
Un esprit libre ne doit rien apprendre en esclave, 128
Uomini,che mascalzoni, gli, 150
Uomini sul fondo, 23–5
Uomo dalla croce, L', 3, 20, 21, 27–30, *29*,
Vanina Vanini, 5, 127, 133, 139
Vannucchi, Luigi, *14*,
Vergano, Aldo, 38
Viaggio in Italia see *Journey to Italy*
Vico, G. B., 127
Vidor, King, 154
Visconti, Luchino, 40, 75, 122 138
Vitelloni, I, 38, 41
Viva l'Italia, 5, 16, *16*, 127, 133, 134, 136
Voce umana, Una', 4, 10, 74, 137, 140, 143, 153
Voix humaine, La (Cocteau), 10 see also 'Voce umana'
Voyage to Italy – see *Journey to Italy*
Vulcano, 70
Weil, Simone, 18, 51
White Ship, The – see *Nave bianca*
Woll, Allen, 70
Wood, Peter H., 161
Wood, Robin, 74
Wright, Basil, 55
Zampa, Luigi, 40, 75
Zavattini, Cesare, 10
Zola, Emiile, 159
zoom, 6, 16, 17, 131
Zweig, Stefan, 14